BRITISH SPECIAL OPERATIONS EXPLORED

Yugoslavia in Turmoil 1941–1943
and the British Response

M. DEROC

EAST EUROPEAN MONOGRAPHS, BOULDER
DISTRIBUTED BY COLUMBIA UNIVERSITY PRESS, NEW YORK

1988

EAST EUROPEAN MONOGRAPHS, NO. CCXLII

Copyright © 1988 by M. Deroc
ISBN 0-88033-139-9
Library of Congress Catalog Card Number 87-82413

Printed in the United States of America

TO MY FATHER (1871-1944)
AND BROTHER (1912-1941)

CONTENTS

Preface	vii
Acknowledgements	xi
General Notes and Explanations	xiii

CHAPTER 1
Belgrade, March 1941 ... 1

CHAPTER 2
Churchill, Hitler and Yugoslavia ... 18

CHAPTER 3
Yugoslavia in 1941: Occupation and Reaction ... 35

CHAPTER 4
The SOE* Steps In: Hudson and "Operation Bullseye" (I) ... 53
    Background and Purpose

CHAPTER 5
The SOE* Steps In: Hudson and "Operation Bullseye" (II) ... 75
    Briefing and Activity

CHAPTER 6
The Leaders (I), Mihailović in Peace and War ... 93

CHAPTER 7
The Leaders (II), Tito 1914-1941 ... 113

CHAPTER 8
Occupied Serbia in 1941: ... 136
    German Administration and Serbian Accommodation

CHAPTER 9
Serbia at Arms, The Uprising of 1941: ... 156
    Main Historical Issues

CHAPTER 10
    Special Operations Executive's Abortive "Russian Project"   194
CHAPTER 11
    Hudson and Mihailović, A Revised Historical Judgement   205

CONCLUSION   217
DIAGRAMS, PHOTOCOPIES, SKETCH-MAPS AND TABLES   232
FOOTNOTES   261
SOURCES   321
INDEX   342

*   The [British] Special Operations Executive

PREFACE

This book challenges the accepted interpretations of the role of Tito and Mihailović in the turbulent history of Yugoslavia in World War II. It also critically reviews the stages of the British wartime response and British policies, from the work of SOE operatives to Churchill and the change of guard at the British "Yugoslavia" desk in London and Cairo. This is followed by a revealing assessment of the post-war grip of Tito's "fan club" on British-Yugoslav historiography.

The subjects of this book are military and paramilitary men, and, predominantly, military events. Nevertheless this is not a military history but a critical record of human problems and politics, and of the strengths and weaknesses of participants. In their Yugoslav context this raises a special problem, and this is best illustrated by comparing it with British ways. In an old cultural milieu sets of values exist which form a common bond. Thus, the immediate British response to the events in occupied Serbia, Yugoslavia, conformed to British Imperial traditions. Even after the change of British policy on Yugoslavia in 1943, the official rationale for it remained British politico-stratetic considerations. By contrast, Yugoslavia had existed for twenty-three years only, and such a cultural cohesion had not yet been achieved. Therefore, in order to under their later actions, the story of the disparate backgrounds of Yugoslav participants must be interwoven with the main narrative.

The narrative is based on a wide-ranging critical comparative examination of various sources, regarding both the events and their background. The main sources are contemporary documents. These are supplemented

—especially in order to add a "human touch"—by interviews and studies of autobiographical works. Finally, major historiographical works are examined in relation to each other, and in relation to the primary sources. All events and their explanations are set in their appropriate context, and care is taken to distinguish between the explanation of events and their interpretation. Particular attention is given to the fact that the events rapidly succeeded each other, so that what was valid at one point in time need not have been so on another day. Many a misunderstanding about these events would have been avoided if attention had been paid to this point. As the story progresses, the reader will come to realize the importance of dates as a check on existing irresponsible historical assumptions and interpretations.

Prominence has been given to all factors in this drama in a series of self-contained yet mutually dependent chapters. Chapter one deals with the March 1941 *coup d'état* in Belgrade, when a group of army officers overturned the government of Prince Paul and brought Yugoslavia into the Allied camp; concurrently British involvement in the coup is reviewed. Chapter two discusses the reactions of Churchill and Hitler to events in Belgrade and the further fate of Yugoslavia. Chapter three is about the Yugoslav collapse under Axis invasion, Hitler's dismemberment of Yugoslavia and the demographic and political consequences of the chaos created there by the Nazis. Chapters four and five detail the intervention of the British Special Operations Executive's (SOE) through its Operation *Bullseye*, including here the adventures of Captain (later Colonel) Hudson in Montenegro and Serbia. Chapters six and seven outline Mihailović's and Tito's backgrounds. Chapter eight examines the German occupation system in Serbia and local response. Chapter nine discusses the main historical issues pertaining to the uprising of 1941, particularly the role of Tito and Mihailović and their relationship. Chapter ten draws (by permission) on still classified files regarding the abortive *"Russian Project."* The SOE endeavoured to raise this project simultaneously with mission *Bullseye*, but foundered because of the opposition of the Yugoslav Prime Minister Simović. Chapter eleven re-examines the relationship between Mihailović and Hudson, and reaches a revised historical judgement of Operation *Bullseye* and its impact on British-Yugoslav wartime relations and post-war historiography. The final chapter, Conclusion, shows that political, and not military, considerations were decisive in the transfer of support from Mihailović to Tito in 1943, and that this political commitment of its wartime protagonists has affected most of the post-war British Yugoslav historiography.

This book grew out of my previous work on this subject, and particularly my doctoral thesis "The Serbian Uprising of 1941 and the British Response" (The University of New England, N.S.W., Australia, 1985), and my articles on this topic. Some details published in my previous works have been updated. For those who might raise the question of my personal relationship with the story of my book, I wish to state that at the time when the uprising and resistance were taking place, I was a POW in Germany (No. 6424 Oflag IVD).

ACKNOWLEDGEMENTS

I am obliged to the following institutions and administrations for copies of wartime and other documents on which this book is based: Auswaertiges Amt (AA), Staatssekretaer, Bonn, West Germany; Bibliothèque de Documentation Internationale Contemporaine (Universités de Paris) Nanterre, France, Bundesarchiv-Militaerarchiv, Freiburg i/B, West Germany; Department of Defense, Naval Historical Branch, London, U.K.; Deutsche Dienststelle, Berlin, West Germany; Ecole Nationale Supérieure de l'Aéronautique et de l'Espace, Association des Anciens Elèves, Paris, France; Foreign and Commonwealth Office, Political Archives, London, U.K; Foreign and Commonwealth Office, SOE Adviser, London, U.K.; International Committee of the Red Cross, Geneva, Switzerland; Library of Congress, Photoduplication Service, Washington, D.C.; Public Record Office (PRO), Kew, London, U.K.; Staatsarchiv-Kriegsarchiv, Vienna, Austria; U.S. Department of Justice, Immigration Branch, San Francisco, California; U.S. Military Academy, Documents Librarian, West Point; U.S. National Archives, Military Archives Division, Washington, D.C. All as cited in the text and footnotes.

I am grateful to Professor Arasaratnam for allowing me the facilities of the History Department of the University of New England, N.S.W., Australia, to do my writing there, and to Jennifer Crew of the same Department for having read and commented on my manuscript, as well as to Geoff Quaife and David Kent. My thanks are also due to the many librarians, governmental officials and private citizens both in Australia and overseas who have assisted me. They can be identified in the text. Brian A. Rice of the Inter-Library Loans Department of the Dixson Library at New England deserves a special mention. To Major R. P. Wade, a wartime British

Liaison Officer to both Mihailović and Tito I am indebted for making it possible for me to meet Colonel Hudson, as well as for many other kindnesses. I remain obliged to Colonel Hudson for his kind support. A particular tribute is due to Noelene Kachel for her untiring, meticulous and efficient typing and preparation of the manuscript, and to Madeleine Hyson for her assistance. To Professor Fisher-Galati of the University of Colorado, Boulder, Colorado, USA, I remain indebted for his kind interest in my manuscript and the decision to print it as a volume of the *East European Monograph Series.*

I appreciate the permission granted by many copyright holders, where such was necessary, to use their material, and especially the permission of the Controller of H.M. Stationery Office to reproduce Crown-copyright records.

My indebtedness to all who have helped, encouraged, or smoothed my path is gratefully acknowledged. Needless to say, I alone bear the responsibility for all opinions and comments as well as for the final product.

GENERAL NOTES AND EXPLANATIONS

−Footnoting,
−Form of personal and geographic names,
−Terminology,
−Titles, ranks, etc.,
−Translations.

Footnoting:

(i) Footnoting follows the following pattern−
Smith, 86   For authors listed once only (the numeral indicates page number);
Smith I, 86   When an author's work has two or more volumes;
Smith, *Britain,* 86 or Smith, *Britain* I, 86
                When an author is listed more than once;
When an abbreviation is used, refer to "Terminology."

(ii) Citing of microfilms−
  (a) Microfilms of captured German army documents, held by the United States National Archives, are identified simply by their coding system, e.g.,
       T501-251-number, meaning "Microcopy No. 501−Roll No. 251−frame No.", e.g. T501-251-00086.
     Contents of these microfils are identified in the Chapter "Sources."
  (b) Other microfilms are identified by source and description.

Form of personal and geographic names:

Unless citing a written or printed source, or a lesser known name, the usual English or Anglicised names are used (e.g. Prince Paul for Prince Pavle, Belgrade for Beograd, Montenegro for Crna Gora, Serbia for Srbija). All other foreign names are spelled as per current practice, that is, as they do it themselves.

When a geographic name has been changed since an event occurred there (e.g. Titograd for Podgorica), this is indicated.

Terminology:

BLO (BLOs)	British Liaison Officer(s)
Četnik	(a) Historically, a Serbian freedom fighter (also "Komita"); (b) In Yugoslav Communist political terminology: a non-defined term for abuse of the Serbs; (c) Serbian military term for volunteers serving in guerrilla warfare companies or "Četa." Mihailović used this terminology in 1941 only; for Mihailović's argument for doing so see text to note 82 in Ch. 9; (d) Colloquially used for the "Yugoslav Army in the Fatherland," 1942-44, commanded by Mihailović: this leads to confusion with the ad-hoc village-selfdefence 'Četniks" in Ustaša-Croatia, which were independent of Mihailović; (e) A term used in 1941-42 by some German auxiliaries in occupied Serbia to describe their own detachments.
Cmd, Cmdg, Cder	Command, Commanding, Commander
CofS	Chief(s) of Staff
DGFP	*Documents on German Foreign Policy*
F&Cth Office	Foreign and Commonwealth Office
FRUS	*Foreign Relations of the United States*
Glasnik *"Njegoš"*	*Glasnik srpskog istorisko-kulturnog društva "Njejoš"*
HQ	Headquarters
JVO	Jugoslovenska Vojska u Otadžbini (Yugoslav Army in the Fatherland: Mihailović's troops)
KPJ	Komunistička partija Jugoslavije (The Communist Party of Yugoslavia)
Luftwaffe	The German Air Force

General Notes

MBS	The German Military Commander in occupied Serbia. The German Plenipotentiary Military Cder in occupied Serbia
NDH	Nezavisna Država Hrvatska ("The Independent State of Croatia," WWII Ustaša Fascist Croat State)
OKH	Oberkommando des Heeres (Supreme Cmd of the Army)
OKW	Oberkommando der Wehrmacht (Supreme Cmd of the Armed Forces)
Partisan	A Russian originated term ("Partizan"), meaning an army-associated freedom fighter. In 1941 in Serbia, the KPJ propaganda claimed that it meant "Followers of all political parties who fight the Fascists."
PRO	Public Record Office, Kew, Richmond, U.K.
PWE	[British] Political Warfare Executive
RAF	The Royal Air Force
RN	The Royal Navy
SOE	[British] Special Operations Executive: for the abbreviations of SOE's HQ titles refer to the chart
Wehrmacht	German Armed Forces

Titles, ranks etc.:

Customarily used titles have been retained (e.g., "Sir", "von", "Dr").

Translation of military ranks into English follows the principle of equivalence: e.g., "Lieutenant General" for "Diviziski general" or "Général de division." A military rank may indicate a member of the regular forces (e.g., Colonel Mihailović, Lieutenant Colonel Clarke), a reserve officer (e.g. Major Mišić), or a wartime appointee (e.g. Lieutenant Colonel Bailey, Brigadier Maclean). Ranks of all Yugoslav army personnel refer to the old Army, unless otherwise shown.

Translations:

Unless it is obvious from the title of a source that it is a foreign work published in English, all translations are by this author (MD).

CHAPTER 1

BELGRADE, MARCH 1941

European war, the prelude to World War II, started on 3 September 1939 and continued for eighteen months. By that time, Mussolini's own sub-war on Yugoslavia's southern neighbour, Greece, had bogged down, and Hitler had decided to intervene there. His urge to act resulted from a mixture of political necessity and propaganda compounded by his wounded pride, and also from a rational military requirement. For political and propaganda reasons, he was apprehensive that the military discomfiture of his Italian Fascist ally might adversely affect his own standing and that of the Nazis. And his wounded pride was involved because of the threat of a landing of the British and Imperial Anzac troops in Greece. Wasn't he, the Fuehrer, adamant that no "English" expeditionary soldier would set foot on the soil of *Europe?* In his own words, he was to repay them for their landing in Greece with yet another "Dunkirk." This goes to show that the same notion may mean opposite things to different people. To Hitler, "Dunkirk" symbolized the expulsion of the "English" Expeditionary Corps from the European Continent in June 1940. To the British, it symbolized the successful extrication of the Expeditionary Corps from the lost allied campaign in France. Finally, as Hitler had decided to launch his *Operation Barbarossa* against the Soviet Union, the rational military corollary required that the right wing and southern flank of the German Eastern Front should be safe and protected. For this reason, south-east Europe, that is, Central Europe and the Balkans, had to be brought under German control. By mid-March 1941, only Greece and Yugoslavia in the south-east were free from Nazi domination. To deal with the Greek case Hitler mounted *Operation Marita*. His intent was to extricate Italians from their Greek fiasco, and also to deal with the Greeks themselves and the "English" troops which had landed there. So it came about that Yugoslavia, which stood between him and Greece, entered Hitler's immediate calculations. Due to her geopolitical location, Yugoslavia presented a twofold risk to Hitler's plans. The immediate risk was in the Balkans where Yugoslavia posed a threat to the safety of the western flank of *Marita* troops deployed in Bulgaria, for attack on Greece. The long term risk was a possible British intervention to bolster the Yugoslav Front. With the British entrenched both in Greece and Yugoslavia, Romanian oil wells and the southern flank of the German Eastern Front would be vulnerable to an allied land attack. If, impressed by the commanding British presence in the Balkans, Turkey also were to declare for Britain, the German overall position could have become very risky indeed. The obvious linchpin in these staff considerations was the attitude of Yugoslavia. To pre-empt any danger of a Yugoslav-British military cooperation, Hitler engaged in an overpowering diplomatic offensive to make Yugoslavia join the Axis powers. Hitherto Yugoslavia had been officially declared neutral in the current conflict. The Yugoslav government resisted Hitler for a while, but then gave in and signed the Tripartite Pact on 25 March 1941. On the same day, *The Times* of London prominently reported the visit of Japan's Foreign Minister Matsuoka to Berlin. Nevertheless, Yugoslav developments must have been judged the main event of the day. This can be seen from *The Times's* late London edition where, beside the heading *The Times,* there was singled out the news "Yugoslav Ministers go to Vienna." Indeed, the Pact was signed in the Belvedere Palace there. At the same time, Sir Alexander Cadogan, Permanent Under-Secretary of State at the Foreign Office (FO), wrote in his diary: "Jugs are signing [the Tripartite Pact] — silly, feeble mugs. . . ." Two days later, in the early hours of 27 March, a group of embittered Yugoslav army officers executed a *coup d'état* in Belgrade. They proclaimed that the boy-king, Peter II, had taken over the exercise of Royal powers, dismissed the Council of Regency, and replaced the Pact-signing government with another one. In Belgrade, and ever since in Yugoslav historiography also, this coup has been referred to as the

"*Puč*", which is obviously a borrowing of the German word "*der Putsch*." Consequently, the officers of the "*Puč*" became known as the "*Pučista*" or "*Pučisti*" officers. Nominally, the head of the conspiracy was the Commander of the Army Air Force, a half-baked soldier-politician, General Dušan T. Simović. The effective head however, was the jovial and outspoken Brigadier General Borivoje (Bora) Mirković, Second in Command in Simović's Air Force. This has made historical writers maintain that the *Puč* was an airmen's affair. It was not. Both Simović and Mirković were originally army men themselves, and this gave them access to officers of the Belgrade army garrison. Thus it came about that the executive *Pučista* organizing the coup in Belgrade was Živan L. Knežević, a selfopiniated Major in the Infantry, commanding a Battalion in the King's Guards Infantry Regiment. The rest of the *Pučisti* were also mostly army (not Air Force) officers, and predominantely Serbs. The *Pučisti* officers immediately invited the formation of a civilian government of all political parties. The latter-day rulers of Yugoslavia, Tito and the Communist Party, were not included, as at the time Tito was only an illegal insignificant foreign agent. The leader of the *Puč*, General Simović, became the new Prime Minister as a non-political or "neutral" member of the new government. A prominent group of British historians, amongst whom was Professor R. W. Seton-Watson, commented:

> since the creation of Yugoslavia, no government so representative of all sections of opinion from Left to Right had ever held office.[1]

But there was also a "Gilbertian" touch in the way in which this government was physically assembled. Its involuntary humour lies in the unforeseen, awkward overtones of the procedure which was adopted. Several junior *Pučisti* officers were issued orders to call at the homes of leaders of the Serbian political opposition on the same night, to wake them up, and bring these elderly gentlemen to the HQ of the Great General Staff. Imbued with his own importance, each officer called at the address he was given. When the door opened on the darkness of the night, the officer, in full field gear, appeared silhouetted against the backdrop of his helmeted patrol with fixed bayonets. Is Mr. X. at home? The officer has come to convey him to the headquarters. Please wake him up and ask him to get dressed. Hurry up, I am on army business. This resulted in assembling a congregation of apprehensive politicians, who, behind the thick walls of the HQ, thought themselves in military custody. The only one whose initial reaction was different was General Petar R. Živković, Guards commander under the late King Alexander. Now retired and a politician, he admonished his escort: "Are you aware, youngsters (actually, he said 'you children,' *deco*), are you aware of what you are doing?" Next, the amassed politicians were amazed when they learned that, no, they were not in custody, but were wanted to form a new democratic government. Petar Živković, however, was left out, as in the days of King Alexander's transient dictatorship twelve years earlier he had been Prime Minister. The generally accepted view is that the *Pučisti* not only overturned the government of the day, but also "arrested" them. This is a fallacy. They did intercept Prime Minister Cvetković, a Serb, on his return from Vienna, and confined him at his home. Whomever else of the Serbs the *Pučisti* might or might not have arrested, it is certain that they never laid a finger on a Croat or Slovene minister of the former government. On the contrary, they invited them to join the new government, which they did. Thus, even if all Serb ministers had been arrested, that still would not justify the indiscriminate claim that the old *Government* was "arrested." Be this as it may, *Pučisti* officers, Serbs themselves, publicly vented their verbal spleen on the Serb ex-ministers only. By doing this, they were barking up the wrong tree. It is indeed ironical that, it can now be seen that the non-Serb, not the Serb, ministers were advocating that the Pact should be signed. For instance, the stand of the leader of the Croat Peasant Party and vice-Prime Minister, Maček, was one of the deciding factors for signing the pact.[2] Despite this, after the *Puč* he became Simović's Vice-Prime Minister, albeit an unwilling one. Simović made Maček his Vice-Prime Minister without first asking for his agreement.

For the six and a half years since King Alexander I Karadjordjević had been assassinated in Marseilles on 9 October 1934, Royal Prerogatives had been exercised by a Regency Council of three me. One of the Regents was boy-King Peter II's uncle, Prince Paul Karadjordjević. Due to his social pre-eminence, Paul in no time achieved ascendance over his two commoner colleagues and assumed the title "Prince Regent." Thus he became identified with the common will of the Regency, and therefore to him fall both praise and blame for the Regency's record. On the night of the coup he was away from Belgrade. With the exception of Brigadier General Jovan

Leko (Lecco), the long-serving Comptroller of the Royal Court and now a Brigade Commander, the willpower of the loyalist brass seemed atrophied by Paul's absence, and they failed to resist the *Puč*. Instead, they allowed themselves to be arrested. This analysis is not to be taken to deny that on that occasion the *Pučisti* represented the best part of Serbian public opinion of the day. Still, Yugoslavia was a multinational State and —as the attitude of their ministers in the Government demonstrated—Croat and Slovene public opinion was not prepared to share the pro-allied sentiments of the Serbs. The internal political situation was as complex as that, and not a simplistic one as it was imagined by the officers whose horizon was restricted to the confines of the Belgrade garrison. It is interesting to observe that historians of Yugoslav affairs have neglected to discuss these points. The question of Paul's whereabouts during the night of 26-27 March, however, is a popular one. Where was he and what was he doing? As it happened, he was travelling in the royal train on his way to holidays in Slovenia, but on the news of the coup returned from Zagreb to Belgrade. There he, the other two Regents, and the overturned government retrospectively resigned their posts. Usually it is asserted that when Prince Paul was in Zagreb he was ordered to return to Belgrade. However this version is strongly opposed by the man who was the ADC on duty in the royal train that night. He maintains that Paul exercised his own initiative in returning to Belgrade. Staff Captain Pomorišac, as he was then, is also the man who woke the Prince to report the news of the coup. When he did so, the Prince paused and then said: "We're finished, in a week or two Germany will roll over us." Pomorišac, a young and proud airman, answered: "Your Highness knows as well as I do that our country is full of mountain ranges so that German tanks will be hard put to master our defences." Prince Paul look at him and added, "Alas,. . ."[3] So that was the mood of the Prince. He wanted to keep his country out of the war. But what was the motive of the *Pučisti*? Was it simple or complex? If it was a complex one, what were its parts? As the Serb *Pučisti* were Yugoslav military officers, it is necessary to examine that body of men to understand their motivation.

The Yugoslav armed forces were created in 1918-1919, after World War I, when "Yugoslavia" was known as the Kingdom of the Serbs, Croats, and Slovenes.[4] In that war, Serbia was on the side of the allies—then known as the *Entente*—whilst Croat soldiers fought for Austria-Hungary, that is, for the losing side. This explains why the victorious allies ordered that the Croat troops be disbanded. This demand was in compliance with the provisions of the protocol of Austro-Hungarian armistice and capitulation, signed at Villa Giusti on 3 November 1918. However, the Allies allowed volunteers from these defeated Austro-Hungarian forces to join the Serbian Army,[5] which played a significant part in the Allied victory. Initially, forces of the Kingdom of the Serbs, Croats and Slovenes consisted of the former Serbian Army, into which was incorporated also the Army of the Serbian Kingdom of Montenegro. This body was then enlarged with volunteers from the Austro-Hungarian forces. The air-squadrons were also a merger of Serbian units with former Austro-Hungarian volunteers. The navy consisted of former Austro-Hungarian naval personnel but no naval craft, as the ships had been reserved for the victorious Great Powers. The new Navy became officially known as *"Kraljevska mornarica"* or the Royal [Yugoslav] Navy, which was not decided upon as a compliment to the British Royal Navy, but as a revival of the previous Austro-Hungarian appellation. As a matter of fact, the Serbs wanted it to be called *"Ratna mornarica"* or "War—", that is, "Military Navy," but failed to convince the Admirals. The old Serbian Army, and later the Army of the Kingdom of Yugoslavia were officially described as the "people's army"; Tito and the Communist Party of Yugoslavia have not invented anything by calling the army of the Republic a people's army. The current usage "Royal Yugoslav Army" for the army of the Kingdom has probably crept into historical writings *via* two channels: by accident, because in World War II Yugoslav exiles found refuge under British protection and so adopted the British style, and for political reasons, because it makes it easier to distinguish between the present-day army of the Republic and the former army of the Kingdom. Initally, the officer corps of the new "Royal" forces consisted of the whole former Serbian complement, Montenegrin officers, and volunteers. The volunteers, the great majority of whom were of South Slavic ethnicity, were recruited between 1918 and 1920. Emigré officers of the former Imperial Russian Army and a few independent individuals of various backgrounds also joined the new army. An illustration of the latter is the case of Flora Sandes, daughter of an English country parson. She came to Serbia in 1914 as a nurse. In 1915 she was enrolled in No. 2 Serbian Infantry Regiment. As a Sergeant, she was in front line trenches on the Macedonian Front. She was wounded and decorated with the highest Serbian order for bravery—the Star of Karadjordje with Swords. In June 1919 she was commissioned a Reserve 2nd Lieutenant, and posted to the Border Guard Troops. She found there a former Russian Colonel as her Yugoslav Sergeant. There were also other women front line soldiers in the Serbian Army in World War I. The best known was Sergeant Milunka Savić, many times decorated for bravery. (It might be that she was not commissioned an officer because of the level of her literacy?) A substantial source of regular subalterns were students from Austro-Hungarian cadet schools. They were commissioned as follows:

> In the name of His Majesty, Peter I, by the Grace of God and the Will of the People, King of the Serbs, Croats and Slovenes, We, Alexander, Heir to the Throne, on a submission of Our Minister for the Army and Navy, and in accordance with the Clause 17 of the Law of Constitution of the Army—commissioned: [the names follow].

These decrees were published in the *Official Military Gazette* (*"Službeni Vojni list"*).

The new officer corps consisted of 2,590 volunteers from the former Austria-Hungary, three Albanian officers from Essad-Pasha's troops, twelve ex-Imperial Russian officers, 3,500 Serbian and 469 Montenegrin officers, a total of 3,074 others and 3,500 Serbians (these figures probably do not include naval volunteers). This mixture appeared an unwieldy group in which it would be difficult to develop a common *esprit de corps*. Had either major component been overwhelmingly superior in numbers to the others, it would have been easier. A particularly delicate problem was posed by the fact that some volunteers from the disbanded Austria-Hungarian Croat units had been personally engaged on the Serbian and Montenegrin front up to this point. This affected the *esprit de corps* of the newly created Yugoslav forces. Transition creates tension, and time was needed to heal these wounds and establish satisfactory personal relationships. However, an army is a body of men which responds to inspiring leadership, and King Alexander I, himself a soldier, was their man. Under his strong leadership the army was consolidating and these tensions were neutralized, although they remained dormant. Had this process been able to continue, it could be expected that the remaining tensions would have dissipated in time and that a supra-national fully "Yugoslav" force would have emerged. All this changed after the murder of the King in 1934, when, under the uninspiring leadership of the Regency—that is, of Prince Paul— demoralization set in and the old tensions resurfaced.

Under Paul's guidance three things occurred that alienated the army. The first was his indifferent leadership, the second a critical change of course in foreign policy, and the third was the manner of the sudden reversal of domestic policies. Perhaps, but for the crisis of leadership, the other two events would not have been critical. It is generally agreed that neither by his temperament nor by his sickly appearance could Prince Paul fulfill the role of an army leader, neither did he bother to establish any rapport with the officer corps. The depth of the chasm between the Prince and the army can best be understood by realizing that it occurred despite the Regency's positive record in the field of rearmament and economic mobilization, as well as in the bettering of the army's material conditions and even increasing the officers' emoluments. In foreign policy, the Regency's innovations went against the grain of the officer corps. Under King Alexander, indoctrination of the whole officer corps portrayed the former "Central Powers" and Italy as enemies, while France, Great Britain and the United States were deemed to be allies.[18] The Regency reversed these postulates, or, at least, it gave the impression of doing so. It is natural to think immediately of the Regency's appeasement of Hitler, and to overlook Yugoslavia's *rapprochement* with Rome. The new policy was inaugurated by Prime Minister Milan Stojadinović (23 June 1935—3 February 1939), and on 25 March 1937 it even led to the signing of an Italo-Yugoslav political agreement. It is crucial to note that ever since the creation of Yugoslavia on 1 December 1918, there had been constant tension and occasional sabre-rattling between Italy and Yugoslavia. Under the Regency the government made overtures to Mussolini, the man who was deemed responsible for encouraging the assassination of King Alexander. It is the task of diplomatic history to explain these changes. Our concern here is that in the country generally, and especially in the army, the rapprochement with Italy was unpopular. So it came about that in the last years of the Regency, officers' frustrations started boiling over into the formation of small groups of malcontents who did not know of each other. The beginning of these cliques appears to coincide with the height of the Regency's "Italian policies," that is, 1937. In domestic policies, also, the

Regency introduced radical changes. This is the period of the prime ministership of Dragiša Cvetković (February 1939–27 March 1941). He is the man who eventually manoeuvred himself into a position where he had no choice but to sign the Tripartite Pact of the Axis powers. Again, Paul's innovations estranged him from the army. Under the late King, officers were indoctrinated to serve and defend a unitarian State. On the French Jacobin model of a *"République une et indivisible,"* the officers were expected to serve and defend a *"Yugoslavie une et indivisible."* When the establishment of a semiautonomous *Banovina* of Croatia was decreed by the Regency out of the blue, on 26 August 1939, public opinion took this to mean the first step in the federalization of the country. Individual officers, disoriented, reacted in unison with their ethnic brethren. This drastic reversal of domestic policies needed careful preparation; this was not done. In 1929 King Alexander I's own *coup d'état* of 6 January succeeded because on that day the King enjoyed the confidence of the people at large, the army, and the Croat politicians. Croat politicians turned against Alexander only when his personal regime disappointed them in their expectations; their subsequent opposition obscured their initial approval. In 1939, Serb public opinion was known to be inimical to Prince Paul and his Prime Minister Dragiša Cvetković, called "Dragiša Gipsy." Prince Paul and Cvetković had the support of Croat politicians (Maček became Vice-Prime Minister), but erred in taking the Army for granted. If it was necessary to proceed in secrecy, then the tensions that were to be created by the establishing of a sole semi-independent *Banovina* should have been forestalled by the simultaneous creation of both a Serb and a Slovenian *Banovina*. Not to do so was a blunder of the first order. It was this blunder of omission that set the Croats and the non-Croats at loggerheads in 1939, and not any "Serb opposition" to the Croats *per se*. This blunder was the main cause of the revival of ethnic tension amongst the military. The other aspects of their career and lifestyle became tainted overnight with political overtones, and the dormant mutual distrust amongst the officers re-emerged.

Frustrations and tensions in the officer corps were only what the words imply, that is, a diffuse feeling. Had Yugoslavia been given a longer span of life, it is quite possible that these ruffled feelings might have subsided again, especially as the Croat Peasant Party began participating in the government from 26 August 1939. Those officers whose patience was exhausted reacted by a display of bravado. Such bravado was that of two Serbs and a Slovene, Guards' Artillery Lieutenants Zvonimir-Zvonko Vučković, Momčilo Smiljanić and Sava Konvalinka. In protest at the appeasement of Germany, they left their posts in March 1941 and entered Greece to volunteer for the embattled Greek army. When crossing the Yugoslav-Greek border, they symbolically left their swords stuck into the ground, together with a note highly critical of Prince Paul's foreign policy. At the other end of the sprectrum is the case of the Air Force Captain Vladimir Kren, a Croat, who could not wait any longer for the fall of Yugoslavia. On 3 April 1941 he left his post and flew to Austria, where he surrendered the air force radio cypher to German authorities and informed them about all Yugoslav landing fields. A week later, on 10 April, Croatia broke away from Yugoslavia. The "Independent State of Croatia" made Kren a General and Commander of the Croat Air Force. The next example of bravado is also the first and last peace time instance where a group of officers organized themselves against the legal government. It is the *'Puč'* which erupted after the government signed the Tripartite Pact of the Axis powers on 25 March 1941. At the time it was not generally known that it was a qualified adherence only. Meeting the Royal Yugoslav government half way, Hitler agreed to emasculate the normal pact obligations. He agreed to guarantee Yugoslavia's territorial integrity, renounced marching or transporting Axis troops through Yugoslavia and declared he would not ask for Yugoslav troops to assist him in the war. Nevertheless, the adherence served Hitler's propaganda purposes, and also ensured Yugoslav neutrality on the right flank of German armies poised for attack on Greece and the British and Commonwealth or "Imperial" troops there ("Operation Marita"). When *The Times* of 25 March reported on the first page "Yugoslav ministers go to Vienna," in the commentary on page four it said also that, "Due to the tension throughout[!] the country, the government has been forced to confine the troops to barracks." Well, yes, but that was not the only reason. To ensure the army's support in case of a Serb anti-Pact explosion, regimental officers were told on the eve of the 25th that the Pact was to be signed and an appeal was made to their self-discipline and loyalty. This step came too late. Faced with the *fait accompli* and without having been conditioned to it, the reactions of the already frustrated officers were mixed. Most of the temperamental Serbs openly expressed a range of feelings ranging from sarcasm to open rebellion and then followed the *"Puč."*

Why did the *coup d'état* or *"Puč"* succeed? It was the misuse of the King's name, *viz.* the pretence that the King was behind the *"Puč"* that explains its success. This was accomplished by broadcasting a purported proclamation of the King over radio Belgrade and telling the listeners that it was the King reading it personally. (Actually, it was read by Naval Lieutenant I Class—*"Poručnik bojnog broda I klase"*—Jakov N. Jovović.) In this manner the acquiescence of the Belgrade population and of Serbs generally was ensured. Even Prince Paul was impressed. Maček, the leader of the Croat Peasant Party and vice-Prime Minister in the overturned government, reported that when, at Zagreb, he suggested to the Prince that the Zagreb garrison should be used against Belgrade, Paul answered: "... such a move would mean revolt against the legitimate King." As a military exercise the coup was brilliantly planned and executed. Politically, it was a disaster. At home and abroad it was expected that the new government would immediately denounce the Pact, declare for Britain, and order a general mobilization of armed forces. Instead, the government complied with diplomatic usage by recognizing the validity of inherited treaties (though Hitler refused all overtures). The point is that, immediately on assuming power, the new ministers discovered that the loyalty of *Banovina* Croatia to the semi-federalized Yugoslavia depended on appeasing Germany to avoid an invasion of Croat low-lands. If the junior officers, such as the *"Pučisti"* Majors, did not know about it they can be excused, as the officer corps was deliberately kept apart from civilian society and was therefore naive in political matters. But it is a sad reflection on General Simović, as the Commander of the Air Force and a recent Chief of the General Staff, that even he was not conversant wit the Croat attitude towards the high politics of the State, or, if he was, then of ignoring Croat views before the *"Puč."* It may be, however, that Simović's post-coup equivocation was not related to Maček's attitude, but to the discovery that Britain would not support Yugoslavia militarily in a war with Germany. British forces in Greece were a token presence only, and not in sufficient force to come to Yugoslavia's aid. Simović might have realized the real position only belatedly. Hence his post-coup prevarication in the negotiations with the British envoys, and his efforts to appease Germany to ensure Yugoslavia's continuing neutrality. If so, then, as a very senior military commander, he was guilty (again) of not being conversant with the current state of British-Yugoslav relatins in the Balkans. Simović, who was popular with his airforce officers, appears to have been quite obtuse in his knowledge and understanding of the domestic situation and international relations. How did he come to hold so many senior positions? The answer is that, apparently, he never held a post for a decent period of time before being shifted sidewise. This deficiency in his makeup became evident also in his tenure of the Prime-ministership. Amidst the national and international post-coup crisis, he lacked the common sense of how to go about it. He should have immediately ordered general mobilization, thus lifting the morale of the people and army, and uniting them around a common goal of defending the country from an attack by the Axis powers. But not Simović. In the event, he had his government neither joined Britain nor demonstratively reaffirmed their country's neutrality. In retrospect it can be seen that Simović's irresponsible lack of action compromised the impact of the *Puč* and bewildered the country. And, by his refusal to mobilize immediately, he left the army unprepared for Hitler's vicious attack.

In the crisis created by the coup, time was at a premium and the succession of events hectic, so that no contemporary observer could have made a reasoned assessment of what was going on and how it was all going to end. Even in retrospect, only two points are certain, and both deal with the historiography of the event. The first point is the infantile claim of the Communist Party of Yugoslavia. When at the end of World War II they found themselves at the helm of State, they devoted considerable propaganda effort to acquire national legitimacy. As at that time the *Puč* of 27 March still signified Yugoslavia's adherence to the Allied cause, and the Allies won the war, the Communist Party pulled out all stops to appropriate the *Puč* to itself. As it happened, this was one of the rare occasions when the "Agitprop" failed (*pace* Djilas, you were its head), and this claim died a natural death even in Tito's own lifetime. A sibling of Titoist propaganda has survived however, in the unsupported claim that the "Yugoslav masses" caused the downfall of the Cvetković government. "Yugoslav" masses? Our confidence must be given to contemporary eyewitnesses, and not to politically committed commentators writing after the events. In March 1941, the witnesses saw only Serbian masses, and particularly the Serb nationalist demonstrations in Belgrade. Even so, but for the officers having taken up the cudgels, nothing further would have happened. Now to discuss the other point, the serious one, which influenced even scholarly historiography for many years. It is about the role which the British sabotage and subversion organisation, the Special Operations Executive (SOE) played in the events in Belgrade. Hitherto it had nothing to show to its credit. On 13 January 1941 Churchill himself "drew the attention of Defence Committee...to the failure of past [SOE] schemes of sabotage, and (expressed) his skepticism about schemes that [they] were currently considering."[6] The Belgrade *coup d'état* was a Godsend for the SOE and particularly for the standing of its head, Dr. Dalton.

How much credit should be given to the SOE for engineering the coup? Had the SOE manipulated *pučisti* officers? Were the officers suborned by the SOE to overthrow the government? Before examining other's investigations, let us first dispose of the issue of subornation. This is the preferred "anti-officers" agrument of former German collaborators. According to them, Professor R. W. Seton-Watson claimed the officers were paid from British secret funds. Seton-Watson's rebuttal of 4 April 1951 reads,

> These men, egged on by a guilty conscience, have tried to represent the coup d'état of 1941 as the work of men in the pay of the British, and thereby to promote the possibility of their own return to power.
>
> ...what forces me to speak now is the publication, in March 1951, of a pamphlet quoting an alleged statement of mine: 'We paid for the entry of Jugoslavia into the war with the sum of £500,000, and we owe the Serbs nothing.'
>
> I hardly need to add that I never made such statement in any form whatsoever, and that these charges, from beginning to end, are to be regarded as impudent and malicious calumnies.[7]

Many British and Yugoslav writers have dealt with the other matters. Yugoslav historiography may be best discussed by the geographical location of the writers, that is, Yugoslav works from Yugoslavia, and those from abroad or the *"emigré"* works.[8] As to British historiography of the event, it is important to realize that it was originally based on the euphoria with which London greeted the news of the coup in Belgrade. This event released all the pent-up tension which had built up in Whitehall during the preceding efforts to have Yugoslavia declare itself against Germany. Relieved at the turn of events, London jumped to the conclusion that the coup was due to the efforts of the SOE:

London was quick to apportion credit for the welcome surprise. The War Cabinet Defence Committee agreed on 27 March to send an 'expression of appreciation' to Dalton 'for the part played by his organization in bringing about the *coup d'etat* in Yugoslavia'[9]

The initial belief resulted in writings appropriating the credit for the event not only to the SOE, but also to this or that other British vested interest. This trend has been reviewed by Wheeler in his decisive style,[10] and more sedately by Stafford in the article on SOE.[11] Stafford's review may be said to be the definite interpretation of the manner and the degrees in which different British agencies deserve credit for the coup. In his assessment of the work done at Belgrade, he says,

> it is clear that there was considerable rivalry between (the Services attachés and the SOE), and that as the direction of the British effort changed, so did the contribution of the SOE and the attachés.... But..., whatever persuasion the British exercised, it is still clear that the initiative came from the Yugoslavs, and only be a stretch of imagination can the British be said to have planned or directed the *coup d'etat*.[12]

Stafford's assessment is correct: the actual *coup d'etat* was the result of a purely domestic military conspiracy.[13] This verdict should not detract from the credit that the SOE operatives deserve for their other work in Belgrade. When they had to move to Turkey and the Middle East, the connections that they made in Belgrade enabled them to re-establish contact with occupied Serbia and gather intelligence more easily. By doing so they might have overstepped their Charter, as they were members of a Sabotage, and not of an intelligence organisation. Still, in their own (and successful) way, they served the best interests of Britain. The question remains, what additional influences combined to translate the diffuse frustration of the army officers into positive action? This issue goes beyond assessment of quantifiable British activities in Belgrade. It deals with the efficiency of British propaganda as judged by the Serb response to it.

First, an analysis of contemporary Serb public opinion is needed. This was the key which made the work of British propaganda much easier. The Serbs, and their army officers, needed no coaching to hate German expansion. Their memories of the First World War had not yet died down. When in 1914 Serbia repulsed two major Austro-Hungarian invasions, Germany stepped in and was instrumental in over-running Serbia in 1915 and bringing about a three-year occupation of the country. The rise and expansion of Germany under Hitler was now resented both for itself and because, since the *Anschluss,* she was also the heir to the former Austria-Hungary. Germany was conceived as the ominous bearer of a renewed *Grand nach Osten.* Thus British anti-Nazi propaganda found in Belgrade a fertile ground for its own action. Its main thrust was to remind the Serbs of their "Kosovo Ethic": defending national honour regardless of consequences. Considering that the Serbian leaders were themselves appealing to the "Kosovo" spirit of their compatriots, British propaganda is seen to have been on the right track. At the news of the coup, there was no rejoicing in Zagreb. However, Serb masses demonstrated in Belgrade with the slogan "Better war than the Pact..." (*"Bolje rat nego pakt!"*); this was conceived as the ultimate confirmation that the "Kosovo" spirit had re-awakened. Stalinist-Communist agitators appeared only in the afternoon after the *Puč,* shouting themselves hoarse with their puny slogan "Mos-cow—Bel-grade," "Mos-cow—Bel-grade." In the euphoria of the day, the people did not mind it. Had anyone stopped to think about it, he would have been struck by the incongruity of this slogan: "Mos-cow" and Hitler were at that time bedfellows, yet the whole drift of the *Puč* was against Hitler. "Better dead than a slave" (*"Bolje grob nego rob"*) chanted the masses. But how much is the "Kosovo spirit" really an all-embracing interpretation of contemporary Serb attitudes? During the centuries of their enslavement under the Turks, the Battle of Kosovo reminded them of the loss of the Serb Medieval Empire. But the Empire was avenged in Serbia's and Montenegro's liberation wars from 1912 to 1918. In revenge for Kosovo, in 1389, Turkey lost the Battle of Kumanovo, in 1912. "Austria," which took over Bosnia and Hercegovina and its mixed population from Turkey after the Congress of Berlin, was defeated in 1918. Now, all Serb lands were geographically gathered in the same Kingdom. But in the Kingdom of Yugoslavia, Serbia ceased to exist. Even the use of the Serb name was forbidden from 1929 to 1938, when everyone was forced to declare himself of "Yugoslav" ethnicity. Even after 1938, the Serb flag was still outlawed. By contrast, the Croats were given an enlarged *Banovina* in 1939, and the use of Croat colours was legal. In this manner the Serbs, whose wars were instrumental in the creation of Yugoslavia, had become resentfull of being second-class citizens in their own country.

It follows that their reaction to the coup of 27 March 1941 was complex. To put officers' frustrations aside, the coup appeared to the Serbs not simply a means of defending national honour against Hitler's encroachments. It was also taken to mean redressing their demeaning domestic position. Hence, on 27 March, one could hear their singing of "Oi, Serbia" beside "Long live the King." In the euphoria of national re-assertion, the streets of Belgrade echoed also to the shouts of "There's no war without the Serbs" (*"Nema rata bez Srba!"*). Whence this martial slogan? It expressed a regained self-confidence, based on the role of the Serbian army in the Allied victory on the Macedonian front in September 1918. The breakthrough was planned by the Serbian Field-Marshal (*"Vojvoda"*) Mišić, and Serbian troops were the spearhead of the Allied advance. According to Ludendorff, then the First Quartermaster General of the German Army, this event "sealed the fate of the Quadruple Alliance." The Chief of Staff, von Hindenburg, agreed with Ludendorff. On 3 October 1918 the two men advised the German government that,

> as a result of the collapse of the Macedonian front, and of the weakening of our reserves in the west, which this has necessitated . . . the only right course is to bring the war to a close, in order to spare the German people and their allies useless sacrifices.[14]

The proposition that the role of the Serbian Army was crucial in the breakthrough by the Macedonian front *and thus* in winning World War I was the foundation of all education in Yugoslav military schools. Serb civilian society was influenced in the same sense by the fireside stories of the returned veterans. Hence the slogan "There's no war . . . ," chanted by the Serb masses on 27 March. It meant, of course, "The Serbs are needed to win the victory." In human relations, firmly held beliefs equal material facts. Even so, in this instance there is still no link which shows conclusively what triggered all these emotional manifestations. What tilted the scales? There can be no doubt that this can be found in British propaganda by wild rumours, which have been hitherto overlooked by historians. The centrepiece of this propaganda was the rumour that Britain had landed 100,000 troops in Greece. The Serbs believed it because they wanted to. It was a brilliant stroke by whoever directed this propaganda offensive: SOE, SIS, service attachés or somebody else. Even after the coup, on his secret visit to Belgrade, General Sir John Dill, C.I.G.S., told Simović that in Greece "half of a projected force of 150,000 was already in place," but on 3 April in a conference at Florina, Greece, General Wilson "immediately put Janković straight regarding Britain's troop strength."[15] It was too late for Brigadier General Mirković, the effective head of the coup, to say to Wing Commander Macdonald, of the Military Attachés office in Belgrade on 5 April: *"Ce n'est pas sérieux."*[16] This belated scorn lends veracity to the report of the newspaper correspondent St. John that, after the coup, "army officers told (him) they believed every word" of the rumours that "a mighty Balkan army" would "help Greece and Yugoslavia defy the Nazis . . . ."[17] It would seem obvious that this finally tilted the scales for the coup.

CHAPTER 2

CHURCHILL, HITLER, AND YUGOSLAVIA

Hitler's retribution for the coup in Belgrade was swift. Within three weeks the Yugoslav army was effectively no more. The *Wehrmacht* saw to this in the Yugoslav and Greek campaign of April 1941. The main characteristic of the April War is that before the event, both friend and foe believed they were dealing with an army firmly steeped in Serbian military traditions. Their belief was based on the knowledge of the prowess of the Serbian Army in the First World War, when Serbian soldiers distinguished themselves as "masters of mountain warfare."[1] This continuing belief in a "Serbian Army" was primarily due to the deceiving packaging—the uniform—of the Yugoslav Army, which had continued to wear the former Serbian regulation dress. Thus, by default, nobody perceived the inner contradictions and the demoralization discussed earlier that affected its *esprit de corps*. This made the observers fail to distinguish between the Serbs as first rate military material, and the Yugoslav Army as an instrument of State. When the Yugoslav Forces collapsed and capitulated on 17 April 1941, this appreciation of the imaginary "Serbian Army" turned into scorn. The pendulum swung to the opposite extreme, and the Serbs carried the onus for what was not their doing. Shortly afterwards, the appearance of Colonel Mihailović, and the news that the "Serbian Remnants" of the Yugoslav Army continued to resist, cheered the Allies and enraged Hitler. Three years later, the pendulum swung again and carried away Mihailović, his brother officers and the concept of a predominant Serbian role in Balkan affairs.

In the days of the post-coup crisis, Churchill wished the Serbs would repeat their World War I exploits, and Hitler was apprehensive that they might. Churchill learned about the coup in Belgrade eight and a half hours after the event. This is revealed in British sources. The coup occurred at 2.20 a.m. local time (1.20 a.m. in London); the telegram bearing this news reached the Foreign Office at 9.55 the same morning. (In comparison, the telegram of the German Legation in Belgrade did not reach Berlin, in the same time-zone as Belgrade, until 11.55 a.m.) Churchill was informed "half an hour" before he had to address the Conservative Council as new leader of the Party. Sir Alexander Cadogan, Permanent Under-Secretary of State for Foreign Affairs, wrote in his diary,

> Thursday, 27 March. Good news arriving at F[oreign] O[ffice], of *coup d'etat* in Belgrade. Went to see P[rime] M[inister] at 11.40. He was due to make speech at 12.

Churchill later wrote that this *coup d'etat* and the consequent Serb anti-Nazi demonstrations occurred "in the moment of (Hitler's) greatest power." Hitler's own words are to similar effect, *viz.*, "In the winter of 1940-1941 . . . . Our Army, . . . was mobilized and, as it were, unemployed."[2] Elated, Churchill informed his audience at the Conservative Council that he had "great news: . . . the Yugoslav nation has found its soul." This lucky turn of phrase brilliantly conveys that, after a period of wavering between Germany and Britain, Yugoslavia had finally opted for Britain. Cadogan claims he gave this phrase to Churchill. An earlier entry by Cadogan in his *Diary* lends credibility to this claim. During the preceding period of tension when both the British and German governments competed in pressing the Government of Yugoslavia to take sides, Cadogan wrote in his diary on Friday 21 March: "Yugoslavs seem to have sold their souls to the Devil," meaning, of course, that they had sided with Germany.[3] In this context, the comment regarding the state of "Yugoslavia's soul" on 27 March can be seen to be the resolution of Cadogan's concern on 21 March. Notwithstanding this academic detail, publicly Churchill was speaking of that composite state, Yugoslavia. Yet privately, on the very day he was bestowed a soul on Yugoslavia, he spoke only of a *coup d'état* "in Serbia" in his message to the Foreign Secretary Anthony Eden. Three weeks later, when Yugoslavia and its army were disintegrating in the war with Germany and her allies, Churchill advised the British Minister in Yugoslavia on 13 April 1941 that the "Serbian Army" should withdraw into the mountains and there continue to fight on. In view of the fact that Mihailović—independently of Churchill's urgings—disobeyed the order for capitulation of his army group on 15 April, the relevant part of Churchill's message of 13 April deserves to be cited. It reads,

> ...We do not see why the King or Government should leave the country, which is vast, mountainous, and full of armed men. German tanks can no doubt move along the roads and tracks, but to conquer the Serbian armies they must bring up infantry. Then will be the chance to kill them.[4]

Churchill went on to speak of the successful defence of mountain regions by the Serbian Army. But that was no Serbian, only a Yugoslav, Army. In the words of Velimir Terzić, a regular captain in the old Yugoslav Army and later Tito's Chief of Staff and a Partisan General,

> There was not anymore the legendary Serbian Army, which was fully supported by the whole Serb people and had an inborne offensive spirit. The Yugoslav Army was a mixture of many different nationalities with different attitudes to Yugoslav unity and State, of whom some were fanatically devoted to the defence of the freedom and independence, some others were indifferent to it, and a third group (the fascists and the national minorities) were ready for treason and cooperation with the enemy.[5]

When Hitler was informed on 27 March about the events in Belgrade, he was at first incredulous and thought that the news about the *"Putsch"* was a "joke."[6] The presence of the Foreign Minister of Japan, Matsuoka, on a visit to Berlin, must have been particularly embarrassing. Hitler immediately ordered that Yugoslavia be ruthlessly destroyed. The terse, impersonal entries in the War Diary of the Supreme Command of the *Wehrmacht* read,

...Prince Paul and the Yugoslav Government resigned.... [In Belgrade] demonstrations outside German Legation.... Towards 1300 hours the Chief of the *Wehrmachtfuehrungsstab* telephoned that the Fuehrer is resolved to destroy Yugoslavia. The commanders-in-chief of the Army and Air Force are already with the Fuehrer.[7]

On the same afternoon, Hitler harangued his aides about his determination to destroy Yugoslavia immediately, both "militarily and as a state."[8] His diatribe at this conference was eventually embodied in formal guidelines for attack on Yugoslavia, the emergency "Directive No. 25."[9] He ordered that the Directive and the army and air force plans be submitted to him the same evening.[10] The original plan "Marita," for attack on Greece, also had to be amended.[11] In Churchill's words, Hitler was "stung to the quick." It is not mere speculation to suggest that his emotional need required much more than the simple destruction of Yugoslavia. He needed to vent his range on something more tangible and picked on what he called the "officers camarilla in Yugoslavia," which, he said, was "always inclined towards a *coup d'état*."[12] From his original position that the "Serbian officers' corps" had affronted him, his next step was the instruction that "the Serbs must be thoroughly squashed."[13] Hitler's emotional malevolence towards the Serbs, engendered by the *"Putsch,"* led him to commit two crucial blunders. First, he attacked Yugoslavia, dismembered it, and opened the door to the genocide of the Serbs in the satellite Croatia. This forced the Serbs to rise in self-defence, and the now famous wartime resistance in occupied Yugoslavia was born. His second blunder was also a consequence of his decision to harm Serbs. In order to dispatch Yugoslavia expeditiously, he had to postpone his planned attack on the Soviet Union, *Operation Barbarossa*. He issued the latter directive on the day of the coup, itself, 27 March 1941, *viz.,*

...employ such strong forces that the Yugoslav collapse will take place within the shortest time. *In this connection, the beginning of Operation Barbarossa* [the attack on the Soviet Union] *will have to be postponed up to 4 weeks.*[14]

As these events recede into the dim past, historians occasionally discuss whether it was the Belgrade coup of March 1941 which made Hitler postpone his attack on the Soviet Union. Surely, Hitler's own directive on the day of the coup cited above, settles this point.

Hitler, as Churchill, had in mind the old Serbian Army, and diverted too many troops to overcome assumed Yugoslav resistance, which adversely affected his original time-table. After the simultaneous attack against Greece ("Operation Marita") and Yugoslavia ("Directive No. 25") had been launched in the early morning of 6 April, Goebbels broadcast Hitler's "Proclamation to the German People." Regarding Yugoslavia, the Proclamation opened with a rambling preamble wailing that Hitler had passed over "all that once [in World War I] had occurred between Germany and Serbia" and that despite this old enmity he prevailed on Yugoslavia to join the Tripartite Pact, which she had done on 25 March. But, said Hitler,

> Hardly had the ministers who signed the pact returned to Belgrade than the elements in British pay, a military clique, which is constantly organizing *coups d'état,* prepared their counter-blow. The Government which had striven for peace with Germany was overthrown, with the explicit announcement that this was necessary in view of its attitude towards Germany.

Claiming, falsely, that many anti-German incidents also had occurred in different parts of Yugoslavia since the *coup d'état* of 27 March, Hitler now put on the mantle of an expert in Balkan history and went on,

> These incidents were provoked by the same creatures who in 1914 drove the world into unbounded misery by the Sarajevo murder. Now, just as then, this military clique of criminals was financed and incited by the British Secret Service. Although the events today are similar to those of 1914, one thing has changed since. The State which is being attacked is not the Austria of 1914 but the German Reich of to-day.

The flourish was added also:

> The German nation will now settle accounts with that Serb clique of criminals in Belgrade who believe they can once more offer the Balkans as a base for a British attack on European peace.[15]

On the eve of his invasion of Yugoslavia, Hitler wrote to Mussolini,

> I realise that this will be a hard struggle against an extremely tough and brave opponent . . . .[16]

Concerned that he was going to fight an army in the mould of the old Serbian Army, Hitler decided to play safe. On land, he assigned 24 German divisions against Yugoslavia, and ensured for himself the overall command of an additional 23 Italian and 5 Hungarian divisions. The armament and equipment of Italian and Hungarian armies were similar to that of the Yugoslav army, while the German divisions consisted of excellently armed and war hardened troops. To oppose this overwhelming Axis onslaught, the Yugoslav army had 31 divisions in all; on 6 April—the day of the German invasion—they were still only partly mobilized. Furthermore, the artillery and supply trains, as well as the higher Yugoslav headquarters (divisional, armies, army groups and the Supreme Command) and the communications services were not yet fully mobilized.[17] To understand the import of this information, one has to be familiar with the organization of the former Yugoslav Army. In peacetime there was no operative armed force (divisions, armies, army groups), but only HQs territorial military areas (e.g., "HQ Divisional Military Area," "HQ Army Military Area"). These were in charge of military administration, training and the establishments (stores, hospitals etc.). They were not at a standard of war preparedness. After a period of equivocation in the vain wish "not to provoke" (!) Hitler, Simović belatedly set the first day of mobilization for the 3rd of April.[18] Even so, it was decided to mobilise by secretly mailing individual call-up notices (*"opšte aktiviranje"*), instead of publicly calling all to arms (*"pošta mobilizacija"*). To top it all, German troops were relying on motorized transport, while the mobility of Yugoslav troops and supply was restricted by the speed of horses and oxen pulling their loads. The impact of this difference can be seen from a description by Robert St. John, a war correspondent. One rainy night he witnessed an ox-cart column on march.

> A team of oxen pulling a peasant wagon. Behind that first team was another and then another. As far as we could see in the light of the headlights there were oxen and peasant carts. Two soldiers walked

beside the head of each of those lumbering, plodding, animals. Inside each wagon there were a few cans of gasoline, or some hay, or some sacks of bread. Supplies for the Yugoslav army.

St. John and his friends counted the ox-carts: "one hundred, two hundred, three hundred . . . ." When he was in Romania, he had witnessed German supply columns:

> Tremendous motor trucks. Any one truck would have held almost as much as all these ox-carts put together. And the truck would have covered in an hour the distance these oxen would cover in a whole day and night.[19]

In the air, against the enemy offensive of 1,500 German and 670 Italian planes, a total of 2,170 planes against Yugoslavia, the latter could put up only 416 planes, of which over a third were old models.[20] To this glaring disproportion of forces and their capabilities must be added yet another fortuitous military factor in favour of the aggressor. Until the *Anschluss* of Austria to Germany in 1938, the only military threat to Yugoslavia was posed by Fascist Italy. Of the other neighbours, Albania was insignificant, and Romania and Greece were friendly. Hungary and Bulgaria were inimical, but could not pose any military threat, as they were emasculated by the demilitarisation provisions of the Neuilly and St. Germain peace treaties of 1919 and 1920. When the *Anschluss* brought Nazi Germany to the north-west frontier of Yugoslavia, the Yugoslav General Staff was obliged for the first time to plan for the contingency of war with Germany. Hitler subsequently garrisoned his troops successively in Hungary, Romania and Bulgaria, forcing Yugoslav war planners constantly to amend their plans. In February 1941 the General Staff started putting into effect its latest war plan, the "R 41" ("*Rat* [19]41," "War [19]41"), which was dispatched to the higher commands of the army, air force and navy on 31 March 1941.[21] The German attack was launched a week later. Due to this coincidence, even without knowing it, the German invasion caught the Yugoslav army in a state of transition on two counts. Yugoslav forces were caught at the moment of mobilisation, and secondly, they were caught at a changeover in war dispositions. This set of circumstances was the worst possible combination for a defender, and an ideal one for the attacker. Given inferior strength, inadequate mobilisation and new war plans it is not surprising that the Yugoslav armed forces capitulated.

The *Wehrmacht* simultaneously attacked Greece, and, despite British and Anzac[22] support, the Greek army also capitulated. An assessment of the reasons for the debacle in Greece may be used as a comparative yardstick for a succint overview of the Yugoslav case. The concluding assessment of the war in Greece is given in the semi-official Australian history of that war. It reads,

> The actual conquest of Yugoslavia and Greece was achieved by a fraction of the troops the Germans laboriously deployed. In the face of such reserve power, detailed examination of Allied [Y] supply problems, the state of the Greek [Y] Army, and the degree of Allied [Y] inferiority in the air, would be prolix.[23]

However there is a striking difference in the way in which the Greek and the Yugoslav governments reacted to the military *débàcle* in their countries. In Greece, the campaign was ended by an illegal capitulation signed by General Tsolakoglou on 20 April 1941; he acted as the head of a cabal of general officers who disobeyed the order of their King and government not to capitulate. Their wilful action added to the other pressures on the King and government to leave Athens. Contrary to the positive war record of the Greek government, the Yugoslav government scurried away in indecent haste while the military campaign was still going on. Before his desertion the Prime Minister of Yugoslavia, General Simović, should have at least tried to see his own instruction of 10 April executed, ordering all units to withdraw to [East] Bosnia and "exercise initiative in engaging the enemy in combat."[24] There he should have combined there a last stand (*"Ils ne passeront pas!"*) and guerrilla action, at the same time following up the initial successes of the anti-Italian offensive in Northern Albania. Instead, Simović and the government lost heart and fled the country, but not before many of them found time to collect their wives, relations and friends. When they left the airfield at Nikšić for Greece and British protection, the eleven senior ministers used the restricted accommodation of the military aircraft to evacuate six wives, four sons, two daughters, one brother, one niece, two political friends and the wife of one of the friends. The *Ban* of Croatia, Šubašić, took with him his wife, and the new Commander of the Air Force, Mirković, his brother and his niece.[25] In view of Churchill's recommendation of 13 April 1941 that they should not leave the country, it is questionable if Yugoslav exiles were welcome. However, once they sought British protection, they were given a faultless reception. The boy-King, Peter II, left on 14 April, Simović and a group of ministers fled on 15 April, and another group on 16th April, 1941.[26]

On 14 April, before abandoning the country, Simović divested himself of the position of Chief of Staff of the Supreme Command. He had assumed it at the beginning of the war, and now had General Kalafatović appointed to that post. Until that date, Kalafatović, a General (Rtd), was Chief of Staff Supreme Command Rear Area. Retaining his capacity as Prime Minister, on 13 April Simović instructed General Kalafatović in writing that his government had decided, *inter alia*, that Kalafatović should forthwith ask the enemy for an armistice. Kalafatović was also instructed that his "decisions" (*"odluke"*) in this matter would be sanctioned by the government as its own and that he was to take "any other measures that might be required."[27] As the German Command refused to entertain any negotiations, the end of the war was embodied in the armistice between the German, Italian and Yugoslav Forces dictated by Germany and signed in Belgrade on 17 April 1941 "at 21.00 hours."[28] On 18 April, the day after the capitulation, the communique of the German High Command read,

> As has been announced already in the *Sondermeldung*, the whole *Serbian Army* [!] capitulated on the evening of the 17th. Battle activity in Yugoslavia will cease at 12 noon on the 18th.[29]

Did General Kalafatović have the competence to accept the German amistice *Diktat* unconditionally? The Prime Minister gave Kalafatović a written instruction specifying that all his decisions would be sanctioned by the government. Kalafatović had no reason to believe that Simović was acting without knowledge of the government.[30] Secondly, Kalafatović was appointed Chief of Staff (CofS) Supreme Command when the IV Army (Croatia) and the VII Army (Slovenia) had already ceased to exist, and other armies were in disarray. Thus, Kalafatović's handling of the political situation was dictated by the situation in the field. Thirdly, Kalafatović was certainly not acting in isolation. According to the *Memoirs* of King Peter II, when he was advised by his Minister of the Royal Court [Professor Radoje Knežević] to fly from Nikšić to Athens he was told that "the Supreme Command would officially announce the capitulation of the Army." According to Čulinović, Miho Krek, a Slovene, one-time Vice-Prime Minister in the exiled government, stated that General Ilić, the Minister for the Army and Navy, had told some ministers on 15 April 1941, at Nikšić, that the "capitulation was signed." Another minister, Sava Kosanović, agrees that he learned the news in Nikšić on 15 April.[31] Finally, as the exiled Royal Yugoslav Goverment of General Simović did not denounce the convention of capitulation on escaping the country, it may be said that the government ratified it at least *de facto* if not *de iure*. Some authors say that the exiled Yugoslav government denounced the convention of capitulation in its first meeting after leaving the country, held at Athens on 17 April 1941. The minutes of this meeting have been published. They do not support this contention, nor could they have done so since the meeting, in two sessions, had been held before the capitulation convention was signed. Indeed, the belated declaration of the exiled government, issued at Jerusalem on 4 May 1941, by no stretch of the imagination can be interpreted as denouncing the convention of capitulation, despite opinions to the contrary. In fact, the statements in the declaration such as "Our confidence in the final positive result of our painful and great struggle is unshakable," and "we are proud again to be on the side of our allies . . ."[32] certainly met political necessities of the day, although they are platitudes. They bring out the fact that Simović and his government had not renounced the capitulation—a situation that was to affect adversely the legal standing of Mihailović and his troops.

The case against Kalafatović is not concerned with his legal competence to act, but with his handling of the whole affair, and especially his authorisation of armistice/capitulation *Diktat*. Terzić, whose qualitative comparison of the Serbian and Yugoslav Armies has been cited earlier in this chapter, argues that,

> While there was still time to do so, the Yugoslav Supreme Command should have instructed that the units be disbanded and the men sent home with their arms (as it was done by Zeta and Hercegovina

Divisions). Alternatively, the Supreme Command should have authorized the commanders of the army, air force and navy to do so. Such an action would have prevented almost a quarter of a million men remaining for four years in the prisoner of war camps. Had the Supreme Command sent the armed men home, conditions for waging the War of People's Liberation would have been better, with bigger reserves of fighting men and of the light and heavy armament and other equipment.[33]

The post-capitulation flurry in the HQ of the Yugoslav Supreme Command ended in "closing all books and passing on the archives" (to whom?). The HQ Yugoslav Supreme Command itself, and the HQ Supreme Command (Rear Area) were closed down on 25 April 1941 at noon.[34] Exit.

While this was happening, General Dušan T. Simović, one-time Chief of the General Staff, Commander of the Air Force, Chief of Staff of the Supreme Command, Prime Minister of Yugoslavia and now Prime Minister of the Government-in-Exile, was received abroad as an Allied anti-Nazi hero. In London, Simović's government fell on 9 January 1942 and Simović vanished into obscurity. Eventually, in 1944, he declared for Tito and at the end of the war repatriated to Yugoslavia, a Republic.[35]

One of the legacies of the April War was that a great number of Serbs remained in German and Italian POW camps until these countries in their turn lost the war. This great number of POWs was due to a combination of different factors: the drawbacks of the Yugoslav territorial war recruiting system, the political dissolution of embattled Yugoslavia (triggering off military rebellions and treason), the handling of armistice provisions by the Yugoslav Supreme Command, and Hitler's instruction that "the Serbs must be thoroughly squashed." Yugoslav war units were mobilized locally. Most Slovenes served in the VII Army, and most Croats in the IV Army. Due to political developments triggered by the setting-up of an independent Croatia on 10 April, the two armies disbanded and by 14 April did not exist. Some Croatian events were a repetition of the last stages of the dissolution of the Habsburg Monarchy in 1918. For instance the Yugoslav 108th Infantry Regiment refused to take its position in the front line, and the 13th Infantry wounded its regimental commander, and killed two battalion commanders and the regimental legal officer.[36] This gave some people the impression that all the Croats committed treason. At the same time, the units mobilized in Serbia and South Serbia (now called Macedonia) were quickly over-run and defeated. The casualties included Brigadier General Mihailo St. Golubović, commanding the infantry of the Toplica Division, Colonels Milo Radunović, of the 20th Infantry and F. Gradišnik of the Air Force; Gradišnik was killed when leading a bomber-attack on a German tank column. When Kalafatović was appointed Chief of Staff on 14 April, he was instructed in writing to ask for an armistice immediately, "Because of the state our army is in after the first reverses, and particularly because because of the delicate position caused by the events in Croatia and Dalmatia...."[37] Kalafatović consulted with his chief assistants. They followed Simović's instruction, and decided to ask for an "honourable armistice," arguing that "total dissolution of our armed forces" had occurred in Croatia, Dalmatia and Slovenia.[38] This formulation of the military situation on 14 April 1941 triggered a lot of political wrangling as to whether it was the collapse of the front in Serbia, or in Croatia etc. that caused the collapse of Yugoslavia. Surely, this is a contrived argument. The collapse of the front in Serbia was of a military nature or the issue of *force majeure,* and in Croatia the collapse was a political issue or a question of loyalty. As the ensuing convention of the armistice required that Yugoslav troops be transported into captivity, the question of Yugoslav prisoners of war requires analysis. This question has two components. What happened in the field? How were Yugoslav prisoners of war treated by German authorities?

According to the German military historian *General der Infanterie* Kurt von Tippelskirch, German forces captured 1,500 officers and 224,000 other ranks (a total of 225,500) during the Yugoslav operations; after the capitulation the total number of prisoners rose to 334,000 "Serbs." He correctly classifies the origin of Yugoslav POWs into those captured in battle, and those mopped up *"nach Abschluss aller Kaempfe"* (when all battle ceased). But he specifies also that

> ...until the end of the [April] war, the advancing [German] troops were not able to overcome the strong Yugoslav resistance at Vranje and in the Upper Ibar [in Serbia].[39]

Discussing the debacle of 1941, Brigadier General Milićević says,

Many field units became prisoners of war without having encountered the enemy at all and even less fired a rifle in anger, while others were rolled over and destroyed by enemy tanks, machinegun fire and concentrated air bombardment.[40]

In some instances the units were even informed that, by the provisions of the armistice, those parts of the country which were conquered in battle would form occupied territory, and the remainder of the country would be under the Belgrade government. The troops of the former territories were to be deemed prisoners of war, and the others were to continue serving. The mobilized men of the latter were to be discharged immediately, and the regular personnel and the national servicemen were ordered to return to their peacetime garrisons and resume duty. It had not yet become known that the King, and Simović with the government, had fled the country. This purported arrangement was reminiscent of the case of France, and in the field all of it was believed. This will be illustrated by the case of the Artillery Regiment of the King's Guards. They and some other units camped for a number of days at Grošnica near Kragujevac, south of Belgrade, awaiting there their entrainment to return to duty. They learned the truth only on 24 April, when the railways transported them from Kragujevac into captivity. Others again, like some artillery officers of the Valjevo garrison south-west of Belgrade, even returned to their barracks only to learn that they had been cheated.

Yet at the same time, on the Italian front in Albania, Yugoslav troops had no word from the Supreme Command and continued with offensive operations. On 20 April (three days after the formal capitulation) one division reached the northern area of Skadar (Scutari, Shkoder). Until the 22nd, when they learned about the capitulation, they continued attacking the enemy although he had superior forces. This was a period of total confusion, which must abound with contradictions. Provided this qualification is kept in mind, the claim of Terzić, cited below, seems to represent a fair assessment,

> The mass capture of POWs was primarily caused by the Yugoslav Supreme Command itself. By its order of 14 April to cease fire, as well as later, the Supreme Command informed its subordinate commands that the armistice had been concluded, and unconditional

surrender was not mentioned. Consequently in the majority of cases the men were not discharged from their units, and the units awaited with their full complement the arrival of German and Italian troops, which then disarmed them and led them into captivity.[41]

Was this a case of intentionally issued false orders, or was it administrative bungling?

Kalafatović made two attempts to end the disastrous war after he took over the Supreme Command. On 14 April, he immediately dispatched a team to negotiate an "honourable armistice" with the invading German command. General Freiherr von Weichs, of the German 2nd Army, refused to comply, then on 16 April Kalafatović appointed a new team to sign the German dictated non-negotiable "armistice." Of the original first team negotiators only Lieutenant General Bodi and Lieutenant Colonel Trojanović carried out their mission.[42] Instructions issued to Bodi contained *inter alia* the following points:

(i) . . .
(ii) Demand a regime as in the case of France and see to it that we retain in our hands as much territory as possible;
(iii) Ask that, until the signing of a peace treaty, we retain a military force of about 40-50,000 men; this force is needed to safeguard public order in the country;
(iv) Our soldiers should not be conveyed into captivity but allowed to [return home] and till the soil;
(v) . . .
(vi) [Demand] that our regular officers and NOCs not be considered POWs, and those not needed for the above Force [see item (iii) above] be discharged from service.[43]

It can be seen that these abortive clauses of initial instruction for negotiating an armistice, and the contents of the final field orders issued—say— to the Guards Artillery, strongly resemble each other. In fact, in this instance the coincidence goes further than the strictures raised by Terzić, who claims only that the troops were not told that the unconditional surrender was an integral part of the convention of armistice. However this evidence, powerful as it is, still remains circumstantial. Conclusive evidence as to who was responsible for these false orders, the extent of this deception, and whether it was a premediated action or an inexcusable piece of administrative bungling, remains buried in the Yugoslav archives. On the other hand, it should be said that the wholesale "capturing" of a capitulated army is the usual procedure. Obviously, the Yugoslav rank and file did not know about it, neither have their historians learned it as yet.

The screening of Yugoslav troops for retention as prisoners of war, or for their release, was initially regulated by the directive of the *Oberkommando des Heeres* (OKH, The Command of the Land Army) of 20 April 1941.[44] The complete listing of those who were to be released read "the *Volksdeutsche,* Hungarians, Bulgarians, Albanians, Dalmatians and Croats." By a supplementary order of 27 April the Rumanians were included also. Serbs, Slovenians and Jews were not listed for release. This is a clear case of racial discrimination. The criterion for the screening of POWs was territorial rather than ethnic. For instance, "Bulgarians" meant people from parts of Serbia handed by Hitler to Bulgaria, and not those of Bulgarian ethnicity. This tempted the individual Serb to seek release by acknowledging the partition of Yugoslavia and renouncing his Serbian ethnic identity. Thus tensions and public divisions amongst the Serbs in the POW camps arose.

How many Yugoslav POWs were there? Historians usually cite 344,000, or 334,000, of which, of course, are the numbers given by Matl and Tippelskirch respectively.[45] Neither of these figures is satisfactory. They are estimates, not a headcount. In order to obtain a meaningful headcount, one has to decide which source and date to use. I decided to approach the International Committee of the Red Cross, which is the international custodian of POW and refugee records. I also decided that the records to consult would be those established when the screening process had been accomplished and all the non-Serbs released. I wrote to Geneva on 7 May 1981, specifying that,

> One of the points which I would like to elucidate is the number of Yugoslav army personnel taken prisoner of war *and registered* by the OKW with the International Red Cross. To the best of my knowledge there are no reliable historical writings on this topic.
>
> Considering that the OKW, after their capture, released a number of Yugoslav POWs, perhaps the *number of POWs in German camps*

at the end of 1941 would be the most convenient figure for this aspect of Yugoslav military history. May I request to be given this information from your achives.

On 17 June 1981 I further requested the Red Cross for information regarding Yugoslav POWs in Italy, Hungary and Bulgaria. The Red Cross supplied me with the official statistics:[46] a total of 172,776 officers and men were in the POW camps in Germany and Italy (for a detailed itemization refer to the table). Therefore, the enclosed table is the best possible record[47] of the total number of Yugoslav POWs of Serb nationality who fought in the (Royal) Yugoslav Army in April 1941. They were either captured in battle or mopped up in the post-armistice confusion. According to wartime German estimates, another 325,000 men who evaded captivity were at large in occupied Serbia.[48] To understand these figures properly, it is also necessary to know that Mihailović's officers and men started arriving in Yugoslav POW camps only from early 1942.[49] The captured Partisans—now treated as POWs—started arriving only from August 1, 1943.[50]

As a *"Post scriptum"* let us attempt to obtain the minimum number of non-Serbians who loyally fought for Yugoslavia *and were captured* in the war of April 1941. To do so, one has to abstract the number of POW Serbs (172,776) from the field assessment of the total number of prisoners made at the conclusion of the campaign. As the Italian field figures are not available, one has to work from German field figures only. It has been shown that most historians accept ether Tippelskirch's estimate (334,000), or Matl's (344,000); let us adopt the mean, that is 339,000. Deducting the number of registered Serbs from this figure, we obtain,

The grand total 339,000
Less the Serbs . . . . *172,776* retained in POW camps, so that
A balance of . . . . 166,224 benefitted from

Hitler's selective racial discrimination against Serbians, Slovenes and Jews, and were repatriated from POW camps. In the true Balkan fashion however, this sample is not reliable enough to allow for any firm conclusion. For instance, these numbers must also contain those Serbs from Croatia who declared themselves "geographically" Croats. To them this was a condition of life to which they were accustomed in the Croatia-Slavonia of the days of Austria-Hungary.

For the remainder of the Second World War the Nazis referred to the Yugoslav army officers as "Serbian officers," including "Serbian" prisoners of war in German camps. At this point it must be said emphatically that the German position was illegal both in terms of international law (these people were Yugoslav POWs), and in the context of Yugoslav national law. Separate Serbian, Croatian and Slovenian citizenships and armies did not exist. The position of the personnel in the Yugoslav Army was similar to that of the British. In Britain the English, the Scots and the others are British civil or military officers when they serve the crown. In Yugoslavia the Serbs, Croats and Slovenes, when army officers, were Yugoslav army officers. One has to stop here and reflect on the long-term impact of Goebbels's propaganda machine. In order to drive a wedge between the Serbs and Croats, the Nazis and the Ustaša maintained that the Serb Yugoslav army officers were "Serbian officers." The implied insinuation was that they were agents of a central government which was, supposedly, oppressing the Croat people. Despite the lapse of time, this thrust of Goebbel's propaganda still lingers in many contemporary writings, and particularly in the Ustaša-influenced media and historiography.

CHAPTER 3

YUGOSLAVIA IN 1941: OCCUPATION AND REACTION

Under the onslaught of the Nazis in April 1941, Yugoslavia collapsed, the Government fled the country, and armed forces capitulated. Hitler then proceeded to carve up Yugoslavia into ten different units. He concurred with Mussolini in creating the Independent State of Croatia—*"Nezavisna Država Hrvatska"* or the NDH, 1941-45. Croatia joined the Tripartite Pact of the Axis Powers on 15 June 1941, declared war on Great Britain and the USA in mid-December 1941, and sent troops to the Russian Front. The British Political Warfare Executive (PWE) referred to "the Croat and Bulgarian declarations of war" in its weekly directive for BBC Yugoslav services 19 December 1941–2 January 1942, specifying at the same time that "Britain does not even recognize that Independent Croatia exists."[1] The Croat Regiment, captured at Stalingrad, was "after the usual purification" transformed into the "Yugoslav Anti-Fascist Brigade."[2] Slovenia was partitioned between Germany and Italy. Further, Montenegro was meant to become an Italian client-state, and a truncated Serbia was put under the direct command of the *Wehrmacht*.

This re-organisation forms the setting for the uprisings of the Serbs across occupied Yugoslavia and in their turn, these uprisings provide the background for the ensuing anti-Axis resistance. Understanding this resistance and its associated events will be incomplete without a clear understanding of the uprisings. In the historiography of these uprisings there is a tendency to interpret them either as a spin-off from the Nazi-Soviet war, or as the direct result of the agitation by the Communist Party of Yugoslavia (KPJ, *Komunistička partija Jugoslavije*). The proposition that the entry into the War of the Soviet Union caused the Serb uprisings is erroneous, although the boost to Allied—including Serbian—morale cannot be denied. Neither was the KPJ responsible for them. Serb uprisings had other causes. The grievances and aims of the insurgents differed from one location to another, and the many risings occurred independently of each other. They can be conveniently classifed according to their location as the uprisings in NDH-Croatia, Montenegro, and Serbia. Only the events in the NDH and Montenegro will be treated in this chapter.

Contrary to general belief, the earliest and most sustained Serb uprisings did not occur in occupied Serbia or Montenegro, but in the territory of the NDH. This was a direct result of the killings organized by the Croat Fascist, "Ustasha," regime. Their leader, Ante Pavelić, was an instigator of the assassination of King Alexander I of Yugoslavia in 1934. Now a head of state himself, he took the title *"Poglavnik"* (Fuehrer), and unleashed the pogroms of Serbs, Jews and Gypsies. What type of man was Pavelić, who willfully created these conditions? This can be seen from the testimony of the Italian journalist Malaparte. He and Raffaele Casertano, the Italian Minister at Zagreb, Croatia, called on Pavelić one day towards the end of the European summer in 1941. On his table stood a wicker basket apparently full of mussels or shelled oysters.

> Casertano looked at me—says Malaparte—and winked, 'Would you like a nice oyster stew?' 'Are they Dalmatian oysters?' he asked the Poglavnik. Ante Pavelic removed the lid from the basket and revealed the mussels, that slimy and jelly-like mass, and he said smiling, with that good-natured smile of his, 'It is a present from my loyal ustashis. Forty pounds of human eyes.'[3]

According to Fitzroy Maclean, wartime head of the British mission to the Partisans,

> Some Ustase collected the eyes of the Serbs they had killed, sending them, when they had enough, to the *Poglavnik* for his inspection or

proudly displaying them and other human organs in the cafés of Zagreb.[4]

The Ustashas were deliberately given their genocidal chance by Hitler, when many Serb populated lands were incorporated in the NDH. The Serbs comprised about a third of the population of the NDH. According to a detailed calculation by the German Ministry of Foreign Affairs on 21 May 1941, Croatia comprised 3,000,000 Croats, 1,925,000 Serbs, 700,000 Muslim, 150,000 Germans, 75,000 Hungarians, 65,000 Slovaks, 30,000 Slovenes, 5,000 Italians, and about 40,000 Jews.[5] The large Serbian minority and the massacres committed by the Croat Ustashas explain much of what follows, and in particular why the Serbs in the NDH were the first to rise. Tomasevich, a Croat-American, suggests the Ustashas had a Serbian policy.

> The formula that was... applied to the Serbian population was simple: about one-third would be expelled to Serbia, one-third would be converted [from Eastern Orthodox Christianity] to Roman Catholicism, and one-third would be exterminated.... The final result bore out the formula.[6]

A German researcher, Wuescht,[7] agrees but argues that German military officers in Croatia urged the cessation of this "senseless slaughter of the Serb population." Another author, Milazzo, considers that the Croat Ustashas' "policy of unrestricted terror" had the result that,

> By the end of the [European 1941] summer at least a third of Independent Croatia's population [the 2,000,000 Serbs?], practically all the nearby Italian occupation authorities, and even several Germans were irrevocably opposed to the Ustashi regime.[8]

Djilas says,

> The killing of Serbs was carried out methodically—first the leaders and the more prosperous citizens, the others right down the line.[9]

In his independent research Karchmar reached the same conclusion.[10]

It was the pattern of these killings, rather than the number, that had long term consequences for the Serbian nation. However Ustasha fanaticism resulted in massacres on such a scale that the original selective pattern was obscured. According to M. R. D. Foot, Ustasha massacres had,

> only two parallels during the war: the hundred thousand people shot in one afternoon at Kharkov, and the three million and more sent to their final end at Auschwitz.
> . . . .
> Against this reign of terror, as frightful as Armenia in 1915 or the Punjab in 1947, only the insensately brave or desperate were likely to be ready to resist; many Serbs were to be found to meet even this challenge.[11]

Nevertheless, despite the initial plans of the Ustasha, and the scale of massacres, these fell short of successful genocide. Karchmar ascribes this to insufficient numbers of Ustasha operatives. They could not act over the whole of the NDH simultaneously, so that many potential victims were warned and escaped.[12] To overcome their lack of man-power, the Ustashas in Hercegovina and East Bosnia set the lower strata of the Muslim population against their Serb-Orthodox neighbours[13] encouraging mutual extermination. Setting Muslim against Serb was not an Ustasha innovation. The Austro-Hungarian authorities adopted similar tactics in the First World War.[14] The Muslim leaders defied the Ustasha and denounced their activity, but in the emotional turmoil of the civil war there civilized stand was ignored and forgotten.

It was inevitable that at the village level, in this civil war atmosphere, some Serb insurgents acting in selfdefense exceeded reasonable bounds, and met terror with counter-terror. Tomasevich translates the comments of Živko Topalović, a Serb who in the later stages of war was a prominent Chetnik personality, as,

> Anti-Croatianism, anti-Moslemism, and anti-Yugoslavism, that is the ideology of the Serbian Chetniks. . . . Experience has shown, however, that in addition to mutual extermination the religious-chauvinistic ideology had one basic consequence—it pushed the Serbs, the Croats, and the Moslems into dependence upon and submission to the foreign conqueror. . . .[15]

When comparing this quotation with the original text, it is found that Topalović's crucial introductory and middle paragraphs are missing in Tomasevich's presentation. In his introductory paragraph Topalović says that the Chetniks from the territory of the NDH professed "Serbism" because their rationale was selfdefence from the Croat "Ustashism."[16] Their attitude was a reaction to the events, and not their cause. Surely this is a crucial qualification by the original author, on which the general interpretation of the rest of the quotation stands or falls. Further, where Tomasevich has three dots after the first sentence of his edited quotation ("Serbian Chetniks..."), implying only a minor omission, two whole middle paragraphs are missing. These two paragraphs are qualifying paragraphs which explain the historical setting relevant to the commentary about the "religious-chauvinistic" ideology. The gist of these paragraphs is that in the area of mixed religions, exclusivism has always been a problem, but that the Ustasha's initial killing of the Orthodox and then the Chetniks killing of the Moslem led to the "most primitive religious and chauvinist divisions and fighting."

At this point it is necessary to look at the effect of the methodical elimination of the Serb literate classes by the Ustasha, which was further aggravated by the transfer of many educated Serbs to POW camps. The result of this leadership crisis was that the early Serb uprisings for self-defence were mostly led by the more resolute local peasants, and the occasional local priest, tradesman or NCO, acting without any support from above or outside. Exiled nationalist writers maintain this circumstance enabled the KPJ activists to step in, take over leading positions, and later claim that they started the whole uprising. The nationalist point about the early characteristic of uprisings is borne out by Tito's own admission as to how the KPJ gained the upper hand, *viz.*,

> ...when the people began to take to the woods and hills to save their lives [from the Ustasha], the Party sent its men to head these unfortunate people.[17]

Was this take-over also attempted in Montenegro? Djilas describes it as follows:

> Communist intellectuals—students, teachers, government employees —had taken refuge in the villages with their relatives. They were on a

higher plane and more vigorous than the local leaders, who were largely peasants with a partial education at best. This disparity necessitated the elevation of newcomers to positions of leadership.[18]

The total number of Serbs massacred in the NDH has been hotly disputed, and most commentators usually consider that Serb propaganda has unscrupulously exaggerated the grand total of the victims. This is slippery ground charged with political emotions. The estimates of the number of victims vary from a conservative figure "probably not less than 50,000 Jews and between 50,000 and 100,000 Serbs,"[19] to between 800,000 and 1,000,000 Serbs and Jews, as claimed by Serb emigrés. In the confidential document over the signature of General (*Generaloberst*) Loehr, the German Commander in Chief in the South-East, dated 27 February 1943, it was said that the Ustashas killed about 400,000 of the "Orthodox population" [that is 400,000 Serbs].[20]

Reliable estimates of the number of victims of the Ustasha are difficult. The thousands of corpses thrown in the ravines and strewn all over the countryside can only be guessed at. Nevertheless there was a government-run centre of mass execution, where the number of recovered skeletons was counted after the war. This find is located in the area Jasenovac–Gradina, straddling the river Sava, Yugoslavia. By October 1981 there had been identified 23 mass-graveyards with 162 mass-graves of from 300 to 3,300 skeletons per grave. It has been calculated that these burial places contain more than 500,000 skeletons. An exact calculation was not possible because some of the area is under water, and some is plowed over and cultivated. The estimates for the whole area may be as high as 700,000 victims. In September 1985, due to an exceptionally low water level, another complex of mass graves was discovered, containing over 360,000 additional victims. The Jasenovac complex is now a public shrine. Between 1967 and mid-October 1981, over 2,600,000 Yugoslav visitors had made their pilgrimage to inspect the graves; by the end of 1985, the number of visitors had risen to over 4,000,000.[21] It is reasonable to assume that these skeletons must comprise also some of Pavelić's non-Serb victims, such as Jews and others. These figures should be compared with the wartime reports of General Mihailović. For instance, in his telegram of 10 August 1942 he estimated that "the Ustashi killed 600,000 Serbs, the Germans about 70,000, the Hungarians 30,000 and the Albanians 10,000."[22] In many current statistics of Ustasha genocide the number of victims shown "in Croatia" or "at Jasenovac, Croatia" is minimal, as the count is restricted to the present-day territory of Croatia. Yet most killings occurred in Serb-populated lands which were incorporated in wartime Croatia or the NDH. (Similarly, the Jasenovac mass-graveyard area is only partly in present-day Croatia.)

This slaughter had two unexpected and long lasting consequences, one at home, and the other abroad. At home, Ustasha activity created masses of destitute people. They became a pool of potential recruits for Chetniks and Partisans. This was also the destiny of many escapees who found refuge in Serbia and Montenegro. The same process was particularly strong and noticeable in the NDH, where masses of terrorised and fearful people remained hiding in the mountains. Tito was to write at the end of 1942,

> I must stress the point that in the ranks of our People's Liberation Army and the Partisan Detachments of Yugoslavia, from inception to the present the great majority are the Serbs, instead of the other way round.[23]

Abroad, at the ministerial level of the exiled Royal Yugoslav Government, the news of massacres caused Serbo-Croat relations to worsen to the point where the ministers could not agree even on a joint declaration of war aims. According to Sir George Rendell, who was at that time British envoy to the Yugoslav government,

> [The evidence of massacres] split the Yugoslavs in London—and indeed all the Yugoslav communities abroad and especially in America —more profoundly than ever. The Serbian and Croat Ministers would hardly meet. I begged the Croat Ministers to issue some clear and unequivocal statement condemning and repudiating the atrocities perpetrated by the Ustashi. But, with what seemed typically short-sighted obstinacy, they refused to be either wise or generous....[24]

This quarrel, and the unrelated Yugoslav military crisis at Cairo (which lasted for the best part of 1942), led to a loss of stature of the exiled Yugoslav politicians, and eventually facilitated the transfer of international support to Tito in 1943.

But to revert to the Ustasha terror which was unleashed in the Independent State of Croatia, and the terror that occured in Serb populated lands occupied by Hungary and Bulgaria. The plight of the high number of scarred and destitute refugees being deported or escaping to neighbouring occupied Serbia caused unrest there also.[25] However, the horrors of genocide could have been avoided by orderly deportations. An examination of German diplomatic documents shows that deportations of sorts within occupied Yugoslavia were initiated by the Croat government. A summary or *"Bericht"* of the resettlement policy was written on the 20th of November, 1941, by the German legation in Zagreb. From this it can be seen that as early as the 13th of May (Yugoslav Forces had capitulated on the 17th of April) the Croat government suggested that the Slovenes displaced by the *Reich* should come to Croatia, provided that a corresponding number of Serbs be deported from Croatia to Serbia. Hitler agreed to this policy on the 25th of May.[26] This was followed on the 4th of June by the first German-Croat conference concerning resettlement. It was agreed that the bulk (*"die Masse"*) of 5,000 "politically tainted persons and intellectuals" should be deported from Slovenia to Serbia, as the Croat government was not going to accept Slovenes who were "politically Serb-oriented Chetniks." Some 170,000 other Slovenes would be sent to Croatia, and the same number of Serbs would be sent from Croatia to Serbia.[27]

An outside observer could perhaps discern some merit in certain aspects of this proposal for exchange of populations, reminiscent of the repatriation of Greeks from Turkey in the 1920s. However, the Ustasha obsession with genocide prevented orderly administration, and the planned resettlement was soon in shambles. This is evident from the minutes of the second German-Croat conference concerning resettlement, held on the 22nd of September, only three and a half months after the launching of the scheme. A comparison of the minutes of this conference and of the information contained in the *"Bericht"* mentioned earlier shows two things. Firstly, there is no doubt that the system had broken down. Only the number of people transported by train could be determined, but not "the remaining figures"; there were "legal" and "illegal" resettlements. Obviously, the term "illegal" was a euphemism for refugees fleeing Ustasha genocide. Secondly, it was admitted that resettlement created "unrest" among the Slovene population in the Reich, and also in Croatia [the 30% of Serbs?] :

this was threatening to give a *"new impetus* and new strength *to the disturbances."* The minutes of this conference contain also a balance sheet of resettlement for the period "up to September 20." However, despite the neat presentation of statistics in this document, the figures do not lend themselves to a clear analysis. They can be disentangled only in comparative reading with the *"Bericht."* This discloses that, with respect to the resettlement in Serbia, 14,110 Serbs had been transported under the German-Croat scheme, and an estimated 90,000 had already reached Serbia by other or "illegal" means.[28]

At the receiving end, that is in occupied Serbia, statistics of arrivals give higher figures than the German documents. This is due to two factors. Firstly, Nazi-Ustasha sources are concerned only with those formally sent from German-occupied Slovenia and the NDH. Serb sources give the sum total of all deportees and escapees who arrived, regardless of their point and mode of departure. Secondly, German figures cover the period from the occupation of Yugoslavia (in April 1941) to September 20th, while Serb statistics span a longer period. For instance, Marjanović says that in 1941 "more than 300,000" displaced persons came to Serbia.[29] (On the partition of Yugoslavia, Serbia was left with about 3,400,000 Serbs—plus others—and the number of arrivals should be related to this initial figure.) An emigré historian, Slijepčević, quotes "more than 500,000" arrivals; his numbers seem to cover the whole period of occupation, that is, 1941-44.[30] Of this number, about 85,000 were children, mostly orphans who escaped the genocide in the NDH.[31]

This formed the crucial physical and psychological background to domestic events in Serbia. The collapse of the state and the ensuing anarchy, enemy occupation, news of the massacres, the influx of refugees, and the sight of Serbian corpses floating down the Drina and Sava to Belgrade, wearing inscriptions *"Meso za Jovanovu pijacu"* ("Meat for the Belgrade Market")[32] unavoidably left their imprint. Perforce, Serbia was an isolated, landlocked, inward looking world, and its particular background and the ruthless conditions of survival must be understood by historians of resistance in occupied Yugoslavia. By the same token, different contemporary utterances by Serb-Yugoslav army officers and Chetnik Commanders cannot be understood if viewed out of the context of these events.

The situation in Montenegro must be examined separately. Local conditions there were different. At the time of the Axis attack on Yugoslavia, historical Montenegro was part of the then Yugoslav territorial administrative unit called *Zetska Banovina*. (A *"Banovina"* was patterned on the French *"Département"*.) Eight years earlier, in 1933, this *Banovina* had had a population of 925,516.[33] After the Second World War, it was calculated that at the end of March 1941 (that is, on the eve of the Axis attack), Montenegro had 425,964 inhabitants.[34] It should be noted that, when dealing with Yugoslav matters, statistics are a mixture of census information, mathematical projections and well-meant or biased propaganda figures, Further, the figures do not necessarily refer to an identical area, and this complicates matters further.

In the distribution of Yugoslav spoils, pre-1914 Montenegro was resurrected and given to Italy, which then truncated it somewhat for the benefit of Italian occupied Albania. There were probably two main reasons for giving Montenegro to Italy. Hitler was determined that,

> For reasons of national policy, Germany did not desire an outlet to the Adriatic. The German people were now oriented toward the Baltic and North Seas, and he would not like to jeopardize this uniform orientation by (the) interests of the southern sections of the Reich in southern seas.[35]

Hitler had also decided that, at the collapse of Yugoslavia,

> in order to keep the Italians in line they are to get everything they want, no matter how absurd.[36]

Hitler's decision to give the Italians "everything they want" seems to have been intended as a malicious practical joke also, for he added, "There is no harm done if, later, they and the Slavs get into one another's hair."[37] Thus favourable conditions were created for the fulfilment of the longstanding Italian aim of encroaching on the east coast of the Adriatic. Historically, this imperialistic aim can be illustrated by referring to the secret treaty of London, on the 26th of April 1915. By that treaty Italy agreed to join the

Occupation and Reaction

Triple Entente, or the "Allies" of the First World War, in return for a promise of certain parts of the then Habsburg-ruled Adriatic littoral (without Montenegro). Eventually Italy was deprived of most of the promised districts when, in 1918-19, they were incorporated into the Kingdom of Serbs, Croats and Slovenes or SHS, and this put Italy at loggerheads with Yugoslavia. Beside the Italian aim of turning the Adriatic Sea into a *Mare nostro*, the Savoyard reigning family had dynastic interests in securing Montenegro. Elena, Queen of Italy, was a daughter of Nicolas I, the last monarch of Montenegro. With teh fall of Yugoslavia the Italian court aspired to see her family, the Petrović-Njegoš, return to the throne at Cetinje.[38]

With Yugoslavia's *de facto* demise Italian national and dynastic interests converged in wanting to secure Montenegro, as well as Albania which had been occupied earlier.[53] However, before the Italian regime in "liberated" Montenegro was fully established, many people escaped from Serbia and Bosnia to the Montenegrin coast. They hoped from there to leave Yugoslavia. Foreign nationals, and Yugoslavs, took the road to Montenegro, including many army officers who refused to comply with the order for capitulation. One of them was the then Lieutenant Zvonimir (Zvonko) J. Vučković, of the King's Guards Artillery Regiment, who was soon to become a renowned Chetnik officer. He came to Herceg Novi a few weeks after the capitulation, and observed that,

> in comparison with the regime in the German zone of occupation, life in the Italian zone was reminiscent of a scout jamboree. Herceg Novi gave the impression of the bustling market town, but all the people milling around were in the main Serbian and Jewish refugees saving themselves from the Nazis and Ustashas.[39]

There he joined a group of officers who were considering their situation. Later, during the uprising in Serbia, Vučković again met the leader of this group at Gornji Milanovac. On the latter occasion he presented him with the pistol of the *Hauptmann* who commanded the first complete German company captured by the rebels. Miloš Rašović, an anti-fascist M.P., arrived at Herceg Novi with the news that a Colonel Mihailović had retreated with a group of soldiers in the direction of North Bosnia-West Serbia. By coincidence, at the same time the Italian secret police set a trap to apprehend Vučković's group. The officers were staying at the hotel called *Hotel na plaži*. The Italian police set their ambush, but an anonymous chambermaid warned the officers, and they escaped. The same evening Vučković abandoned his plans to leave the country and decided to join Colonel Mihailović immediately.

Vućković's impression of the relatively lenient conditions in the early period of Italian occupation is at variance with the more usual 'black and white' occupation history. Yet his statements are supported by other eyewitnesses. Thus, Milan Bandović, who was one of the elected rebel commanders in the July 1941 Montenegrin uprising, says that when the Italian occupation troops arrived they behaved correctly and peacefully toward civilians. According to Jovan Kontić, a teacher and publicist, "the Italians" opened stores selling victuals very cheaply, and did their best to impress people with their friendliness.[40] The account of one man who was the KPJ delegate in Italian occupied Montenegro in 1941, Milovan Djilas, agrees with the statements of Vučković, Bandović, and Kontić about the early Italian regime, *viz.*,

> It was striking to see how well the Italian troops behaved on entering the Montenegrin towns. In contrast to the simple Italian soldiers, who played marbles with the children . . . , the Black Shirts stood out threateningly. Yet there was no plundering, no arrests, no use of force.[41]

Djilas also makes a significant admission. He says that "Communists openly walked the streets and sat quietly in cafés." Nevertheless, although Vučković thought "Mussolini failed to change the easy-going Italians into German martinets", scholarly works show that Italy's introduction of a "liberal system of occupation" and the provision of food supplies[42] was a planned policy. All this changed in the wake of the Montenegrin uprising.

Before the uprising, Italian policy makers were deliberately courting Montenegrin public opinion in a "softening-up" process, which they intended would lead to the installation of an Italian client-king on the putative throne of Montenegro. One of the early steps in this direction was the offer of the throne to Prince Mihajlo Petrović-Njegoš, a grandson of the last King of Montenegro and a nephew of his daughter, Queen Elena of Italy. The Italian consul at Frankfurt, Serra di Cassano, was charged with the mission to Prince Mihajlo. There are two versions of the interview of 29 May 1941. Both versions agree that the Prince refused the offer of the crown, but, on the face of it, disagree about his arguments. In his own version,[43] Prince Mihajlo claims that he refused the crown by reminding the Italian consul of his loyalty to Yugoslavia and King Peter II. In the ensuing conversation he further told di Cassano he would have reacted in the same way irrespective of who made the offer, and that his attitude was independent of his opposition to the regimes in Germany and Italy. Yet following Ciano's record of the interview,[44] the Prince told di Cassano he did "not want to compromise himself" because he believed in Allied victory and so considered "any present solution" to be "transitory and ephemeral." Thereupon the Nazis interned him. Following this refusal the Italian authorities changed their tactics. They arranged that on the 12th of July[45] a Montenegrin Assembly at Cetinje would proclaim "The Independent State of Montenegro."[46] As the throne was vacant, the King of Italy was requested to designate a Regent. All of this was a blatant reversal of the decision of the Great Montenegrin National Assembly at Podgorica (now Titograd), on the 26th of November 1918, when union with Serbia was proclaimed.[47]

On the 13th of July 1941, the day after the meeting of the Italian-sponsored assembly at Cetinje, a general uprising started in Montenegro.[48] What was the role of the KPJ in it? According to Djilas, who was at the time the KPJ delegate and commander in Montenegro,

> we, the leadership, didn't learn of [opening] battles until later.[49]

Yet Partisan historiographers have appropriated for the KPJ the honour of starting and leading the Montenegrin uprising. For example Terzić states

> the people, led by the Communist Party, on the 13th of July rose in rebellion. . . .[50]

This is also the official Yugoslav line. In emigré or nationalist historiography it is maintained that the uprising, led by army officers, resulted from the interplay of different factors, such as Communist agitation, deliberations of local notables and army officers, and the revulsion of the ordinary people against the setting up of an Italian sponsored Montegrin "State."[51] However, as nationalist history deals with the losers in a civil war, generally it has attracted neither the number of writers nor the enthusiasm of those who have dealt with the Partisans. Karchmar, whose doctoral dissertation probably contains the most detailed treatise of this matter to date in English, after comparing the claims of the two opposing schools of history concludes that,

> on the whole, the nationalists appear to be more justified in their assertions, [provided we think in terms of a] chaotic, amorphous mass movement without an overall direction.[52]

This, of course, corresponds to the image of earlier Serb uprisings (*"ustanak"*) and rebellions (*"buna"*) in their first stages of development.

Nevertheless, both Partisan and nationalist schools of history are deficient in having overlooked the impact upon local developments of the mass of Serb refugees and returnees who came to Montenegro. Their presence made further demands on already scarce food supplies. Emotionally, their influx became "a big issue,"[53] although not to the extent it was in Serbia. The refugees were people who either escaped the persecution and killing of Serbs in adjoining Italian Albania and Ustasha occupied Hercegovina, or were forcibly deported from these areas. Destitute and desperate, they told their stories, which increased the emotional pitch of the intolerance of occupation and counteracted the Italian attempts to winning Montenegrin friendship. To understand the latter point, one must take into account that these areas of anti-Serb terror, Albania, and Hercegovina under the Ustasha, were at the time both under Italian control. But the Serbs across the occupation borders were of the same kin. Therefore the Montenegrins must have thought that, while professing their friendship for Montenegro, the Italian administration was actually setting their neighbours against them. A scholar might argue that this was primarily the result of Italian administrative muddle and inefficiency at the political level of decision making. It is a loss for historical studies of Yugoslavia in the Second World War, that—for instance—no lessons are drawn from the characteristics of different occupation systems and their failures or relative successes. Indeed, if the Italian planners really thought that in each of these adjoining lands they could simultaneously court local chauvinism at the expense of their neighbours, they had overreached themselves. It took the Italian army one month to quell the rebellion. This was followed by a split among the nationalists. Some came to an accommodation with the Italians immediately, other nationalists and the communists went underground or withdrew into the mountains to recuperate. Italian authorities abandoned the policy of creating a Montenegrin client State, withdrew their troops into a few garrison towns, and patrolled the main highways in the daytime only. The countryside was practically left in the hands of the insurgents, whereupon many nationalists in the mountains returned home.

One would think that this result would indicate that a small people had won an overwhelming victory over an imperial power. Yet the KPJ, who used the lull to reorganize its ranks and committees,[54] disagrees. Joined by the committed Yugoslav and foreign pro-Partisan writers, it has raised the cry of nationalist collaboration with the enemy, and even since then partisan historiographers have made an issue of this. The accusation of collaboration can be challenged on two grounds. Firstly, the charge of collaboration with the Italian authorities can be refuted on the ground that "collaboration" is a political alignment with the other party. In Montenegro, however, throughout the war the main nationalist grouping (the Montenegrin Chetniks led by army officers such as Djurišić), made it clear that the Italian presence was unwelcome (*vide* the uprising), and that the length of their transient occupation was at the mercy of Allied war plans. Secondly, nationalist writers insist that the accommodation (not collaboration) was originally the best way to stop Italian post-uprising reprisals, and in particular to stop them using vicious Albanian auxiliaries. The sole reason for the Montenegrin Chetniks later exploiting this accommodation was to safeguard their own people from communist engineered terror and killings. In support of this argument they produce Tito's own admission that "Force was used rather than persuasion"[55] in 1941 by the KPJ followers in Montenegro.

Tito's interviewer and the main English-speaking biographer of Tito so far, Phyllis Auty, describes crisply the kind of terror that was waged by the Montenegrin communists. In her own words,

> They raged through Montenegro burning, pillaging and slaying.
>
> ....
>
> [They] . . . began to organize the most extreme form of government through soviets, killing off opponents and wreaking vengeance.⁵⁶

It is the main nationalist argument that this abuse of force amounted to starting the civil war under foreign occupation. The aim of these excesses was to liquidate any potential opposition to their future government. In those circumstances, many army officers as well as others might have thought the former Yugoslav government justified in outlawing the KPJ as a terrorist organization in 1921.⁵⁷ Contemporary British Intelligence assessments contain similar information about this complex problem. Thus, in a nineteen-page typewritten intelligence report of the Director of Military Intelligence of 27th April 1943, it is said, *inter alia,*

> When the revolt against the Axis had begun in the summer of 1941 MONTENEGRO had been one of the earliest scenes of Partisan activity. The Italian garrison . . . throughout the ensuing winter had in effect been blockaded in the more important towns while the rebels controlled the country-side. The triumphant Partisans, however, began to make themselves very much disliked by the local peasantry. Their antipathy to Serb nationalism and their doctrinaire insistence on Communist dogma combined to make them odious in the eyes of the Montenegrins, who . . . glory in their Serb ancestry.

In the coming spring Chetnik bands began assisting the peasants "to eject from Montenegro the unpopular elements," and to this end obtained food and arms from Italians. The M.I. 3b's report continues,

> The Italians were delighted that local elements . . . should cooperate in clearing the hills of Communists: the Chetniks saw a chance of restoring peace to the tortured country-side and were under no illusion as to the use they would ultimately make of their weapons.⁵⁸

Obviously, whichever source of information were used by M.I. 3b, it is remarkable that, the anonymous British intelligence professionals were then already in the possession of data which nowadays historians are still only

Occupation and Reaction

gathering. The M.I. 3b's report provides the rudiments for the framework of a considered political assessment of the Montenegrin *imbroglio*. It deals neither with heroes nor villains, but, in turn, discusses the probable motivations of the various main participants. By introducing also the role of the Italian commander, General Pirzio Biroli, what occurred has been recreated more realistically than ever would have been possible by discussing the Chetniks and Partisans only, and recounting their skirmishes and the usual accusations and counter-accusations.[59]

All these uprisings across occupied Yugoslavia had in common that they were a Serb manifestation. In addition to this, in both Serbia and Montenegro those army officers who recognized Mihailović's authority were the national leaders. It should be noted that in the case of Montenegro and in the NDH the pattern which was to emerge all over Yugoslavia could be seen already. As has been demonstrated by Tito's and Djilas's admissions, the KPJ would send its delegate from outside into a district there to organize their own supremacy through a Partisan movement. In contrast to this procedure, local Serb nationalist groupings were endeavouring to establish contact with Mihailović who was elsewhere. Usually it is said that Captain Pavle Djurišić was the first Montenegrin officer to establish contact with Mihailović in Serbia (Djurišić later became a central Chetnik figure in Montenegro and Sandžak). However Karchmar contends that Djurišić's legendary journey to meet Mihailović and their interview is a myth. It was a Slovene, says Karchmar, Captain [later Major] Rudolf Perhinek, who made the successful journey in October 1941 and obtained Mihailović's directives for organizing the command structure in Montenegro.[60] Due to the remoteness of Montenegro, however, the events there had hardly any effect upon other lands in occupied Yugoslavia. The one exception is that—as in the past—Montenegrins brought succor to their Serb brethren across the border in Hercegovina. In the past, they had helped them against their Turk overlords, and in 1941 they did so against the Croat Ustashas. The remoteness of Montenegro from other lands in Yugoslavia was due to its peripheral location with respect to the political, economic and cultural mainstream of life, and to the main transport lines, which all ran along the axis Belgrade—Zagreb—Ljubljana.

Yet regardless of the place that Montenegro in 1941 might occupy in Yugoslav history, an event occurred there which ensures it a place in the history of British wartime dealing with Yugoslavia. It is the story of the first British attempt to gain a foothold in the Axis occupied Balkans. In the lull between the suppression of the Montenegrin uprising and the start of open civil war in Montenegro, the first British military mission to occupied Yugoslavia landed there from HM submarine *Triumph,* passed through Montenegro and proceeded to Mihailović in Serbia. Actually, this was a combined British-Yugoslav endeavour, organized by the Special Operations Executive (SOE) and code-named *Operation Bullseye.* Its British member was Captain (later Lt. Colonel) D. T. ("Bill") Hudson of the SOE.

CHAPTER 4

THE SOE STEPS IN: HUDSON AND "OPERATION BULLSEYE" (I), BACKGROUND AND PURPOSE

Soon after the suppression of the 1941 anti-Italian uprising in Montenegro, the first British-Yugoslav military mission to occupied Yugoslavia, called "Mission Bullseye," passed through Montenegro. This mission was an enterprise of the British Special Operations Executive (SOE). What were the genesis of the SOE and its role in Yugoslavia, its relationship with Yugoslav exiles, the organization of the mission, its composition and command structure, its purpose and its journey to Montenegro?

The creation of the SOE was one result of the Anglo-French military crisis of May 1940. Faced with the possibility of France's collapse, British military and civilian authorities examined alternatives for continuing the war. On 25 May 1940, a month before the French armistice of 22 June, the Chiefs of Staff submitted to the Cabinet a paper suggesting that Germany could be defeated by a combination of economic warfare and subversion, and that a special organization was needed to co-ordinate the latter activity.[1] This paper had thirteen paragraphs; it discussed the co-ordination of action leading to "revolt within the conquered countries," and subversion, blockade and the air offensive as "potential weapons of victory."[2]

On the 1st of July a meeting of key personnel chaired by Foreign Secretary, Lord Halifax, agreed that a controller of propaganda and subversion was needed. Prime Minister Churchill approved this proposal, and on the 16th of July asked the Minister for Economic Warfare, Hugh Dalton, to add subversion and sabotage to his portfolio and create an appropriate organization. On this occasion Churchill referred to the new organization as "the Ministry of Ungentlemanly Warfare," and exhorted Dalton to "set Europe ablaze."[3] On the 22nd of July, the very day it refused Hitler's offer of peace, the British Cabinet approved Churchill's action in setting up the Special Operations Executive (SOE).[4] Dalton's enthusiasm for his new job is seen from his secret paper of 19 August, in which he advocated that subversion should become recognized as the "Fourth [Fighting] Arm."[5]

The charter of the new organization was signed on July 19th, 1940, by Neville Chamberlain.[6] According to Sir Colin Gubbins, who was first director of SOE's training and operations, and then SOE's executive head, nobody was "ever informed officially or in writing of what the charter of S.O.E. was."[7] Theatre commanders and resident ministers were never formally informed of the creation of SOE. This secrecy adversely affected the initial attitude of the Middle East Command to "the operations in the Balkans of the Special Operations Executive."[8] Gubbins made his comment in the context of the question of "why it took so long" for GHQ ME to realize that in Yugoslavia "they had on their hands...a major war." Gubbins' testimony illustrates how stringently the ruling that there was to be "no public announcement" of Dalton's new ministerial responsibility was observed, and that the knowledge of SOE's responsibilities should be limited "within a very restricted circle."[9] Its formal charter is still a classified document, the major purport of which can only be recreated from other sources.

Two historians given access to all SOE files, Butler and Foot, agree as to the wording of the crucial part of the charter. Butler conceals the fact that his statement is a direct quotation from the charter by omitting the quotation marks. Foot, using the very same words, cites it as an extract. The SOE was,

> to co-ordinate all action, by way of subversion and sabotage, against the enemy overseas....[10]

SOE: Background and Purpose   55

In the conference of 21 August 1940, the Vice-Chiefs of Staff had agreed with Dalton that "his organization would be responsible for offensive subversive activities which did not involve the use of officers and men wearing uniform."[11] This, of course, is reminiscent of the private agreement between Majors (later Major-Generals) L. D. Grand and J. C. F. Holland when they were in charge of Section D of the Special or Secret Intelligence Service (SIS) and Section GS(R) of the general staff at the War Office.

What action constituted "subversion and sabotage"? The controversial nature of such a definition may be one of the reasons why this charter is still a classified document. The details must be gleaned from elsewhere. For instance, Donald Hamilton-Hill, one-time second in command of SOE's training schools, was present at Tempsford SOE airfield in Bedfordshire on the departure of the Heydrich assassination squad.[12] Yet Sweet-Escott reveals that although in the (European) autumn of 1940 Whitehall had "on several occasions" suggested that the SOE "ought to be able to arrange for the disappearance of Middle Eastern politicians who were actively working against the allies," no such order was ever issued. He concludes that "after all cold-blooded murder was not part of our code": "007 has not yet been invented."[13] If this instance is typical it would seem that the SOE personnel, when acting on their own initiative were more determined than Whitehall.

SOE was formed by combining two existing sectins already engaged in clandestine activities. On the "subversion" side Dalton took over the "Black propaganda" section of Electra House of the "EH."[14] To acquire a sabotage section, SOE bypassed the Chief of SIS (or "C"), Colonel (later Major-General Sir) Stewart Menzies, and without his leave appropriated his Section D.[15]

The genesis of the Special or Secret Intelligence Service (SIS), which was known also by its military title MI 6, and the establishment of its Section D is shown in the Table. The SIS had immediately established the Belgrade outpost of its newly created Section "D." The first head of "D" in Belgrade was a local British businessman, (Colonel) Julius Hanau, known as Caesar.[16] In the European summer of 1940 the "Balkan section of 'D' was the only operative part of the organization."[17] When the SOE was created in July 1940, Belgrade D Section of the SIS became Belgrade SO(2) Section of the SOE. (Colonel) Tom Masterson became its first head in November 1940.[18] At the time of the collapse of Yugoslavia, in April

1941, Belgrade was the main centre of SOE activities in the Balkans. Belgrade operations came under the SOE's Balkan country section in London.[19] Beside sabotaging German supply transport in transit through Yugoslavia, the main activities of Belgrade D/SOE centred on influencing Serbian public opinion and Serb opposition political parties. This meant establishing good personal relations with the people considered to be pro-British who might be prepared to subvert and perhaps even replace "Prince Paul's" government.[20] Among the many close acquaintances of D/SOE people in Belgrade were Miloš Tupanjanin, of the Serb Agrarian Party, and Jovan Djonović, a republican and an expert on Albania, where he had been King Alexander's plenipotentiary minister. After the collapse of Yugoslavia, Tupanjanin's and Djonović's names continue to appear in SOE Balkan activities directed from Istanbul. The Istanbul SO(2) section had been established by Hanau to conduct operations into the Balkans, but in August 1940 it was taken over by Bailey, earlier Hanau's successor in Belgrade.[21] Before his posting to Istanbul, where he was in charge of SOE's Balkan activities, Bailey was ordered from Belgrade by GHQ ME to meet them at Cairo, and was then sent to Istanbul to run SOE Balkan activities from there.[22] It is interesting to note that Bailey's trip and the duplication in Istanbul of SOE's Belgrade Balkan centre followed closely on the establishment of Yugoslav-Soviet diplomatic relations. It would be rewarding to establish the motive for duplicating the existing Belgrade post with the one in Istanbul. The Yugoslav-Soviet rapprochement can be viewed either as the first step of unopposed Soviet penetration of Balkans, or as the first step to a Balkan war between Hitler and Stalin. The best British response for either contingency would have been to establish a British intelligence post adjoining this area. Hence Bailey's summons for consultation in Cairo and his posting to Istanbul? At Istanbul, Bailey made Julian Amery his chief assistant.[23] Eight months later, after a spell in Britain, Amery resumed his duties with Bailey in the Middle East,[24] and was able to assist with the influx of Serbian refugees fleeing German occupation of Yugoslavia.

After the collapse of Yugoslavia, and until the first news about a Serbian resistance started trickling out of the country, British officials must have been wondering what had gone amiss with their planned guerilla action in occupied Serbia. In the last stage of Prince Paul's regime, D/SOE had carefully discussed these arrangements with the leadership of the Serbian

SOE: Background and Purpose

Agrarian party of SZS (*Srpska zemljoradnička stranka*). Beside subsidies to assist the SZS in maintaining opposition to the foreign policies of the regime,[25] British SZS contacts were supplied with weapons, explosives and ammunition. These were smuggled into Yugoslavia through D/SOE channels,[26] and—nominally at least— were not meant to be used against Yugoslavia's own national authorities.

D/SOE activities can be gauged from Yugoslav sources. Thus, in a statement given to the foremost Yugoslav Partisan historian, Dr. Jovan Marjanović, it is claimed that the "English Intelligence Service" started supplying SZS with weaponry from November 1940 onwards. This material was partly stored in the villa of the Party's President, Dr. Milan Gavrilović, and partly in SZS HO rooms, and then distributed across Serbia. The same statement contains also the answer to the riddle of what eventually happened to this enterprise. It reads.

> When [*the Coup d'Etat* of] 27th of March occurred, all this weaponry was passed on to the nearest Yugoslav military commands, . . .[27]

This was a gesture of civic loyalty, but, as Hitler swiftly reacted to this *coup d'état* by ordering the *Wehrmacht* to overrun Yugoslavia, this ertswhile British and then SZS-Yugoslav Army guerila arsenal was swept away in the general *débàcle*.

With the arrival of Serb refugees from Yugoslavia in Turkey and Palestine, Bailey's ad hoc intelligence service, purely a British enterprise, was soon duplicated by Yugoslav improvisations. Yugoslav endeavours must have been motivated not only by the desire of exiled Serbs to remain in touch with their occupied country, but also by their intention to enhance their own standing as an independent ally. On the SOE side, no doubt, Yugoslav activity was seen as a potential widening of the scope for gathering intelligence from the Balkans. Furthermore, as the Serbs were dependent on their Belgrade SOE acquaintacces for material facilities and support, this gave the SOE a good chance—hopefully—to remain in ultimate control of the exiles' endeavours in this field. According to Deakin, liaison with occupied Yugoslavia was the joint function of Royal Yugoslav officials at Istanbul and Cairo, and on the British side by the SOE, "most of whose members" were hitherto active inside Yugoslavia.[28] The main in charge of Yugoslav officials was Jovan Djonović, who had already established good relations with the SOE in Belgrade. Before the exiled Yugoslav government left Palestine for London, Djonović was appointed its Resident Delegate in the Middle East.[29] General Simović, the Yugoslav P.M., on leaving Cairo for London asked Colonel Bailey "to work closely" with Djonović and "with the Yugoslav General Staff who would remain in Cairo,"[30] but the cooperation did not run smoothly.[31]

Djonović faced several problems in organizing his group—what was its aim, and whom should he employ? Deakin's statement that Djonović employed "mainly [Yugoslav] regular army officers"[32] must be questioned. It was established practice in the Serbian and later in the Yugoslav army that no military personnel could be managed by civilians. Headed by a General as War Minister, the whole military structure was based on the principle of non-interference by civilians. The rationale for this system was that hot-blooded Balkan tempers required that the Army be managed by non-political and a-political military professionals. This tradition was adhered to, according to Djonović's own account. He used consular personnel and refugee press attachés. His main intelligence centre relied on the Yugoslav consul at Istanbul, Hadži-Djordjević; the propaganda service was based at Jerusalem and headed by a refugee Press Attaché, Branko Denić; the third post, at Cairo, was organized under the former Press Attaché at Bucarest, Petrović.[33] It should be added as well that Colonel Žarko R. Popović, formerly Director of Military Intelligence in Belgrade, and then Military Attaché in the U.S.S.R., was appointed Yugoslav DMI in Cairo.

The early reports obtained from Yugoslavia by Djonović's agents dealt "with German bestialities" in Belgrade, and the general situation in the Serb lands. An escapee from Yugoslavia, Lieutenant Stanislav Rapotec, a Slovene, reported on the extermination of Serbs in Pavelić's Croatia.[34] On the strength of this and other information, on the 7th of August Djonović instructed his "propaganda services" to brief the foreign press accordingly. At about the same time in Istanbul Djonović interviewed Dragomir Rakić,[35] an industrialist from Mladenovac in Serbia, who informed him that two resistance groups existed in Serbia.

According to Rakić, the bigger and better organized group was led by a General Staff Colonel, Dragoljub Mihailović, accompanied by a number of officers and men who had refused to surrender to the enemy. Mihailović's HQ was at the Suvobor Palteau, in the villa of the late Field-Marshal or

SOE: Background and Purpose   59

"*Vojvoda*" Mišić in the village of Struganik. With the Serbs, Mišić's name evoked the victory on the Macedonian or Salonika Front in 1918. Indeed, even Liddel Hart rated "the campaign in Macedonia in 1918 under Voivode Mišić's brilliant command... amongst the finest examples of generalship in the First World War."[36] Mišić's elder son, Major Aleksandar Mišić, was on Colonel Mihailović's staff.[37] This group was creating a military organization in West Serbia. However, the funds voluntarily raised within Serbia were insufficient to meet Mihailović's needs, as he was paying peasants for all his supplies. He therefore appealed for funds from abroad.

The other resistance group, said Rakić, consisted of Communists. Unknown to Djonović, Yugoslav Military Intelligence in Cairo (Colonel Popović) learned from another source that, beside Army Chetniks, there were also Partisans in Serbia. This news was brought by two Polish officers who escaped to the Middle East *via* Yugoslavia.[38] Rakić stated further than before the Nazi-Soviet war, the Communists betrayed Mihailović's followers to the occupying authorities. "Following these denunciations many honourable people and householders lost their lives at the hands of the Gestapo." Nevertheless the Communists, who refrained from resistance until the Nazi attack on the Soviet Union, rose in arms after the Nazi-Soviet war started,[39] and by occasionally killing a German they provoked retaliations. Villages were razed and one hundred Serbian lives were exacted for every one German soldier killed. Thereafter the Communists would recruit the surviving people into their own ranks. Rakić explained that, to avoid risking such reprisals, Mihailović engaged in combat only in selfdefence, while the Communists had no such concern. Their main aim was assitance to the imperilled Soviet regime.

Djonović was moved by Mihailović's financial straits and his appeal for funds from abroad. The exiled Yugoslav government had not given him any funds for such purposes, and Djonović "contacted the English [intelligence] service at Istanbul" for the necessary loan.[40] Yet following the Nazi-Soviet war Bailey re-planned the objectives of his Balkan SOE activities. He emphasized that, the

> first essential was to build up centres of resistance in the different Balkan countries and seek to influence their character by giving them money, arms and political guidance.[41]

The SOE's HQ in London had approved this policy and therefore, when towards the end of July[42] Djonović acquainted Amery with Rakić's situation report, Amery singled out those points of the report which seemed to favour immediate action by the SOE. He noted that Colonel Mihailović, whom he personally knew from Belgrade as an advocate of guerrilla action,[43] was now in the mountains with men under arms, and that,

> Their headquarters was at Suvobor, a high plateau in Serbia. They requested that we send an aircraft with liaison officers and wireless sets to establish regular contact with them.[44]

Where Djonović's immediate worry was to ensure the physical survival of Mihailović and his men, Amery reacted in terms of executing the standing SOE Balkan policy. It may be assumed legitimately that their different reactions caused each man later to single out and publish different aspects of the same interview. Their summaries in fact complement each other to complete a fairly consistent picture.

It was already known that Montenegro and Serbia had risen. Amery, gratified that at least one of the headquarters of rebellion and its leader had been identified, left Istanbul for Cairo. There he endeavoured to obtain "approval and facilities" to organize a mission to Mihailović, "establish regular communication" and explore possibilities for further action. However the Cairo office of SOE was in "chaos."[45] This "chaos" resulted from the August 1941 purge of the Cairo SOE office and field detachments. London SOE headquarters was becoming concerned that the Middle East SOE organization had done "nothing very constructive" regarding Rashid-Ali's pro-German coup in Iraq, Axis occupation of the Balkans, and the Syrian campaign.[46] Furthermore, when with the fall of the Balkans, Belgrade and other Balkan SO(2) people regrouped in the Middle East, there occurred sustained in-fighting between them and the personnel of the SO(1).[47] This infighting affected British-Yugoslav relations also. In their meeting of 25 September 1941 Masterson told the Yugoslav Minister for War: ". . . you reported to General Simović [Yugoslav PM] that many different people had contacted you in the name of the Secret Service. Simović told my chief about it, and I have been sent to coordinate all British services. From now on, only I or Bennett in my

SOE: Background and Purpose

stead will liaise with you." The Minister however replied that he had successfully cooperated "with Lt. Colonel Bailey and Captain Julian Amery" and that he would prefer to see this arrangement continue.[48] What was the cause of this upheaval? SO(1) Section of the SOE were charged with "Black propaganda" in enemy and enemy occupied countries. Before the fall of Balkans they were not interested in that area, so that SO(2) stepped in a handled this activity as part of subversion and sabotage activities. Now SO(1) insisted that SO(2) desist from further action in the field of propaganda. The GHQ ME became dissatisfied with the local SOE and complained directly to Hugh Dalton, the Minister in charge of the SOE, and to the War Office in London.[49] Eventually, when the GHQ ME started "hinting at grave irregularities" among SOE staff in the Middle East and asked for a visit by the head of the SOE's Section SO(2) or the "CD," Sir Frank Nelson, action followed within a matter of days. Sir Frank, with Terence Maxwell, a banker who was designated to take over the Cairo SOE office from George Pollock, left London for Egypt. They were accompanied by Sweet-Escott who was, for the occasion, "promoted to the dizzy rank of a Major."

The timing of these events can be deduced from circumstantial evidence. The SOE HQ party was given a lift in the Catalina taking Air Vice-Marshal Coningham from Plymouth to Egypt to take up his new post as C-in-C Western Desert Air Force.[51] Coningham took over from Collishaw in August 1941.[52] Amery says that, following his letter of 15 August to his father, "Dalton prodded Maxwell in Cairo." This shows that Coningham's passengers, Nelson, Maxwell and Sweet-Escott were by then in Cairo, so that the flight has to be set not later than the middle of August, 1941. This reconstruction can be verified in official records, which show that, in Cairo, "Maxwell was installed as Head of SOE in the Middle East with effect from 15th August [1941]."[53] At this time, C-in-C ME was already General (later Field-Marshal) Sir Claude J. E. Auchinleck—"AUK" (July 1941-August 1942).

However, this was not the first time that the Commander-in-Chief, Middle East, had asked that the local SOE be reorganized. Sweet-Escott and the other officials who were newly appointed to deal with the crisis of 1941 may not have known of this earlier crisis. This had occurred at the end of the previous year when Wavell was in C-in-C ME. On that occasion Pollock brought to London Wavell's proposals of steps he wanted taken. London decided that Pollock should return to Cairo in January 1941 and "take charge of all SOE operations in the Middle East." Dalton wrote a letter to Wavell which reads,[54] *inter alia*,

> Henceforth the distinction between SO(1) and SO(2) will only apply in this country and will consequently disappear in year area. There will henceforth be only one SOE Organisation in the Middle East, under the general control of POLLOCK, who, while remaining responsible to me, will operate under your direction.
>
> The functions of the SOE Department will cover:
>
> (i)   Subversive propaganda
> (ii) Political Subversion
> (iii) Raiding and Sabotage.

It is seen that, had Pollock fulfilled his brief of January 1941, the final SO(1)–SO(2) clash in the Middle East and the subsequent crisis might have been avoided.

Sweet-Escott, "who played a principal personal part in the [SOE Cairo] reorganization" of August 1941,[55] provides sufficient details to reconstruct the event briefly, he was asked to report on the GHQ ME papers supposedly incriminating the SOE people there. He found them to be a combination of "rubbish" based on gossip and papers which "could have been obtained only from (SOE) files." Sweet-Escott maintains that the papers he saw do not support Lord Chandos's contention in his memoirs that there was "incontestable proof" of wrongdoings by the Middle East SOE. Meanwhile, in discussions with Auchinleck and Lyttelton, Sir Frank Nelson concluded that the main issue was to regain the confidence of the military. Nelson's solution was to take "drastic action." He sent a telegram to Dalton recommending the removal of a number of senior SOE officers, and placing both SO(1) and SO(2) under Terence Maxwell.[56] Dalton's approval arrived within twenty-four hours, and the next day Nelson gave the senior officers their marching orders and returned to London.[57] Among the people relived of their SOE duties were Lt. Colonel George A. Pollock (the SO(2) Cairo head who had been expected to assert himself as the overall Cairo SOE head), his deputy, Lt. Colonel S. W. Bailey (Head of the SO(2) Balkan desks at Jerusalem), Colonel C. J. M. Thornhill (SO(1) representative in Cairo) and Lt. Colonel

Kenneth Johnstone (SO(1) representative at Jerusalem).[58] By coincidence at the same time in London it was decided to transfer the Section SO(1) from the SOE organization to the specially created Political Warfare Executive (PWE) under the Foreign Office.[59]

Julian Amery, who came to Cairo to advocate a mission to Mihailović, now found himself without a superior who would be conversant with local policy and activities. Pollock and Bailey had been removed. Maxwell was new in his job and preoccupied with office reorganization. Bailey's successor, Tom Masterson, an old Balkan hand, was still in London. Believing that the mission to Mihailović should be given urgent attention. Amery wrote to his father on 15th of August in the hope of obtaining Churchill's ear.[60] This letter, which seems hitherto to have escaped the attention of historians although it marks a crucial moment, read in part,

> ... The reorganization of our Middle East activities is now being carried out too late to be of any use but just in time to hold up important—and I think essential—action in the Balkans....
>
> Briefly I believe the time has come to launch a general revolt in the Balkans
> ....

In support of this view Amery pointed out that "something like a general insurrection" was underway in Serbia and Bosnia. He also said that "the peasants there and in Greece" had not yet been fully disarmed by the Germans, and, finally, that,

> the fortunate coincidence of Democrat and Communist, Anglophil and Pan-Slav interests (created) a solid anti-German block... south of the Danube.

If these circumstances were exploited immediately, either the Germans would not be able to spare troops from the Eastern Front to quell the rebellion, or, if they were to divert troops for this purpose, this would create a diversion which would "help the Russians to hold out" [that is, the Balkan battlefield would become a virtual second front].[61] Amery adds that his father contacted Churchill, who "prodded Dalton," who—

in turn—"prodded Maxwell." So, the issue of a mission to Mihailović was taken in Cairo from the pending tray and given first priority.⁶² The end result was Operation Bullseye.

Deakin, however, has a different view as to the origins and purpose of this operation. His opening statement is the text of Churchill's minute to Dalton of 28 August 1941. It reads,

> I understand from General Simovic that there is widespread guerrilla activity in Yugoslavia. It needs cohesion, support and direction from outside. Please report briefly what contacts you have with these bands and what you can do to help them.⁶³

Curiously enough, Deakin offers two versions of Dalton's answer. In 1962 he stated at Oxford that Dalton's "immediate" answer to Churchill's enquiry about the contacts with the guerrilla bands was "nothing," "because there was no contact, no information and no knowledge."⁶⁴ Nine years later, in 1971, Deakin stated that in his answer to Churchill's minute Dalton reported that, "The sum of £20,000 was being sent to Mihailovic by courier from Istanbul," and that "a mission was to be despatched to study the situation inside the country."⁶⁵ Deakin characterises the dispatch of this mission as at "the most decisive historical moment."⁶⁶ As the story develops, Deakin will continue to contradict himself on other points also. What really happened on this occasion will shortly be examined in depth. In any case, both Amery and Deakin agree that Churchill was the chief instigator whose intercession resulted in sending the mission. They differ in who prompted him. According to Amery, Churchill interceded when prompted by Amery Snr. According to Deakin, Churchill did so when approached by the Yugoslav Prime Minister, General Simović.

It appears however that at least a substantial part of a proper answer is to be found in Elisabeth Barker's published research into wartime British-Yugoslav relations. After drawing attention to the fact that from July the neutral press and other sources contained news "about guerrilla fighting in western Serbia, Bosnia and Montenegro" Barker refers to Simović's initiative when he,

> asked Churchill to send a submarine to contact a 'working committee for action' in Split, [Dalmatia,] which had sent out a courier.⁶⁷

SOE: Background and Purpose   65

Despite Simović's intercession "nothing came of this request."[68] The date of Simović's intercession for the committee in Split is crucial: the 14th of August.[69] This date should be related to the date cited by Deakin as the date of Churchill's minute to Dalton, the 25th or 28th of August. Thus, in addition to the evidence that no mission resulted from Simović's approach to Churchill, there is also the evidence of a time gap of ten to thirteen days from Simović unsuccessfully contacting Churchill, to Churchill's minute to Dalton which resulted in the dispatch of the mission "Bullseye."

However, and this is a turning point, although Simović's intervention caused no immediate positive action, "Churchill's interest in Yugoslav resistance was kindled."[70] Amery Jnr. states that he wrote on the 15th of August to his father asking for his support, and his father then approached Churchill. Assuming that this letter took five to seven days to reach Amery Snr., it would have been in his hands on the 20th or 22nd of August. This would have allowed sufficient time for Leopold Amery (Amery Snr.) to contact Churchill, and for Churchill to find time to make up his mind and to act on the 25th or the 28th.

When Dalton's enquiry (on behalf of Churchill) landed on Maxwell's desk in Cairo, he had nobody sufficiently experienced to turn to for assistance. By a fortuitous chance however, Churchill's enquiry was preceded by the latest Djonović—Bailey—Amery Yugoslav intelligence from Istanbul. This included the request for money for Mihailović. At the same time, Amery was persistently calling at Maxwell's office for a mission to be dispatched. "I returned to the charge several times . . . ." says Amery.[71] Thus, profiting from these circumstances, Maxwell was able to satisfy Dalton of Cairo SOE's efficiency. Within two days of his minute, on 30 August Dalton reported to Churchill that contacts and financial help for guerilla bands were being organized. Financial help— money to Mihailović—had been discussed already. As to "contacts," Maxwell now instructed his staff to proceed with the dispatch of a mission to Yugoslavia, and gave it the code-name "Operation Bullseye."[72]

Originally, the mission was to consist of a purely Royal Yugoslav team, but a British member was added to it at a later stage.[73] He was Captain (later Colonel) D. T. ("Bill") Hudson of the SOE, in civilian life a mining engineer.[74] Later, in Serbia, he was known by the *nom de guerre* "Marko," and also as the Englishman who liked to drink milk, asking, *"Majka, daj mleko!"* ("Mother, give me some milk").[75] Hudson

> had volunteered for the job but was only called upon to go because Jarko Popovitch insisted that there must be a British officer.[76]

Popović might have done so in order to start British-Yugoslav cooperation in the field. Yugoslav members of the team were three Serbs from Montenegro, Majors Mirko I. Lalatović and Zaharije I. Ostojić with their *"radio-telegrafista"* (W/T operator) a Sergeant Dragićević of the Yugoslav Air Force. Lalatović and Ostojić were Airmen and Staff Officers: Dragićević was in civilian life a W/T operator with the Yugoslav airline. This was a parallel British-Yugoslav team, Deakin says that the mission was "under the command of Major [sic] Hudson"; Auty, for her part, claims that the "head of mission" was Captain Hudson.[77] This is incorrect. Despite these assertions to the contrary, there was no question of Hudson "commanding" or even "heading" the mission. On another occasion Deakin admits "This mission was a joint British—Royal Yugoslav operation and *there was no question of command.*"[78]

Actually, the exiled Yugoslav government was given assurances that no Yugoslav army units would be directly commanded by British officers, although this arrangement "seems never to have been embodied in a formal document."[79] As it happens, in Colonel Popović's wartime papers there are some documents which seem to support Bailey's statement that an agreement about command structure was reached but there was no "formal document." In the August 1941 purge of Cairo SOE, Colonel Bailey was relieved of his post and replaced by Colonel Tom Masterson. Popović's papers contain the minutes (in Serbian) of the meeting between Yugoslav Defence Minister General Ilić and Colonel Masterson, when the later came to advise the Minister of his taking over SOE's Yugoslav work. The minutes are headed "Tok razgovora. . . ." ["The course of the conversation between the Minister for Army and Navy, General Bogoljub Ilić, and the Chief of O.E.S. [sic] on 25 September 1941 from 0900 to 0930 hours in the building "Villa Aida," 20 El Mansour Mohammed Street. Present [also] : Colonel Ž.R. Popović, Captain John Bennett."] They contain an exchange which might be construed as pertaining to the verbal agreement regarding the command of Yugoslav units. Page four contains the following demands by General Ilić:

SOE: Background and Purpose

    (i)   There must be absolute frankness in cooperation, without any ulterior motives;
    (ii)   No action to be undertaken without my knowledge, all reports to be addressed only to me, all jobs given to Yugoslav personnel, all instructions, orders and supplies [materiel?] to be sent only through me.

Masterson replied,

> That was just the reason of my visiting you immediately so that we may reach a frank understanding. So I may now report to my chief that the understanding has been reached.

On the next day, 26 September, John Bennett brought to General Ilić at noon the "Memorandum of meeting at the Yugoslav Ministry for War... [when] certain decisions were reached regarding future work back in Yugoslavia."[80] Popović's papers contain both a Serbian and an English copy of this document. They are identical and although enumerating other points of agreement, there is no mention of the chain of command. But it is also seen that, regardless of claims that SOE was not a policy making body,[81] some at least SOE's local instructions were definitiely of a policy making nature.

    The purpose of the mission can best be deduced from Dalton's answer to Churchill when he was enquiring as to what contacts there were with guerilla bands in Yugoslavia. Deakin's works contain two versions of this. Deakin's original version has been quoted as stating in 1962, that, Dalton had nothing to report because "there was nothing," "no contact, no information, and no knowledge."[82] Therefore—again following Deakin's first version—Hudson was sent to investigate the situation in a "completely blank scene."[83] This proposition, of course, leaves all avenues open to conjecture and commentaries in and out of context, such as the forceful undercurrent that it was wrong initially to liaise with Mihailović instead of immediately supporting Tito. Yet Tito's name was mentioned for the first time, by Mihailović himself, only on 5 November 1941,[84] whereas here we deal with the events of August and September 1941. In 1971, in his later version of Dalton's answer, Deakin cites him as having reported that "plans [for helping guerrillas] were in hand," Mihailović was being sent £20,000, and a mission was due to go and "study the situation inside the country."[85] It is inconceivable that in the period from Deakin's first to his second version there was an actual change in the text of Dalton's report to Churchill. Assuming Deakin's second version to be more credible, this does not give licence (with further investigation) to conclude that—because Mihailović is mentioned—this mission was directed, while still in Cairo, to procede directly to Colonel Mihailović's GHQ in Serbia. Indeed, Deakin insists that, before leaving Cairo, Mihailović's "very existence" was unknown to Hudson.[86] Furthermore, Deakin considers that Hudson had been in Montenegro for some days before he was ordered to procede to Serbia and join Mihailović on the 9th of October. This order, says Deakin, followed upon "a chance radio message picked up in Malta" on the 10th of September, which "revealed to the British the presence of a Colonel Mihailović in Western Serbia." Historians are supposed to cross-check their sources—yet, in this instance, Deakin's error has been uncritically followed by many others.[87] The first occasion on which Mihailović made contact with the British was in the middle of August, and not only in October.[88]

Thus, one is facing here an array of arguments based on Deakin's work which are seemingly supported by data from British archives, although (again) no references are provided. Opposed to these arguments is Amery's explicit claim that the mission was "a mission to Mihailović," sent in response to his request for British "aircraft with liaison officers and wireless sets." Like Deakin, Amery provides no references, but he claims that his account is autobiographical.[89] His own claim makes Amery a primary witness. Deakin admits that he was posted to Cairo SOE only in late 1942. But, as he said at the St. Antony conference, "I have a few notes"[90] (presumably from his briefing, the files he saw and the eyewitnesses he chatted with?). There are, however, other sources both on the British and the Yugoslav side.

On the British side, there is first the man who, in the Cairo purge, seems to have become (under Masterson) head of Yugoslav SOE's desk in Istanbul. Hitherto he was on the Istanbul SOE strength, and before that he was at Belgrade. He is Hugh Seton-Watson, who cannot be accused of being partial to Mihailović. In his own words,

> The British military authorities, . . . decided, as soon as they received information about Mihailovic, to send a British mission to

arrange wireless contact between him and the British Command in the Middle East. The first British officer, Captain Hudson, arrived [in Serbia] in October 1941.[91]

Sweet-Escott, who—as has been shown—was intimately connected with the Cairo purge and reorganization, states,

> Maxwell had induced the navy to land Bill Hudson . . . on the coast of Montenegro in the hope that he might make his way to Mihailović's headquarters.[92]

On the Yugoslav side, there is also significant testimony. Soon after landing, the Bullseye party made contact with local people and were conducted by them to the village Radovče where they met Djilas. At that time he was the Delegate of the KPJ for Montenegro. Neither then, nor in his subsequent career was Djilas at any stage a partisan of Mihailović. Yet he says,

> The mission stayed with us for five or six days. They made it clear from the start that they intended to go to Serbia, to Colonel Draža Mihailović.[93]

Thus, as far as the purpose of the mission is concerned, Amery's explanation is seen to have been vindicated. The Bullseye team (including Hudson) was originally set up and dispatched to go to Colonel Mihailović's headquarters. They were sent to the reported fighting remnants of the Yugoslav Army, Colonel Mihailović commanding: "at the time a liaison with Mihailovitch was the only proposal under consideration."[94]

Let us now chart the journey. At present—in the mid 1980's—the best known version of the Bullseye history is contained in pages 126-34 and 202 of Deakin's *Embattled Mountain*. According to Deakin, the mission left on its journey from Alexandria by air on 13 September 1941 for Malta, where on 16 September they boarded a submarine and landed on the Montenegrin coast near Petrovac[95] on the 20th of the same month. Although he is usually sparing in providing references, in this instance Deakin has followed the information regarding the landing date and site by referring to the log of HM Submarine *Triumph*. However, whereas from

Deakin's own extract from *Triumph's* report it is seen that *Triumph* left Malta on 16 September, he provides no annotation to support the landing date. Search for more details is facilitated by the fact that Deakin concludes his reference with the remark that a British officer, "not named in the report of the Commander of HMS *Triumph*," accompanied the mission to the Montenegrin coast. "He was Captain Julian Amery."[96] This information is confirmed in a totally independent, official source, as Amery's journey to Yugoslavia was mentioned in the Minutes of the Ilić–Masterson meeting of 25 September.

Amery's own account of these events is contained in pp. 242-56 of his book *Approach March*. Although Amery has not spelled out the dates, his detailed account enables one to do so. The mission left Cairo on 8 September by air for Alexandria. On the same day they boarded there a Sunderland for Malta and arrived there on the 9th; on the 13th they left Malta in the submarine *Triumph*. Captain of *HMS Triumph* was Commander Woods.[97] Eventually the party landed "A little to the north of Petrovatz, . . . [In] a sandy cove, Perisicadol Bay," during the night of 17-18 September. Captain Amery and *Triumph's* Sub-Lieutenant Douglas Don[98] went ashore with the party and then re-embarked in the *Triumph*. Amery adds that landing started at ten-thirty in the evening of the 17th, and ended "towards one o'clock in the morning" of the 18th. In his post-war statement to Phyllis Auty, the other British witness and the man in the centre of it all, Colonel Hudson, also states that the landing occurred "on the coast of Montenegro near Petrovac on the night of 17-18 September."[99]

Therefore it is necessary to ascertain which landing date to adopt: 20 September (as suggested by Deakin without citing evidence), or 18 September (as stated by the two British participants). An enquiry from the Naval Historical Branch brought the reply that,

> . . . the Admiralty War Diary includes a signal time 1852B on 27 September 1941 addressed to Captain (S) one which includes the sentence: Special operation completed (? night) (20th?). The words in brackets—in this case vital . . .—were received corrupt and were interpreted in the best way by the War Staff based on other known assumptions. You will not that there is no reference to BULLSEYE as such.

An official account of this period in the war written in 1955 states:

> On the 20th TRIUMPH was off *Peljesac,* preparing to land her Jugoslav party. This was successfully accomplished that night although some difficulty had been experienced in recognizing landmarks 'despite or perhaps because of native aid' (from the Jugoslav officers). This trouble was of frequent occurrence in many other theatres of war. Local guides, or people claiming special knowledge were, when it came to periscope work, frequently worse than useless.[100]

When this information is related to the earlier discussion regarding operation Bullseye, two comments may be advanced.

One, in the signal from the Admiralty's Diary there is nothing definite either to support Deakin's date (20 September), or to discredit Amery and Hudson's date (18 September). Two, regarding the account written in 1955, it is known that apart from Operation Bullseye in September 1941 no other sea-landing of a British-Yugoslav military team occurred on the Adriatic coast of Yugoslavia. It is suggested that, perhaps, in deciphering the information, a better known name (Pelješac: "Pet" or "Pel". . . "ac") came to mind instead of the unknown Petrovac ("Pet". . . "ac"). Pelješac is a peninsula, and Petrovac an anonymous village—hence the deciphering mistake. Therefore a landing "off Pelješac" could not have taken place.

A further search in the Naval Historical Branch and in the Public Record Office in London produced HMS *Triumph's* Log and Captain's Report dealing with operation Bullseye.[101] Thus, this fascinating work of historical detection can be successfully brought to its final conclusion. The log contains all the technical data necessary to resolve the question of sailing on mission and landing the party, as well as other details of interest. Thus on 14 September, the last Sunday in the base at Malta before sailing on mission, one of the entries reads, "0930 [hours], hands to Divine Service in Base." On the last day before sailing, Monday 15 September, under "No. on Sick List" the entry reads "Nil," and under "Leave granted to Ship's Company" it is entered "Blue and White Watches 1830-0700; C.P.O.s and P.O.s 0730."

On Tuesday 16 September there are a number of entries which prove that it was *Triumph's* sailing day from Malta. Already the heading of the Log reads "From Malta to Patrol and at Malta." The entries of interest to the present research read,

0815 Hands employed in compartments at storing and preparing for sea.
1319 Slipped from No. 3 Buoys. . . .
1745 Harbour stations. *1807. Slipped and proceeded on M/M* [? Main Motors]. *1813, Gate.*
1934 . . . Commenced zig zag.

On Wednesday 17 September the heading of the Log reads "From Malta to Patrol." On Thursday 18 September, under the same heading, it is noted —*inter alia*—that at "0815 (was) sighted one merchant Vessel escorted by one destroyer," at 0844 were "Fired 1, 2 and 3 [torpedo] tubes." Three minutes later, at 0847 the entry reads "One hit on M[erchant] V[essel]." But the destroyer started "hunting and depth charging," so that the entry at 0950 reads "44 depth charges." In the afternoon *Triumph* passed "Crotone Harbour." On Friday 19 September the heading reads "From Malta to Patrol and at Patrol Area (Adriatic)." On the same day, the total time sailing submerged is the greatest of the journey and reads "15 hrs 20 mins."

Considering that the journey from Malta was not broken, Log entries in the evening of *Saturday 20 September* refer to landing the Bullseye mission. The entries of import read,

. . . 2011, Depth 60 ft [? fathoms].
2040 *Surfaced.* 2106, Canoes on deck. Position 2500 yds from Beach. *2124, First Canoe left.* Submarine lying quietly 1½ cables from shore. *Proceeded with landing party.*

On the next day, Sunday 21 September, the first entry in the Log reads,

0015 *Completed operation.* All canoes stowed. . . .
0028 Commenced zig zag.

The exact location of the submarine could be ascertained by plotting the technical data entered in the Log of 20 September. However, this is not necessary as the Captain's Report contains both sufficiently descriptive and very vividly presented information about it. Commanders Woods' report reads *inter alia.*

Saturday 20 September.
1400 Arrived off PETROVAC. Some difficulty was experienced in recognizing landmarks despite or perhaps because of, native aid. The ship had been set 9 miles NW in spite of continuous ENE wind. 2 aircraft and one red bus were seen during the day. Selected landing place in PERISICADOL Bay. The wind was dropping and conditions were ideal for landing the JUGOSLAV party.
2100 It was decided to postpone charging until after landing to give the party ample time to get clear by daylight. Surfaced 1½ miles offshore. Launched first canoe containing Captain Hudson, Sub Lieutenant DON and one JUGOSLAVIAN officer ½ mile from the beach. There was now a fresh NE wind, with very strong gusts coming down off the mountains, but little sea and no swell. The wind made handling canoes difficult, and it was an hour before the first canoe returned to report that the landing place was ideal. A second canoe was launched to complete the landing, three more trips from each boat (manned by Cpls DAVIES and ROLF of No 2 Commando) being required. As soon as it was evident that there were no sentries ashore closed to 300 yds from the beach, where the submarine was hidden by cliffs except from the beach and from seaward, and in sheltered water.

Woods' report of happening on the next day, the 21 September, is fascinating as well, and, in addition, even contains a surprise (shown in italics when transcribing). These extracts read,

Sunday 21 September
0015 Withdrew to seaward having struck down canoes. Searchlights were active at the entrance to KOTOR.
1848 *It was noticed that the light-houses were still flying Jugoslav colours.*
2045 Surfaced. There was no blackout at DUBROVNIK or on neighbouring towns.

Commander Woods has also provided a description of the landing bay, and a summary of the trip, including a list of equipment provided by the

Triumph to the men of *Bullseye*. All of this forms an interesting footnote to the history of the mission.

It has been finally ascertained that HM Submarine *Triumph* with the Bullseye team aboard left Malta harbour in the afternoon of Tuesday 16 September 1941, at seven minutes past six. At the Ilić—Masterson meeting of 25 September it was known already that the submarine sailed on 16 September; information was announced by John Bennett. The landing occurred at Perisicadol Bay [? Perišića Dol] near Petrovac on the Montenegrin coast. It started at twenty four minutes past nine in the afternoon of Saturday 20 September, and ended at fifteen minutes past midnight 20-21 September 1941. Having reached a final conclusion and thus completed this aspect of the historical investigation of Operation Bullseye, one must point out that the end result contains both a surprise and a warning. The surprise is that Amery's account, full of detail that can be verified, somewhere went astray in its chronology. Both he and the other participant, Colonel Hudson, are seen to have erred in indicating 18 September as the date of the landing. Yet Deakin's date—20 September—which is cited without supporting evidence, emerged as the correct information. The warning is that this experience is really a classic example of the need for total vigilance when engaged in historical research.

As an overall conclusion on SOE and Yugoslavia, it may be said that, three observations have to be made. First, in the days when Britian was preoccupied with her own survival and had no inclination at the governmental level to be distracted by Yugoslavia, the small band of D/SOE volunteers in Belgrade kept the British presence felt. Although their job was supposed to be primarily the sabotage of Germany-bound transport, they exercised rewarding initiative in nursing personal contacts with the leading Serb anglophile element. Second, after the collapse of Yugoslavia, their further initiative and personal ties with the Serb exiles enabled them to keep more closely in touch with the news or "intelligence" from occupied Yugoslavia. Exercising initiative again, they assiduously followed the aim of ensuring the renewal of the British presence in the Balkans. At the first opportunity the SOE organized Operation Bullseye and sent in Captain Hudson, who was later followed by others. And, third, *Triumph's* Bullseye patrol may be said to have initiated British seaborne communications with the resistance in Yugoslavia.[102] The latter case, however, requires a qualification: one ought to adopt an historical and not a political attitude, and view Yugoslavia as a State and not as a regime.

CHAPTER 5

THE SOE STEPS IN:
HUDSON AND "OPERATION BULLSEYE" (II),
BRIEFING AND ACTIVITY

What happened to the Bullseye party, which was conducted to Radovče where it spent most of its time before leaving for Serbia? Controversy surrounds six major issues: the purpose of the mission, its briefing, its landing and stay in Montenegro, its departure for and early days in Serbia. The briefing and the question of W/T sets and communications is at the forefront of the historical debate. The controversy surrounding the briefing of the mission, which would reflect its general background and purpose, stems from a number of factors. The mission was a parallel Yugoslav-British team, hurriedly raised, in which each national component was briefed by its own superiors. Whereas care has been taken to reconstruct Hudson's briefing, no attempt has been made to explain some rather puzzling details, while innuendos dominate the reconstruction of the Yugoslav briefing. Having been directed in Cairo to proceed directly to Colonel Mihailović, Hudson's brief required him to collect and report military intelligence about the enemy,[1] collect and report intelligence about [local] forces resisting the enemy,[2] and, finally *advise the Yugoslavs to fight for their own benefit, and not for the interest of any foreign power.*[3]

A part of Hudson's brief to investigate and report on everyone resisting the enemy, "regardless of nationality, religion or political belief,"[4] is puzzling. It does not make sense in the contemporary Yugoslav context, yet nobody commented on it. The British authorities in Cairo knew Yugoslavia was a Kingdom of Serbs, Croats and Slovenes, and national minorities such as Germans and Hungarians.[5] Considering that, except for Croat Ustashas and the Axis minorities, the others were expected to resist the occupation, what was there to look for "regardless of nationality, religion or political belief"? The answer must be looked for outside the Yugoslav context, and two independent witnesses of opposite political persuasions, Amery and Djilas provide it. Their testimonies complement each other. Julian Amery's assessment of possibilities opened by the Serbian revolt emphasized the development of a "solid anti-German block." This view was strengthened by the Albanian experience which revealed that local resistance to the Italians comprised royalists and anti-royalists.[6] This is contrary to the situation in Montenegro and Serbia, where, based on SOE sources, it is alleged that it was Hudson who discovered the potential resistance value of *Communist-led* guerrillas. Independently of Amery, Djilas reports that "(Hudson) was particularly interested in . . . Miljan Radonjić of Montenegro, [and] Gani-beg of Kosovo . . . ." These names were totally unknown then, as well as now, to anyone not familiar with local Montenegrin and Albanian affairs in 1939-41. The one place where something can be learned about these people is Amery's account of his Albanian work, for they were the people he conspired with before the German invasion of Yugoslavia.[7] On the strength of this evidence it is obvious that, in Hudson's instructions, the item concerning potential resisters "regardless of nationality, religion and political belief" primarily meant the Albanians, and not the Yugoslavs. This detail is of crucial importance. Besides clarifying the reference to different nationalities (etc.), it reveals also the identity of the British briefing officer. It was Julian Amery. Indeed, this evidence concurs with Amery's own claims that at Malta he briefed "Hudson and his colleagues collectively and separately"; this is not contradicted in SOE files.[8] Amery was also interested in Bulgaria,[9] and Hudson was instructed to provide intelligence about Bulgaria as well. In his correspondence about Hudson's brief, Amery says explicitly,

> . . . Hudson's briefing all took place in Malta and in the submarine. . . . I did the briefing myself and as you [that is, MD] rightly suggest (the brief) also asked him to examine the situation in Albania—Gani

Kryeziu. It also asked him . . . to try and find out whether there was any Bulgarian resistance developing on behalf of the Peasant Party, the Army or the Proto Gueroffist wing of the Macedonian Movement.[10]

But to revert to the existing historiography.

The claim that Hudson was instructed also "to coordinate" resistance forces might be too formalized a version of his own wartime statement to Major (then Captain) Rudi K. Perhinek, to whom he said that he came *to assist* everybody fighting against the Axis Powers.[11] Indeed—unless someone blundered in Cairo—it is hard to entertain seriously the suggestion that he, as a Captain, was meant to "coordinate" whatever a Staff Colonel and Senior Officer in the Field (Mihailović) was doing in his own country (Yugoslavia). If he was really meant to "coordinate" anything, Hudson should have been sent in at least with a field-rank, if not with the rank of full Colonel, so as to be equal to Mihailović in the military hierarchy. Cairo somewhat belatedly grasped this point, and, late in 1942, *Lt Colonel* S. W. Bailey was appointed the Senior British Liaison Officer with Mihailović. Eventually, a Brigadier was appointed to each Balkan guerrilla as the Senior British Liaison Officer. In contrast to the work done in reconstructing Hudson's brief, the reconstruction of the Yugoslav briefing for Operation Bullseye is little advanced. The best known version of their brief is contained in Deakin's *Embattled Mountain*. Unfortunately, he "created" a problem by referring to "secret instructions" and "certain directives" given to Yugoslav officers. The tone of Deakin's approach might have been influenced by a post-war statement of a former Yugoslav P.M. in exile, General Simović.

Deakin cites a translation of his statement *in extenso;* it reads,

> the mission was sent without my knowledge but on the basis of my *preliminary talks* with [War Minister] General Ilic. *Before I went to London* the Yugoslav command in Cairo, in agreement with the British Intelligence Service, sent Ostojic and Lalatovic into the country . . . with the task of making contact with the *forces* of resistance in the country and to send reports on the situation there. I heard later that they had received *certain instructions* but what and from whom is unknown to me . . . . "[12]

There are no emphases in the original quotation; but these help focus the following discussion.

Simović's "preliminary talks" with General Ilić regarding the Bullseye mission will be studied further in chapter 10, on the "Russian Project." His claim that Ostojić and Lalatović were sent "into the country" *before he (Simović) left* the Middle East for London is erroneous. Mission Bullseye was raised and dispatched in August-September 1941, yet Simović had already left the Middle East and arrived in England on 21 June 1941, where he stayed. The "forces" of resistance are obviously a sop offered to the new regime, as Simović made his statement after his repatriation to Tito's Yugoslavia. Surely, if, as an exile in 1941, he really thought in terms of any "forces" resisting in occupied Yugoslavia, as a loyal professional soldier he could and would have to conceive of them only as an instrument subordinate to the exiled government. Indeed, all his interventions asking for Churchill's and Eden's intercessions with the Soviet Government prove this point. Thus, Simović wrote to Eden on 13 November 1941, that he had instructed the Yugoslav Minister in Moscow to "immediately ask the Russian [sic] Government to warn the Communists in Yugoslavia to help Colonel Mihailovitch, and to collaborate with him against the Germans." At the same time Simović asked the Soviet Ambassador in London, Maisky, to "also use his influence with the Russian [sic] Government, to this end."[13] Therefore Simović's statement, cited by Deakin, is worthless as to its main claims.

However, Yugoslav "secret" instructions, a novelty introduced by Deakin, were not so secret after all. According to Deakin himself, the two Yugoslav Majors were directed to,

> contact and reveal the exclusive existence of national bands loyal to the King and led by their fellow officers from the dissolved[14] Yugoslav army. They had been informed in Cairo that a certain Colonel Mihailovic was at the centre of a skeleton nationalist resistance movement based on the heights of Suvobor in Western Serbia, and their orders were clearly to proceed, through nationalist channels in Montenegro, to Mihailovic's headquarters.[15]

Other writers have not contributed any new points to Deakin's summary. It appears that few endeavoured to locate and interview witnesses who dealt with the Yugoslav end of Operation Bullseye. This is surprising as ever since the war an invaluable Yugoslav witness, Colonel Popović, has lived in London. At the time of the raising and dispatch of the Bullseye mission he was Director of Yugoslav Military Intelligence in Cairo; earlier he was Director of Military Intelligence in Belgrade, and thereafter Military Attaché in Moscow. Late in 1942 he left the Yugoslav Army and became a Colonel in the British Army. His evidence has been invaluable. According to Colonel Popović, one day in September 1941 he was unexpectedly visited by John Bennett and Julian Amery, who demanded that he immediately transfer to them a team of men to be sent to Yugoslavia.[16] He indicated that he had no authority to do so, and reported the matter to the Yugoslav GHQ in Cairo, in order to assist the British. The reason for this sudden calling on Colonel Popović is explained by Amery. It had been planned that the mission to Mihailović should go by air, but at RAF headquarters "the difficulties of an air operation were judged insuperable." Maxwell then arranged that a Sunderland should fly the mission to Malta, from where they were to proceed by submarine. As Djonović had volunteers ready to go to Yugoslavia, Amery had telegraphed John Bennett in Istanbul to send them to Cairo.[17] On 5 September Bennett arrived in Cairo with the news that a "Voivoda Vasili Turbitch and another Yugoslav officer" followed. On meeting them however, it was found that Trbić ("Turbitch") was too old (over sixty), "although his morale was high." They had lunch together in Amery's flat. Trbić "thought he was going to be landed by air,"[18] but when Bennett and Amery began to brief him and he learned that he was supposed to travel by submarine and go to Serbia via Montenegro,

> Nothing would induce him to go there. He knew little of the country or its people and disliked the little he knew . . . . He would not go to Montenegro.[19]

Meanwhile, while awaiting the arrival of the team from Istanbul, Hudson had volunteered for duty as the British member. But now, twenty four hours before flying out, Trbić's refusal to go on created a crisis. This forced Bennett and Amery to call on Colonel Popović who undertook to do what he could.[20] He went to his superiors. When Popović reached the Yugoslav GHQ, he found the War Minister,[21] General Ilić, and the

Commander of the Air Force, Brigadier-General Borivoje (Bora) Mirković, chatting in the drawing room drinking black coffee.[22] The Generals acted quickly, selecting an airman and General Staff officer, Major Boško Stanojlović. However they sustained Colonel Popović's objection that, as an "urban child" Stanojlović would be fair game to the enemy in the countryside.[23] Thereupon Mirković suggested Majors Ostojić and Lalatović, and the minister approved them. Why were airmen posted to the Bullseye mission? The answer is simple. The Air Force Commander happened to be with the War Minister when postings were suddenly required, and so he proposed his own staff officers.[24] It may be assumed that, but for the accidental presence of the Air Force Commander, Popović would have advanced to the Minister names of artillery officers, as he was himself an artilleryman and staff officer. (So much for the perennial argument of *"raison d'état."*)

This leaves another question: why Ostojić and Lalatović, and not someone else? The only witness—Colonel Popović—says,

> I do not know General Mirković's motivation in putting up their names. I assume however that he wanted to move Ostojić away from Cairo, because he clashed with the British military in the camp where he was....

When Popović called at the Yugoslav GHQ with the Yugoslav team the next morning, the Minister (Gl Ilić) and the Air Force Commander (Brig.-Gl Mirković) happened to be entering their car to go to Palestine on sick leave. Lalatović nudged Ostojić to go and greet the Minister, but he loudly swore and added in the same voice,

> Why should I go and greet him, when he obviously has no time to spare for me. All he wants is to exploit me to ensure his return to power, but I am not going to oblige him.[25]

For his part of the briefing, Colonel Popović says that when he was instructed by the Minister to "explain to them the situation in Yugoslavia," he acquainted the Yugoslav team with the intelligence provided by the two Polish officers. "As to my own briefing," he says,

SOE: Briefing and Activity

> I added that they should ask Colonel Mihailović to let me know if he wanted me there too.

The two colonels were lifelong friends, so that this claim seems reasonable. Then he exhorted the two officers to heed Serb interests, which—of course—*in those days* meant to keep in mind that in Yugoslavia only Serbs were still on the Allied side. The Ustaše and the Communists were not pro-Ally (Popović had learned about the Communist activity from the two Polish officers). As to whether the Yugoslav Bullseye component was briefed by the British military also, Colonel Popović says,

> I do not know that British briefing they received, but I assume it must have dealt with sabotage issues, as the section organizing it was a sabotage section.

Their British briefing officer was Amery, who, incidentally, "tried to discover what private instructions Popovitch might have given" them, but "they did not give much away." He formed the opinion that "the Communist danger was very much in their minds."[26] There is only one statement about this briefing attributed to a team member. Lieutenant (later Captain) Nedjeljko B. Plećaš was parachuted into Yugoslavia during the night 5-6 September 1942. Soon afterwards he met Lalatović, who told him that in Cairo he had been received by the War Minister, who asked him to locate and assassinate a Colonel and ensure that the country welcomed back the exiled government.[27] It seems that the Yugoslav military were caught by surprise, and that there was no substantial briefing. However, if Deakin's statement is divorced from too much formalism and a "certain" undercurrent of mistrust, his and Colonel Popović's statements may give the best approximation of what really happened.

The question of the mission's landing and stay in Montenegro gives rise to a minor and a major historical problem. The minor problem concerns the manner in which they got in touch with the local guerrillas. This issue seems to have arisen through the insensitivity of many urban-bred writers to the spontaneity of rural mass-movements, and their tendency to describe everything in terms of regimented forms. Thus, Auty says Bullseye landed in the territory "at that time held by *Tito's forces*"; Deakin speaks of "local guerrilla units who were *posted* in the hills overlooking the coast."[28]

Yet Howarth says that the party "had the good fortune to meet a Franciscan friar, who was looking for his goats."[29] In my interview with him in London in 1985, Colonel Hudson confirmed that Howarth's version was the correct one: "I gave him this information" he said. On the other hand, no Yugoslav Partisan source says other than that the Bullseye party "immediately sought contact with our [sic] guerrilla units" and was "assisted" by Montenegrin partisans.[30] Nevertheless, it is erroneous to designate as "Partisans" all insurgents who were led by the KPJ in 1941. At the time, in Montenegro the whole medley of insurgents was known as "guerrilla." Even Deakin says that Hudson found there "patriot forces," and that "at no point was there any indication of the existence of local Communist leadership."[31] The division into "Partisans" and nationalists occurred only when the KPJ distanced itself from the mass of the insurgent people. According to Djilas himself, the division could not have occurred before mid-October 1941.[32]

The major historical problem regarding the mission's stay in Montenegro is the problem of the mission's W/T set and communications. Deakin claims that after Hudson "received orders from Cairo to move to Serbia," on 9 October[33] his "Royal Yugoslav companions" started sending their own telegrams to Malta without consulting Hudson.[34] Deakin has overlooked the fact that the party was a parallel party of British and Yugoslav personnel. Whereas common sense required their cooperation, surely there was no legal obligation to submit themselves to one another's censorship. In the context the whole discussion may be considered as contrived. To build up his case, Deakin cites the text (or extract?) of a telegram dated 13 October, which, he says, is "clearly an example" of acting "without (Hudson's) knowledge." Deakin's introductory remark reads: "the following *summary of messages* was sent to Malta in French, and presumably over Hudson's set from Montenegro."[35] The import of this point requires that the text be cited fully:

> Instructions have been delivered to our group which is operating in Montenegro not to co-operate with those leaders of Chetnik *odreds* who do not recognize the Yugoslav government. No other report which you have received and which states the contrary should be dealt with.
>
> It has equally been so settled that Colonel Mihailović is receiving orders to *refrain from sabotage except against railway tracks,*

locomotives etc., where explosives are not needed, so that the population will not be too exposed to reprisals. The group has been ordered to confine itself for the time being to preparations and collecting material with the aim of co-ordinated and well organized action at a moment which will be ordered later.

We have received a telegram which confirms that this message has been received by the group in Montenegro.[36]

Deakin also makes the point that the message is "contained in the Mihailović files in Belgrade." Despite all this, his explanations somehow do not sound convincing. Karchmar contends that,

Deakin completely misinterprets this telegram, which he pretends was sent *from* [sic; MD] Lalatovic in Montenegro *to* Malta; its contents make it obvious that it was sent *from* Malta to Mihailovic (in whose files, AS DEAKIN NOTES, it was found). This would also account for its being in French.[37]

Karchmar's speculation sounds reasonable *qua* speculation. Its weakness is that Karchmar's rebuttal of Deakin's version is based on the Deakin posited proposition that the message—"AS DEAKIN NOTES"—is contained in Mihailović's files in Belgrade. In order to break out of Deakin posited parameters, one ought to look elsewhere. As it happens, in Kljaković's article "Velika..." one can locate a quotation identical to Deakin's.[38] There, Kljaković states that *summaries of Hudson's telegrams were being passed on to the Yugoslav government.*[39] In other words, these were British summaries prepared for their Yugoslav ally. Furthermore, Kljaković states verbatim that in the Yugoslav government's file of received summaries, this particular message is entered as follows:

On 13 October 1941 *received* the following text *in French:* Summary of telegrams received from Montenegro . . . . " [The Deakin and Kljaković text follows.][40]

It is obvious therefore that this summary of telegrams was an intergovernmental communication (which explains also why it was in French, as—at the time—French was stil the international diplomatic language). It is held in Belgrade *amongst the material* pertaining to Mihailović. This is not the same as Deakin simply saying "Mihailovic files," which allows for the misunderstanding that the document was found amongst Mihailović's own October 1941 papers. Karchmar was misled by this fact. In this light, all that remains of Deakin's argument is the possibility that "over Hudson's set from Montenegro" it was not necessarily Hudson himself who confirmed the receipt of messages received. But then, is not the acknowledging of messages received a routine matter, ordinarily dealt with by the radio operator? Finally, Colonel Popović's papers also contain the record of an early decision regarding the resistance which, when related to the summary of telegrams discussed here, leaves no doubt that this summary is a summary of instructions *sent to* Montenegro. This is seen from clause two of the summary, which deals with the directives *to concentrate on railway sabotage.* This decision was taken at the Ilić—Masterson meeting of 25 September, and it is recorded in the Memorandum of this meeting.[41] The originator of the railway sabotage proposal was Masterson. Its result would be felt only "5-600 km later," that is, outside Serbia, so that the Serb population would be safe from German reprisals.[42] The summary of telegrams is the proof that the high-level decision taken in Cairo was then transmitted down-the-line to the field personnel.

On or about 13 October (that is, after the receipt of orders was acknowledged), Hudson and Ostojić set out from Montenegro for Serbia.[43] They were accompanied by Mitar Bakić and Captain Arso Jovanović.[44] Lalatović and the W/T operator, Dragićević, stayed behind with the Bullseye's W/T set. Deakin finds this arrangement "significant."[45] Lalatović was "clearly bent," he says, on preventing any further British contacts with the local Communist Partisans, and to secure all communications and any British material aid exclusively for nationalists and the supporters of the Royal Yugoslav government.[46] To illustrate this point, he adds,

> On 24 October the following signal was received in Cairo, presumably from Lalatovic; 'Everything is ready to receive material aid at Radovce *according to the plan drawn up,* which will be valid on 21-22-25-26-27 October.'[47]

At that time the Royal Yugoslav Government was Lalatović's legal government. However, lest someone should think Deakin was praising Lalatović

SOE: Briefing and Activity

for loyalty and devotion to duty, he immediately comments "The message provokes speculation" and proceeds to a number of rhetorical questions. His last "speculation" reads,

> Or did the message come from Lalatovic on his own set and refer to *separate and secret* arrangements to send supplies to other nationalist bands in the area?[48]

Kept "secret" from whom? Hudson, namely the British? In his book *Wartime*, published in 1977, six years after Deakin's, Djilas contributes what is probably the answer to the above question, *viz.*,

> [While staying at Radovče] With the help of our officers, Hudson set out to measure the plain of Radovče, to see if aircraft could land there. It was concluded that, with a little leveling of the ground, it would be possible, but there the matter stood.[49]

However, but for observing what *Hudson* was doing (surveying and discussing leveling the ground), Djilas cannot be said to have been a party to Bullseye's W/T traffic and other arrangements which followed. Neither were these arrangements sinister and, perhaps, anti-Hudson—(not to say "anti-British") as might be implied from Deakin's commentary. The real situation was very different. A week after Lalatović's telegram was received in Cairo, General Dill wrote to the Yugoslav P.M. Simović, to tell him about the advice he had received from Cairo as to the help they would render to Yugoslav patriots. *Inter alia*, in a matter of days the RAF was to make a night sortie and parachute *at Radovče* a Yugoslav agent, arms, ammunition, bandages and "gold." His letter is published by Marjanović,[50] who is the foremost partisan historian. So it seems that, the other archival material, Djilas' testimony and Dill's letter to Yugoslav Premier destroy Deakin's interpretation. In any case, the drop at Radovče did not eventuate. Be this as it may, Lalatović does not seem to have waited for it and, together with Dragićević, set out to follow Hudson and Ostojić on the journey to Serbia.

Hudson's arrival in Serbia causes the foregoing pattern of historiographical meanderings about Operation Bullseye to reach its climax. It also reopens arguments about Bullseye's W/T set(s). For instance, to quote Deakin again,

The historical misfortune in Colonel Hudson's case was that he had trouble with his wireless communications and the one set that he had when he reached Mihailović—I think I am correct in this—was in fact *more or less* impounded by Mihailović.[51]

According to Auty,

> Shorty after Hudson arrived [in Serbia], and *after he had sent the message suggesting an end to [Chetnik] hostilities against the Partisans and a mission* [sent] *to Tito,* he lost control of his own radio transmitter. One story was that Mihailović took charge of it, another that is was confiscated by the Germans who had broken his cipher.[52]

Deakin's hypothesis that a W/T set could be simultaneously both impounded and not impounded was made in 1962, Auty's speculations were published in 1970. In 1973 Roberts claimed:

> Lalatovic and Dragicevic had not yet reached Uzice [from Montenegro] when Hudson and Ostojic set out [from Uzice] for Ravna Gora on October 25.
>
> Shortly thereafter, Lalatovic and Dragicevic arrived in Uzice, but while Lalatovic went on [to Mihailovic] at Ravna Gora, Dragicevic refused to join him and instead stayed, with Hudson's radio set, at Partisan headquarters [in Uzice].[53]

In the same year, independently from Roberts, Karchmar observed that,

> In any case, Hudson's probelm was not the loss of the radio but of the radio operator, who was a Communist and went over to the Partisans shortly after the mission arrived in Yugoslavia.[54]

But meanwhile (in 1971), and in contrast to his other statement, Deakin himself had written:

> ... Lalatovic had reached Uzice from Montenegro, together with the radio operator Dragicevic. The latter had already fallen out with

both Yugoslav officers attached to the mission, and refused to follow Hudson to Ravna Gora. He was to remain with Partisan headquarters and to become their chief radio operator.

This time Deakin also admits that the Mark III W/T set, "brought up from Montenegro by Lalatovic and Dragicevic" was "left in Uzice."[55]

Fortunately, the history of Operation Bullseye's progress from Montenegro to Serbia, and its early days in Serbia, is not nearly as complicated as its would-be historiography. On the strength of all the evidence its main outline may reasonably be reconstructed as follows. Hudson said that in Cairo he was issued with two radio sets. One was the "most antique" imaginable Mark III set, wieghing about 55 lbs and running off electricity. The other was "a small 'J'" set, which could not operate longer than half an hour at a time, otherwise it would burn out. Its range was such that it "could just get Malta" from Montenegro, but "not from Serbia."[56] On leaving Montenegro for Serbia, probably about 13 October, Hudson and Ostojić were accompanied by Arso Jovanović and Mitar Bakić. On their way through Sandžak and other areas, the presence of the latter two [communist functionaries] gave Hudson the opportunity of,

> meeting the various troops and loosely formed associations of patriots, partisans, and various people who at this time had not aligned themselves completely, but who were dominated or controlled by a Communist organization.[57]

He saw no evidence that Mihailović had any organization there "then" [later this was to change]. On 23 October Hudson and the party arrived at Užice in Serbia,[58] where they met Tito. Whereas Major Ostojić proceeded without delay to Colonel Mihailović's headquarters to report on duty, Hudson stayed behind.[59] Probably instructed by the Colonel, Ostojić returned to Užice for Hudson, and the two men "moved on to Ravna Gora" on 25 October.[60] At the time of Hudson's arrival Mihailović was at the foot of the mountain Ravna Gora at Brajići, so Hudson went there. On meeting Mihailović, Hudson passed on to him the cipher and codeword "Villa Resta," which he was given *in Cairo* especially for Mihailović. This is admitted by both Auty and Deakin,[61] who thus contradict attempts to deny Hudson's knowledge of Mihailović before he was told about him in Montenegro.

Meanwhile Lalatović, still in Montenegro, attended to finalizing arrangements for an RAF sortie at Radovče, and set out for Serbia in late October together with Dragićević.[62] They had not yet arrived at Užice when Ostojić and Hudson moved to Ravna Gora. "My wireless set," says Hudson in a crucial statement on the matter,

> My wireless set was a bulky thing and had to come down by mule and it came about ten days after I arrived on the scene, mainly because I crossed at speed with Arso Jovanovic and Mitar Bakic having passed through their communications—and *the set was too heavy and too slowmoving to be brought with us.*[63]

This must have been the Mark III set, the small "J" set had burned out in Montenegro already. All straight forward and nothing sinister about it. When Lalatović and Dragićević arrived at Užice about ten days after Hudson,[64] Dragićević declared himself for the Partisans, and retained Hudson's remaining radio set with him; Major Lalatović proceeded to Mihailović to report on duty. On 27 October, as if anticipating the loss that would be caused by Dragićević, Hudson used Mihailović's transmitter to request air-supply of "A.C. and accumulator W/T sets," but to no avail.[65] Shortly afterwards, Majors Ostojić and Lalatović serving now under Colonel Mihailović, and Sergeant Dragićević having opted for the Partisans, the original Anglo-Yugoslav composition of Bullseye mission ended. Captain Hudson remained mission "Bullseye" on his own, and Mihailović started using his own cipher—"Villa Resta."

Even the final fate of Hudson's transmitter gave rise to controversy. Let's start with Deakin. He says that the fate of Hudson's set "left [sic] in Uzice, has not been completely clarified."[66] Nevertheless he does say that on 29 November, when German troops entered Užice, Hudson withdrew "with Tito and his staff," but after "a 'two day rout'" decided to return to Serbia.[67] He took this decision *"After crossing the Uvac river on the borders of the Sandzak,"* and, returning to Ravna Gora, also brought with him his radio set.[68] Djilas is more explicit. According to him, partisans "were spilling out [of Užice] in panic" (and the Germans were entering) only in the afternoon of the 30th.[69] At first he says that Tito and Hudson left in "Tito's limousine," yet only three pages later one gets the impression that Djilas is now saying they left Užice on foot.[70] Eventually, *when the Partisans crossed the River Uvac from Serbia into Sandžak,*

SOE: Briefing and Activity

Hudson told them at Radonja that he wanted to "rejoin Draža Mihailović," and was given his radio set to take back.[71] Yet there is also a third version, hitherto not published. According to Major Perhinek, Hudson told him that,

> When he went on 29 November to recover his set from Tito and sat there chatting with him, a Partisan barged into the office shouting, 'Run, here come the Germans.' Hudson asked Tito what were Partisans going to do, and Tito answered 'We'll defend ourselves.' Hudson [who was a well-built and strong man] loaded himself with the radio set and started running away together with Tito. Whenever Hudson was aksing where would the Partisans stop and fight, Tito would say 'On the next hill.' *When they reached Kokin Brod* Hudson had enough of it. With the intention to recover it later, Hudson buried his radio set. Having witnessed that the Communists could not resist the Germans he returned to Mihailović.[72]

Deakin's version is secondary information, Djilas's is an incomplete eyewitness account, and Perhinek's is a mixed eyewitness and reporter's account. Three questions arise. What is the correct date of German retaking of Užice, why had Hudson left the Partisans to return to Mihailović, and, what happened to Hudson's own W/T set. As to the date (29 or 30 November), the answer is to be found in the Operations War Diary (*"Kriegstagebuch, Fuehrungsabteilung"*) of the German 342 Infantry Division. Under the date 29 November the main entries concerning Užice are a record that the offensive on Užice resumed at 0730 hours, then, at 1310 hours that orders were issued to attack Užice on the same afternoon, and at 1510 hours the report is entered of [the Attack Column Group North A (?)] advance units that Užice was taken and the German war standard (*"Reichskriegsflagge"*) raised.[73] As to Hudson, Deakin does not discuss his motivation, although he does say Hudson decided to return to Serbia "after 'a two days [Partisan] rout'." Djilas says there was "talk" amongst Partisans that Hudson was "partial to Draža [Mihailović]," which is rather an insinuation and not an explanation. Perhinek contends Hudson told him himself that he had had enough of continuous retreat.

Nevertheless, there is more to it. Simply mentioning that Partisans crossed from Serbia into Sandžak before Hudson's decision, gives the impression of an ordinary guerrilla move from one district to another. In this instance however the crucial point is that, by doing so, Partisans had escaped from the German occupation zone into the Italian. Says Djilas,

> ...(Germans) had driven us across the Uvca [sic] River. This was the boundary of the Italian zone,... Having cleared their own territory, (Germans) left it to their Italian allies to contend with the remnants.[74]

But the Italians did not bother. In retrospect, it is obvious that most German anti-guerrilla actions in Yugoslavia aborted due to the non-cooperation of the Italian army, so that the pursued could always find a refuge in the Italian zone of occupation. But this is not the point. The point here is that a British Captain, posted to Serbia and—*inter alia*—required to report on anti-Axis resistance, now suddenly witnesses a total rout of the most vocal resistance group. Hudson only decided to leave them and return to Serbia after—in Hudson's words—"Tito and Co." had voted with their feet to abandon Serbia. Deakin cites Hudson's own signal,

> I got the impression everywhere that British help was best concentrated on Mihailović.... I told Tito and Co. this and made my way back in a wave of Germans and Quislings.

At that stage, Partisan leaders showed no intention themselves of returning to Serbia.[75] A grim picture indeed; Deakin adds also that Hudson was "captured three times on this fearful journey."[76] Therefore it is hard to give credence to Deakin's simultaneous claim that Hudson was carrying his radio set with him all the while, and that he brought it with him on his return to Ravna Gora.[77] Yet by combining Djilas and Perhinek's accounts a reasonable and acceptable proposition emerges. Chronologically, Hudson is seen to carry his own set during the rout (*vide* Perhinek), then at Radonja Djilas wanted to spirit the set away but Tito ordered its return to Hudson (Djilas) and, finally, Hudson decided to bury it for the time being and recover it later (Perhinek). There is a sequel to this. According to Perhinek, Lieutenant Vuk Kalaitović's soldiers

("Chetniks") found the set, and early in May 1942 Perhinek was charged with the return of his radio set to Hudson. The handover took place on Čemernica, where Hudson informed Perhinek of his adventure.[78]

In reviewing mission Bullseye's record, and in particular the problem of its W/T sets, it is amazing how some historians have complicated the story unnecessarily. Instead of reconstructing a given event, some historians seem to have been preoccupied in demeaning Mihailović. Now this rebounds on their credibility. What their readers could not know, is that Colonel Hudson had volunteered all the necessary information. In a symposium of historians he even stated unequivocally,

> I would like to clear all points on which I am competent to give an answer.

He made this statement at the conference at St. Antony's in 1962.[79] Yet, by studying the "Proceedings" of this conference, one cannot escape the impression that he was prevented from doing so. The proposition could be entertained that he had displeased his audience, or part of his audience, by his remark,

> I think is seriously compromises the work of a serious historian who comes out with a statement that Mihailović did not, on any occasion, fight the enemy.[80]

The general impression gained from following Hudson's repeated attempts to intervene in the discussion at the conference is that he met with obstruction from some historians with committed views. Eventually he was dismissed by snubbing him as if he were a little boy. *Inter alia*, he was being referred to as "...our dear Hudson...."[81] (No wonder that, since this experience, Colonel Hudson has become reticent about volunteering any further statements and giving interviews.)

Yet concurrently with what appears to have been an obstruction of the chief witness, the conference was treated to high sounding talk about a historian's lot, such as,

> The greatest difficulty for all of us is undoubtedly the problem of sources.[82]

To take this statement as a yardstick to apply to Bullseye's historiography, it is hard to see that sources were the "problem." The official British position is that, in Cairo, early SOE records were burned in the northern summer of 1942. It is really remarkable therefore how so many British authors have at their disposal abundant information on Operation Bullseye and its radio equipment. Furthermore—and this has been shown also—the exiled Yugoslav government's wartime files are kept in Belgrade. They include summaries of Hudson's early W/T traffic. Thus, it appears that the problem is not so much the lack of sources as an oft-encountered tendency for their selective usage and interpretation.

It has been seen that the historiography of *Mission Bullseye* suffers from a contrived anti-Mihailović interpretation. This is only one link in the larger contect of the biased historiography of the resistance in Yugoslavia in World War II. As well as its general bias, that part of the historiography which relates to the KPJ and Yugoslav Partisans, is also voluminous. By contrast, almost nothing serious has been written about the Mihailovićs, Ostojićs, Lalatovićs and their brother officers. This is a failing. One needs to be familiar with their background and role, in the same way as one ought to be aware of the uncritical and romanticized Partisan picture. One way of trying to redress this imbalance is to assess the background and personalities of the representatives of the two groups of people, that is, of their respective leaders. Indeed, from the moment that Captain Hudson met Tito at Užice and Mihailović at Brajići, both the army officers and the KPJ-Partisan management enter British calculations. This reinforces the importance of the question "Who were the two leaders?"

CHAPTER 6

THE LEADERS (I),
MIHAILOVIĆ IN PEACE AND WAR

Who was this man Mihailović, who attracted so much politically committed animosity? Wat is his doing, or was he a scapegoat of international politics? Considering that he was a professional staff officer, we have to begin by examining his military background and his views. At the time of the Yugoslav Regency he was a full Colonel. As all the previous years of his *curriculum* led to this point, let us take it from there. Beside the other problems of foreign and domestic policies, the Regency had to grapple also with the military consequences of the rise of Hitler (1933) and the new German *Wehrmacht*. At the same time the unconventional views and behaviour of Dragoljub (Draža) M. Mihailović, a Colonel in the General Staff Corps, came to the notice of his superiors. Born in 1892, a full Colonel in 1935, he was then 43 years old. The re-emergence of revisionist Germany as a great power in the mid- and late-1930s caused the end of the Europe of Versailles, a regrouping of European powers and a military soul-searching about how to counter a *Blitzkrieg*. By accident, the death of Alexander I (1934) coincided with this European military upheaval. In his lifetime the European doctrine of warfare on land was based on the "Queen of the Battle," the infantry. In those days artillery support and the use of other technology depended on the size and the wealth of a country. Use of cavalry, although already anachronistic, was still advocated by some, while others switched over to "mechanized cavalry" *viz.*, light tanks. Yugoslavia was an agricultural country, and this added weight to the use of infantry as an instrument of victory. Its use was based on the doctrine of movement. The final argument in such warfare would be resolved by a decisive bayonet charge. Detail of this drill is illustrated in notes written in 1929 by the then 17 years old Military Academy Cadet, 1st Year, Lance Corporal Jovan V. Derok. As a bonus, this description ends with a humorous twist. Here is an extract from his account of a bayonet rehearsal[1]:

> Yesterday we had a terrific exercise at Gradac.... In the past we only observed Gradac from Beli Kamen, where we attended to our war field-service instructions. In the direction of Leskovac,[2] a steep hill used to jut out out the fog: we knew it was Gradac, but yesterday we also 'felt it.'
>
> The night before it rained, and we were hoping to get a day off, but it was not to be. We started at 06.00 hours.
> ....
> As we were coming closer to it, Gradac appeared to grow higher and higher. The mud weighed down our boots, and our dress was mud-splattered. We advance, section leaders order to open fire. We run in twos and threes from the left and the right wing.
>
> We reach the hedge, our last natural cover below the enemy's position. High above me rises the pyramid marking the triangulation control point. The whole firing line moves forward; the slope is so steep that we slip backwards and have to crawl the best we can. Just below the summit I wanted to pause to cathc breath, but the new command flung me on: 'Bayonet charge! Forwards—urah!' We 'Urrr-aah!' at the top of our voices, and charge. I debouch into the enemy position, from all sides appear yet more bayonets, the hill resounds with the din of our shouting. Of the enemy troops we found only a demoralized and bewildered hare, running to and fro to force an exit through the besieging steel. Djuro, a Montenegrin, in order to wipe out every last one of the enemy, charged the hare with his bayonet for the kill, but the hare jumped over the barrel of his rifle and escaped.

When the German Panzer Army rose out of the ashes of the Weimar Republic, and Germany incorporated Austria in 1938 to become Yugoslavia's neighbour, there was no way that Yugoslavia and her army could have been a match for the new Great Power. Yugoslavia had a land frontier of 2,000 km. The arrival of Germany in the Balkans left Yugoslavia only with the Romanian and Greek borders in friendly hands, and in 1940 even Romania came under German control. Beside her size, which was no match for Germany, Yugoslavia had neither finances nor credit to buy sufficient updated arms and planes. Furthermore, as it was the rise of Hitler that caused the need for these new arms, they were now needed by the Big Powers themselves. This, regardless of any other arguments, precluded Yugoslavia from obtaining the armaments, spare parts, equipment and ammunition that she needed. Under the changed circumstances, it was imperative that Yugoslavia should review her military chances and policy. Elsewhere, people like Majors Holland and Grand were in Britain researching on their own initiative ways to wage "unconventional" warfare. Their problem was to devise means of propaganda and sabotage in neutral, enemy, and enemy occupied countries. Yugoslavia, exposed to a direct German land attack, had a different problem. Here, "irregular" warfare in support of the regular army's operations had to be considered. Classic guerrilla tactics meant harrassing enemy troops and their lines of communications. Under the conditions of *Blitzkrieg* the problem was how to force a man to man combat? In a mountainous country, the answer seemed to be either to ambush the enemy at his natural halts (refuelling, personal needs, overnight stops), or to force him to halt and leave his vehicles (mine damage to his tracks and wheels, destroyed highway bridges, obstructions in mountain passes). This required an organization, personnel, training, material, stores and transport. The discussions and steps which took place in Yugoslavia have not yet been studied, and this is an attempt to fill the gap. The only known writing by a Yugoslav officer who studied guerrilla warfare is a 118 page book by Captain Derok.[3] (He was soon to become "one of the principal Četnik commanders in West Serbia"[4] in the uprising of 1941.) As Yugoslavia had declared its neutrality in the European War, the Yugoslav Department of External Affairs and the General Staff allowed only an emasculated version of the book to be printed, so as "not to offend the Bulgarian and German governments."

In practice, a belated attempt was made to prepare for guerrilla warfare. In 1940 six Army Četnik Battalions were set up. In officers' circles it was rumoured that they were meant "to cut the wires of enemy aeroplanes" and do other sabotage work. The British military attaché in Belgrade reported that,

> In April [1940] it was decided to form six battalions of guerrilla warfare troops, one in each of the armies existing in peace.... Their function in war will be to operate independently against the enemy troops in rear areas and against his lines of communications....[5]

When some Croat politicians objected to the name "Četnik," the battalions were renamed "Assault battalions" (*"Jurišni bataljoni"*), and this took the wind out of their sails before they were even launched properly. It is interesting to compare these arrangements with Serbian guerrilla arrangements in the war with Austria-Hungary in 1914.[6] The latter can be seen from the instruction issued by the Chief of Staff of the Serbian High Command ("as approved by the Minister for the Army"). Guerrilla action was classified under "When we advance" and "When we retreat." In the case of withdrawal, Četnik Detachments had to remain in the evacuated areas and attack the enemy's encampments, communications, supply lines etc. "day and night." In enemy occupied territories specially formed Četnik teams were to be detailed to assassinate higher enemy commanders. This was a revolutionary provision, as in wars ordinary people get killed, and senior commanders are usually spared. "Fear and panic" was to be spread in enemy ranks. Both in offensive and defensive operations, Četnik detachments remained under the command of prescribed army corps commanders. (In the Second World War, the chain of command of Soviet Partisans was similar.)

In occupied Yugoslavia, German occupation authorities discovered three documents relating to Četnik matters in the Archives of the Intelligence Department of the Yugoslav General Staff. Their contents can be seen in a German summary dated 4 September 1941.[7] From this a number of vital conclusions can be drawn regarding the setting up of the six battalions and the instructions they were (or were not) issued. The first document originated in the HQ Četnik Command at Novi Sad

("*Tschetnikkommando in Neusatz*") on 7 June 1940.[8] As the original Yugoslav document could not be located when writing this book, its writer should be assumed. In 1940, at Novi Sad there were located Major Palošević's 1st Assault (Četnik) Battalion, and the HQ Četnik Command under Lieutenant General Mihailo Mihailović. It seems safe to ascribe this document to the latter. Addressed to the Intelligence Department of the General Staff, it is a request for information about the organization, field employment and armament of the *franc-tireurs* ("*Freischaerler-*") and similar troops in the Sino-Japanese, Spanish, Russian, and "the present" war.[9] It appears that the Intelligence Department had no relevant information. On 14 June 1940 the General Staff requested all military attachés abroad to obtain and forward the requested information.[10] After Yugoslavia established diplomatic relations with the Soviet Union, the same information was requested from the military attaché in Moscow also on 22 October.[11]

How much preliminary research and discussion took place in Yugoslavia before the Četnik battalions were set up, and what briefing (if any) was given to them? Or were they to rely on a regular officer's common sense as to how to harrass the enemy? At about the same time the belief spread in the officers' ranks that an invading German armoured army could be kept back "by our mountains and our muddy highways."[12] As yet, there is still no documentation to explain what briefing was given to Četnik battalions. However, one of the points which drew them to volunteer for these new units was the chance to be trained as parachutists.

This brings our research to Colonel Mihailović and his views on the best war plan for Yugoslavia. It will be shown that he and Colonel Clarke, the British Military Attaché in Belgrade, seem to have held closely related professional opinions. The difference between the two men was that Clarke seems to have had a better grasp of what was politically feasible and what was not. (But then, Clarke was an outside observer and Mihailović was in the thick of it.) As this is not a biography of Mihailović,[13] only two incidents will be discussed. The first incident illustrates Mihailović's concern about Yugoslavia's prospects in the coming conflict with Germany, and the second illustrates his attitude to Great Britain. Both incidents gave rise to a lot of guesswork by historians. For Mihailović both incidents led to thirty days arrest. The term "arrest" is used here because other authors have done so. In Mihailović's case the punishment was meted out by the Minister for the Army and Navy, exercising his discretionary powers in disciplinary matters; it was not a court martial. These disciplinary punishments were called *"pritvor"* and *"strogi pritvor."* They were a form of confinement to the barracks, office, or the private abode, after hours.[13] What makes these punishments unusual is that at the time of punishment Mihailović was a full Colonel; he was promoted to the rank on 6 September 1935. On 1 November 1939 he was punished for having submitted a memorandum to the Intelligence Department of the General Staff in which "the morale of the troops and the general situation in Slovenia were over-pessimistically described."[15] The contents of this memorandum can be only conjectured. Apparently, he advocated separate Serb, Croat and Slovene units,[16] fortifying the southern instead of the northern border,[17] and withdrawing the troops into the West Serbian, Hercegovinian and Montenegrin *Hinterland* and coastal area of the Adriatic Sea.[18]

It is interesting to compare Mihailović's concept of concentrating the army in the *Hinterland* area with the opinion held by Colonel Clarke, who wrote,

> From a purely strategical point of view it seems inevitable that General Staff should... ['concentrate their forces for the active defence of Serbia'] despite the fact that this would entail sacrifice [of] much territory and abandonment of defences on Northern frontier (...) on which so much time and energy have been expended.[19]

This disposition, thought Clarke, would enable the Yugoslav army to "hold a length of line (...) more in proportion to the number of troops available."[20] But,

> movement of forces away from Croalia and Wesnia [sic; decoding error?: probably 'Croatia and Slovenia'] might...be ruled out by Government and...army might therefore be forced into this strategically unsound position for purely political reasons;...[21]

Clarke's despatch is dated 13 November 1940. On 25 November 1940 Prince Paul told Ronald Ian Campbell, the British Minister in Belgrade, that it was "politically impossible" to relocate army defences from the north further to the south "as it would mean leaving Croatia defenceless."[29] Colonel Stojanović,[23] when he was acting head of the General Staff Section of the Ministry for Army and Navy, became conversant with the case of Mihailović. He claims Mihailović was punished when some politicians learned about his memorandum. In the light of Prince Paul's statement, this, of course, confirms Clarke's speculation about the "purely political reasons" in the matter of Yugoslav national defence. Emigré writers claim that the first of Mihailović's misadventures and punishment by the Minister for Army and Navy, General Milan Dj. Nedić, occurred in 1938 when Mihailović was commanding the No. 39 Infantry Regiment in Celje.[24] Yet Milan Nedić, who is not to be confused with his brother, General Milutin Dj. Nedić, was minister from 26 August 1939 to 8 November 1940, so that the dates do not tally. But in the German *curriculum vitae* of Mihailović based on Yugoslav archives,[25] which has not been used hitherto, it is stated that Mihailović commanded the 39th from 19 April 1938 to 30 April 1939.[26] From that date until 17 December 1939 he was Chief of Staff, HQ, Fortifications Construction Command.[27] He was punished on 1 November 1939, not in 1938. It is obvious therefore that, when writing his memorandum, Mihailović was not speaking out of turn (as a regimental colonel on matters which were not of his competence), but intervened as an outspoken chief of staff about matters of his concern. His minister *was* General Milan Dj. Nedić,[28] who punished him under political pressure on 1 November 1939, and not in 1938. Karchmar critically reviewed the chronological exposition of this chronology in émigré historiography, but was waylaid by some of his sources and reached wrong conclusions. *Inter alia,* he says that Mihailović was not censured for his memorandum in 1938, which is correct; instead, Karchmar claims that, because of the political embarrassment Mihailović caused by his "strong arm methods" against the local Nazis, Mihailović was "removed" from the command of the 39th and "disciplined" in 1938.[29] But on the contrary, Mihailović was not "removed" from his command: one of the conditions for obtaining credit toward promotion to a Brigadier General was that a General Staff Colonel must command an infantry regiment for one year. As shown, Mihailović commanded the 39th from 19 April 1938 to 30 April 1939, that is, for one year. Therefore he served his full term.[30]

The incident of Mihailović's second punishment illustrates problems and tensions that occur in a small neutral country when buffetted by Great Powers who are at war. The data of this incident is straightforward. Colonel Mihailović, without authorisation and in uniform, attended a function Colonel Clarke held for the Association of Yugoslav reserve NCOs. Thereupon, on 3 November 1940 Minister Nedić punished Mihailović with another 30 days arrest.[31] He also instructed that Mihailović be demoted from a General Staff oficer to an infantry officer, and that he be put on the retired list. Luckily for Mihailović, Nedić resigned on 8 November 1940 and the new minister, General Petar Pešić, spared Mihailović his demotion. It is reasonable to assume that Minister Nedić reacted unfavourably as soon as he learned that Mihailović had been involved in yet another political incident, especially as this time there was also the risk of a diplomatic incident with the powerful German neighbour. What were the arguments of the confidential investigation into Mihailović's case, which increased Nedić's irritation with Mihailović? The available evidence points to the fact that Mihailović was found to have compounded the breach of discipline (i) by being present at a function where Stalin's name was cheered,[32] and (ii) by using the occasion of the function "to disparage Germany and Hitler" and to advocate that "Yugoslavia should enter the war."[33] Mihailović committed the first breach of discipline because he contravened the contemporary Yugoslav military regulations whereby all "communist activity" or "taking part" in such activity was banned. And the second point was that, by calling publicly for Yugoslavia to declare against Germany and enter the war, he, as a serving officer, transgressed into the political field. The last straw was when the German envoy, Viktor von Heeren, having learned about Mihailović, lodged a protest with the Yugoslav Minister for External Affairs.[34] Mihailović was censured. By contrast, the same misadventure earned Mihailović the confidence of the British agencies in Belgrade, and thus was a contributory factor in gaining him British support in the early days of the German occupation of Yugoslavia.

Five months later, in the April War, Mihailović refused to comply with the orders to surrender and, with a group of officers and other ranks, headed for the "forests" ("*u šumu*").[35] He was not the only Yugoslav army officer to do so. Many others headed for the "forests" as well. Besides those who eventually joined Mihailović, there was also Brigadier

General Ljubo Novaković, who had been unsuccessful in his bid for leadership. When Mihailović became the national leader, he entered the international scene. This has affected the historiography of Mihailović to the extent that hardly anyone is interested in the history of the man, but rather in his image. His service as a staff officer in the war of April 1941 has been ignored. It is as if he came into existence only after he left his staff post and became a resistance leader. Even Jovan Marjanović did not bother to reconstruct Mihailović's record in that war, although earlier parts of his biography of Mihailović[36] deserve serious consideration. Yet Marjanović himself must have been impressed by the *émigré* interpretation of Mihailović's leaving his post and heading for the "forest" to start guerrilla warfare. He instinctively over-reacted to this interpretation. Marjanović seems preoccupied with doubts as to Mihailović's leadership qualities and relates little evidence of his actual role in the war. He points to the indifferent war record of the Yugoslav 2nd Army[37] in which Mihailović served, he says, as Assistant Chief of Staff, which he was not.[38] He holds Mihailović responsible for that Army's lack of achievement. "The Army showed no example of the *will to fight*" says Marjanović.[39] But the 2nd Army, in accordance with the Yugoslav War Plan "R 41," had the job of delaying an offensive coming from across the Hungarian border by retreating slowly southwards towards Bosnia.[40] Even if Mihailović had been the commander of the 2nd Army he would have had to comply with these instructions.

Except for Marjanović's uneven account, there is only one other known work which deals with this period. It is an article which was written by Miodrag M. Vuković, who as a General Staff Captain served in that war under Mihailović.[41] What wollows is a critical interpretation based on the information provided in Vuković's article, expanded by such other evidence as has become available. Vuković's last peacetime posting was in the HQ Bosna Division in Sarajevo. On 3 April 1941, the first day of mobilization, he reported on duty in the HQ 2nd Army at Kiseljak, west of Sarajevo.[42] Commanding the 2nd Army was General Dragoslav Miljković; his Chief of Staff (CofS) was General Staff Brigadier General Bogdan Maglić.[43] Together with a class-mate, General Staff Captain Jovan "Hadžidamjanović" [actually, Hadži-Damjanović], Vuković was detailed to serve under the Director of Operations of the 2nd Army Colonel Mihailović. He assigned the care of the Operations War Diary to

Vuković. Although they were far removed from the enemy, Mihailović instructed him also to keep entering on ordnance maps intelligence about the enemy's movements, saying,

> They taught you in military schools that to beat the enemy is the main job. To do so we must be informed of his location and movements.[44]

Vuković seems to have been overimpressed by this commonsense instruction. He might have though HQ 2nd Army was too far away from the enemy? If this was so, Vuković must have been thinking in terms of mounted troops (he was a cavalry man), and not in terms of motorized troops.

The 2nd Army was meant to take 24 days from the 3rd of April to mobilize, concentrate and deploy. Mihailović commented,

> The enemy is not going to oblige and attack only after we complete our deployment.[45]

In his opinion, the *Wehrmacht* was going to repeat the Polish and French *Blitzkrieg*. Mihailović went to argue with Miljković and Maglić that the HQ should immediately proceed to the deployment area and there await the troops, instead, as required by the war plan, to be last to go there.[45] The CofS, Maglić, opposed Mihailović's request, arguing that the planning was done by the General Staff, and if everyone were to follow Mihailović's initiative, that would result in general chaos in the movement of troops. But the Commanding General eventually gave into the Mihailović and allowed him to proceed to the Hungarian front; Mihailović took Vuković with him.[47] Although there is no known independent corroborating evidence to support Vuković's testimony, it appears a reasonable account. Mihailović emerges from this account as a competent and conscientious staff officer who was conversant with German war doctrine, and a man of initiative and courage. All of it agrees with the characteristics displayed by Mihailović earlier, in his clashes with the military establishment. Mihailović and Vuković went to Djakovo, north of the Sava, the initial front line location for the HQ of the 2nd Army on the Hungarian front. Their quarters were in the palace of the Roman Catholic Bishop who received them with great friendliness although they were Orthodox Serbs.[48] Hardly had they arrived, when reports of Croat rebellions and desertions from the army started arriving:

> This made me very depressed, [says Vuković], but Colonel Mihailović remained cool. He gave a lot of thought to these reports, analysed them, and said that it was all the work of the Ustasha and the fifth columnists, against whom the appropriate measures should be taken immediately.[49]

One of the most often quoted of these incidents is the rebellion of the Infantry Regiment No. 108 of Croat war conscripts. It rebelled and deserted in order not to take up a position on the Hungarian front, and then took over the city of Bjelovar and settled in.[50] Even the Croat leader, Maček, sent his emissaries to have the rebels return to colours, but to no avail.[51] The 108th was a part of the Slavonia Division, 4th Army, I Army Group, adjoining the 2nd Army, II Army Group, in which Mihailović served. The divisional commander was Lieutenant General Ratko Raketić. In his typewritten, unpublished *"Dnevnik"* ("Diary")[52] the following entries are of interest here:

Under 4 April (entry on p. 2).
   The 108th Infantry Regiment should start marching tonight. In answer to my query, the regimental commander assures me . . . that he has confidence in his soldiers. He paraded them and asked that everybody individually kiss the regimental colours, which they did . . . .
Under 6 April (entry on p. 25).
   Today we heard that Belgrade was bombed, but I do not know if war has been proclaimed.[53]
Under 8 April (entry on p. 27).
   My commander of the infantry, [Brigadier] General Kragujević, who was marching with the 108th, came to report that the whole regiment had rebelled, burned the colours and returned to Bjelovar. He hardly saved himself. Now I've got the [area in the] direction of Virovitica completely bare of troops.[54]

Under the same date, 8 April, Operations War Diary No. 1 of the German

XLVI Army Corps reveals that at "14.30 hours" the 14th *Panzer* Division reported that there were no Yugoslav troops in Virovitica.[55] This report was confirmed four hours later and already at 7:30 that evening the entry reads "[German] bridgehead extended from Barcs [in Hungary] to Virovitica."[56] On the next day, 9 April, Raketić entered on p. 27 of his Diary, "The Germans are fanning southwards towards Virovitica," and the German Diary reads,

> At 13.30 hours the 2nd Army ("2 AOK") ordered by telephone that the XLVI Army Corps advance with the 14th *Panzer* Division on 10 April from the Barcs bridgehead over Virovitica and Bjelovar on Zagreb . . . .[57]

On the 10th, Raketić wrote on p. 29,

> The Croats have proclaimed an independent State . . . .

and the Diary of the XLVI Corps reads on 11 April,

> 14th *Panzer* Division entered Zagreb on 10 April at 10.45 hours, just when a new Croat government was proclaimed . . . . Jubilation of the civilian population is indescribable.[58]

By 11 April the majority of the units of the Yugoslav 2nd Army had disbanded also, and many of the remaining units were considerably weakened.[60] To this should be added the effect of the indecisiveness and even desertion of regular officers and NCOs regardless of ethnicity, rebellions of mobilized soldiers and the widespread arrests of "Serbian" [sic] officers by the rebels. In the span of only a few days, all of this resulted in general anarchy reigning in the area between the river Sava and the Hungarian front. On 10 April the Yugoslav Supreme Command instructed the II Army Group to withdraw south of the Sava, and the Army Group transmitted this order ot its 1st and 2nd army.[61] The remnants of the Yugoslav troops started withdrawing higgledy-piggledy to the south of the Sava, the 2nd Army mostly to Bosnia. There were constantly harassed by Ustašas and deserters.[62] The 2nd Army that re-crossed the Sava into Bosnia on 11 and 12 April had the real strength of a weak infantry division and 12 batteries of artillery.⁶³ In this situation two actions of Mihailović's stand out—namely his initiative in reorganizing the troops and ensuring the safety of their rear area, and secondly his decision not to obey surrender orders.

Mihailović and Vuković re-crossed the Sava over the bridge at Brčko, "at about 6 in the evening,"⁶⁴ probably on 11 April. The remaining troops of the 2nd Army were re-crossing the river on 11 and 12 April and Mihailović, having crossed the bridge, spent that night and the next day gathering and marshalling the troops dribbling in from the north.⁶⁵ This suggests that Mihailović came to Brčko on 11 April, as the 12th was the last day of evacuation over the bridge. When he and Vuković crossed the bridge, Mihailović personally awaited the struggling troops coming from the north and marshalled them for the defense of the river crossing.⁶⁶ At midnight 11-12 April he roused Vuković and instructed him to take over, adding,

> When a complete unit arrives wake me up. I want to use it for waging battle.⁶⁷

Vuković took over. At about 3 a.m. a complete artillery battalion in regulation formation arrived, led by Artillery Captain Jovan Derok, whom Vuković knew personally. A graduate of the Staff College, Derok was at the time a trainee General Staff Officer. In view of the earlier discussion of the general anarchy and the disorganisation of troops, the exchange that followed between Mihailović and Derok throws additional light on these events. Colonel Mihailović shook hands with Derok, congratulated him for having brought along a whole unit, and asked: "How have you done it?" Derok answered: "Nothing to it. I kept strict discipline. . . ." The Colonel ordered him to take up battle position at the bridge.⁶⁸ Afterwards a detachment of the Infantry Regiment No. 41 arrived in marching order, Sergeant-Major (later Lieutenant) Boža ("Božidar"?) Perović carrying the regimental colours. The other—mobilized—soldiers had deserted the regiment, and this detachment was a unit composed of the Serbs from the 41st.⁶⁹ When the 41st Regiment crossed the bridge, the bridge was blown up.⁷⁰ The engineer-officer charged with the demolition was a man by the name of Tarović, who was later a POW. From this meeting at Brčko, Perović and the regimental colours of the 41st remained with Mihailović throughout the later guerrilla warfare.

Earlier in the morning Brigadier General Maglić, Chief of Staff of the 2nd Army, had reported sick with appendicitis and earache, and Mihailović hitherto Director of Operations, was appointed to take over as Chief of Staff.[71] (This change in Mihailović's posting led to the historiographical confusion between Mihailović's last peacetime posting [*Assistant* Chief of Staff, Seacoast army area] and his last wartime posting, *Chief* of Staff, 2nd army.) At Brčko, infantry fire was heard from the north in the afternoon, signalling the arrival of the remnants of the Infantry Regiment No. 60, harassed in its retreat by the Croat Ustašas. Under the protective fire of the troops he had marshalled, Mihailović brought the 60th across the river in commandeered small boats.[72] By the end of the day a detachment of the German XLVI Corps appeared across the river; German records show that it engaged in "sharp" combat, and it withdrew after losses in vehicles and wounded.[73] While these events were taking place, Colonel Eta Spajić, commanding the cavalry regiment of the 2nd Army, was ordered by Mihailović to protect the eastern flank of the troops fighting at the bridge. Instead of obeying his orders, Spajić deserted his post.[74] Major Stanković, the witness and chronicler of the event, adds that on that occasion Mihailović "said a sharp word on account of Colonel Spajić." The tactical problem facing Mihailović and the 2nd Army was that during the retreat across the river Sava into Bosnia, the west flank of the army would become threatened by the eastward drive of the German 46th Motorized Corps on 11 April.[75] On 12 April, the commander of the 46th Corps received orders to wheel his front southwards in the general direction of Sarajevo, that is, across the Sava into Bosnia.[76] Fortunately for the Yugoslav 2nd Army, its retreat beyond the Sava was already accomplished. However on the next day, 13 April, the rear of the 2nd Army became endangered by the German 14th Armoured Division coming from Banja Luka. In addition to this, on 13 April the 2nd Army's west flank was confronted with an Ustaša rebellion and their occupation of Derventa.[77] They had risen to assist the Germans who had crossed the Sava at nearby Bosanski Brod. Mihailović's reaction was swift. He required the Vrbas Division to send some infantry, tanks and motorized vehicles to the 2nd Army's new HQ at Gračanica.[78] This *ad hoc* detachment was either named, or, in any case became known as, "*Brzi odred*" ("Rapid Mobile Detachment"). Mihailović commanded it personally, and used it to restore the situation in the area Doboj—Derventa—Brod. His energetic counter-measures, and personal command in the field, illustrates what he meant at Djakovo, when he advocated immediate "appropriate measures" against the fifth columnists.[79]

In the Doboj–Ševarlija area some Yugoslav artillery under Major Misita opposed the advance of the German 14th Armoured Division.[80] So also did a unit of light tanks.[81] Although the Yugoslav army had only obsolete French light tanks, they were pitted against modern German armour. An attempt to identify with certainty the commander of the light tanks at Ševarlija remained unsuccessful, but it may have been a Captain (later Major) Ljubiša T. Terzić. He later escaped from captivity in Germany and reached Cairo, and was then parachuted to Mihailović in July 1942. It is interesting to observe that the men who fought in the withdrawal combats in this general area, Mihailović, Misita and Derok, soon were to become prominent in the Serbian 1941 uprising, and Terzić joined Mihailović via Cairo a year later.

What made Mihailović head for the "forests"? Why did he decide not to surrender? It has been shown that the final capitulation was preceded by a period of confusion on governmental level. The capitulation was already determined but the troops in the field had no inkling that Simović with his government was heading for the airfield at Nikšić. A hectic sequence of events followed which affected Mihailović personally. Not only days but hours are of crucial importance here, and a brief outline of events is necessary. The Prime Minister, General Simović, who was also Chief of Staff of the Supreme Command, divested himself from his military post on 14 April. On the same day at about 7 a.m. General Kalafatović took over as the new Chief of Staff. Prime Minister Simović immediately instructed him to ask for an armistice. Then:

• Some 14 hours before the dispatch of the first team of armistice negotiators, at 9.30 a.m. on the 14th, Kalafatović contacted all commanders of Yugoslav army groups and the armies by telephone, and instructed them to ask for local armistices.[82]

• The commander of the German XLVI Corps, who had received orders to wheel southwards in the general direction of Sarajevo on 12 April, refused to negotiate any local armistice. Instead, at 5 p.m. he issued an ultimatum demanding the immediate capitulation of all Yugoslav troops barring his way to Sarajevo. This concerned the Yugoslav II Army Group, including its 2nd Army, which Mihailović had taken over as Chief of Staff. The German Commander later relented and extended his ultimatum so as to allow Yugoslav commanders to get in touch with their Supreme Command.[83]

- Either in the morning of 14 April, or early next morning, the commander of the 2nd Army General Miljković, **accompanied by Vuković,** left the HQ 2nd Army and went to Tuzla to confer with the commander of the 2nd Army Group.[84]
- Mihailović remained behind as the senior officer at the HQ of the 2nd Army.
- On the morning of 15 April, in reply to the ultimatum of the German XLVI Corps, Mihailović received the following order from his Supreme Command:

> Armistice has been concluded with the enemy facing our 2nd Army Group. . . . Order all troops and establishments to remain in place and cease fire. If any German troops come by do not resist but surrender arms. . . .[85]

Mihailović refused to comply with this order and left. As a staff officer he had no troops under his immediate command; even so, he was joined by some personnel of his *ad hoc* "Rapid Mobile Detachment." Why did he take this decision?

Mihailović took his stand on 15 April (that is, when his Army was ordered to surrender), and not, as it is usually said, on the 17th (the date of the general capitulation). About the latter he apparently heard only on the 20th.[86] It is reasonable to suggest that Mihailović was resentful of an order to surrender specifically addressed to the army group in which he served. This assumption is further reinforced by the observation that this order coincided with the first proper combat engagement of Mihailović and the units of the 2nd Army with the enemy. Therefore a logical conclusion is that on the 15th Mihailović disobeyed his instruction, not in order to go "into the forest" as is usually asserted, but to find and join the troops he assumed were still in the field. Mihailović believed that it was only the 2nd Army group that had been ordered to surrender. This is consistent with his decision to march in the direction of East Bosnia and West Serbia, where he expected that a last stand by the Yugoslav army should be made.[87] Mihailović's own statement bears out the above reconstruction, *viz.*,

I did not want to capitulate and so I refused to comply.... I decided to reach the Drina and expected to find a front established there, and became disappointed when I found no battle front.[88]

Mihailović's movements from 15 April to his arrival at Ravna Gora in Serbia have been recreated by Radoje Knežević and Lucien Karchmar. It is doubtful whether this compilation can be bettered until Yugoslav archives become accessible to independent researchers; therefore, except for two historiographical issues, this matter can not be pursued here. The first issue that must be taken up is the information that on his march to East Bosnia and West Serbia Mihailović endeavoured to have the railway line Zavidovići—Han Pijesak demolished on 22-23 April.[89] Marjanović is very critical of this action. He says that,

> Railway line Zavidovići—Han Pijesak was a dead-end track of a narrow gauge forest railway line. Why would a General Staff Colonel waste two days on demolishing a dead end track of a forest railway after he had learned [presumably on 20 April] that the whole army had capitulated? Here no harm was done to the enemy. In the case of the railway Brod—Sarajevo it would have been a different matter.[90]

Should one remind Marjanović that Mihailović was marching along the Zavidović—Han Pijesak track, not along the Brod—Sarajevo line? Regardless of the point that the date when Mihailović learned about the general capitulation has not been established, but is only guessed at, on the question of whether the railway demolition did in fact take place, Marjanović's criticism is ill placed. Mihailović was looking for a front on the Drina, and was anxious to demolish supply lines to this hypothetical front. In a mountainous countryside barren of communications the Zavidović—Han Pijesak railway had strategic importance. It ran north-west to south-east, and terminated just short of the Serbian border on the Drina and the Užice region of West Serbia. This narrow gauge forest line with a daily capacity of four trains of 40 axles[91] played a major role when Austria-Hungary launched its unsuccessful invasion of Serbia in 1914 across the Drina.

The second issue in the historiography of the march of Mihailović from Doboj to Serbia arises from the methodology of Matteo J. Milazzo, and concerns Mihailović and the local Muslim population.⁹² Two incidents occurred. On 25 April Mihailović repulsed an attack by armed Muslims from the village of Olovo,⁹³ and then continued his march. The second incident occurred on 26 April, when Mihailović was advised that the local Muslims were attacking Serb villages. Mihailović had two Muslim village dignitaries from Žepa brought to him. He advised them not to follow the German anti-Serb propaganda and to abstain from starting a war of mutual extermination, saying,

> If today a Serb village is extirpated tomorrow it will be the turn of a Muslim one, and this will lead to mutual annihilation in this district.⁹⁴

Milazzo discusses these happenings and telescopes the two events into one, and then claims there is confusion between the sources and—not only more important, but vital—he omits mention of Mihailović's talk with the Muslim leaders. He writes

> The details of these incidents are, to say the least, somewhat vague. While Knezevic claims that Mihailovic, on 25 April, beat back an attack by the group of Muslims armed by the Germans near the village of Olovo, Stankovic asserts that the clash took place on 26 April at Zepo.⁹⁵

He goes on to make a totally irrelevant comment, *viz.*,

> At any rate, in view of Mihailovic's later directives to his subordinates in Bosnia and Montenegro and the whole Chetnik treatment of the Yugoslav Muslims during the war, the incident was one of the first and typical examples of the officers' military strategy and was part of a major pattern of the civil war in wartime Yugoslavia.⁹⁶

When Milazzo's version is compared with his own sources it is obvious that he distorted them and thus he is misleading his readers. Having done so, he then draws conclusions which contradict the characteristics of the events as presented in his sources. At issue here is Milazzo's methodology, and not his conclusion *per se* (although it must be mentioned that his "conclusion" is based on insinuations about the "officers' military strategy" and the "treatment" of Muslims instead of producing examples which could be discussed). The point is that, under the guise of historical investigation, Milazzo is here conveying to his readers definite misinformation.

Another charge used against Mihailović is the claim that he was inimical to the Croats. What does his war record reveal about this? Fortunately for an historian, the writings of witnesses who had to deal with Mihailović in the April war unintentionally produce a consensus in this regard. The special importance of these testimonies is that they deal with Mihailović's reaction to the events when the Ustaša Croat State was set up. According to Vuković, when the commander of the Vrbas Division, Lieutenant General Milosavljević, told Mihailović at Djakovo that the "Croats in his Division were deserting," and added, "The Croats are going to betray us and join the Germans," Mihailović answered that he agreed *the [Croat] Ustaša* were part of the German army.[97] Milosavljević, reminiscing most probably about the same incident, relates that when he said to Mihailović that he was concerned about the possibility of a Croat betrayal in the war, Mihailović retorted, "I also am concerned that *a part* of the Croats may betray us."[98] Stanković reported to Mihailović the disbandment of the 41st Infantry and his retreat through the rebellious countryside. When he said that "At Vinkovci the Croats have set up their own military command," Mihailović commented "Yes, yes, *the Ustaša* at Vinkovci . . . [etc.]."[99] Mešković, who later joined Mihailović on his march to East Bosnia and Serbia with the remnants of the 1st Assault or Četnik Battalion,[100] does not report any comment of Mihailović's regarding "the Croats." Neither is there any report of his animosity to the Croat people in any testimony of his peacetime life and career. His reported concept that each ethnic group should have had its own military units cannot possibly be held as a proof of animosity toward anyone, but rather as a staff officer's search for efficiency in a multinational military constituency. Therefore it is obvious that the claims deprecating Mihailović's attitudes in these matters are politically motivated: they do not rest on the sources.

In conclusion, different traits of Mihailović's character in peace and war have emerged. As a staff officer, he appeared well versed in the current military doctrines, including the *"Blitzkrieg,"* and thought of ways to parry it. He was also self-motivated and exercised initiative, taking responsibility and standing firm by his opinions. When in his professional opinion he thought government's military policies detrimental to the country, he argued they be amended. When he felt that the foreign policies—the alignment in the Second World War—endangered the future of his country, he staged a one-man protest bravado by openly visiting Colonel Clarke. Later this firmness of character led to collisions with the British agencies in the Middle-East. Mihailović had drive and courage, and was cool and composed in times of adversity. A former Serbian officer, he is seen to have carried over the best officer traditions of that army. Mihailović never complained or spoke of his personal problems or of himself. Except for his "sharp word" regarding the deserter-regimental commander, no witness has reported anything that would indicate Mihailović's innermost feelings regarding the disaster that was going on around him in the April War. A true professional soldier, he was composed and correct to the end. This civilized selfcontrol was to his disadvantage in the later civil war with the Partisans, when ruthlessness was the order of the day.

CHAPTER 7

THE LEADERS (II):
TITO 1914-1941

Mihailović made his own historical reputation when, in April 1941, he refused to obey orders to surrender. The reputation of Mihailović's opponent and enemy, Josip Broz *alias* Tito, the Communist leader of the Partisans, resulted from the secret military decisions of the Tehran Conference (27 November–1 December 1943). Roosevelt, Stalin and Churchill had agreed there on 1 December that

> the Partisans in Yugoslavia should be supported by supplies and equipment to the greatest possible extent, and also by commando operations.

Two days earlier, on 29 November 1943, at the second session of the "Anti-Fascist Council of National Liberation of Yugoslavia" (AVNOJ), at Jajce, Tito was proclaimed "Marshal" of Yugoslavia. His actual name, Josip Broz, was on that occasion revealed for the first time. How did Tito's proclamation as Marshal come about? Djilas supplies a romanticized version, whereby when Kardelj, a Slovenian, told Tito on the 28th he was to be made a Marshal, Tito "turned red in the face." But Djilas also adds that Tito started "pacing" the room they were in, *"as if to think the matter over* while pacing." Duretić, the Yugoslav-Serbian historian who debunked the mythological Tito in his book on the Allies and the Yugoslav war drama and then made him a politician *à la mesure humaine*, goes a step further. He reveals that Tito's proclamation for Marshall was done "in consultation with the Soviets." The idea was thus to manufacture for both the Partisans and the West a mental picture or "symbol" of association of the Partisan leader with the Soviet Marshals who were "fighting in the Russian steppes." This, of course, throws a new light on the Churchill-Stalin relationship at the Tehran conference. It has been observed that in the matter of the Yugoslav Partisans Stalin had adopted a reserved stance, and let Churchill advocate their case. At one stage, Stalin even chided Churchill for exaggerating the number of Partisans. Now, after Duretić's revelation, Stalin's duplicity in the conspiracy to build Tito into a mythical figure has become evident.[1]

Who was this man Josip Broz, the professional revolutionary whom General Sir Henry Maitland Wilson ("Jumbo") addressed as "Mr. General Tito" in his first message? What were the main steps of his rise to prominence? Which aspects of his pre-war life enabled him to play his role as a guerrilla leader in the Second World War? To obtain an appropriate answer, one has to study how his major politico-military training and experiences formed his personality. As Broz was not a theoretician, but a Stalinist field worker and organizer, the study will center on his activities rather than on his ideas.

The crucial stage in Broz's career was his service as an *apparatchik* or an employee on the payroll of the Communist International or the Comintern, where he was known under the name Valter. He was virtually the only Yugoslav Communist leader who was not liquidated by Stalin purges of the 1930s. Indeed, is was Moscow who appointed him Secretary General of the Yugoslav Section of the Comintern or "The Communist Party of Yugoslavia" (KPJ, *Komunistička partija Jugoslavije*). The Soviet administration keeps meticulous personal records, and I approached the then Chairman of the Presidium of the USSR, Leonid I. Brezhnev, for declassiffied information on Valter-Tito. This was declined and I was advised to write to Yugoslavia.[2] I knew that when Phyllis Auty started gathering material for her biography of Tito, she was told in Yugoslavia that everyone has to start with Dedijer's biography of Tito. This she "found to be true."[3] Tito himself had established the framework and the choice of topics for his biography in a series of interviews which he gave to Dedijer. The latter, in turn, edited this material and expanded it; its English edition is called "Tito Speaks."[4] Consequently, our enquiries will start by critically assessing and completing the information contained in Dedijer's authorized work. As Dedijer's writing is somewhat disjointed, a logical framework must be devised first. Therefore study of Broz's public life is marshalled here into four consecutive phases. They are (i) Broz's experiences in the First World War (1914-19), (ii) his period as a Communist agitator or an apprentice revolutionary (1920-34), (iii) his service as an *apparatchik* of the Comintern or a paid professional revolutionary (1934-1940), including here his absentee secretaryship of the KPJ and, (iv), the fourth and final phase, his taking over as the "Boss," when he settled in Yugoslavia in 1940 and actively took over the secretaryship of the Party (1940-41). Broz-Tito's post-1941 activities are referred to in other chapters.

Broz's Experiences in the First World War (1914-19)

Son of a Croat father and a Slovene mother, in civilian life a mechanic, in 1914 Tito was a NCO in the Hungarian Branch of the Habsburg Armies. Tito told Dedijer that he served in the 25th Home Guards in Zagreb.[5] When the war broke out in August, his regiment left Zagreb for the front. What happened next? In answer to this question, Tito provided two conflicting versions. He told his biographer Dedijer, that, because he was opposed to the war, he was imprisoned at Petrovaradin. From this version it appears that he was released from prison at the latest in the second half of September 1914.[6] Tito also made a "taped statement" whereby his arrest was due to a "clerical error" and that he was jailed for one day only.[7] Obviously, Tito's statement to Dedijer served the political purpose of building up his credentials as a long-time revolutionary. Shortly after his release, Tito told Dedijer, his regiment was sent to the Carpathians on the Russian Front. But where was the regiment meanwhile, and when did it leave for the Russian Front? Auty believes the 25th was "in reserve" north of Belgrade outside Serbia, whence it left for the Russian Front in September 1914.[8] Documentary evidence invalidates this interpretation. A search in the State Srchives in Vienna confirmed that a *Zugsfuehrer* Josip Broz was serving in the Royal Hungarian Honved-Infantry Regiment No. 25 (*k.u. Honvéd-Inft.-Regt. Nr. 25*).[9] This regiment was in the Royal Hungarian 42nd Honvéd-Infantry *"Truppen-Division,"* which fought on the Serbian Front until December (not September) 1914. The 42nd Division was transferred to the Russian Front only in January 1915, where it joined the Czibulka Corps.[10] The question is—what was Broz doing in the three months of 1914 which have been omitted in Dedijer's work?

It has been shown that Tito's regiment was engaged in fighting the Serbians. That does not mean that, *ipso facto,* Broz fought with the regiment. Yet in his *Wartime,* published in 1977, Djilas reports that in 1914 Tito "fought as an Austro-Hungarian" in northwestern Serbia. It is significant that in 1941, when he was a Partisan leader in Serbia, Tito started talking about it and was cautioned not to do so "because the Serbs were sensitive on the subject."[11] Djilas adds,

> This was . . . hushed up, especially in Dedijer's otherwise extensive biography of Tito.

Is Djilas right? How can this be checked? As it happens, when writing twenty years before Djilas and some thirteen years before Auty, Tito's friend (Sir) Fitzroy Maclean stated in his *Disputed Barricade* that before "Josip Broz's regiment was sent to the [Russian] Front," "Josip had already seen some fighting against the Serbs. . . ."[12] In the light of this cumulative information, it appears that *Zugsfuehrer* Broz was fighting the Serbs in the three "lost" months of 1914. This shows that Dedijer's joint silence with Tito about Broz-Tito fighting the Serbians in 1914 was politically motivated. It was a case of a deliberate doctoring of the past, and not an oversight.[13]

In the second half of March 1915, the battalion in which Broz served on the Russian Front, the III/25th, was transferred from the 42nd Hungarian Honvéd Division to the Imperial and Royal (*k.u.k.*) Austro-Hungarian 72nd Infantry Brigade of Major General von Luxardo.[14] Broz claims that he was wounded there and made a prisoner of war.[15] The question is how to verify his claim of captivity in Russia? The point is that the international prisoner of war records do not bear out his POW claim. Answering persistent enquiries about it, the final letter from the Central Tracing Agency of the International Red Cross reads,

> . . . we regret to say again that we are unable to provide an attestation of captivity concerning the late Mr. Josip Broz (alias 'Tito')

for we did not find any information about the above-named in our First World War records.[16]

However, further research in the Austrian State Archives gave positive results. Reports filed there by the delegates of the International Red Cross, as well as by the visiting sisters of the Austro-Hungarian Red Cross, contain references to a POW in Russia by the name of Josip (Josef) Broz or "Brož." The man was from the 25th *k.u.* Honvéd Infantry and was made a POW either on 22 or 23 March 1915.[17]

While he was in Russian captivity. POWs of South Slavic nationalities were enabled to volunteer for the Serbian army and fight Austria-Hungary to free their homelands from foreign rule. Broz did not volunteer. Considering that he was an acknowledged latter day Yugoslav leader, this raises the question of Broz's attitude to the Yugoslav idea, or, to be precise, to Serbia as the contemporary "Piedmont" of this movement. The answer could be looked for in his Austro-Hungarian anti-Serb indoctrination. The Austro-Hungarian press claimed that,

> these abominable Serbs were murderous savages. They cut off noses and ears of their prisoners, gouged out their eyes, and castrated them into the bargain.[18]

"Even the officers believed in this tale."[19] This anti-Serb indoctrination resulted in atrocities committed by the invading Austro-Hungarian army in the first invasion of Serbia in 1914. In Serbia, "all humanity and kindness of heart are out of place" read the instructions issued by an Austro-Hungarian army corps.[20] How much had the effect of this propaganda to do with Tito's decision not to be a Yugoslav volunteer? Or was he, as a soldier, simply loyal to Francis-Joseph, his Habsburg King and Emperor? For the time being this must remain a moot point. It is interesting however that, later, both as a Communist agitator and politician, Broz was preoccupied with anti-Serb policies. In any case, instead of fighting for a Yugoslavia, it is claimed that he joined the Bolsheviks. Auty examined this question and concluded that Broz-Tito's

> Communist Party membership is given as registered with the Omsk party on 19 January 1919. But this was a time when Omsk was in the hands of Kolchak.[21]

The implication is that on 19 January 1919 the Omsk Party did not exist, and therefore Broz could not have joined it. But there are also independent circumstantial indicators which make it possible to query the import of this information regardless of its dating. At the time, the Bolshevik anti-Church revolutionary emotionalism was in mortal conflict with the Christian emotional conservatism. Yet Broz married Pelagia (Polka) Beloussova in a Russian Orthodox church at Bogolyubskoe near Omsk. It is unlikely that, as a "Bolshevik," Broz would have gone to church to marry. After his repatriation Broz had a few children who died as infants, and he gave them—in Auty's words—"the usual Christian burrial." The tombstones at Kumrovec prove this point. Would a "Bolshevik" have done so? It is clear that the import of the claim that Broz was an early Bolshevik remains open to questioning. Indeed, in an autobiographical letter which he wrote in 1945, Tito stated himself that his part in the October Revolution was "insignificant," and that he does "not count" his 1918 membership at Omsk, but considers himself a member since 1920.[22] Further, it is said that at the end of the "Great" or the First World War, Broz returned home in early 1920 as a former Red Guard. This in no way conflicts with indications that, at the time, he was not necessarily a converted lifetime Bolshevik. This observation requires an historical elucidation. It is that across Europe in 1917-1920 the impact of the Bolshevik Revolution was keenly felt. The tangible expression of this state of affairs was the umpteen thousands of soldiers and demobilized soldiers who were in empathy with the Bolshevik revolution. The newly created Yugoslavia was no exception. There, the influx of returning disgruntled ex-Austrohungarian POWs from Russia, who had fought for a different outcome, bore heavily on the normalization of life. This flood contained many who boasted that they had been "Red Guards" in Russia. In this context then, Broz was only one of the many. This was not necessarily a lifetime commitment, but rather symptomatic of the times. As a matter of fact, Tito stated himself that he served [only] at Omsk. In those "few months" ("*više mesjeci*"), he said, he and the other Red Guards there were engaged in guard duties and working at the railway station called Marjanovka. Although Kolchak with his "Whites" was fighting the Bolsheviks there and eventually took Omsk, and the Czech Legion occupied Marjanovka, Broz himself was not engaged in combat.[23] Indeed, until he bestirred in 1923, there is no evidence that Broz had been a communist activist. In his later years however, in order to boost his revolutionary legitimacy as Leader, he and his propaganda machine engaged in retrospect to create for him an untainted Bolshevik past.[24]

Communist Agitator and Apprentice Revolutionary (1920-34)

When Broz left for war, his native land, Croatia-Slavonia, was in Austria-Hungary. On his return from Russia, he found Croatia-Slavonia a part of the new Kingdom of the Serbs, Croats and Slovenes (renamed "Yugoslavia" by King Alexander I on 3 October 1929). Soon after his return, elections for the Constituent Assembly were held and on 12 December 1920, the Assembly met at Belgrade. The Communist Party of Yugoslavia had 58 seats. Two weeks later, on 29 December the Party was banned by the government's decision which is known as the "*Obznana.*" Why? Tito told Dedijer that,

> we were third [in strenght] among the dozen parties that contested the elections. Alexander's reply a few weeks later was the *Obznana* (Proclamation), outlawing the Party....[25]

This interpretation is not supported by historical record. It is misleading in two respects. One, the Karadjordjević monarchy was still a parliamentary one, the same as it had been hitherto in Serbia; Alexander I's personal regime began only in 1929. Secondly, by drawing attention to the electoral success of the Party, Tito implies that this was the reason for the ban. It was not so. The genuine reason for this act is to be found outside the purely political numbers game. Yugoslavia had been created only a short time previously, and its government was not yet consolidated. Of 419 elected deputies only 342 attended the Constituent Assembly. Deputies of Radić's Croat Republican Peasant Party (HRSS, *Hrvatska republikanska Seljačka stranka*) had proclaimed themselves to be the "Croat National Representation" on 7 December and refused to leave Zagreb for Belgrade.[26] This action endangered the existence of the State. Exploiting this circumstance, a coal miners strike took place in Slovenia on 17 December, and spread to Bosnia within four days. Communist agitation for a general strike added to its record of fomenting disturbances, and aggravated the situation. The government reacted on 24 December. It conscripted the railwaymen and the miners, put both under martial law, and ordered them back to work.[27] The government's motivation is self-evident: the prevent the lack of coal supplies in mid-winter, which would worsen the already explosive political situation. But the KPJ went ahead, and called the general strike for 29 December. And here comes the crunch: on 28 December the Chairman of the Central Committee of the KPJ, Pavle Pavlović MP, harangued a public meeting in Belgrade to proceed to "action," "tomorrow or the day after."[28] The government of Milenko Vesnić struck first, and on the "morrow," 29 December 1920, proclaimed the *Obznana* to uphold law and order *during the session of the Constituent Assembly.*[29] It banned the Communist Party but not its deputies; they remained in the Parliament as private individuals. Six months later, on 28 June 1921, Communist elements attempted to assassinate Alexander, when seven onlookers were wounded. In another assassination attempt, on 21 July, they mortally wounded the minister responsible for the *Obznana*. Tito admits these two events.[30] The Parliament met in a special session on 30 July and voted the *Law for the Protection of Public Safety and Order in the State*.[31] This Law was known by its short title "*Zakon za zaštitu države*" ("The Law for the Protection of the State"). On this occasion Communist deputies were expelled and Communist activities proclaimed a criminal offence. This law remained in force for the duration of the Kingdom.

What was Bronz doing all this time? He claims that he took part in several strikes, and that in 1920 he lectured the unionists of Zagreb on the anniversary of the October Revolution that "The workers can conquer only with the help of arms!"[32] Early in 1921 Broz suddenly left Zagreb for the village Veliko Trojstvo.[33] His move to a rural environment from urban Zagreb and its proletariat followed closely on the *Obznana* of 29 December 1920. The first ascertainable turning point on Broz's road to becoming a professional revolutionary occurred only two years later. One day in 1923 he was contacted by another ex-prisoner of war in Russia, Stevo Šabić.[34] Tito recalled that

> With Šabić and some other workers and peasants in the neighbourhood who had been active before the *Obznana* we secretly started our political work again.[35]

Early the next year he was elected a member of a district party committee.[36] As the Communist Party of Yugoslavia had been outlawed,

Broz's new activity eventually attracted the attention of the police. He was arrested for the first time on 14 July 1927.[37] In February 1928 he was elected secretary of the local committee in Zagreb.[38] This point marks the end of his workingman's existence. Broz "never had a job as a mechanic again," says Auty, and continued his career as a Communist political official.[39] On May Day 1928 Broz was arrested again, after having broken up a public meeting of Social Democrats and caused a brawl.[40] Evidently, Broz was by now a fully fledged Communist agitator. On 4 August 1928 he was arrested for distributing Communist literature and possessing unlicenced arms,[41] and sentenced to five years imprisonment on 13 November.[42]

Broz now entered the crucial formative period of his life. Serving his sentence, he profited from Alexander's liberal regime for political prisoners,[43] and acquired a thorough communist training. The man responsible for Broz's political and improved general education was the son of an old Belgrade family and his prison-mate, Moša (Mojsije; Moses) Pijade, a Jewish Serb[44] who was a prominent member of the party. In Tito's own words, "the penitentiary was really a university for many of our people"; it was there that he (Tito) "learned most."[45] When Broz left his Communist "University" in the prison in 1934, he was employable in ways beyond that of the former poorly educated agitator. Born in 1893, he was then 41 years old. It was only after his release from his "University" in the jail that Broz started asserting himself. Tito's image can be "doctored" but not "improved" by pretending otherwise. Most of Broz's biographers follow Dedijer in that they tend to project Tito's later standing back onto the first period of Broz's indifferent public record. This is a historiographical failure. The two periods of his life should be separated in the historiography the same as they were in his own life.

An "Apparatchik" and Absentee Secretary (1934-40)

Tito's rise to become the dominant personality in the Communist Party of Yugoslavia started soon after he left prison. On his release, he was elected to membership of the party's committee for Croatia,[46] and sent to Vienna to establish contact with the Central Committee of the party, which had taken refuge there. Broz came to Vienna in July 1934 and was given an assignment to carry out in Yugoslavia. The job done, he returned to Vienna. Having been co-opted into the Politbureau in August

1934, he attended meetings of the Central Committee held in Vienna in September and October of the same year. On that occasion his first involvement with military issues in Yugoslavia occurred: the Committee asked him to prepare two reports on military matters there. One dealt with workers' "defence companies," and the other with "anti-militaristic work in Yugoslavia."[47] Dedijer cites extracts from other reports written by Broz, but gives no details about his military submissions to the central Committee in Vienna. This complicates the historian's task of ascertaining Tito's early military concepts. One must make assumptions about what these reports might have contained. Whereas Broz's arguments cannot be reconstructed, the parameters of his submissions can be confidently inferred from the contemporary military doctrine of the Comintern and the activity of the KPJ in Yugoslavia.

The Comintern's military *dicta* from 1919 to Broz's release from jail in 1934 aimed to achieve the politico-military goal spelled out in the invitation to the First Congress of the Communist International in 1919.[48] This was amplified in the "Platform" adopted by the first congress of the Comintern:

> the disarming of the bourgeoisie, of the counter-revolutionary officers, of the white guards, and the arming of the proletariat, of the revolutionary soldiery, of the red workers' guard; . . .[49]

In the above instance, the juxtaposition of the "counter-revolutionary officers" and of the "revolutionary soldiery" is clear: it is based on the proposition "if you are not for me, you are against me." Nine years later, after lengthy discussions, on 29 August 1928 the sixth congress adopted the Comintern's theses about "just" and "unjust" wars. Communists were to join bourgeois armies, there to engage in anti-militaristic work. In the case of a war which would be "unjust" in the Comintern's eyes, the proletariat should contribute to the "defeat of its own government" by transforming this war into a civil war.[50] The fourth congress of the KPJ in its own resolution of November 1928 "followed" the Comintern's lead.[51]

The KPJ had inherited an anti-militaristic tradition from the Serb Social Democratic Party, and in 1919 called for the "abolition of the call-up,"[52] only to veer soon afterwards towards the official Comintern line. The second congress of the KPJ, in June 1920, called for arming the "workers and poor peasants" and creating an "active" Red Army as the defender of the Revolution.[53] By adopting the Comintern's resolution to create illegal revolutionary cells in the army, the KPJ took the first practical step from theory to practice. Even so, after the early 1920s, the closest that the Party came to subverting an army unit occurred whilst Broz was serving his sentence. The Party failed: the communist conspiracy in Maribor garrison in Slovenia fizzled out in the court-martial of June and July 1932.[54] The results were disappointing for the Party, and in 1928, 1934 and 1935 the Party's congresses and conferences castigated this poor performance.[55] In the year of Broz's arrest and sentencing, 1928, the party even called for "armed insurrection," only to meet with disastrous consequences in the clashes with the Gendarmerie.[56] It is interesting to note that at the time of his last arrest, 4 August 1928, Broz was in possession of unlicensed arms. Commenting about it, Tito's biographer Phyllis Auty says,

> Broz had been acting in the spirit of the Comintern instructions which urged communists to go over to armed action against the authorities in their countries.[57]

Twenty years after the event, in his report to the 5th Congress of the party in 1948,[58] Tito condemned these tactics in retrospect as "One of the main mistakes" of the leadership, which embarked "on a course of armed insurrection . . . with a Party isolated from the masses." He added that this was "an ordinary adventure and criminal behaviour." He did not think so in 1928.

None of this contributes to the understanding of the development of Broz's personality as the future *military* leader of the Partisans. However, the occasion of writing military reports on workers' "defence companies" and "anti-militaristic work in Yugoslavia" to the Central Committee in 1934 is an exception. It gave him the chance to marshal the result of his *political* training in firmness of purpose for an alternative army as the instrument of revolution. Later he successfully applied this doctrine as a guerrilla leader.

After another assignment in Yugoslavia, Broz crossed his Rubicon. He was sent to Moscow to work for the Comintern. Arriving in Moscow by the end of 1934, he was put on the Comintern payroll under the name "Valter"[59] and became a Stalinist *apparatchik*. Broz never looked back. In 1936 Moscow appointed him Organizing Secretary of the Communist Party of Yugoslavia (KPJ), under General Secretary Josip Čižinski (*alias* Milan Gorkić).[60] It is important to note that henceforth Broz led an itinerant life: he was not permanently stationed in Yugoslavia. Charged with various duties, "Valter" commuted between Moscow, Yugoslavia and Paris until 1940.[61] In Paris, his main job was transport officer organizing the travel of Yugoslav volunteers joining the International Brigades in the Spanish Civil War,[62] but he never went to Spain himself.[63] "Yugoslav volunteers" with whom Broz dealt were not necessarily only those from Yugoslavia, but also "Yugoslavs" from Canada etc. (Later, in World War II, British authorities trained a group of Croat-Canadian communists in guerrilla warfare and parachuted them to Tito's Partisans.) In 1937 Čižinski-Gorkić was liquidated in Stalin's purges.[64] "Valter" stepped into his shoes, first as acting Secretary General of the Communist Party of Yugoslavia;[65] he was confirmed as SG "early" in 1939.[66] Broz returned to Yugoslavia permanently only in March 1940. In 1941, as "Tito," he assumed leadership of the Communist-led Partisans.

For the whole of the period since 1934, only two claims have been made that Broz was involved with politico-military matters. The case of his writing of the two reports for the Central Committee in Vienna in 1934 has already been discussed. An additional claim has been raised by Tito in his tales about his first stay in Moscow, in 1935. He told Dedijer that there he

> also made a serious study of military literature, first of all Frunze, works by Russian writers and then especially the German classics, Clausewitz and others, and during my stay in Moscow I greatly expanded my knowledge of military problems.[67]

Djilas, in the know as Tito's former associate and head of the Agitation and Propaganda of the KPJ, comments that "Like most of Tito's statements... this must be subjected to careful scrutiny."[68] Djilas argues that, when in Moscow, Tito was too busy to have had time for all he claims.

Foreign students at the Moscow Party schools,—says Djilas—were, indeed, required to take courses in military tactics, but the instruction was general and superficial.

"Far more valuable," concludes Djilas, was Tito's "experience during World War I as a noncommissioned officer in the Austro-Hungarian Army."[69] So, Tito's claim to have studied Clausewitz has no sounder base than the image of him as a student of Tolstoy, Turgenieff and other classics.

Taking over as the "Boss" (1940-41)

It has been noted that Broz, *alias* "Valter" *alias* "Tito," was mostly absent from the country, and that he returned permanently to Yugoslavia only in March 1940. His latest absence had lasted eight months: half of this time he worked in Moscow.[70] Yet meanwhile the Party went on as before. Who was it then who ran the Party? Auty shows that by 1938 Tito had formed an "inner, decision-making" core of new, younger men. They ran the Party in his absence.[71] Regardless of this, Tito told Dedijer that on the eve of the Second World War, his "basic problem" was to "prepare my country to meet the difficult days on the horizon."[72] What he was really saying, is, that he was personally handling Party affairs at that time. How did he go about it? He raised three claims, and I will critically examine each in turn.

His first claim deals with his activity in the wake of the Soviet-Nazi Pact of 23 August 1939. He told Dedijer that, despite the Pact, "we" continued with "our vigilance in preparing for the defence of the homeland."[73] Considering that he made this statement when he was interviewed as an internationally renowed Yugoslav leader, the royal "we" naturally reads as "I, Tito, and my Party." How does this compare with the historical record? How did Valter brave the Soviet-Nazi Pact and act "for the defence" of his Yugoslav homeland? As a theoretical proposition, his claim could be refuted by observing that the Comintern was an exceedingly centralized organization, which ruled dictatorially from Mahovaya Street in Moscow. The whole issue of the interpretation of the Pact was under the firm control of the Comintern.[74] Its activities were designed to further Soviet foreign policy, and not necessarily Yugoslav or anyone else's national interests. At the time of the signing of the pact, in August 1939, Valter had just arrived in Moscow for another of his working visits.[75] However, full documentation to establish what he did there is lacking. Avakumović exposes this lacuna when he says,

> For understandable reasons (Tito) and his biographers have preferred to concentrate on his problems in crossing bourgeois frontiers with forged passports....[76]

How did the KPJ handle the question of the "defence of the homeland"? How much was Broz really personally involved with it? It is hard to visualize that during his absence he had anything to do with the day-to-day running of the Yugoslav party, although he might have influenced its policy. Still, as he claims that "we"—he and the party—were vigilant in preparing for the defence in Yugoslavia, he identifies himself with whatever was done. Therefore the Party's major activity in the military field must be singled out anew, we are faced with the KPJ's efforts to subvert the army. This consisted of endeavours to undermine—not to strengthen—the country's preparedness for war. Before the fall of France, the Party went so far as to claim that "at the moment" Hitler presented "no danger whatsoever to the independence of Yugoslavia" and protested against the military defence measures undertaken by the government.[77]

Ironically, in the whole of this period the party achieved its greatest success early in the piece. When the European war had started in the early days of September 1939, Yugoslavia partly mobilized, and the KPJ engineered the rebellion of the mobilized Yugoslav 106th Infantry Regiment at Karlovac, Croatia.[78] The mobilized Croat soldiers were stirred by the propaganda that they were to be sent to join the Allied front in France. But Broz was at that time in Moscow; how did he get involved in it? After his return from abroad, in October 1940, Broz approved of the "slogan against mobilization," adopted by the party in the autumn of 1939.[79] Surely, this evidence compromises Broz's latter day claim to his and his Party's contemporary Yugoslav patriotism? Avakumović, who meticulously examined this period of the KPJ's activity, demonstrates that "nearly all (the party's) efforts" were directed against the West, but that this has been camouflaged in the existing historiography. Considering that his judgement deals both with history and the writing of history, it ought to be cited in full.

The lack of significant anti-fascist activities in the period in question accounts for the unwillingness of the Yugoslav Communists to publish in full the various party resolutions and manifestoes for the period September 1939 to May 1940. Tito in his report to the fifth party congress and Dedijer in his biography of Tito confine themselves to a few meagre extracts from leaflets and manifestoes published after the fall of France.[80]

Indeed, policies of the Comintern's agent in Yugoslavia, the KPJ, started slowly changing only after the fall of France in June 1940, and reflected the deterioration in Soviet-Nazi relations.

Tito's second claim about his post-Pact work deals with his activity in the six months from his return to Yugoslavia in 1940 to the fifth party conference in October 1940. Referring to it in his report to the fifth congress of the KPJ in 1948, Tito singled out his purge of the "remnants of the fractionalists and group-formers," the organizational strengthening of the Party, political indoctrination, and work on the "rallying of all progressive forces" against the "fascist danger."[81] This, of course, enabled him to hold a conference in which he had no opposition. This conference is also an ascertained instance when an action of the KPJ coincides with Tito being there. By now he was 48 years old with six years of Moscow training behind him. The Stalinist hallmark of his action is evident: the purge was ruthless. In fact, the latter trait, and Tito's gift for choosing the appropriate people ("core") as collaborators, already bear the mark of the future Partisan leader.

The conference was held in Zagreb from 19 to 23 October. Tito told Dedijer that the conference reviewed past work, adopted a resolution about the danger of war spreading to the Balkans, criticised Prince Paul, elected a new Central Committee and Politbureau, and dispatched loyalty telegrams to Moscow.[82] As shortly Tito was to become Partisan leader, this puts the focus on discussion of military matters at the conference. "I was in charge of a special military commission" charged to "organize Party work in the army" Tito told Dedijer.[83] However, Mitar Bakić was doing the work.[84] What was the content of Bakić's report? Was there any discussion; which arguments were raised? Did Broz intervene? What was his line of thinking? Could we discern that he was already contemplating the possibility of guerrilla warfare? Was he, perhaps, still content with advocating the previous Comintern's anti-militaristic line? Again we are not told anything about this in Tito's authorized biography. Yet we are dealing with the biography of a man who made his name as a Partisan commander. There is nothing about his military views! There is no information which would allow us to discern his progress in this matter. To repeat: we have travelled full circle from Tito's military submissions to the Central Committee in 1934 (of which Dedijer says nothing), to this conference in 1940 (about which, again, Dedijer says nothing). Yet the latter was the last peace-time conference of the party, and one ought to be told Tito's strategic thought at that point in time. Did he have any? Dedijer does not say. Without this information, one is entitled to give full weight to the view that Tito came round to the concept of guerrilla warfare only when the Comintern explicitly ordered him to do so after the 22nd of June. Tito's other biographer, Auty, is no more helpful. Instead of informing us what the conference actually did, she entertains us with small talk. Though an historian, she restricts herself to generalities and how the delegates travelled to the conference, and about the accommodation and catering arrangements for the conference.[85] She praises the party's platform, and tells us that the conference was "an historic occasion" in Tito's curriculum.[86] Yes, but what is the meat in the sandwich? She does not tell us. Thus we see that the main biographies of Tito in English are unsatisfactory in this respect. Nevertheless, there is an interesting historical post-script to the resolution of the conference: it was doctored after it was adopted. Avakumović points out that the "resolution" of the conference which ended on 23 October, carries a reference to the war in Greece, which started only on the 28th.[87] It is inconceivable that the resolution could have been tampered with without Tito's involvement.

The third and last claim deals with the last of Tito's own acts before the 1941 Serb uprisings: the meeting of the KPJ's Central Committee at Zagreb, after the fall of Yugoslavia. Djilas refers to it as the Zagreb "consultation."[88] This terminology will be adopted, in order to avoid confusion with the Zagreb conference of October 1940. The evidence advanced by Dedijer and Djilas points to the consultation taking place either in the last days of April, or in early May 1941. Therefore Tito's statement to the 5th Congress of the party that it had been on 10 April, the day when the *Wehrmacht* entered Zagreb, is an error. On the 10th Tito had conversations only with the people who happened to be on hand.[89] The occasion of the formal consultation—not on 10 April—is also the earliest of the manifold claims that on a particular occasion "the majority" of the members of the party's Central Committee dispersed to the countryside to prepare "the Party and the People" for the uprising. In Zagreb, on the same occasion,

> It was decided to form a military committee with the secretary of the C[entral] C[ommittee] at its head.[90]

Dedijer expands this information by adding that the uprising had to be "of the broadest nature," and directed against both the invaders and their collaborators. This then, is presented as the first act of the Partisan saga.

It is only when consulting Djilas's *Memoir* that the foregoing innocuous nationalist version of the consultation obtains its proper, revolutionary political flavour:

> At this consultation Tito established a new thesis: the possibility of a direct Communist take-over of power, a denial of the need for the revolution to go through two stages, bourgeois-democratic and the proletarian, which had been the party position until then, following Comintern decisions. Tito also postulated a *Communist takeover after the defeat of Germany, to prevent any other party or organization from doing so* . . . . Tito said that we Communists had to organize ourselves militarily . . . , and thus be able to take power.[91]

But Tito was a pragmatist, not a theoretician. One may safely disregard the above dialectical justification of his orders for action, and examine the latter. These orders should be related to Comintern's *dicta* about the wartime role of the "Proletariat" (read: the Communist Party) in bringing down their national government by *turning the war into a civil war.*[92] So we discern here that Tito elaborated on the fact that the Yugoslav government had collapsed already. Therefore—as Djilas testifies—Tito ordered immediate action for a "Communist takeover after the [pending] defeat of Germany." The necessary decisions as to how to go about it were taken immediately. It was decided to "denounce the army officers," who were "hiding in the mountains of west Serbia," and to "begin an armed struggle against them . . . ."[93] It is obvious that the original decision was to fight

Yugoslav ("Serbian"?) officers, and not the Nazis. Significantly, the latter struggle became the order of the day only after 22 June, when Moscow so ordered. This circumstance also gives a different meaning to the decision to "collect arms and set up military committees attached to party committees."[94] All of it could be viewed also as Tito's expanded application of Comintern-dictated "anti-militaristic" work, which he discussed in his report to the Central Committee of the party in 1934. It also sheds new light on claims that—five months after the Zagreb consultation—it was Mihailović who engineered the civil war. Djilas's account of the consultation is the first testimony of Tito's political acumen. Indeed, here we see Tito exercise his gift to foresee, plan, instruct and guide. He was to develop this quality fully in Partisan warfare, and exploit it in acquiring Churchill's support in 1944, when prevaricating by assuring him repeatedly that he was not going to introduce a communist regime in Yugoslavia.

The objection could be raised, however, that Djilas' testimony is not supported by other evidence. As a rejoinder, it may suffice to cite Dedijer's summary of Tito's intervention at the Zagreb consultation:

> Tito made a statement on the subject [of the uprising] in which he emphasized that the people of Yugoslavia were very bitter against the King and the former government.... That meant that the *former civil authorities should be destroyed and replaced by a new, people's authority.*[95]

Thereupon, says Dedijer, the decision to collect arms, and "form shock troops" followed.

Until this point in time, in all his public career Broz-Tito demonstrated no particular South-Slavic feelings, either as a Yugoslav revolutionary, or as a Croat patriot. The most that could be said of his public life over this span of time is that, until the collapse of the Habsburg Monarchy, he was a *Kaisertreu* soldier, and later he transferred his loyalty to another supranational agency, the Comintern. Until his condemnation by Stalin in 1948, when he as a 56-year old man underwent a personal crisis for survival, Broz-Tito had been consistently a foreign servant. This explains his personal motivation when Yugoslavia collapsed, and he followed his Stalinist training. He thought of how to destroy the remnants of the Royal Yugoslav authorities (e.g., the "counter-revolutionary officers" and the "civil authorities"), and not how to get rid of the occupation. Stalin would take care of Hitler in due time. He, Tito, would prepare the "takeover." In this manner, Tito justified his Comintern training and found a role in life by endeavouring to turn the collapse of the State to the profit of his anational political Party.

For the next two months nothing much happened on Tito's part. This is not to deny that the KPJ followers probably did engage in collecting arms. The interpretation of this activity, however, should be kept in its proper perspective. With the members of an illegal revolutionary party, collection of arms amounts to an obsession; they would do it under any circumstances. On the other hand, as long as the Soviet Union and Nazi Germany were allies, it was out of the question for KPJ's collection of arms to have been meant against the "Fascist Aggressor" (which the Nazis were not to them as yet, although their own country was occupied). Meanwhile, Tito, a would-be "anti-Fascist" leader, deserted the centre of the home-grown Fascists, Zagreb in Croatia, and let them rule their Ustaša Fascist State in peace. Instead of firing at them in anger, he moved to German-occupied Belgrade in Serbia. There he settled down to the sheltered life of a home guest at Ribnikars', one of the well-to-do influential Belgrade families. A few hours after the German attack on the Soviet Union was launched on 22 June 1941, "Grandfather" ("Deda," viz. Dimitrov of the Comintern) wired the Yugoslav Communist Party new instructions. "Germany's treacherous attack upon the USSR," read his telegram, gave the Yugoslavs "the opportunity to create a general liberation struggle against the German invaders" and thus "facilitate the just war" of the Soviet people; at issue was not a socialist revolution.[96]

Auty comments that this released "pent-up energies in the Yugoslav party," and, as these new orders now "coincided with national feelings," the party was able to "appeal for patriotic support for immediate resistance."[97] But was it so? The answer should be searched for in Tito's proclamation which on the same day (22 June) resulted from Dimitrov's injunction. As cited by Auty, the proclamation read:

> The fateful hour has struck. The decisive battle against the ancient enemy of the working class has begun . . . . Proletarians of all regions of Yugoslavia, to your places in the first fighting ranks. Close ranks around your vanguard, the Yugoslav Communist Party . . . . Do not

allow the precious blood of the heroic Soviet people to be shed without your participation.[98]

This quote does not support Auty's contention that "the party" canvassed "immediate resistance." She even herself qualifies this proclamation as "cautiously inexplicit." Consequently our attention is attracted to the parts of the text which have been omitted by Auty (". . . ."). And indeed, when reading the same text in another publication, it is seen that Auty's second ellipsis (". . . .") stands for a critical sentence. In between ". . . Communist Party" and "Do not allow . . .", the missing part reads,

> . . . Without wavering and with discipline, fulfill your proletarian duty. *Prepare yourself* without delay for the last and decisive battle. Do not allow (etc.).[99]

Here we have Tito's own thought of the moment, and there is no need for historians to lend him theirs.

On the day of the crisis, the 22nd of June, Tito kept his "pent-up energies" (*pace,* Auty) in check, and did not call for "immediate resistance." He did so only when on 1 July the Comintern explicitly ordered him to get up and fight. To cite again the Comintern text,

> The hour has struck when communists must launch an open fight against the invaders. Without wasting a moment, organise partisan detachments and start a partisan war behind the enemy's line . . . . Acknowledge receipt of these instructions, and notify facts to show fulfillment.[100]

This was a testy admonishment: stop procrastinating, organise detachments, start a partisan war, and "notify facts to show fulfillment." A strict taskmaster was chastising his slack errand-boy. But this time the response was immediate: "Tito did as he was ordered," says Auty. A new proclamation was issued on 4 July, and re-issued on the 12th.

> 'Now is the time,' read the text, 'the hour has struck to rise as one man for the battle against the invaders and hirelings, killers of our people.'[101]

We see that, on Moscow's orders to get up and fight, Tito's first reaction was to procrastinate. This was but a passing wavering which makes this mythological figure human. The second observation is that he called on others to start armed resistance, yet he himself remained in comfort at Ribnikars for three months longer. It was only in mid-September 1941, when he felt Belgrade was becoming too hot for him, that he left for the Serbian mountains and guerrilla warfare. All this time, Mihailović and his men have ben in the forests. For good measure, Tito left Belgrade with a genuine collaborationist identity card, and in the company of a *Volksdeutscher*. What work was he doing while basking in comfort at Ribnikars' from 22 June to 16 September?

In English-language writings about the uprising, the one work which stands out because it lists its sources, is Phyllis Auty's *Tito*.[102] Her description of Tito's preoccupations while he remained in Belgrade is naive. She says he had to try to "keep control of all military operations," deal with the acquiring and distribution of arms, receive Ranković's "intelligence reports" and so on. Her source of informatin was Dedijer's Diary. But, as will be shown in the Conclusion, the part of Dedijer's diary which deals with this period of the uprising is not a contemporary document. It is a propaganda work manufactured after the event. Regardless of this circumstance and as a matter of methodology, Auty should have exercised caution. She should have been aware that the uprising started as a countryside phenomenon "organized" and "led" by no central authority. At that stage, its leaders were the anonymous local prompters. This found expression in the saying *"Moja puška prva"* ("My rifle was the first").[103] Auty's description reads as if she was projecting the work of the HQ of the British Long Range Desert Patrol (LRDP) onto the Serbian irregular theatre of war. She fails to recognise that guerrilla ambushes in Serbia of solitary enemy personnel were an *ad hoc* event, and not a foreseen and garrison-rehearsed operation of regular troops. This issue is complicated further when one observes that in her discussion of what Tito was ordered to do by Moscow on 1 July 1941, her text again provides ellipsis (thus:...) in lieu of a critical part of Moscow's order.[104] The missing part will surprise all those historians who believe Tito was the initiator of guerrilla war tactics by the Partisans. The truth is that Tito was explicitly told by Moscow how to go about it. Furthermore, shortly the Chief and Deputy Chief of Staff of Tito's Partisan HQ became two regular Captains of the (Royal)

Yugoslav Army, Terzić and Jovanović. The latter was Mihailović's student at the Higher School of the Military Academy or the Staff College, where Mihailović is reputed to have taught also guerrilla warfare matters. The part of Moscow's text which is missing in Auty's quotation reads:

> ... Set fire to war factories, stores of inflammable material (petroleum, gasoline, and others), airports; destroy and demolish the railway, telegraph, and telephone network; do not allow the transportation of troops and munitions (of war material in general). Organize the peasantry to hide their grain and drive the livestock into the woods. It is indispensable to use all means to terrorize the enemy, to make him feel as if he were within a besieged fortress.[105]

Therefore, as far as Tito's story is concerned, this period is viewed best as a transitional period of his life, leading from his peacetime political underground work, to his wartime guerrilla activities. He had still a lot to learn. Those historians who project the image of an accomplished partisan leader of the latter day Tito's saga back onto the events in 1941 Serbia, risk their credibility. The others would do better not to be fainthearted when citing the contemporary documents.

Significantly, Tito was not moved when the Nazis had overrun Yugoslavia. This is today acknowledged even there. Thus, Koštunica and Čavoški in their monograph[106] state explicitly,

> right up until 22 June 1941, the C[ommunist] P[arty] of Y[ugoslavia] had never condemned fascist Germany as the aggressor and initiator of the Second World War, but maintained instead that the English and French imperialists *attacked* Germany, that is, that they, and not Germany, provoked and instigated the Second World War.[107]

Yet now, when the Nazis turned against the Soviet Union, Tito suddenly woke up that the Nazis were "invaders" (of whom? when?) and "killers of our people" (whose people?). So much for the contemporary empathy of this latter day Yugoslav patriot with his Nazi-enslaved Yugoslav compatriots. Were the Yugoslavs—and in the first place the Serbs—for him but cannon-fodder to be sacrificed on the altar of international Stalinism? The authoritative answer to all these questions confirms our earlier conclusions.

The answer is contained in Tito's eight war-cries which he launched on the occasion of the 22nd of June. Here they are:[108]

> Long live the Great and Invincible Land of Socialism, the Soviet Union!
> Long live the Heroic Bolshevik Party, the Soviet Communist Party!
> Long live the Leader and Organiser of the past and future Victories of the Powerful Soviet Union, Comrade Stalin!
> Long live the Communist International!
> Long live the Communist Party of Yugoslavia!
> Long live the international solidarity of all the down-trodden ones and the exploited!
> Long live union and struggle of the working masses of Yugoslavia!
> Down with the Imperialistic-Fascist criminals, headed by Bloody Hitler, Mussolini and the other Satraps!

That is all very well, but where is the declaration of Yugoslav patriotism? What about "Long live Yugoslavia"? Where is the call for the liberation of Yugoslavia? There was none of it. So much for the history of the day and its historiography the day after.

CHAPTER 8

OCCUPIED SERBIA IN 1941: GERMAN ADMINISTRATION AND SERBIAN ACCOMMODATION

Mihailović established himself on Ravna Gora in hilly west Serbia on 11 May 1941.[1] He found his homeland occupied by German troops and governed by a German military administration, which was assisted in local Serbian matters by a German-nominated Serbian "Commissioners" (*"Komesari"*) placed in charge of former Yugoslav ministerial departments. Shortly afterwards Mihailović became the mainspring and centre of the first resistance organisation in Serbia. The Partisan organization also arose in Serbia, albeit only after Hitler's attack on the Soviet Union on 22 June 1941. Obviously, the rise of both anti-Axis resistance organizations had a common background in Nazi occupation, which first needs to be examined.

Nature and policies of the occupation regime.

Hitler had viewed the Belgrade *coup d'état* of 27 March 1941 as a personal affront, and decided to dismember Yugoslavia and to humiliate Serbia. His instructions to this effect were embodied in the "Provisional Directives for the Partition of Yugoslavia." These "Directives" were issued by the head of the supreme command of German armed forces [OKW], Field Marshal Wilhelm Keitel, on 3 April,[2] three days before the German invasion of Yugoslavia. This document defined the spoils which were to be retained by Germany, and those to be given to Italy, Hungary and Bulgaria. It prescribed that an independent Croatia was to be set up,[3] and specified, given to Italy, Hungary and Bulgaria. It prescribed that an independent Croatia was to be set up,[3] and specified,

> The territory of *old Serbia* (should be) placed under German military administration under the High Command of the Army [or the OKH].[4]

Under "old Serbia" (*"Alt-Serbien"*) Hitler meant Serbia on the eve of her 1912 war for liberation and unification with those Serb districts which were still under Turkey.

Even this territory was to be further dismembered on Hitler's orders, by excluding areas currently occupied by Italy and Bulgaria. To this rump *"Serbien"* there was added West Banat from the Yugoslav-Romanian border on the east to the river Tisa (Tisza, Theiss) on the west, and from the Yugoslav-Hungarian border on the north to the Danube on the south.[5] Hitler first intended to give Banat to Hungary, but, faced with Romanian hostility, he changed his original instructions.[6] General Halder, Chief of Staff of the Army, noted in his diary on 2 May 1941 that one could buy off Romania by the return of Bessarabia, and then give Banat to Hungary.[7] In practice, a fully *Volksdeutsche* administration was set up in Banat, although the German or *"Volksdeutsche"* minority there (120,450 people) amounted to only 20% of the population.[8] This administration was virtually independent of the local Serbian authorities in Belgrade. In the war of April 1941 Belgrade had been proclaimed an open city, and German troops entered it without any Yugoslav resistance on 13 April. By his *Befehl* of 20 April, the Commander-in-Chief of the Army, von Brauchitsch, ordered that the military administration of occupied Serbia start functioning on 22 April 1941 at 12 o'clock noon.[9]

The German military occupation of *"Serbien"* was established in two stages. During the Yugoslav campaign, Lieutenant General Schmidt-Logan, commander of the Rear Area of the 2nd Army (AOK 2), was in charge.[10] At the conclusion of the campaign a specially appointed *Militaerbefehlshaber in Serbien* or MBS (Military Commander in Serbia) took over.[11] The first MBS was Air Force Lieutenant General Foerster, who took over on 22 April.[12] The basic document or "constitution" as it were of the military governance was von Brauchitsch's *Befehl* of 20 April with the enclosure "Service instructions for the military commander in Serbia," dated

17 April.[13] In the latter, Clause "C 1" specified that the commander in Serbia (MBS) was,

> the head of the military administration there. He (could) take all decisions which by their nature and importance are not reserved for the commander-in-chief of the army or reserved by the commander of the AOK 2. He (could) proclaim legally binding ordinances. . . .

He was also required to safeguard the "militarily important communications," and last but not least, he was charged with keeping local Serbian authorities under the strictest control.[14]

The HQ establishment of the MBS evolved from the "Liaison Unit South" (*"Verbindungsstelle Sued"*), which was also known as "Unit 08633," although nominally, "Unit 08633" was only its field post-code. This unit was set up by the OKH on 25 March 1941; on 17 April the unit was renamed the HQ of the Military Commander in Serbia (MBS) and ordered to depart from Germany to Belgrade, where it arrived on 23 April.[15] The HQ consisted of two major departments: one for military matters (*"Kommandostab"*), and the other for administrative matters (*"Verwaltungsstab"*).[16] The other subordinates are listed in Executive Order No. 1 of the MBS of 28 April 1941.[17] Initially there were four *"Feld-"* or "Field" commanders under the MBS (one for each Serbian remnant of the former Yugoslav territorial *"Banovina"* and one for the City of Belgrade), nine *"Orts-"* or *"Kreis-"* commanders (as counterparts of the local *"srezovi"* or counties), four *Landesschuetzen* or territorial defence battalions (*Ls-Btl.*), and two POW transit camps. As the field troops of the AOK 2 were setting up their own *"Standort"* or "location" commands, on 2 May 1941 the Military Commander in Serbia ordered that his *"Orts-"* commands be renamed *"Kreis-"* or district commands.[18]

In addition to the Commander in Serbia, two other men of senior status were posted to Belgrade in 1941. They could not be called either his subordinates or his nominal equals, although all the evidence points to the fact that for the smooth running of the administration the cooperation of the three men was required. One was the economic plenipotentiary in Serbia (the *Generalbevollmaechtigte feur de Wirtschaft"* or GBW), Franz Neuhausen, an appointee of Goering's. The other man was Felix Benzler, representing the department of external affairs. His terms of appointment illustrate the concern in Berlin regarding Serbia. In Hitler's directive of 28 April 1941 establishing the position of the "Plenipotentiary of the Department of External Affairs with the Military Commander in Serbia," Hitler emphasized that his task was to,

> prevent the activities of Serbian political elements harmful to the political interests of the Reich.[19]

The status of the commander in Serbia (MBS) should have resulted from the executive chain of command from Berlin to Belgrade. Clause 2 of the *Befehl* of 20 April specified that the MBS was subordinated directly to the high command of the army (the OKH), with the proviso that, as long as *"Serbien"* remained in the operational area of the 2nd army (the AOK 2), the MBS was to defer to the commander of the 2nd army. Reflecting this framework, the MBS exercised his authority in the names of the commander-in-chief of the army and the commander of the 2nd army.[20] Clause 4 of the same *Befehl* re-emphasized the direct subordination of the MBS to the OKH. It stressed in the strongest possible terms that, except in economic matters, only the OKH was the superior of the MBS. It read,

> The highest authorities of the Reich, as well as the High Commands of the Air Force and the Navy on one hand, and the Military Commander in Serbia on the other, will not correspond directly with one another, except in economic matters when instructed or authorized by the *Reichsmarschall* to do so.[21]

This stipulation was, of course, based on Hitler's directive of 3 April that *"Alt-Serbien"* was to be "placed under German military administration" controlled by the high command of the army.

The "highest authorities of the Reich"—the Nazis—reacted by passing the MBS and setting up their own little empires in Belgrade, starting with the Gestapo and the Police. In time, other agencies were added to the administrative conglomerate built up in Belgrade. As they had no local overall boss, or even a coordinator, they engaged in mutual rivalries which reflected power games played in Berlin. These arrangements and the consequent rivalries which occurred repeated the pattern of occupied Europe in general.[22] Nominally, the status of the MBS was that of a senior politico-military army post. In practice the actual authority of the MBS in Belgrade depended on the strength of his personality. The case of the head of the own *Verwaltungsstab* of the MBS, *SS-Obergruppenfuehrer* Dr. Harald Turner,[23] illustrates this point. Commanding generals came and went but Turner stayed put. In the critical phase of the uprising in Serbia, he parted ways with his current superior, Air Corps General Danckelmann, and joined forces with a martinet, General Boehme, only to share in his shame for the inhuman treatment of the civilian population of the city of Šabac, west-south-west of Belgrade.

Besides the overbearing attitude of the various Nazi officials in Belgrade, the MBS was hampered also by the military arrangements which were adopted. The employment of well disciplined troops in an occupied country should guarantee the necessary coercive power to maintain the occupation and its administration. In Serbia, German arrangements were deficient. Hitler was intent on a speedy build-up of his forces for operation "Barbarossa" (attack on the Soviet Union), and, on 13 April ruled that when the campaign in the Balkans was concluded, most of the army formations were to be withdrawn. "It is planned," he directed, to leave

> one or two divisions in Greece, one further division in Salonika, [and] two or three divisions in Serbia.[24]

The withdrawal of troops started immediately. The AOK 2 was completely withdrawn from Serbia, and the "AOK 12, left in Greece, had at its disposal only the Headquarters XVIII Corps of General...Boehme" and some other units.[25] The vacuum was filled by Italian and Bulgarian troops, and in some instances by Croat soldiers. While the territory of the "Military Commander in Serbia" (the MBS) was still in the operational area of the AOK 2, the relationship of the two commands was regulated by a "Directive" issued by the AOK 2 on 26 April.[26] The AOK 2 stated unequivocally that it was the "unrestricted" (*"uneingeschraenkt"*) command authority for all subordinate troops, and prescribed the procedure the MBS and his *"Feld"* and *"Orts"* [*"Kreis"*] commands were to follow when requisitioning the help of field troops. This led to a twofold chain of command and competence, and contributed the final qualification to the status of the "Commander in Serbia." Despite his title, the MBS was shown to be only a military governor, in charge of administration and public order, who had at his direct disposal a few *Landesschuetzen* battalions (*Ls-Btl.*) for guard duties.[27] This double-command arrangement soon led to friction, so that on 13 May Halder wrote in his diary: "Relationship between the AOK 2 and the MBS is not smooth."[28]

Despite repeated requests by the MBS and even despite the intervention of the chief of staff of the army, Halder, nothing substantial was done to increase the strength, armament and mobility of the troops of the MBS. Yet at the same time the *Wehrmacht* had a healthy respect for the Serbian Četnik of pre-World War I and World War I fame, and orders were issued to guard against Četnik or guerrilla warfare. German authorities had not realized that in the twenty years of Yugoslavia's existence the seemingly insoluable "Croat question" had sapped Serbian strength and resolve, so that there was never any serious preparation for a guerrilla war. The *Wehrmacht* titlted at a windmill of its own invention. The reports from German troops in the field deserve serious consideration by historians, as the reports of German intelligence analysts are often blinkered, seeing a pre-war organized Četnik under each bed. Preconditioned in this matter, German commanders were wary of the Četniks and guerrilla warfare from the moment they set foot in Yugoslavia. In reality, Mihailović's *ad hoc* military organization started from scratch.

When, in the April War, the AOK 2 entered Serbia and encountered occasional attacks by isolated remnants of the Yugoslav army, it overreacted. Instead of relying on the deterrent effect of the visible presence of German field troops, or, perhaps, restricting itself to the reprisals permitted by the usages of war, the AOK 2 introduced a reign of terror. The barbarian streak behind this reign of terror is seen in an order by General Weichs of 28 April 1941. It read,

> Anyone found in Serbian uniform, if armed, is not protected by the usages of war and is immediately to be shot. *The corpses of the shot are to be hung up and left to hang.*[29]

In time, the terror was extended to the civilian population. However, one cannot ascribe barbarism indiscriminately to all German army commands. Individual generals reacted differently, probably largely due to the different nature of their reponsibilities. The general public became aware of these different attitudes amongst their German overlords. In the same way as Field Marshal Rommel is set apart from many others in British eyes, in the history of the uprising in Serbia Lieutenant General Foerster, the first "Commander in Serbia" was set apart. Colonel Živanović wrote,

> Foerster appeared to have remained an upright man regardless of wearing a Hitlerite uniform. This might explain why he was soon dismissed from his post . . . .[30]

Considering that Foerster and von Weichs were in Belgrade at the same time, the favoured picture of the former may have arisen from contrasting Foerster's ways and Weich's barbarism. And even in the crisis of the uprising, the MBS who was dismissed in favour of the martinet Boehme, Danckelmann, said on 29 August 1941 that,

> It was not in the nature of the German soldier, when the fight against the military enemy is over, to treat the civilian population as an enemy.[31]

Despite their dread of a Četnik-inspired Serbian uprising, the requirements of planning for "Barbarossa" prevented German authorities from reinforcing their garrisons in Serbia. On the contrary, they had to deplete them. However measures were taken to replace the departing field troops of the AOK 2 by four infantry divisions (the 704th, 714th and 717th in Serbia, and the 718th in Bosnia, west of the Serbian border), grouped in a special formation, the "Higher Command LXV" (*"Hoeheres Kommando"* or HK LXV). Their soldiers were from the so-called "15th wave."[32] All this took time, and the turning point of the month of June, when Hitler attacked the Soviet Union, was fast approaching. The HK LXV of Lieutenant General Bader completed its arrival in Serbia on 11 June, and took over from the AOK 2 on 17 June.[33] The precise nature of Bader's initial command relationship to the other commander in Serbia, the MBS, cannot be determined due to lack of documents. Nevertheless, existing evidence suggests that Bader simply relieved the troops of the AOK 2 of General von Weichs, but did not accede to his seniority[34] over the MBS. For a few days in July 1941, Bader was acting MBS,[35] probably because he was the senior officer present. By Hitler's directive No. 31 of 9 June, the commander of the AOK 12 in Greece, Field Marshal List, was also appointed to the newly created post of the "Commander of Armed Forces South-east," thus Serbia, as well as German occupied parts of Greece, came under his command.[36] On the 22nd of June Hitler invaded the Soviet Union.

For the last seven weeks the Serbians had witnessed a steady withdrawal of field troops from occupied Serbia and Greece.[37] The wholesale withdrawal of troops started on 5 May 1941. In Berlin Halder noted on 8 May 1941 that,

> Return march from the Balkans (was) progressing according to plan.[38]

Indeed, at one stage eleven German divisions were withdrawing through Serbia.[39] What appeared to be *"planmaessig"* success in Berlin, was not necessarily so in Serbia. Both German authorities on the spot, the MBS and the AOK 2, were critical of the new arrangements. Replacement divisions were inadequate, and mobile reserves were needed for effective suppression of any disturbances.[40] There were never set up. In addition, Bader's replacement divisions were dispersed all over the country, "in some cases 120 km apart from each other," and were themselves immediately engaged in "extensive guard duty."[41] To top it all, Serbia was in the grip of unrest unconnected with external events.

The origin of the unrest can be related to clause 1 of the protocol of the capitulation of Yugoslav forces of 17 April, which stipulated that all military personnel should become prisoners of war. But some 325,000 men had evaded captivity[42] and were are large in Serbia. On 15 May 1941 the MBS, Lieutenant General Foerster, issued a proclamation ordering registration of all POWs of Serb and Slovene ethnicity who had evaded captivity, and promised in return that they would be issued with identity cards as "POWs on leave of absence."[43] Registration started at the end of May and in early June. To cite Partisan historian Marjanović,

> It turned out that in some districts this was not an ordinary registration, but [an excuse for gathering and] deportation of men into POW camps in Germany,[44]

and on 12 June the Serbian Commissioner for the Department of Interior, Aćimović, lodged a protest with the Administration Department of the MBS.[45] Outwardly, this event appeared to be a case of misplaced zeal by some German authorities. Nevertheless, in their reaction the potential "POWs on leave," and their relations and acquaintances, and the people at large were at one. The general unrest must have been considerable. The Serbian department of the interior recorded on 15 June that,

> many are now escaping into forests, and thereby are endangering public order; at the same time there is the danger that fields will remain untended and the harvest not collected.[46]

When searching for an explanation of this extreme reaction, one must conclude that the people were probably guided by their experience with *Wehrmacht* procedures in the April War. On that occasion the POWs were taken from point "A" to point "B," to point "C". . . under the constant promise of "registration and release" at the next point, until the barbed wire closed around them. Why trust the German administration to be true to its word this time? Documentation now available justifies the Serb reaction. In a confidential MBS instruction to *"Feld-"* commanders on 14 June 1941, it was stated,

> Under the guise of these proceedings (*'unter Schildung des Sachverhaltes'*) attend to the arrest of the professional military personnel (officers, . . .) as well as of troublemakers and the other unwanted elements (*'unliebsame Elemente'*) and send them to the nearest POW camp for further transporation to Germany. Arrest is to take place when [after their registration] they return for their identity cards. . . .[47]

The chronology here is all important. Yugoslav archives revealed by the Partisan historian Marjanović suggest that this move into the forest started before the 22nd of June. At that time the Communist Party of Yugoslavia (KPJ) was not yet in the field. Mihailović and his officers were.

At the same time a purely political event occurred which fanned the pre-22 June unrest in Serbia. Almost a month to the day after the proclamation of the MBS of 15 May, under 13 June in the war Diary of the unit 08633 (Ia) we find the following entry:

Rumours that the Banat will be given over to Hungary increase the upheaval ('*Unruhe*') of the Serbian population.

A similar observation is made in Wisshaupt's report to the Commander South-East on the insurgency in Serbia, under the general title "August 1941."[48] The correct dating, of course, affects our understanding of events. Whereas this particular date is not critical in the context of Wisshaupt's report, when related to the intervening watershed of 22 June, it became critical for historical interpretation. Obviously, the chronological determinant here is the earlier and explicit date of the rumours: it is mid-June 1941. To revert now to Wisshaupt. He adds that this rumour caused "disturbance" also amongst the "Germans, Bulgars and Hungarians." This detail, which illustrates the contemporary Serbian scene, requires clarification. Many MBS documents reveal that the Hungarians had paid scant regard to the MBS installed administration in the Banat, which resulted in a series of incidents. What would have befallen the German minority if Hungary was to become the official overlord there? That though must have been sufficient to cause "disturbance" amongst them. As to the "Bulgars," there was no Bulgarian minority in Serbia, but only Bulgarian troops in different districts. They must have resented a possible increase in the status of Hungary, as she was their competitor in scavenging Serbian spoils. And the rumours made the Hungarians themselves impatient to conclude the final transfer of the Banat to the Crown of St. Stephen, which caused an upsurge of Hungaro-German incidents. All of it was at Serbian expense, and contributed to their ever increasing unrest.

Therefore, looking beyond Partisan historiography, a different picture emerges. In the Serbian context, war in the east and the subsequent agitation of the KPJ were additional components, superimposed on the existing complex internal situation. In this combination of circumstances one should not overlook the effect of the influential BBC broadcasts nor the intense, wishful war-newsmongering of a subjugated population. It is crucial to realize that the KPJ, through its militia the "Partisans," skilfully exploited this situation, but did not create it. The turning point seems to have been the departure of the German troops which had conquered Yugoslavia and Greece, and the arrival of Bader's replacement occupation troops. This development enabled the Serbians to express their hate fot the German occupier. Mihailović later commented that, when the Germans started evacuating the territories of Western Serbia, we all jumped to arms.⁴⁹

Serbs rose as a nation, not as partisans of any political party.

Why did Some Serbs Assist the German Administration?

At the time of Hitler's invasion, Yugoslavia was territorily divided into eight (formerly nine) "Banovina" and the Directorate (*"Uprava"*) of the City of Belgrade. One of the banovinas was called *"Banovina* of Croatia," but Serbia, as a formal unit, did not exist. Furthermore, when the establishment of the semi-autonomous *Banovina* of Croatia was decreed in 1939, Yugoslav governmental authority and the civil service were passed on to it. After the *Luftwaffe* bombed Belgrade on 6 April 1941, Dr. Vladko Maček, the undisputed leader of the vast majority of the Croats and Vice-President of the Yugoslav government, resigned his post in the government and returned to Zagreb. On 10 April a former Austro-Hungarian Lieutenant Colonel and then a Yugoslav Colonel, by the name of Kvaternik, proclaimed the "Independent State of Croatia," German troops entered Zagreb, and Maček had the following proclamation read over Zagreb radio:

> Croatian People! Colonel Slavko Kvaternik, the leader of the nationalist movement, proclaimed today the liberated and independent Croat State over the whole territory of Croatia, and took over the government ('*vlast*'). I call on the whole Croatian people to obey the new government. I call on all followers of the Croat Peasant Party who hold executive posts in the administration of the country ('*koji su na upravnim položajima*'), as well on all district councillors and the others, sincerely to assist the new government.⁵⁰

In this manner, the whole civil service of the *Banovina,* and the Gendarmerie were passed over to Axis-aligned Croatia.⁵¹

In contrast, to this, in April 1941 Serbia found herself in a legal, administrative, and political limbo. This was due to the precipitate flight of the Yugoslav government and leading politicians and to the lack of any legal status as the Royal Government of Yugoslavia had partitioned Serbia into faceless banovinas.⁵² There was no authority or representative body between naked German power and the hapless Serbian population. The local councils and police (Gendarmerie), continued functioning in accordance with international usage and the protocol of capitulation of 17 April, but they could not rise above their station. Therefore, while national euphoria was the order of the day in Croatia, in Serbia fear and chaos reigned.[53] This, of course, was what Hitler wanted when he ordered the establishment of a truncated Serbia. Furthermore, the borders of this rump-Serbia remained open to adverse review.[54] The fear of further encroachments on Serbian territory by the Italians, Albanians, Bulgarians, Hungarians and Croats had a direct impact on Serbian attitudes. The question of borders was not only a Serbian "national" issue, but literally a question of most immediate importance in the lives of ordinary people. This can be illustrated by the written request from the Serb population of Nova Varoš and the Stari Vlah district to the German military command, asking for protection from the undisciplined behaviour and excesses of Croat troops which had taken over from the *Wehrmacht*. The petition read,

> Because of (Croat excesses) the whole Serbian population lives in fear and terror and we plead that these circumstances and conditions by urgently remedied. We, the undersigned, and the whole population put our trust only in the disciplined German troops to restore peaceful conditions and public order here.[55]

These complaints had no effect on Berlin's policies regarding *"Serbien."* Because of this policy the local population had no other redress but to rely on the goodwill of the military occupation authorities and the effectiveness of their control. Shortly, the influx of destitute Serb refugees from pogroms in Ustasha-Croatia, and instances of communist excesses (or "left deviation") in the uprising of 1941, added further dimensions to the original fear for public safety, and—emotionally—even for national survival. These circumstances must be singled out at this point, otherwise it would be hard to grasp the rationale of the Serbian accommodation with the occupation authorities.[56]

Already the *"Anordnung"* of the high command of the army of 31 March,[57] which regulated the procedures to be followed in "Operation 25" (war with Yugoslavia), directed that local authorities be retained and German ones superimposed.[58] At the same time it was in German interest to establish some sort of Serbian central authority and save their own manpower while retaining control. In 1941, in Hitler-defined *"Serbien"* the MBS successively installed two Serbian administrations. The first administration (30 April-28(?) August) consisted of a number of commissioners in charge of former Yugoslav ministerial departments, and is discussed in this chapter. The second administration (from 29 August onwards) consisted of a number of ministers under a Prime Minister, known since as the "Government of General Nedić."[59] Nedić's "Government of National Salvation," which was formed to combat the uprising and was a self-declared anti-Communist body, will be discussed in chapter 9 ("Serbia at Arms").

On 22 April, the day that Foerster took over as the MBS, he submitted a list of men to the commander of the AOK 2 whom he wanted appointed (*"Ich habe. . . ernannt"*) as commissioners of ministerial departments.[60] Negotiations leading to this preceded Foerster's arrival. Turner, the chief of civil administration of the MBS, had come over from the AOK 2, where Schmidt-Logan was nominally in charge of *"Serbien."*[61] Turner appears to have been instrumental in the Belgrade negotiations and in obtaining Foerster's immediate signature. However, this particular document was never executed. One of the appointees refused to comply, so that the appointments had to be renegotiated, and a team was not officially announced until 30 April.[62] As in the initial team, the new list of commissioners was headed by Milan Aćimović, who in Milan Stojadinović's government was Minister for Interior when *rapprochement* with Hitler's Germany took place. Thirdly, at the foot of the document of 22 April the following annotation has been added by hand:

> Head of police [Dragoslav-Dragi] Jovanovic. 1st Mayor Dr. Miloslav Stojadinovic.

The first German made appointment was to make the Head of Police Special Branch, Jovanović, head of the Belgrade police. It may be assumed that the above annotation is the official record of his appointment. He had had official dealings with his German counterparts in peacetime and probably renewed contacts when the Nazis came to Belgrade as conquerors. To hold it against Jovanović, as Yugoslav historiography does, that he was known to the Germans is nonsense. There are jobs which require international cooperation, and police administration is one of them. Jovanović had dealings with other foreign police, and not only with the Germans. One may disagree over the political interpretation of the German-made appointments in occupied Serbia, but in terms of western customs, as well as in terms of the Yugoslav protocol of capitulation, police had to stay at their post and continue doing their professional job. When Jovanović was appointed, under the occupation, ~~to head the occupation~~, to head the Serbian metropolitan police, the situation in Belgrade was desparate. Hitler's *Luftwaffe*, without a declaration of war, had bombed Belgrade and left it

> in ruins, with charred buildings and the streets full of broken glass; there was no water to be had, and so using toilets was forbidden. The Germans, oblivious of any civilians in the street, proceeded to shoot dogs and cats
> ....
> All streets were plastered with the posters and decrees of the army of occupation; almost without fail they always ended with the threat of capital punishment.
>   The atmosphere in Belgrade went from bad to worse, especially when the news of Ustaša, Hungarian, Bulgarian and Albanian atrocities started arriving....[63]

At the same time the food supply to the city was interrupted, and a humanitarian action of the American minister in Belgrade stands out. To alleviate the distress of the population, Arthur Bliss Lane

> opened the first soup kitchen and increased their number to thirteen. These served 227,000 meals between April 12 and May 9....[64]

It is difficult to write a history of this period. Yugoslav Partisan historiography takes no notice of the chaos and insecurity into which Serbia was plunged with the fall of Yugoslavia. The Partisan school of history discusses everything and everyone in the post-22nd of June Stalinist mould, and then projects this interpretation backwards in time. Thus, Marjanović says,

It is obvious that the Germans relied in Serbia on that section of the bourgeoisie on which they had relied earlier, before their attack on Yugoslavia.[65]

These people, says Marjanović, influenced many others in April 1941 "to put themselves at the disposal of the authorities of occupation." He classifies them into four categories—firstly, those who believed in a German "mission" in Europe; secondly, those who wanted to profit from an occupation they thought temporary only; a third group, who believed in German victory and "wanted to assure the future of Serbian bourgeoisie"; and a fourth group of time-servers, who "seem to have been the majority." Marjanović should have allowed also for people motivated by sheet patriotism, and a personal commitment to alleviate the conditions of existence which were inflicted on their compatriots.

In contrast to the administrative authorities, such as the police (Gendarmerie) and the local councils, the body of commissioners, which was set up by the MBS as a local central authority, had no standing in international and/or Yugoslav law, and literally depended on the whim of their German overlords. It was Milan Aćimović, a former minister of interior as well as a former head of the Belgrade police, who took the initiative for an accomodation with the enemy.[66] When Aćimović consulted prominent citizens on the alleviation of the rigours of the occupation, he also approached the leader of the Yugoslav right wing movement "Zbor," Dimitrije Ljotić. Ironically, the man whom he chanced to ask where to find Ljotić was Milosav Vasiljević, a "Ljotić-ite" whom Aćimović had had arrested on political grounds and had kept imprisoned for two months in 1938.[67] Eventually, commissioners were appointed from amongst people with a wide range of political backgrounds, although with few exceptions none was a delegate of any political party. The exceptions were the Ljotić-ites. Ljotić refused to be a commissioner himself, but appointed his delegates who, as commissioners, did not owe their loyalty to their colleagues but to their leader, Ljotić. In time his influence and posturing were to interfere with the solidarity of the commissioners. Soon afterwards, when Ljotić organized his own private army to combat both Mihailović and the Communist-led insurgents,[68] in the days of the government of General Nedić, he became a committed Nazi collaborator. It is interesting therefore to note that, originally, Ljotić was not a German choice. But it should be noted also that we are referring here to "Communist-," not "Tito-led" insurgents: there was no public mention of Tito in 1941 (although he was leader of the Party).[69] At the time, the Communist war-cry was "Stalin." Tito's name was put forth only two years later, when he was declared a "Marshal" at the second meeting of the Anti-Fascist Council at Jajce in November 1943.

German authorities were notified beforehand about the conditions under which the commissioners would manage the administration of Serbia.[70] They consisted of details derived from international law, and included the requirement that the photographs of King Peter II remained displayed in offices, and that the courts of law continue administering justice in the name of the King. "The Germans" (Turner?) did not agree to the latter. Let us sum up the four short months of their administration, in which the commissioners endeavoured to pull the country out of chaos. They introduced subsidies for the families of prisoners of war and payment of pensions to those public servants who could not be offered continuation of employment; they obtained agreement to set up a Serbian Red Cross, and organized reception and regular help for refugees arriving in Serbia. The commissioners were supposed to pay 6,500,000 *Reichsmark* per month to the MBS for "expenses of occupation," in addition to paying for "war damages."[71] They did what they could to reorganize police service and the economy, and, generally, had to serve as the unwilling servants of occupation authorities. They refused to comply with the demand to bring in an anti-Jewish law.[72] The internal and external events that occurred in the month of June, and the ensuing unrest and uprising undid the commissioners' work of recovery. The local reaction to the drastic measures of repression, introduced by the occupation authorities on orders from Berlin, worsened the position of the commissioners. The mentality behind these orders can be judged from an order by the supreme commander of armed forces (OWK) of 29 July, whereby,

> death sentences pronounced for sabotage should be executed by hanging, *und auch alle sonstigen, den Gebraeuchen der Landeseinwohner entsprechenden Mittel zur Abschrekung anzuwenden* ('. . . and it is also necessary to apply other fearful deterrents which are in customary use by the inhabitants of the land.')[73]

In whose customary use were "fearful deterrents"? Nazis' or Serbian? In any case, after 22 June the commissioners' administration was fast losing control over events in the country. On 28 July, and independently of the above order but in the same spirit, a "deterrent" of unmitigated barbarism occurred.[74] In the early morning of 27 July two sergeants of the 1st Company of the German 64th Police Reserve Battalion were ambushed on the road from Užice to Valjevo, one was killed and the other reported missing.[75] On the next day, the 1st Company, assisted by a unit of the *"Feldgendarmerie"* and a detachment of Serbian genarmes, combed a wider area, arrested 81 people and brought them to the scene of the ambush. They were shot and the corpses left lying on the highway.[76] Živanović says[77] that on that occasion Colonel von Stockhausen, [*"Feld"* commander of the FK 816 in Užice], personally ordered Serbian gendarmes to shoot and kill the arrested people. When the gendarmes refused to comply, he threatened to have them shot first. In this predicament, says Živanović, the gendarmes complied, but after returning to their base they abandoned their post: some went home, and the others joined Colonel Mihailović. This event was the proverbial "last straw" and worsened the crisis of the already shaky commissioner administration. Shortly afterwards the commissioners resigned. How much of Živanović's reconstruction and interpretation can be verified from contemporary German sources?

Firstly, the report of the 64th Battalion attests to the fact that Serbian gendarmes executed the people: the 81 Serbs were *"am Tatort durch die serbische Gendarmerie erschossen."*[78] Secondly, Benzler's confidential telegram of 1 August 1941 to the Department of External Affairs in Berlin confirms that the Gendarmes were forced to do so under the threat of German rifles aimed at them (". . .*durch deutsches Militaer mit vorgehaltenem Gewehr*").[79] Colonel Trišić of the Serbian Gendarmerie wrote on this subject on 15 August that,

> . . . lately . . . German authorities are forcing our gendarmes to shoot and kill our innocent people without any [legally pronounced] sentence. This is contravening our national laws and the international laws [of warfare] also. Furthermore, when our country was free, the Gendarmerie never executed death sentences.[80]

Thirdly, can it be proven that, beside the Nazi police, Colonel Stockhausen of the *Wehrmacht* was involved also, and in that particularly barbarian fashion? The police report does not mention his presence at the place of execution, nor any other involvement. But there is a significant paragraph in Benzler's telegram, which definitely implicates a "Feldkommandant." It reads,

> Unfortunately, our endeavours [to pacify the country] have been caused a serious setback by an irresponsible act (*'Vorgehen'*) of an otherwise very fatherly figure of a *Feldkommandant* who has obviously become nervous.[81]

He had, says Benzler, disregarded the regulations of the MBS and arrested 80 [sic] wholly irreproachable people (*"unbescholtene Personen"*) who were working on their crops in the fields, and had them shot by the Serbian gendarmes. There is circumstantial evidence which indicates that Colonel von Stockhausen might have been the officer in question. He was the *Feldkommandant* at Užice. He had also a company of the 64th Police Reserve Battalion at his disposal for use against "communist and nationalist" disturbances,[82] and the police company involved in the killing was stationed in Užice.[83]

What were the political consequences of this killing? Živanović's version is borne out by Benzler, who reported that, following the event, Aćimović and his Ministers-Commissioners were "seriously considering resignation."[84] By the end of August political developments in Belgrade had a wider ramification and had reached their critical phase. Benzler notified Berlin on 27 August that,

> The provisionally appointed [*Komissarische*] government is in the process of dissolution.
> ....
> The installation of the new Serbian government body of popular men who are willing to fight communism vigorously encounters difficulties but is nevertheless being attempted. Negotiations are in progress.[85]

From the availble evidence details of the "process of dissolution" are not clear, except that a discordance in timing emerged between the Ljotićites, who were faithfully following the guidance of their leader, and the other commissioners, who acted according to their consciences. Benzler's final telegram from Belgrade, on 29 August, notified Berlin that the MBS called on General Nedić, "who is a known adversary of the Communists," to form a new government. Point three of this telegram reads, in part,

> In order to enhance General Nedić's authority with respect to his colleagues in the Ministry and in the country, he will bear the title Minister President and his collaborators will be designed as Ministers.
> It has been made sure, however, that the de facto new government body will be given no substantive powers exceeding those given to the old provisionally appointed government. . . .[86]

The irony is that, from the historical perspective, the ambush and killing to which the 1st Company of the 64th Police Reserve Battalion overreacted was not a Partisan antifascist accomplishment as claimed by Marjanović. The brutal "deterrent" of the 1/64th which led to the Belgrade crisis was provoked by an act of primitive highway murder and robbery. Boots and socks were stolen from the corpse, and the rifle left.

Whey were there some Serbs who were prepared to work with the Germans? Certainly not for glory without power. Their generation knew the 1915-18 occupation, when Austria-Hungary ruled Serbia without setting up a governmental façade. Was the ethically pure patriotism, which Marjanović would not allow for, a sufficient driving force to make these people in 1941 take a course of action which had no precedent?[87] So many questions, so many answers; only ideologically committed people could be dogmatic here. Perhaps the closest that one can come to a fair answer is that the expression of their patriotism was affected by the prevailing anti-Serbian circumstances. In this context, three elements must be noted. The shock of the sudden collapse of the State, the rise of a Fascist Great Croatia with the correlated persecution of the Serbs there and in the other satellite occupied territories, and the very real concern that Hitler and his Nazi cohorts would cripple the Serbian people for ever. Originally, except for the ideologically committed anti-Communist Ljotić-ites, the anti-Communism of the people accommodating with the Germans was an accident. It was a condition superimposed after 22 June, derived from the concern that the Communists *alias* "Partisans" were doing the job of the Nazis by provoking reprisals, such as the wholesale shooting of people, burning down of villages etc. The Nazis could use this chance also in Serbia to inflict irreparable biological and economic damage, which appeared to be going on everywhere else in occupied Yugoslavia. In the final analysis one has to ask if those who made an accomodation with the German occupation authorities in Serbia, were in their own light motivated by the classic case of the *Salus rei publicae suprema lex*.

CHAPTER 9

SERBIA AT ARMS, THE UPRISING OF 1941: MAIN HISTORICAL ISSUES

The German-Soviet war is seen as the major factor contributing to the uprising in occupied Serbia. Yet was it? Chaos had prevailed in Serbia since the collapse of Yugoslavia, and dissidents escaped into the forests before the German-Soviet war. The best known of them was Colonel Mihailović. The withdrawal of German first-line troops from the Balkans in May-June 1941 reminded the Serbians of a similar German move in September-October 1918, which preceeded the collapse of Imperial Germany. In 1941 however, the German northward trek was followed instead by war on the eastern front. Nevertheless, the Serbians believed that the events of 1918 would repeat themselves and result in a quick collapse of Nazi Germany. Existing unrest readily escalated into an uprising. The provisional Serbian "Commissioner Administration" lost control and the German authorities in Belgrade installed General Nedić as the head of the new Serbian "government."

The early part of this chapter will deal with the aspirations and failures of the German-appointed "Prime Minister of Serbia," General Nedić, as well as with the relevant policies of his German overlords and the inter-relationship between the two parties. The second and longer part of the chapter will study the main features of the anti-Axis resistance endeavours, aims and tactics, both of those of Mihailović and of the Communists. The problems of the German command in occupied Serbia and the solutions found to those problems will be paid due attention. At the same time, and so as to achieve a reliable reconstruction of the whole imbroglio and to discern what was really going on, various historical works will be critically examined in the light of the contemporary documents and in relation to each other.

The first issue to examine is the "case Nedić." As usual in Yugoslav matters, historians tend to substitute opinion for evidentially based conclusions. There are three schools of opinion. Some unreservedly support Nedić's record, but others equate his role with that of Pétain and other with that of Pavelić. Are writers justified in comparing Nedić with Pacelić and his Ustaša regime? What cane be seen from a factual comparison of the two men and their regimes? Two points have to be made. One, as the ideological collaborator of the Axis, Pavelić was instrumental in the political collapse of Yugoslavia in World War II. Nedić has no such record, and he has not even been criticised for his command of a Yugoslav army group in the lost April War. Two, as the head of the Croat State of 1941-45, Pavelić has remained identified with the pogrom of one-fifth of the population of wartime fascist Croatia. The 1941-45 "Nedić's Serbia" has no genocide record. On the contrary, even the Croats who took refuge there were not discriminated against. For instance, Josip Broz, *alias* Tito, a Croat refugee, lived with false papers undisturbed and comfortably in Belgrade, whence he left of his own free will for the Serbian forests and Partisan warfare.

The second school of though compares Nedić with Pétain in France, implying a man who sacrificed himself to save whatever was left of the national wreckage. But this ought to be qualified, and Nedić's submission of 27 August 1941 to the commander in Serbia, *General der Flieger* (Lieutenant General, Air Force) Danckelmann must be assessed. This submission contained Nedić's formal listing of conditions under which he would be prepared to set up his Serbian government. This document supports the proposition that Nedić was expecting to achieve an autonomous status for Serbia akin to that of unoccupied France. At the time of the capitulation, the Yugoslav army was full of rumours about "occupied" and "unoccupied" Yugoslavia. The officers corps—at least its Serb component—was French aligned, and in this crisis, the case of unoccupied France seemed a partial salve to their wounds—not so much a provisional legal solution, but as a remnant of free territory. But here the comparison between Nedić and Pétain should stop. In unoccupied France, fascist elements manipulated the senile Marshal to establish a Nazi-aligned regime. In Serbia, Nedić's Fascist hangers-on, Ljotić and his cohorts, remained a foreign canker on the national body. Armed and employed by the German occupying authorities, they fought both Mihailović and the Communists, and proved themselves a very efficient anti-guerrilla formation.[1] (In fact, after the main body of the Communists was expelled from Serbia at the end of 1941, the Ljotićites, fighting their own civil war, remained Mihailović's main domestic foes in that territory.) Finally, in their respective national legal systems, the constitutional position of Pétain and Nedić was different. Pétain presided over an unoccupied part of France; Nedić did not preside over unoccupied Yugoslavia, but over a *Wehrmacht* constituted *"Serbien."* Consequently, the majority of Serb army officers refused to recognize Nedić's authority.[2]

What did Nedić want? He wrote his submission to Danckelmann on 27 August, two days before he was appointed Serbian "Prime Minister."[3] In the opening paragraph of his submission Nedić specified he would accept the post if the German commander in Serbia agreed with his "work program" (...*unerlaesslichen Arbeitsvoraussetzungen*). He presented his "program" in two parts: "I. General" and "II. Particular." In the first part, Nedić spelled out his views of the competence of the government he would form, *vis.,*

1. Under the supervision of the Military Commander in Serbia, the Serbian government will administer all State and National matters of the Serb people in this territory with respect to upholding the military political and economic interests of the Reich.

In other words, Nedić was after autonomy within the occupation regime. He required the formation and arming of a Serbian Gendarmerie and Auxiliary Troops, which would maintain public order by authority of the Serbian government. All sick POWs, those POWs over 55 years of age, and those needed for the economic reconstruction of Serbia were to be repatriated; and the Serbian government must be permitted to supply the POW camps with food. The economic and administrative conditions of Serbia should be improved by an appropriate increase in the territory of the Commander in Serbia. Persecution of Serbs in occupied, partitioned Yugoslavia, must cease—

5. An effective stop [must be put] to murder, pauperisation and persecution of Serbs in Croatia, Bulgaria and Hungary.

In the second part of his submission, Nedić stipulated that a Serbian Political Council be formed. The next clause, Clause 2, and particularly its sub-clause b), is a critical clause in the context of the German reaction to the uprising in Serbia:

2.a) The fight against Communism is primarily the task of the Serbian people and its government. The *Wehrmacht* will support this action when the means of the Serbian government are insufficient.
2.b) When acts of sabotage against the *Wehrmacht* occur, reprisals must be restricted to the guilty, and in no case may the non-guilty be made to suffer. Therefore the reprisals will be undertaken only after a prompt cross-check (*nach rascher Erholung*) of the relative data with the Serbian government.

It is symptomatic that the unknown Nazi official reading Clause 2.b), drew in its margin a heavy exlamation mark. (This exclamation mark should be viewed against the background of the trials of German war criminals in the wake of the Second World War. A great number of cases consisted of orders for the mass-killing of innocent hostages and other civilians.[4]) Nedić's apologists claim that he asked the commander in Serbia also for "Serbian troops" to serve under the Serbian flag, and for them to take the oath to the émigré-King, Peter II. Although it is a fact that in his governance of Serbia Nedić did maintain monarchical emblems, in his submission of 27 August Nedić exercised circumspection: Clause 3.c) reads only, "Considering that the *Wehrmacht* has set up Serbia, it is necessary to allow the use of State and National emblems." In his conclusion Nedić stressed that his program would allow the mastering of the current difficulties [with the Communists] and ensure the survival of the Serbian people.

His government was formed on 29 August 1941. On 1 September Nedić addressed the Serbian people over the radio for the first time. He concluded his appeal for pacification of the country by saying,

> Today the greatest powers in the world are settling their accounts. In this fight we can neither help not hinder.
>
> Let us not interfere in other peoples' affairs. Whoever meddles in the business of others, burns his fingers.[5]

The "Others" in Nedić's mind were, of course, "England" (Mihailović), and "Russia" (the Communists). About three or four days later, the Provincial Committee for Serbia of the Communist Party of Yugoslavia commented in a pamphlet that,

> The job of the 'government' of Milan Nedić is to create an internal front of fanning the civil war in Serbia and the killing of each other for foreign interests.[6]

Whereas Nedić was a self-confessed, overt anti-communist, his private attitude to the then Colonel Mihailović must be established from German confidential intelligence material. Thus, in a German assessment of Mihailović's organization of 24 October 1941, it is noted,

> General Nedić considers that any action against Mihailović, be it in the press, over the radio or by arms, would remain ineffective (*nicht unternommen werden kann*), as Mihailović is extremely (*allgemein*) popular with the people.

Yet when Boehme was putting Serbia to fire and sword, he wrote on 15 November 1941, that Nedić asked that the rebellious towns (*Ortschaften der Aufstaendischen*) should be bombarded, and that Mihailović's followers should unconditionally capitulate.[7]

What was the attitude of the local German authorities in 1941 to Serbian issues? Their major administrative problems and solutions were reviewed in the previous chapter. Here, their policies will be discussed. Surprisingly, in many instances they followed their own counsel instead of obeying Hitler's directives. The major area of this independence was on the question of how to quell the Serbian uprising. The probelm was the insufficiency of troops in Serbia, and three reactions may be distinguished. The commander in Serbia, and the foreign office (*Auswartiges Amt*) representative in Belgrade (Benzler), sought to overcome the problem by political manoeuvring. Their intent was to involve the Serbians themselves in mastering the uprising and then maintaining public order and the functioning of the economy—hence the Nedić experiment. To boost Nedić's prestige in the country, he was designated the Serbian Prime Minister. Viewed from Berlin however, there were inherent risks in this experiment, and Ribbentrop wrote to Benzler on 2 September:

> If the new government has the inner strength expected of it for crushing the communist forces, it is to be expected and feared that it will afterwards use this strength to make troublesome demands of one sort or another of the Reich government. Please therefore watch this jointly with the Military Commander, and prevent the new government from turning against Germany in its mental attitude and conduct. We must retain the possibility at all times of imposing the necessary limits on the new government or of recalling it.[8]

Such a quandry is, of course, a perennial problem of any power occupying a foreign country. Hence its general interest, which transcends the present discussion. In this instance, even the advocates of more power to a local Serbian government were conscious of Ribbentrop's admonishment, and never elaborated a persistent policy of how much arms and auxiliary troops Nedić should be allowed. Superimposed over it all was Hitler's resolve that the insufficiency of troops in Serbia should be made up for by the application of terror and mass-killing of hostages and other civilians. Hitler's primitivism in this matter was supported by his sycophantic assistants in the senior hierarchy. The command in Serbia was finally brought in line on 16 September 1941. On this day Hitler charged the commander in the South-East, Field Marshal List, with the supression of the "insurgent movement," with a view to

> securing in the Serbian area the traffic arteries and objects which are important in the entire area on a long term basis *by the application of the most severe means.*[9]

Hitler's chief of armed forces, Keitel, on the same day elaborated on the meaning of the "most severe" means.[10] The *"severest means,"* said Keitel, should be employed so as to "break down this movement in the shortest time possible":

> Only in this manner, which has always been applied successfully in the history of the extension of power of great peoples, can quiet by restored.

Then he ordered that,

> Each incident of insurrection against the German armed forces, regardless of individual circumstances, must be assumed to be of Communist origin.

(This, of course, affects the reliability of sources regarding the situation in 1941 Serbia. While it is positive the victims of reprisals were Serbs, there is no record that they were first interrogated as to their political convictions.) Keitel went on that there a human life "frequently counts for naught," and "a deterring effect can only be achieved by unusual severity," so that

> the death penalty for 50 to 100 Communists must in general be deemed appropriate as retaliation for the life of a German soldier.

But Keitel was still not satisfied. So he added, "The manner of execution must increase the deterrent effect." (It took Hitler's minions three more years of warfare until they realized that violence breeds violence, and so changed their manula of anti-guerrilla warfare in 1944.)

The man sent to Serbia to take over from Danckelmann and quell the uprising was *General der Infanterie* (Lieutenant General, Infantry) Boehme. He was appointed *Plenipotentiary* Commanding General in Serbia, so that he was both field and territorial commander. This made Danckelmann's post of the "Commanding General in Serbia" superfluous. Boehme proceeded in line with Hitler's and Keitel's *Weltanschauung.* One of his orders regulated reprisals for losses incurred from insurgents. Boehme's solution was to order mass-killings and the destruction of property.[11] His order read, *inter alia,*

the territorially competent commanders up to the regimental commanders are to decree the shooting...
   a. For each killed or murdered German soldier or ethnic German, (man woman, or child) 100 prisoners or hostages;
   b. For each wounded German soldier or ethnic German, 50 prisoners or hostages.
The shootings are to be carried out by the troops....

The troops had daily to report all such instances, including the information "whether and to what extent the reprisal measure is carried out or when this will be furnished." He added,

Localities which have to be taken in combat are to be burned down, as well as farms from which troops were shot at.

This was not the first time that the killing of Serbs in the ratio of 1:100 was ordered. Von Weichs, commanding the 2nd German Army in the campaign of April 1941, on 28 April ordered that in reprisal for German losses "100 Serbs are to be shot, without consideration, for every German soldier who comes to harm."[12] Boehme dispensed with Keitel's qualification that only the "Communists" should be shot. He extended the application of reprisals as well, from a means of protecting his own soldiers, to avenging the *Volksdeutsche* civilians also ("... German soldiers or ethnic Germans"). The latter innovation was definitely not derived from the more-or-less applied or misapplied customs of war on land. *Inter alia,* Boehme's attitude compromised also the respect the German army had won for its chivalry in Serbia in 1915. On his posting to the Serbian front in 1915, Field Marshal von Mackensen had issued his troops the following order which is repeatedly cited in Serbian historiography:

...You are leaving for battle against a new enemy, dangerous, stubborn, brave and tough. You are going to the Serbian front and against Serbia. The Serbs are a people who cherish liberty, and fight and sacrifice themselves to the last man. Take care that this little enemy does not eclipse your glory and does not tarnish the successes that the glorious German army has achieved.

Mackensen's troops responded to this positive coaching. Consequently, until the Nazis came, both the Serb military and the civilian held a grudging respect for the German soldier. Now, in 1941, Mackensen's linear descendant on the Serbian front, Boehme, issued the following order of the day:[13]

> Your mission lies in carrying out reconnaissance of the country in which German blood flowed in 1914 [sic], through the treachery of the Serbs, men and women.
> You are the avengers of these dead. An intimidating example must be created for the whole of Serbia which must hit the whole population most savagely.

And then came Boehme's punchline:

> Everyone who wishes to live charitably sins against the lives of his comrades. He will be called to account without regard for his person and placed before a court martial.

This sounds familiar. It is. In its concept and intent, if not in its wording, this negative exhortation is identical to the order of that Austro-Hungarian army corps in 1914, that in Serbia "all humanity and kindness of heart are out of place."

To the credit of the German name, however, many occupation administrators in Serbia were against this savagery in 1941. The commander in Serbia (Danckelmann), and the diplomatic agent (Benzler), have been mentioned. Danckelmann's chief of staff, Colonel Kewisch should be added. He believed one should try to "win the cooperation of larger circles of the Serbian population."[14] Lieutenant General Foertsch should not be omitted. In 1941 he was a Colonel and chief of staff to Field Marshal List in Athens, after the war he was acquitted of war crimes by the Military Tribunal in Nurenberg; his and Boehme's boss, List, was sentenced to life imprisonment. Boehme also was brought to the court at Nurenberg. Left now without the supporting scaffolding of military accoutrements, this erstwhile martinent suicided in his cell after the indictment was read.[15]

Yet when he was in power, Boehme hardly distinguished between the guilty and the innocent. On occasions his orders caused resentment among his own commanders and sometimes became political issues. As the

Plenipotentiary Commander in Serbia, Boehme was also in charge of the Higher Command LXV, which had the 718th Infantry Division posted in Croatia. The uprising of the Serbs was spreading there, and Boehme exercised his last "Hooray." Although Bader of the LXVth was appointed his successor on 4 December 1941, on 8 December Boehme ordered the 718th Division to "shoot 650 hostages" to avenge the "soldiers of his Division recently killed and wounded in fighting the Četniks." *Generalmajor* (Brigadier General) Foertner of the 718th immediately rang the German General in Zagreb, Glaise von Horstenau, to consult with him.[16]

> 'These hostages,' said Foertner, 'are to be shot . . . near Sarajevo. (Boehme's command) would supply the hostages from concentration camps at Šabac and Niš, that is, from old Serbia, and transport them to Sarajevo by train.'

Foertner was required to execute this order by 15 December; instead, he agreed with Brigadier General Glaise von Horstenau to ask Boehme for a postponment. Glaise followed up Foertner's telephone call by writing immediately to the German minister in Zagreb. His arguments deserve to be cited fully. He wrote,

> . . . I would strongly advise against the manner in which this mass-action is planned. One need not change one's opinion about the ethic and the real necessity for shooting hostages, but, in the present instance this issue is turned into ridicule (*"Groteske"*), as the hostages are to be provided from the territory of another state. Undeniably, there are many connections between the uprisings in Serbia and Croatia, yet malevolent critics could see in providing hostages from Serbia for revenge in Croatia, a sign of recognition of the continuing existence of the Yugoslav State. However, regardless of this secondary observation, one can visualize the impression on the inhabitants of Sarajevo, if the German soldiers were to proceed to shooting this mass of people there, who not only had nothing to do with the misdeed, but—at least in the light of the Fuehrer's provisional arrangements—have not even the slightest connection with the land in which the misdeeds occurred which require shooting of hostages.

He went on to suggest that, in Bosnia, the shooting of hostages should be done by the Croat authorities. Otherwise, he said, if the *Wehrmacht* was to continue doing it, "this could be easily interpreted as a *post-factum* approval (*als nachtraegliche Zustimmung*) of the Ustaša raging fury by the German armed forces." The implication is obvious: the Serbs in Croatia had rebelled because of the Ustaša "fury" against them. Concerned to spare "German blood," Glaise enquired if it were not better to "abandon Croatia to the Italians." In historical works one comes intermittently across statements that Glaise suggested abandoning Croatia to Italy, yet nowhere has it been stated how this came about. This is now explained. Eventually, on 30 December 1941, Glaise notified the Commander South-East and the German minister in Zagreb that the OKW had overruled this suggestion.[17]

A year after Boehme put Serbia to fire and sword, Nedić sent to the Plenipotentiary Commanding General in Serbia, Bader, a long memorandum critical of the regime introduced in Serbia.[18] The gravamen of his complaint was that on the occasion of forming his government, the then Commander in Serbia, Danckelmann, promised his autonomy in the discharging of governmental responsibilities. At that time "reigned chaos and total lawlessness" in Serbia. He pacified the country, said Nedić; his government achieved this despite insufficient armed auxiliaries, and despite the adverse psychological conditions caused by the influx of 400,000 refugees escaping from mass murder in Croatia. Since the Communist uprising had been quelled, his government had successfully rehabilitated the country and "led the Serbian people on the proper way of collaborating with the Great German Reich," so as to ensure a better future [!]. When "London and Moscow" exhorted the Serbians not to till the land, saying the whole harvest would be taken away to Germany, he obtained a promise from the German authorities that all the food would be left in Serbia (. . . "for consumption by the people and the occupation troops"). Yet despite all these successes the freedom of action of the government was daily being eroded. After all this, when the government thought it had won the confidence of the German occupation authorities, Bulgarian troops were brought in to occupy the heart of Serbia, the districts of Niš, Leskovac, Kruševac, Jagodina and Kragujevac. Now the German authorities ordered the German and Bulgarian troops to requisition food from the population.

This order caused a real panic and brought about such excitement, that one has to fear the worst—such as fleeing into forests, disturbances and similar.

There is no question anymore, said Nedić, that the Serbian government has any autonomy in governing the country, especially since the SS took over.

By this point one would expect to hear of Nedić's resignation. But no: his letter went on for three more pages, to finish in a wimper on the fourth —if these things were to be remedied, Nedić's government would remain in office. It is obvious that, although resignation is implied, there was no formal threat proferred of resignation "now." Herein lies the Nedić enigma: although reduced to a German plaything, he endured it. Why? His apologists maintain that he was blackmailed by the Nazis. Politically, Nedić continues to be remembered chiefly as the man who resolutely came out against the uprising of 1941.

In English-language writings about the uprising, the one work which stands out because it lists its sources, is Phyllis Auty's *Tito*. Her chapter 10 deals with Tito's role in the uprising. Early on, by way of explaining Tito's preoccupation from April to June 1941, Auty cites Zilliacus[19] that Tito was confident the "war had given him an opportunity to lead a communist revolution in Yugoslavia." Zilliacus and Auty are probably using this argument to illustrate that Tito was impatiently awaiting the chance to start a national war of liberation. But he was not impatient to start such a war. As we have shown in chapter seven, Tito was intent to organise the Communist takeover. He counted on Stalin to take care of liberation. Be this as it may, Tito's release from the constraints of the Nazi-Soviet pact of 1939 came on 22 June 1941, although at first he only marked time. It was only the sharp reprimand from Moscow that made him call for an uprising on the 4th of July.

Meanwhile an incident occurred confirming the image of the punctilious German bureaucrat. For the duration of the Nazi-Soviet pact, the German authorities in Serbia did not interfere with the local Communists. It was only after the actual outbreak of war on the eastern front that the German bureaucracy changed its tack. On that day, 22 June, Dr. Turner, the head of the civilian administration under the military commander in Serbia, acted. He wrote to Aćimović, Serbian Commissioner of the Interior, requiring that leading local Communists be arrested on the night of

22/23 June.[20] But the news of the war had been broadcast on the morning of the 22nd, so that, by the nightfall of 22/23 the proverbial horse had bolted before the door was locked.

Auty maintains that the proclamation of 4 July "achieved a major effect in Serbia and Montenegro where conditions were conducive to revolt." Unless Auty has additoinal reliable sources to prove her point, which she has not revealed in her notes, it is hard to construe any connection between the proclamation of 4 July in Belgrade, and the uprising of 13 July in Montenegro. Djilas, who was the party's delegate in Montenegro, does not mention it; he even admits that the party leadership was surprised when the insurrection errupted.[21] As to the impact of the proclamation of 4 July on developments in Serbia, Auty's summary must be qualified. The first remark is a reminder: it has been shown that the situation in Serbia was chaotic, independently of and before the 22nd of June. Life was insecure in the countryside. The escapes into forests, which were on the increase, were a visible symptom of the prevalent malaise. This can be further illustrated from the war diary of the German commander in Serbia. Numerous entries for May and June referred to growing sabotage especially of telephone lines.[22] This surge of activities should be related to the withdrawal of German frontline troops from Serbia.

Another interesting entry is a Croat War Department note of 23 June to the German HQ in Belgrade that a Croat, [formerly a Yugoslav] NCO, after release from POW captivity in Bulgaria, encountered Serb Četniks on his return through Serbia on 16 May.[23] The NCO reported that:

> Their leader was General Staff Colonel Draža Mihailović. The others were Major Paloševič, Captain (Cavalry) Reljić, Captain (Gendarmerie) Uzelac, Lieutenants Ilić and Ratko Martinović, and a number of other ranks and soldiers from different arms of service. The Liaison officer of this group was Major (Reserve Corps) Aleksandar Mišić, son of the late Field Marshal Mišić.

This information was correct; however, as Mihailović is said to have come to Ravna Gora mountain plateau on or about the 11 May, one may surmise that the Croat NCO must have spent at least a week or two there: Mišić was not in Mihailović's original group, and was contacted later. The un-named NCO supplied also the location of the Četniks, and added that the teachers in that area, local mayors, and the commander of the Gendarmerie Detachment at Gornji Milanovac were acquainted with it. This complementary information by the denouncing NCO confirms that he must have spent a short while with Mihailović: the latter did not liaise with all those people immediately. But it also shows that the NCO, although a Croat, was shown no animosity at Mihailović's HQ, but was free in his movements. German efficiency was not evident in this case: German authorities disregarded this report. The one conceivable reason for this is that the informer was not a German soldier, and he was of lowly rank. Yet at the same time the German military and police authorities continued with their own investigations to discover the leadership and organization of the military Četniks. They exercised constant vigilance so as not to be surprised by an attack from the very same quarters. The *Wehrmacht* had enough to worry about. In a rumour entered in the war diary of 7 June 1941,[24] it was said that two armed and well supplied Četnik regiments were in the hills and forests around Gornji Milanovac.

Therefore it is obvious that when the Communist Party entered the lists, they were not faced with the problem of first overcoming the apathy of the Serbian population. After the urban communists escaped from the cities to avoid the arrests of 22 June, they joined their rural comrades and staged red terror in the countryside. Their attacks were not directed against the enemy-German (or "Fascist") Forces, but against the "class enemy." Indeed, in a report of the Operations Department (Ia) of the German commander in Serbia, dated 2 August 1941, it is specified that *the first attack on the deutsche Wehrmacht* occurred only on 18 July.[25] The question is, can this claim be substantiated by independent testimony? As it happens, the corroborating statement is contained in the chief Partisan history of events in 1941 Serbia. Its author, Jovan Marjanović, has also compiled a list of the purported Partisan "*Akcija.*" For the period 1 July to the 18th, his list contains 49 entries. The fiftieth entry (under "18 July at 16.30 hours) mentions the Lontscha incident[26] and so bears out the German contention. Before this entry, 12 instances of cutting telephone wires and cables are listed (which is nothing new, and therefore not necessarily a Partisan endeavour). What is "new" is that 13 attacks were made on the Serbian Gendarmerie posts and individual Gendarmes. A further six attacks were made on private property and persons. These activities were accompanied by continuing with peacetime propaganda against the "agents of London," who were "preventing the workers and peasants from establishing a Soviet aligned workers' and peasants' government."[27] To compound the trouble caused by the red terror, the Nazi-directed killing machine proceeded to shoot people in reprisals, although —as it is seen—Partisan action was not yet directed against German power.[28]

At about the same time as the Lontscha incident, that is, in mid-July, the Communist Party toned down its naked class war and abandoned the anti-Allies slogans. Karchmar, the only western historian beside Avakumović, who researched in depth the events in 1941 Serbia, conjectures that in mid-July Moscow reminded the Yugoslav party that "'London' was now a Soviet ally," and

> the United Front, not exclusion and subversion of the non-Communists, was to be the watchword of the resistance.[29]

"As part of the new policy," says Karchmar, the party now endeavoured to get in touch with the [military] Četniks of Mihailović. It may be added that, if the party received new instructions from Moscow, it would have been a reprimand repeating the orders given on 22 June. In the Comintern's instruction of that date to Tito, it was spelled out *inter alia* that it was "vitally necessary" to

> develop a movement under the slogan of a united national front and the earlier united international front of struggle against the German and Italian fascist brigands, for the protection of the peoples subjugated by fascism.[30]

In other words, Tito was ordered to launch a wartime *Front populaire* and not an overt "Socialist revolution." He was not supposed to launch an open class war under the occupation. Obviously, due to the worsening military situation, at this stage of the war Moscow exercised restraint in order not to provoke a political disagreement with London. Consequently, in Serbia nationalist slogans were superimposed on Stalinist clichés. This, then marks the turning point which enabled the party successfully to recruit the responsive peasant masses. Considering that pro-Partisan historiography treats Tito as an oracle, an independent researcher finds it hard to determine if the adaptation of the Comintern's order was Tito's or someone elses brainchild. Was it Tito who deserved credit for it, or, rather, Žujović "Crni" ("The Black", "Swarthy"), who in 1941 was the head of the party's military committee in Serbia? As a Serb, he would have known how to approach the Serbian peasant.

In any case, only after this volte-face occurred, is it possible to accept Auty's commentary that, by the end of July "there were so many Partisans in Serbia" that the German command began to realize it had to deal "with a general resistance movement."[31] Indeed, it was this that eventually compelled the German authorities in August to call on Nedić for help. There is a contemporary German Intelligence ("Ic") assessment, which deserves an historian's attention. It is a document dictated by *Rittmeister* (Captain, Cavalry) Picht, and titled "Report of activities of the Department Ic [of the Commander in Serbia] for the period July, including the end of June 1941." Written sometime in early August 1941,[32] it argues that, beside the communist propaganda, the following circumstances have contributed to the uprising,

> (German) reprisals, which have often hit the innocent, and the shock caused by the expulsion of the Serbs from the neighbouring countries into Serbia. The expulsions were particularly brutal (*Brutalitaet*) from Croatia.

This is followed by the statement, "And a temporary lack of bread in Serbia, which has not yet been fully overcome, worsens the situation." The report goes on to say that, as the persecutions and killings in Croatia "occur under the eyes of German soldiers," [in Serbia] this has adversely affected the standing of the German army. It is clear that this report is full of information which allows valid historical lessons to be drawn. There is the lesson of the boomerang effect of indiscriminate reprisals in an occupied country (in this instance, deliberate Nazi policy). Another is the impact which the influx of destitute and desperate refugees into Serbia had on developments there. The German authorities in Belgrade were aware of this and asked that the flow of Serb refugees be brought to an end. It was the destitute young among these refugees created by the Ustaša pogroms who responded to Partisan propaganda. In Serbia itself, by provoking German reprisals, the Communists created a local destitute class which provided them with Partisans—proof of the maxim: Whose house doth burn, must soldier turn.

The new orientation of Communist propaganda may be obtained from a German assessment of the "political situation in Serbia" of 23 July 1941. It noted that the people were told Stalin had reverted to the Orthodox Church and was praying for the great Slavic victory.[33] Another propaganda line was that Stalin had betrothed his daughter Svetlana to the exiled King Peter II of Yugoslavia.[34] On the other hand, the reason for the miserable failure of the Nazi anti-communist propaganda in Serbia offers further insights. The same document which related the myth of Stalin in communist propaganda, makes the following admission: "German radio propaganda remained totally ineffective. Descriptions of Russian bestialities, such as at Lvov, are dismissed [in Serbia] with the remark that the Croat terror over Serbs is their foremost concern...."[35]

After their first approaches to army Četniks, the party leadership insisted that an agreement must be reached with Mihailović. They wanted the agreement just with Mihailović. Why? This becomes clear from an internal party document of 20 August. After saying the interest of the Soviet Union required that the uprising in Serbia become widespread, the following injunction is made: "It is necessary to endeavour to obtain the agreement of Draža Mihailović and the men around him for a joint démarche. *It is extremely important* that his signature be appended also."[36] This injunction reveals that at this stage the party was still the underdog, and Mihailović was the most popular leader of the resistance. For the same reason, until the outbreak of the civil war later in the year, the Partisans always correctly titled Mihailović the Commander of the Yugoslav Army's "Military Četnik" Detachments. It was only after the civil war that these units became labelled "Draža's Četniks" and/or simply "Četniks." This led intentionally to the historiographic confusion about "which" Četniks are meant: the army's anti-German ones (Mihailović), or the collaborationist civilians (Pećanac). But there is also another side of the picture. In the field, the maze of different "Četniks" bewildered the overworked German command. Boehme's Chief of Staff, Colonel Pemsel, attempted to sort out this entanglement on 3 November 1941, by requiring rigid differentiation between the "loyal" and the "enemy" Četniks.[37]

The story of Mihailović's relationship with Tito in 1941 is treated in the same manner as Tito crossing frontiers with false passports. The reader is distracted into trivia (e.g., at a meeting "Mihailović plucked at his beard"), and the importnat issues are passed over. Such a methodology

Serbia in Arms

leads nowhere as no issue can be brought to its logical conclusion. Instead, the basic problem must be spelled out. In this instance, the historiographical problem parallels that of the field problems between Tito and Mihailović. The former wanted to reduce Mihailović to a military technician on the Partisan HQ (the role later given to Royal Captains Velimir Terzić and Arso Jovanović). Mihailović simply could not comprehend that anybody could entertain the idea of replacing the army by a foreign controlled political party's militia. He expected Tito dutifully to accept his command as a Yugoslav citizen. No argument could sway either Tito or Mihailović, neither can any amount of argument sway committed historians and readers one way or the other. What really happened in the field and the British response are studied here in chapters dealing with the intervention of the Special Operations Executive or the SOE and Captain Hudson.

The last point to discuss is the numerical strength of Serbian Partisans as compared with that of the Army Četniks. This is a beloved ploy of committed writers. Caution is necessary and reasons will shortly be obvious. Firstly, neither Mihailović nor Tito kept a roll-call of men or a daily record of supply requisitions. Secondly, Mihailović's and Tito's approaches to manpower were different. Mihailović was guided by the military principle of keeping under arms only the necessary minimum. The other men were relegated to the army reserve and directed to stay at home and till the land: they would be called up when required. By contrast, Tito followed the revolutionary practice of keeping all followers constantly afoot. Therefore any general numerical comparison of their respective mobile strengths is out of the question. And, thirdly, men kept crossing from one organization into the other as the two leaders had concluded a formal agreement allowing this practice. All this makes nonsense of any pretentions to speak in numbers. All one can do is to make approximations, and the statements of two contemporary figures will do. The first witness is Tito. In one of his early conversations with Fitzroy Maclean in 1944, Tito recalled his meeting Mihailović "near Užice" [at Brajići, in October 1941].

> In those days, (Tito) said, the Cetniks had the advantage. Now [in 1944] the Partisans were the stronger and it would be for them to impose their terms.[38]

The other witness is Djilas. When Djilas returned to Serbia from Montenegro and rejoined Tito either in later October or early November 1941, he found that the Četniks had "achieved a numerical preponderance."[39] As these admissions cut across the entrenched historiography, which claims otherwise, an interesting question can be put. Who should be believed? The two foremost Communist and Partisan leaders, Tito and Djilas, talking about their own observations, or the secondary writers who, after the event, embroider the experiences of the very same witnesses?

Case studies, such as the ordinary man's experiences in guerrilla fighting, throw further light on this issue. A good example for such a study is the case of Gornji Milanovac, a town in Western Serbia. The guerrilla actin here contained all the elements of a drama and a variety of sources: softening up of the German garrison, combined Četnik-Partisan attack on 28-29 September 1941, conflicting claims as to who captured the German garrison, the chance of verifying historical writings in the light of the enemy's intelligence records, and the testimony of an independent witness. The attack on Gornji Milanovac was one of the most successful guerrilla operations in 1941. It occurred at a time when "everywhere in Serbia there was vigorous insurgent activity."[40] The *Wehrmacht* garrison was the 6th Company of the 920 *Landesschuetzen* Battalion, which came there from Niš in mid-July 1941. The men expected nothing worse than the boredom of guarding the ammunition-booty in the former Yugoslav barracks there.[41] However, any complacency that they might have entertained as to their welcome by the Serbian population was soon to be shattered. The turning point affecting the further fate of the garrison occurred in mid-August, when the garrison was weakened by the departure of the additional 50 men from another unit and the first attack on a patrol of three men occurred.[42] From a report by the Captain commanding the 6th/920 of 3 September, it can be seen that the Company now suffered constant attacks. The nearest German troops were 25km to the south, and the Captain requested immediate reinforcement. Reinforcements were refused.[43] Five days later, the 6th/920 renewed its request for help by a telegram which took three days to reach the HQ in Belgrade: the telegram was sent on 8 September, and received by the HQ/Ia only on 11 September.[44] A Major Weyhe, commanding the *Feldkommandantur* 610 also intervened; his telephoned message to the HQ in Belgrade is entered in the operations war diary (Ia) as follows:

The [6th] Company is besieged by the insurgents (*"Banditen"*) and was compelled to vacate the previous accommodation [in the Artillery Barracks] and withdraw to the centre of the town. The [920] Battalion is requesting that the road be opened and secured [so that the 6th Company] may leave either for Kragujevac or for Čačak. There is the danger that, in case of a massive attack by the insurgents, the Company would be overwhelmed. . . . [45]

A search of German documents shows overwork and impotence to be another effect on German staff officers of the contemporary sabotage and guerrilla action. In the operations section (Ia) of the Commander in Serbia, the case of the 6th/920 was handled by a Lieutenant-Colonel Kogard. He planned to use an infantry battalion to extricate the *Landesschuetzen* company, but could not do it as the insurgents had seriously damaged all roads and also dug anti-tank trenches. The only reminder of this abortive operation is a great number of handwritten notes and a chain of neatly typed, impotent operation orders. Eventually *Herr General* Bader, commanding the LXV Higher Command, intervened personally. On 26 September at 21.15 hours he telephoned the Operations (Ia) of the Commander in Serbia and instructed that a battalion from Čačak should extricate the Gornji Milanovac garrison. His directive was dutifully elaborated in the appropriate orders, but the situation had already deteriorated for the Germans so much that the orders had to be dropped by aeroplane.[46] The only result of Bader's personal intervention was a bureaucratic one: the first four ensuing documents were signed personally by his chief of staff, Gravenhorst,[47] and then Kogard took over again.

Finally, local Četnik and Partisan commanders agreed to attack during the night of 28-29 September 1941. The Takovo Četnik Detachment was commanded by Lieutenant Zvonimir (Zvonko) Vučković, formerly of the Royal Guards Artillery Regiment, an the Takovo Partisan Detachment was commanded by Branko Rakić, a teacher, and his political commissar Bogdan Oklobdžija. The Četniks were attacking from the north-west, along the Takovo highway, and the Partisans from the south, from the plain "Ržanik." The attack started on Monday 29 September at 3 a.m. Vučković's first target was the tavern outside the town, housing the German guard.[48] He and his soldiers crawled at first along the shoulders of the highway, and then past some low bushes and the first houses on the outskirts of the town. At the moment when two of his soldiers felled the unsuspecting German sentry, Vučković and a few others ran to the door of the tavern. With his finger on the trigger of his carbine, says Vućković, he and his soldiers now burst into the tavern, fully set to fall on the enemy. Instead, he tripped over a bench. The bench fell with a bang. That was all. No enemy was to be seen around. To make matters worse, several doors led to the other parts of the house. Where to now? The publican, a woman intervened. Spontaneously, to help her own side, she pointed to one of the doors. Vućković kicked it, yelled *"Haende hoch!,"* and was confronted with the following scene:

> Three soldiers had already jumped out of the bed. They were keeping up their longjohns with one hand, and with the other they tried to get hold of the rifles hung above their beds. When Vućković materialized, they froze. The others jumped out of bed and stood at attention. Shaking with fright they mumbled something, the loudest one saying *"Ich bin Oesterreicher"* ("I am an Austrian"). He must have thought the Germans would be killed.

A Četnik soldier, Ljubiša Milenković, in civilian life a Serbian peasant small-landowner from the village of Mojsinje, disarmed the enemy soldiers. Their first task accomplished, the Četnik Detachment proceeded to close upon the bulk of the enemy.

Unfortunately there are no personal experiences extant by Partisan fighters in this engagement. Yugoslav sources are preoccupied with politics. In this instance they argue that, although "60 Četniks" participated in this operation, it was the Partisans who defeated the German garrison. Nevertheless on one point both the Partisan and the Četnik sources are in agreement: on 29 September 1941 the captured German garrison was taken away by the Četniks. This was the first time ever that a whole *Wehrmacht* Company surrendered to a guerrilla unit. They were taken to the POW camp at Planinica, close to Mihailović's HQ; the camp commander was Lieutenant Stanoje Letica. As Avakumović points out, this was "the first POW camp in the history of any resistance movement against Hitler."[49] Captain Maurice Vitou of the British Army, an escaped German POW, and another escapee, an Australian Lieutenant, happened to be at Mihailović's HQ at the time, which, says Vitou, they were "amazed" to find really well organized.

Near the H.Q. was a camp for about 200 German prisoners—prisoners of war in their own territory. They were treated in accordance with the Geneva convention relating to prisoners of war....[50]

The German command in Serbia established a special file to investigate the case of the 6th/920. This file also contains the records of interrogation of those German NCO's who escaped from the POW camp at Planinica.[51] The summing up of the interrogating officer, *Rittmeister* Prince von Holstein, bears out Vitou's commentary. Holstein reported:

> The insurgents... designate themselves as the free, national Serbian Army, whose only aim is to expel the Germans. They consider themselves soldiers and abide by the laws of war, and their treatment of prisoners of war is particularly correct.

A German witness, *Unteroffizier* Egger, one of those who escaped from Planinica, described to Price Holstein how he became captured:

> Then came a Četnik *parlementaire* and aksed that we surrender our arms.... The Company Commander refused it, and the battle continued for about half an hour. The *parlementaire* then came again, and offered that the company may, under arms and a Četnik escort, freely withdraw to the West. The fire now ceased. The Četniks often came out in the open and stood about in the street. There were about six hundred men, all armed.
> ....
> When we started on our march, ahead of the Company, around us, and behind us, marched numerous Četniks.

Egger saw no Partisans, that is, fighers with a Red Star as a badge. Following another escaped *Unteroffizier,* Dirnberger, the Company surrendered only after the third assault (*"Sturmangriff"*) by the insurgents.

After the German *Wehrmacht* company was marched out of the town into the open, "a Četnik officer" [Vučković] ordered the Company to halt and surrender arms; finding himself in a hopeless situation, its commander, *Hauptmann* Zerlacher, complied.[52] (The moral of the story is, when negotiating a surrender, do not assume anything: Zerlacher should have negotiated his return to German lines, and not just a safe passage "to the West," out of the town—which he was given). Thereupon the officers and men of the 6th/920 were declared prisoners of war. At that time, Mihailović's officers had standing orders to allow the Partisans a half of their booty and prisoners of war. On this occasion, Vučković complied only partly. He allowed the Partisans a half of the booty, but refused to "divide" the prisoners of war with the Partisans. It is interesting to note that Partisan historiography claims that it was the Partisans who had passed on the POWs to the Četnik, after the *Wehrmacht* soldiers had first surrendered their arms to the Partisans.[53] But surely, a soldier knows who captured him, and how. The German investigating officer, Holstein, bluntly states in his report that the Commander of the 6th/920 "personally supervised that each soldier surrender his arms to the Četniks."[54] That morning must have presented a motley picture on the western outskirts of Gornji Milanovac. In the midst of their part of occupied Europe, there was the regimental *Feldgrau* of German POWs, surrounded by armed men in a combination of Serbian peasant and military wear. Vučković himself wore the peasant garb and the hand-knitten embroidered peasant socks of heavy wool; his only insignia was an artillery officer's badge on his headgear. While Vučković was engaged in supervising the marshalling of his POWs, suddenly Captain Derok appeared. He was dressed in dark blue "ski" trousers, officer's blouse and the artillery officer's badge on his forage cap (*"šajkača"*). Vučković had met him for the first time nine years ago in the "Prince Tomislav" Artillery Regiment in Zagreb. They had met last in Herceg Novi on the sea coast, after the capitulation. Derok was the man who on that occasion took it upon himself to organize the officers who sheltered there to escape surrender (this has been related in chapter three). Vučković was elated by his arrival. "As a token of my respect," Vučković wrote in his papers, "I presented him there and then with the pistol of the surrendered German Company Commander." Sergeant Krsta Kljajić then took the POWs to Planinica camp, and Derok returned to Mihailović's HQ. Only the day after, when he was ordered to join Derok, who was on his way to coordinate the attack on Čačak, did Vučković learn that Derok was Mihailović's delegate in that region.[55]

Vučković's engagement at Gornji Milanovac occurred in the period of cooperation between Mihailović and Tito. Prior to this, Mihailović persisted in his refusal to join in the uprising. This raises the question "why?" Considering that Mihailović was a regular officer, the answer must be looked for in his military background. In the military view, an organized uprising—as distinct from a spontaneous movement by the masses—must make politico-military sense. As an academic proposition, in the political case of "grand strategy" in a wartime alliance, an uprising might be necessary as a diversion to improve the overall strategic position of the allies. On a national level, an uprising is justified only in conjunction with an existing national or allied front, or in conjunction with a forthcoming national or allied landing. Even in the latter case this issue is not clear cut: for instance, in the liberating invasion of Europe in 1944, the French, Belgian and Dutch *populations* were officially enjoined *not* to rise, although the 'resistance' was active. Mihailović's long-range planning was based on the likelihood of a British landing in the Balkans, and he did not expect this so soon after the collapse of Yugoslavia and the British retreat from Greece. Consequently, in his view an early uprising in Serbia was not justified. In opposition to Mihailović, the local Communists preferred a Soviet alliance to that of the British. They also ardently believed that the arrival of their Russian brothers was imminent. The KPJ proceeded with the uprising, but the "Russians" did not come. The *Wehrmacht* put down the uprising, and exacted 34,900 Serbian lives for the wounding of 378 and killing of 160 German soldiers.[56] But to obtain a grand total of losses in Serbian lives in the uprising of 1941, to these military statistics should be added the thousands of civilians arrested, tortured and executed by the Nazi political and police agencies in occupied Serbia. In the Serbian context, the uprising misfired.

This leaves the political argument open: if the 1941 uprising did not help Serbia to achieve its liberation, was it at least successful as a diversion in helping the Soviet Union? How many German divisions had to be withdrawn from the Eastern Front and sent to Serbia? The existing documentation shows only one division, the *113. Infanterie Division* from Ukraina was so re-directed. But it does not seem that the Division was withdrawn from the front line. Its commander, Lieutenant General Friedrich Zickwolff, warned his troops that it was not going to be so peaceful in Serbia as where they were on the eastern front: *"So friedlich wie im Raum von Shitomir wird es nicht sein."*[57] It is clear that, in return for over 34,900 Serbian lives, the effective help of the Communist Party of Yugoslavia to the Soviet cause was nil.

Nevertheless, let us ask if Mihailović's assessment of the situation in 1941 corresponded to that of the British planners? It did. Two British actions make this quite clear. Firstly, when the first British Liaison Officer (BLO), Captain Hudson, arrived in Serbia in 1941, he brought the message that the Serbs should fight for their own aims, and not for any foreign power. And secondly, even when the uprising in Serbia was in full swing, the British Chiefs of Staff considered the uprising still to be "premature" on 15 October.[58] It is as well to recall that "to fight the enemy" and "to raise an uprising" are not synonymous actions. To be at war does not mean actually to fight twenty-four hours a day for five consecutive years. In this sense, Mihailović did continue to "fight the war," and his only military miscalculation occurred in the (northern) autumn of 1941. The *Wehrmacht* was then withdrawing its garrisons from West Serbia, Mihailović thought the "favourable" time for uprising had arrived,[59] and he joined in. But the Germans did not vacate Serbia: they only re-grouped their forces, and then struck back.

If Mihailović considered an early uprising in Serbia premature, was he engaged in active fighting anywhere else at the same time in 1941? If he was, what was his motivation and policy? To reach an answer, one has to proceed from the situation in Serbia. There, to the east of the river Drina, after the initial hangings and shooting, the *Wehrmacht* had settled down and the countryside was left to its own devices. West of the Drina however, in East Bosnia and Hercegovina, the genocide of the Serbs by the Ustaša was in full swing. This made Mihailović give priority to protecting the Serbs west of the Drina, while in Serbia intelligent sabotage was to go on. Using Serbia as his base, Mihailović posted his officers and troops to East Bosnia. Steady crossing of the Drina by Četniks going from Serbia into Bosnia are referred to in reports of German authorities in Serbia. Reports of the XLV Higher Command's 718 Infantry Division, stationed in Croatia, repeatedly mention the influx of troops from Serbia in support of the anti-Ustaša uprising, and show that Mihailović was engaged there in heavy fighting. Mihailović's preoccupation with the events in Bosnia is seen also from the fact that, even when the uprising in Serbia was in full swing (in August and September 1941), he continued posting officers to Bosnia. His foremost commander there was Major Dangić, and in Hercegovina Major Boško P. Todorović. But what was the actual situation in Bosnia? What were the Ustaša doing? Here is a brief extract from Major Dangić's circular of 2 September 1941. It reads, "Pavelić's bandits" are

> demolishing our [Orthodox] churches, and killing priests and important persons.... They impale the Serbs, tie them to crosses, gauge out their eyes...pack their mouths full of soil, scorch them with boiling water and skin them alive.... They cut off their fingers and flesh and make them eat it and drink their own blood. They burn live people and whole villages with their inhabitants....

Who was doing it? "We are fighting against a well organized and properly supplied army" says Dangić. His own "Companies (were) commanded by private soldiers, and the Battalions by Sergeants." By contrast,

> to the enemy, aeroplanes bring orders and ammunition, and machine-gun our ranks. Enemy units [maintain communications] by radio transmitters, whereas our infantrymen couriers have to trudge through ravines, fog and rain for hundreds of kilometers.
> ....
> We are cut off from the whole world.... Help![60]

However, due to the impact of events in Serbia, the case of Bosnia and Hercegovina, and its effect on Mihailović's early policies, has been overlooked by historians. Hence there has been lopsided discussion and further misunderstanding of Mihailović's actions. One would know more about it if the record of Mihailović's last plea at his trial in Belgrade in 1946 were accessible. For instance, *The Times* of 12 July 1946 carried on page 4 the following summing-up by its "Special Correspondent" in Belgrade:

> (Mihailović) spoke for over four hours without oratory, withour rancour towards political opponents or private enemies, lucidly and in detail. It was the professional soldier presenting a military report, compelling because of its simplicity.
> ....
> Throughout, General Mihailović's care for detail was astonishing. ...He went through action after action, place by place, until the time when the British mission left him [in 1944].

"The Correspondent" concluded his dispatch by saying,

What he said had the ring of truth, and at least it will be among the documents which history must sift.

But the text of Mihailović's plea cannot be obtained.[61]

Whilst Mihailović intervened in Bosnia from his HQ in Serbia, Communist-provoked German reprisals in Serbia turned this land into a slaughterhouse also. Mihailović concluded that he should counteract Communist excesses by giving effective military leadership to the uprising. This was a contributory factor which made him join the uprising. But the Communists would not be bridled. Although they fought the Germans, they would not desist from fighting for the Revolution also. In practice, this revolved now around the question of how to administer liberated towns. The bone of contention was the application of the Mihailović-Tito agreement to run two parallel town commands. In conformity with the requirements for organizing rear areas, Mihailović would set up town commands with the minimum number of people, leaving the running of the administration to the civilian authorities. The Partisans would then over-run these HQs with their fighters and proceed to arrest all army officers they could round up, including Mihailović's own people.[62] This done, they would replace the former local government with their revolutionary "Committees of National Liberation." These, and other similar incidents, caused friction between the two resistance groups. This was manifested by revolving quarrels, setting up of investigating commissions, peacemaking, renewed accusations, counteraccusations, drafting local "agreements," new quarrels and so on. All of it led to civil war. The Communist Party ("Partisans") also set up its Soviet "Užice Republic," now euphemistically called "Liberated Territory of 1941." Its seat was at Užice, hence its name. Užice (now called "Titovo Užice"), which was (by order) evacuated by the *Wehrmacht* garrison, was "liberated" by the Partisans some days later. Having entered Užice, the Partisans hoisted the red flag with hammer and sickle.[63] Tito established himself there, and proceeded to play out a Balkan version of Stalin and the Soviet leadership. The anniversary of the October Revolution (7 November) was commemorated with parades, Tito and the Communist leadership high up on a "review stand."[64] A fortnight later, Lazović, Četnik co-Mayor of Čačak, went with a delegation to Užice for parleys with Tito. Lazović's description of their meeting place deserves to be cited:

The passage way from the entrance to the conference hall was brightly lit and entirely smothered in red. Guards were posted along both walls of the corridor, so that one would have thought one was in Moscow. In the hall itself, where we met in conference, everything was again smothered in red, gingered up with stars and Stalin's portraits. The long [conference] table was also covered in red.[65]

Concurrently, Communist revolution in the countryside proceeded apace. It is hard to see what all this had to do with the liberation of Yugoslavia, the latter claim being the cornerstone of postwar Partisan and associated historiography.

But to revert to the situation in Serbia. In order to reconquer the country, the German high command brought the following front line troops to Serbia: 125th Independent Infantry Regiment from Greece, 113th Infantry Division from Ukraina and the 342nd Division from France, plus some smaller units, including tanks. And now came the turning point. Boehme, appointed Plenipotentiary Commanding General in Serbia, undertook a two-pronged action. Besides using the troops as soldiers to fight the uprising, he used them also to perpetuate terror over innocent civilians. An example of his methods is the evacuation of all males aged between 14 and 70 from the town of Šabac on 24 September, and their removal to a concentration camp in Croatia.[66] Their guilt? They were inhabitants of a town which was besieged by a combined Četnik-Partisan Force (Cer Četnik Detachment under Captain Drag. S. Račić and Podrinje Partisan Detachment under Nebojša Jerković). Shootings on the scale 1:100 were strictly applied. Četniks' and Partisans' reaction to mass executions differed. As they could not protect their compatriots from Boehme's reprisals, army men started talking about the perfectly normal military solution: truce! On the other hand, Partisans showed no compassion for civilians. After having provoked a reprisal, they would—unconcerned— withdraw to their mountain hideouts. This callousness was but the result of their Stalinist indoctrination; to borrow Karchmar's definition, for them the "political label determined personal attitudes."[67] These opposite reactions in the two anti-Axis resistance groups made them irksome to each other. The reaction was not uniform and even less synchronized.

In the one location where combined Četnik-Partisan operations were set up by personal agreement between Mihailović and Tito, they continued for a while. This was the renowned siege of Kraljevo (HQ Siege Command: Major Radoslav Dj. Djurić and Captain Derok for the Četniks, and Mole Radosavljević "Abas" with his political commissar Ratko Mitorvić for the Partisans). The cooperation continued for a while also at the siege of Valjevo. One of the Četnik commanders who made his name there was Lieutenant Neško Nedić. The name(s) of Partisan commanders have not yet been established. According to the Četnik officers, Mihailović personally took part in the combat there.[68] When Captain Hudson arrived from Cairo, Mihailović took him to inspect Valjevo battlefield. Said Hudson,

> During the siege of Valjevo in October-November 1941, when I went with Mihailović, his troops were half way round the town, the other half were surrounded by partisans (Tito's men) and I saw the engagement of Četnik tanks, I saw the wounded coming up— all Četniks—and I went down to the space where the tanks were withdrawn after the engagement and I went over the terrain.

Hudson made this statement at the conference at St. Antony's College,[69] in response to the manifest tendency there to ascribe all the resistance to the Partisans. He added,

> ... I think it seriously compromises the work of a serious historian who comes out with a statement that Mihailović did not, on any occasion, fight the enemy.

But the civil war was coming closer. At Čačak and Požega armed conflict between Partisans and Četniks occurred; Mihailović and Tito patched it up. Elsewhere, the Četniks simply left and went home: they would fight the Germans, but not a *"gradjanski rat"* (civil war) againt their Serbian brothers. Thus the so-called moral factor came to the fore: newly converted doctrinaire Partisans were firm and ruthless, Četniks were wavering. This was a confused transition period. Any writer who talks about it in black-and-white terms has not done his homework properly.

At the other end of the scale, many military men, particularly those NCOs who had remained on the sidelines hitherto, made up their mind that Mihailović was too soft with the Communists. They reported on

Serbia in Arms 185

duty to Nedić, and, armed by the Germans, assisted to "pacify" the country. But the Germans could not count on them to fight Mihailović's Četniks. Finally, completely to the right was a number of ideological anti-Communists. They banded together in Ljotić's volunteer detachments and fought both the Communists and the Četniks with great determination. The leader of those who were attached to the 113th German Infantry Division as auxiliaries earned even the commendation of its Commander, *Generalleutnant* Zickwolff.[70] Before the uprising chaos prevailed in the Serbian countryside, now it became mayhem. This forced Mihailović to abandon his conciliatory attitude towards the Partisans.

At this point it is necessary to assess the situation in Serbia at that time. The objective elements of the situation can be reasonably reconstructed to have been as follows:

(i) The uprising had received no reinforcements from abroad, either in men or the necessary materiel;
(ii) The erstwhile evacuation of German front line troops from Serbia had proved to be only temporary—the enemy had brought in operational replacements and deployed them to quell the uprising;
(iii) The German Command and the Nazi civil authorities disregarded the restrictions of the Hague Convention on land warfare and proceeded to inflict unbridled reprisals on civilians. To speak only of the major instances of mass executions, on 2 October 2,100 people were shot,[71] and in the week ending 29 October "In Kraljevo 1,700 male Serbs were executed, in Kragujevac 2,300."[72] Army Četniks were powerless to protect their compatriots from this terror.

The existing enemy terror was worsened by the Communists, who persisted in goading the *Wehrmacht* to further reprisals. In opposition to such a policy, Mihailović was determined not to allow a repetition of the Serbian uprising of the Toplica District in 1917. This uprising had been meant to be coordinated with the Allied breakthrough on the Macedonian Front, but the offensive was postponed yet the uprising went on. Its consequences, 8,767 Serbs killed in reprisals, and 43, 484 buildings burned down,[73] could not be justified. Now, while provoking the external enemy's reprisals, the Communists profited from the national liberation war to wage an internal class war also. By propaganda and action they attacked all vestiges of the former Yugoslav civil administration: district and town offices, records, archives and administrators, country gendarmerie stations and policemen. Indeed, their first "national liberation" enterprise was the killing of two Serbian gendarmes in the village of Bela Crkva on 7 July 1941, and not an attack on the soldiers of the *Wehrmacht*. The killing of Bela Crkva is now feted in Yugoslavia as "The Day of Uprising" in Serbia. Neither were private citizens safe; whoever was not a party follower was liable to be described as a "collaborator," "traitor" and "enemy of the people." What was now needed in Serbia was a *de facto* truce with the external enemy. In Mihailović's eyes, this would have brought about two positive results. First, it would sap further Communist activity. Future governmental organization would be left to the competence of the post-war Constituent Assembly, and not be pre-empted by agents of a foreign power. And secondly, a truce would allow him to revert to rebuilding the Army structure for the day of reckoning with the Nazis. Meanwhile, Allied interests could be served best by persistent intelligent sabotage. Mihailović found that, generally, his appreciation of the situation in the field concurred with the instruction of Prime Minister Simović, who told him on 28 October 1941 "not to risk any losses but to await from here [*viz.*, London] directives when to start operations."[74] Obviously, Mihailović had to extricate himself and his troops from the present predicament and save the organization for another day. The point was, how to go about it?

With respect to the Communist action in Serbia, Mihailović had gone the full circle. When his officers asked him for the first time how to deal with it, he commented, "I do not know who they are and what they want. Our policy is, nevertheless: whosoever is against the enemy occupant—we will join forces even with the Black Gypsies." However, after receiving a Communist delegation early in September 1941, Mihailović admonished his staff by saying, "Do not arrange any more that I meet these irresponsible criminals and rabble, for they do not know what they are doing; they wish to kill even those who were spared by the Germans."[75] (Not that he stopped meeting them. He curbed his criticism, and, in an endeavour to achieve national unity, he later received Tito.

This conciliatory patience was held against him by some of his more impulsive officers.) As has been shown, the question was now how to withdraw from the uprising? Colonel Branislav J. Pantić, a friend of Mihailović's, was one of the people who wanted Mihailović to approach the authorities in Belgrade. The idea was to negotiate the ending of German "punitive expeditions."[76] Pantić and *Hauptmann* Josef Matl (not "Matel"), otherwise a Professor in the University of Graz, Austria, were instrumental in the preliminaries which led to the meeting arranged between the German Command and Mihailović at a village called Divci. The only leading participant in the meeting itself who wrote about it is Pantić. He sent a lengthy letter about it to Bor. M. Karapandžić for his book *Gradjanski... [Civil War in Serbia 1941-1945]*. Besides this letter, the only special study devoted to it is Marjanović's lengthy article "Četnicko-Nemački...."[77] Pantić's letter is a totally unreliable document, where neither the chronology nor the events are correctly described. The only exception from this general assessment is Pantić's description of how and why Mihailović decided to parley with the enemy. It deserves to be cited. In a meeting of his inner staff, says Pantić, all present prevailed on Mihailović to contact General Nedić for ammunition for his infantry, to stop the Communists from provoking further German "punishment" reprisals. The only officer against contacting Nedić was Major Mišić. According to Pantić, Mihailović then made the following statement:

> As the present situation compells me to parley, I will parley with the enemy [and not with his underling Nedić]. I am entitled to it by the international laws of warfare....[78]

Marjanović's study of the meeting at Divci is an unreliable document also. Pantić's letter is a muddled document in which an old man has confused dates and happenings with wishful thinking. Marjanović's study is a deliberate political concoction trying to prove that Mihailović was a covert collaborator all along. Where Marjanović went wrong is that he "protested too much" and finished by saying all sorts of things, instead of concentrating on the proper historical study of the event.

But German documents about the meeting are in existence, and accessible. They can be obtained either on U.S. microfilm, or directly from the West German military archives in Freiburg. By extracting relevant documents from the general file of the Commander in Serbia/Ic (Microcopy T314-Roll 1457), one can establish a fully documented dossier on the matter. One of the documents in such a dossier is the minutes of the meeting at Divci. They show that the following persons took part in the meeting, which was held on 11 November 1941 from 19.15 to 20.35 hours:[79] "On the German side"—Lieutenant Colonel Kogard, Counsellor Dr. Kiessel, Captain Dr. Mattel [sic], *SS-Obstuf.* Wienicke and *Sonderfuehrer* Matern. "On the Serbian side"—Colonel Draža Mihajlović [sic], Major Alexander Mišić, "both in uniform," Colonel Pantić, Captain Mitrović, "both in mufti." The meeting started with Kogard reading a prepared statement to the effect that the *Wehrmacht* was not going to parley with Mihailović, and refused his offer to cooperate with the German Army and Nedić government against the Communists. "Regarding your declared intention to save Serbian blood," said Kogard, "I am charged to advise you that you have only one choice, namely stop further fighting and surrender unconditionally." He concluded by warning, "If Colonel, you do not comply with the conditions I have put to you, the fight against your Četniks will continue in the same manner as is already afoot against the Communist bands . . . ."

Instead of summing up Mihailović's rejoinder, let the man speak personally, Parts of his rejoinder amount to a policy statement. These parts are, in fact, his only policy statements accessible to the western world, and therefore it is imperative that they be noted in full. Mihailović told Kogard.[80]

> I am neither an agent of London nor of any other country. Therefore I am not interested either in your past intentions nor in your future ones. However, in Serbia you have introduced measures which shed the blook of the innocent. The Communists are still continuing with surprise attacks, so that [then] you kill the innocent.
>
> . . . .
>
> It is not my intent to fight you, because, as a general staff officer, I am aware of the strength of both parties. I am neither a Communist, nor do I work for you. But I attempted to alleviate and hinder your terror.
>
> . . . .
>
> (The Communists) wish that the highest possible number of Serbs be killed, so as to ensure their own later success. No agreement could

be made with them. My only intent [in dealing with them] was to hinder their terror, which is as terrible as yours, the German one. At the moment the innocent people suffer from the terrorist acts of you both. The terrorist acts of the Communists are calculated so that you shoot those whom you arrest.

As a soldier I am not ashamed to be a nationalist. In this capacity I will serve only my people. . . . It is our duty as soldiers not to surrender as long as we can fight. Therefore you cannot reproach us for not surrendering.

. . . .

I intend to continue the fight against the Communists, which I started on 31 October. . . . We need ammunition. This need brought me here. . . . I expected this night already to obtain a certain quantity of ammunition, and thought we would discuss this question.

. . . .

The Communists have an ammunition factory and ammunition dumps in Užice. I ask you in the interest of the Serbian people as well as in your own interest to supply me, if possible, with ammunition this very night.

. . . .

Otherwise, that is, if I am not given any ammunition, the Communists will again obtain sway over Serbia. . . .

This was a voice of anguish and desparation, a blunt soldier appealing to the temporary mutual interest of enemy parties: "I request that this issue be tackled to the advantage of both of us." Kogard's answer was shattering: "My only instruction from the Commander in Serbia is to ask Colonel Mihailović if he is unconditionally capitulating or not." Mihailović commented, "I do not see any sense in your invitation to come to the meeting if this was all you had to say. You could have done it through the middlemen." After Mišić and Pantić had their say, Kogard declared the meeting closed. *"Darauf allgemeine Verabschiedung"* ("Thereupon everybody took leave") reads the last sentence of the minutes.

Was Mihailović entitled to negotiate with the enemy? From Colonel Pantić's account it is clear that Mihailović considered himself "entitled to it by the international laws of warfare." In this context one should distinguish between two levels of negotiations. The competence of a field commander is to negotiate field or local, that is, tactical matters. Strategic or global negotiations are in the competence of the political power, that is, of the national government. At the conference at Divci, Mihailović was neither the Commander of "The Army in the Fatherland," nor the War Minister in the *émigré* government. However, he was the Senior Yugoslav Officer in the field. As to the contents of negotiations, the party which initiates negotiations expects advantages from it. In other words, anything can be negotiated. Therefore the only question that arises in the case of Mihailović, is, what was his competence to negotiate? The Yugoslav Army had capitulated, and *Oberstleutnant* Kogard reminded Mihailović at Divci that, "The warfare you wage, Colonel, is illegal."[81]

In Mihailović's own mind, the warfare he was waging was "irregular," not "illegal." "It (was) in line with our war service regulations that an army which is left without a front has to organize Četnik units" he said later at his post-war trial in Belgrade.[82] He must have relied on a liberal interpretation of the definition of an irregular combatant in the Hague Convention. The Hague Rules required that the irregular troops should be "commanded by a person responsible for his subordinants," that they wore distinct insignia, "carry arms openly," and *"Conduct their operations in accordance with the laws and customs of war."*[83] (In his liberal interpretation of these conditions, Mihailović was in fact the precursor of the post-WWII concept of extension of rights to and the protection of "Partisans.") It is interesting to observe—as will be shown later—that some German field commanders in Serbia wavered in their interpretation of the Mihailović phenomenon. They tended to reciprocate Mihailović's observance of the "laws and customs of war," and thus departed from Hitler's orders.

However, the negotiations Mihailović held with Kogard had political overtones. He required the enemy to provide him with means (the ammunition) whereby he could prevent a committed group of his co-citizens from continuing to risk the lives of the majority of citizens. There is no country which abstains from using the army as *ultima ratio* in maintaining public order and civil peace—provided that the ultimate control remains with the political authority. Nevertheless, the aborted negotiations of Divci had nothing in common with the approach of the Partisan leadership to the Germans in 1943. On that occasion the Partisan leadership notified the *Wehrmacht* they would fight the British troops in case of their landing on the Dalmatian coast.[84] This incident offers a good opportunity to digress for a moment from our main narrative, and compare western attitudes to Mihailović with the ways Tito was accommodated. For his negotiations at Divci, Mihailović has been roundly condemned. Nowadays, when the minutes of the meeting are freely accessible, it has become obvious that the censure of Mihailović has been based on a specious, selective use of that document. Yet, to cite from Nora Beloff's *Tito's Flawed Legacy,* when Tito's dealings with the Germans became known in the West,

> Phyllis Auty, one of Tito's staunch defenders, . . in a letter to *The Times Literary Supplement* (27 November 1970), said that she had consulted Tito personally about the reported deal and had been told it was untrue.

The punchline, Auty's conclusion, reads as follows:

> I see no evidence to doubt Marshal Tito's word on this and know of no credible evidence to refute it.

"But refuted it was," says Beloff.[85] She is right. Furthermore, in addition to all the evidence adduced by Beloff, Auty's loyalty was abused by Tito himself. In Yugoslavia, in 1985, a monograph was published on this question, titled *Martovski pregovori 1943* [*The Negotiations of March 1943*]. Its author is Mišo Leković, a Yugoslav military historian. When interviewed by *NIN,* in defence of these negotiations Leković cited *inter alia* Tito's own oblique admission, when he said,

> Who is the one to censure us today for having done something which boosted our strength. . . .[86]

What about the goose and the gander, though with one qualification: Mihailović never considered fighting the Allies.

But to revert to our own study of Mihailović: the question remains, was Mihailović authorized by his government to do what he did? At this stage of historical knowledge, an answer can be construed only on the basis of circumstantial evidence. From German archives it is clear that

"London's" broadcasts (the BBC?) referred twice to Mihailović's negotiations with the enemy's command in Serbia. The crux of the matter is that, in its broadcast of 10 November, "London" announced that Mihailović had refused to comply in his negotiations "yesterday" with the demand to capitulate. From German records it is seen that Mihailović was meant to meet Kogard on 9 November.[87] Therefore the broadcast of 10 November was meant to be a "report" of what had happened the day before. Yet Mihailović could not attend the meeting on 9 November, and it took place only on the 11th; that is, Mihailović refused to capitulate only on the day after it had already been broadcast. It is this slip in the chronology of the news-service that allows for the proposition that Mihailović's action was known by the Yugoslav government before the event.

Mihailović and his staff had been given safe-conduct to return whence they came, regardless of the outcome of the conference, and the *Wehrmacht* observed it scrupulously. In a letter he wrote some fifteen years after the event, Professor Matl, who was actively involved, stated that the German "police companies" wanted to use the occasion to arrest Mihailović but were prevented.[88] The other point of interest in his letter is his claim that it was Boehme's Chief of Staff, Colonel Pemsel, who insisted that Mihailović must capitulate.[89] Pemsel himself, in his report to the Commander South-East of 12 November, described Mihailović as "a remowned enemy of Germany," whose action was caused by his Četniks being in a weak position. In the conference "it was obvious" that his offer of cooperation was not a sincere one, but "calculated to win time," and when his circumstances improve (*bei guenstigerer Gelegenheit*) to renew his fighting the *Wehrmacht*. This conclusion is interesting. It was based on the impressions of Colonel Kogard, who chaired the meeting.[90] There is another document in German files related to the conference at Divci on 11 November—Kogard's sketch of Mihailović as man and soldier. In his memorandum, titled "*Oberst* Mihailović," the relevant part reads,[91]

> His appearance makes a good impression. He is of middle height, selfconfident, and has an extraordinary capacity for selfcontrol. Even when greatly disappointed, his expression does not change. He came [to the conference] believing we would negotiate with him; when he was enjoined unconditionally to capitulate, the

expression of his face did not change. His request for ammunition had to be refused. This must have been for him a very great disappointment, yet he showed it in no way.

He appears also very fit. In the morning of Tuesday [*viz.*, the 11th of November] he was with his troops which were fighting in the area of Pozega, departed at 10 a.m. and arrived at 19.00 hours. He crossed the rugged mountain terrain on foot, horse, and by cart, yet he showed no trace of being tired. He made the impact of a trained mountain fighter.

In earlier discussion of Mihailović's reaction to the debacle of the April War, his selfcontrol was singled out. It is valuable also to cite the observation of a British officer who witnessed the moment when Mihailović learned over the BBC broadcast that he had been finally abandoned by the Churchill government. Captain Michael Lees wrote in the *Sunday Express* of 26 March 1946,

> ....(Mihailović) rose from his seat and turned off the radio. We sat embarrassed, looking away as his sad eyes rested on each of us [British BLOs] in turn. He spoke calmly:
> '...I realize, Gentlemen, that this decision is no fault of yours. If I may do so, I still regard you as my friends and the friends of Yugoslavia. I shall do every thing in my power to help you to escape safely.
> 'Perhaps we shall meet again in happier circumstances after the war. You will always be welcome here.'

"It was the gesture of a very gallant gentleman who had lost all but his pride," commented Lees. And then he added the observation based on his service with him,

> Mihailović was unusual in his absolute confidence of ultimate British victory.[92]

At this time, 24 May 1944, Mihailović had been fighting on the Allied side for three years.

CHAPTER 10

SPECIAL OPERATIONS EXECUTIVE'S ABORTIVE "RUSSIAN PROJECT"

Before we continue with the story of the events in Serbia proper, let us digress to study the intended twin-mission of the *Operation Bullseye*. Its historical importance is that it was an attempt at British—Soviet—Yugoslav cooperation. Its history shows that a wartime alliance of uneven powers brings about more casualties than just the freedom of action of smaller powers. The obstruction of a small power may damage the relations of its more powerful allies. Such was the case here. Even so, there is one saving grace in its story. In contrast to the case of the *Bullseye,* no subsequent historical writings have intervened to confuse its purpose and course. One of the men who was involved in the organization of the intended inter-allied mission was Captain (later Major) John Bennett, who was an SOE operative in Belgrade until the German-Yugoslav April war, and after the Yugoslav débâcle moved to the Middle East. The *Bullseye,* which sailed from Malta, obtained its code-name from Terence Maxwell, the newly intalled head of the Middle East SOE. Its intended twin mission, which was to take off from an airfield in the Soviet Union, was left nameless. However, in a retrospective report to the SOE headquarters in London, Bennett referred to it as the *"Russian Project,"*[1] and this name is retained here.

There are only two published sources regarding the Russian Project. Both are written by leading participants. There is a short reference to the

Project in Julian Amery's *Approach March,* and a mention in an article by Jovan Djonović, Amery's wartime Yugoslav contact. These two brief references to the *Project* triggered this investigation. The genesis of the *Russian Project* lies in the reaction of Colonel Bailey, an Englishman, to Hitler's attack on the Soviet Union on 22 June 1941, and in the reaction of Jovan Djonović, a Montenegrin Serb, to the uprising of 1941 in occupied Serbia. At the time of the start of the Nazi-Soviet war Bailey was in charge of the Balkan Section of the Middle East SOE. After he left Belgrade in 1940, Bailey was stationed in Istanbul from August 1940 to April 1941, when he established himself in Jerusalem. According to Amery,[2] in the wake of the 22nd of June Bailey consulted with his staff, and submitted to his superiors that Britain should "build up" and guide anti-Nazi resistance in the Balkans. A vital point of this plan was that Britain should engage Soviet support for this work before the Soviet power become too assertive. "Our headquarters in London," says Amery, "accepted these views." Somewhat later, by the end of July 1941, Djonović, Yugoslav Government Delegate in the Middle East, learned in Istanbul that both the Communists and the nationalists participated in the Serbian uprising.[3] The nationalist leader, a Colonel Mihailović, had his HQ on the Suvobor mountain plateau, and asked for liaison officers and W/T sets to be flown in by air. Djonović immediately relayed this request to Amery and the Soviet representative in Istanbul.[4] Evidently, thanks to Bailey's earlier initiative, Djonović's action met with instant British support: Amery left for Cairo to arrange a mission to Mihailović. Even the Soviet authorities offered Djonović an aircraft to take a combined Yugoslav, British and "Russian" military team to Mihailović; if necessary, the aircraft was to "make a crash landing."[5] Before he left Cairo with the mission *Bullseye,* Amery learned that Bennett was to recruit "another Anglo-Yugoslav team" and procede to Leninakan in Soviet Armenia to board the promised Soviet aircraft; but the Yugoslav government, "suspicious of the Soviets," opposed the project, and Cairo had to countermand it.[6] Djonović mentioned the event five years before Amery.[7] The two versions agree that it was Djonović who started the ball rolling, that Moscow's reply was positive, and that the reaction of the Yugoslav government aborted the mission. Djonović's version is more detailed. He states that beside contacting Bailey and a Soviet representative in Istanbul, Colonel Nikolaev,[8] he also contacted his own superior, Vice-Prime Minister Jovanović in London. Djonović suggested to Jovanović that an eventual conflict between the two parties in the uprising, the nationalists and the Communists, could be prevented by joint Yugoslav–British–Soviet planning of any military missions sent in.[9]

At first view it appears that no primary sources about the event are available as the SOE's Cairo archives were largely destroyed when Rommel reached Egypt.[10] Some relevant SOE documents have been preserved in London, although they are still classified. Fortunately, permission has been given to obtain information from these records and to use them in this study.[11] Thus Bennett's memorandum, which was mentioned earlier in this chapter, shows that he came from Jerusalem to Istanbul on 4 August 1941, where Djonović saw him, and suggested they should enquire from the Russians "whether they could provide means of infiltrating people into Yugoslavia with W/T sets." Bennett agreed, and Djonović established contact with Nikovaev. Djonović followed up with Bennett the same matter he took up with Amery: the need to contact Mihailović, whose location in Serbia was now known. Djonović enquired about the "means" of infiltrating into Yugoslavia. There is no record of any discussion concerning the composition of the team to be sent. Indeed, at this stage it was assumed that a team of Serbs would go. In a telegram of 6 August Bennett reported that Djonović now suggested using a French aircraft from Syria to send to Yugoslavia two of his collaborators in Istanbul; they would take with them a W/T set for use by an operator to be found in Yugoslavia. The two men put forward by Djonović were Dušan [M.] Radović, formerly a Colonel in the Yugoslav Air Force, who would pilot the plane, and a civilian, Vasilije Trbić, as his passenger. This option had more substance than may appear, as Radović was a versatile pilot whose experience included French machines. Bennett's reaction was akin to Amery's: he was anxious to get a mission afoot. He made his own inquiries, and five days later, on 11 August, reported from Istanbul that Hudson, who was there, volunteered to join Radović and Trbić. (Hudson, of course, was later of *Bullseye* fame.) Bennett's and Amery's boss, Bailey, also took an active personal part. On 15 and 19 August he reported that he was investigating arranging air or sea transport for despatch of agents into Yugoslavia, including obtaining a French aircraft from Syria, but indicated that his "main hope" was rather to obtain a plane in Malta. The speed of such activity was exceptional given war-time conditions, and the different national administration involved. Only two weeks after

Djonović's initiative, three irons were already in the fire—potential routes *via* the Soviet Union, Syria and Malta.

Probably to speed up the Soviet alternative, Bailey contacted London for permission to deal directly with the Russians in Istanbul. However London had a SOE mission in Moscow which could handle the matter directly. At first the mission was headed by Bobby Guinness, a sapper, who was succeeded shortly after by Brigadier George Hill.[12] The Moscow SOE contact was with the NKVD who preferred to keep matters in their own hands. The Foreign Office was concerned that direct SOE-Soviet negotiations in Istanbul might upset the neutral Turks. The *Wehrmacht* controlled the Bulgarian border with Turkey, and the Red Army was in retreat on the Eastern Front. Consequently, on 20 August London told Bailey to mark time, as the SOE man in Moscow was "exploring generally the possibilities of co-operation with the Russians." On 23 August London indicated that discussions in Moscow for establishing "machinery" for collaboration in the Balkans were under way but that contact was not to be made in Istanbul, although "there was no wish" to interfere with Djonović's negotiations. In his turn, Djonović expected "any day" a reply from Moscow about "parachuting Serbs into Yugoslavia." Bailey came from Jerusalem to Istanbul, to be on the spot. In reviewing the situation on 31 August, he submitted that "the only chance" of success before the onset of the European winter was to despatch a team from Cairo, either by aircraft or submarine. Obviously, the Syrian option had fallen by the wayside, and Bailey was still uninformed about Moscow's reaction to the Russian Project.

Suddenly, things started moving. On Friday 5 September Amery asked from Cairo that Radović and Trbić come there immediately, in order that they be sent to Yugoslavia with a W/T operator "next week." On the 6 September, Nikolaev told Bennett and Djonović in Istanbul that as Moscow had "no current communications with Yugoslavia," it was

> keen to establish them . . . and planes, W/T sets and operators were immediately available.

Yet Djonović had asked only for W/T sets and transport. The Soviet authorities offered W/T sets with operators. Logistically, this was certainly a turning point toward a speedy despatch of the mission and an efficient, guaranteed radio service. Politically however it was dangerous. A selfcontained Soviet W/T team would have given Moscow a communications and command monopoly in local events within Serbia.[13] One can imagine Bailey's reaction when he was faced with this possibility. He stepped in. Accompanied by Bennett and Djonović, he saw Nikolaev later on the same day (6 September). Bailey reported that at the conference

> it was suggested that [Colonel] Radović should go immediately to Moscow and should be flown from there to Suvobor to contact Mihailović, taking with him as couriers three or four Yugoslav officers from Amman [the Yugoslav airmen's camp].

In his report Bailey recommended that this be approved, and that, beside the mission *via* Moscow, Trbić should be sent on his way *via* Cairo; thus two missions would be on the road simultaneously. Significantly he also recommended that British officers be attached to each mission.[14] Bailey's initiative of 6 September, that British officers be attached to the two missions, seems to be the first time that this was considered, or—at least—the first time that it was put on paper. Thus it came about that a team, which was originally meant to consist of Serbs only, was expanded to include Soviet and British personnel. On the eve of the meeting with Nikolaev, Amery in Cairo asked for Radović and Trbić. Bailey replied that the former would remain in Istanbul, but that Trbić, accompanied by another officer, would be sent to Cairo. Despite the insistence by Cairo (including the new head there, Maxwell), Bailey remained firm. He may have been motivated by the animosity between Radović and the Yugoslav Prime Minister, General Simović. Radović refused to leave neutral Turkey for Cairo, which was the seat of the Yugoslav War Minister, General Ilić. Radović believed that Ilić might stop his mission to Yugoslavia; Bailey clearly wanted him in the Russian Project.

Who were Trbić and Radović, and why did the *Project* come to grief?

Trbić came to Cairo from Istanbul, but when he learned he was to be landed first in Montenegro on his way to Serbia, he refused to go.[15] Majors Ostojić and Lalatović, with their W/T operator, joined by Hudson, took the place of Trbić and his companion Grdanički. Trbić wrote about this period in his still unpublished memoirs.[16]

From his memoirs, it is clear that he was a man with wide connections, including senior Turkish personnel of the Istanbul police and the railway police. Early in June 1941 Bailey sent him to Istanbul to report to a man named Thompson, and henceforth Trbić passed on to him any intelligence from Yugoslavia.[17] When the news about fighting in Serbia "and the other parts of occupied Yugoslavia," came from different sources in the later part of July, Bailey "immediately" came to Istanbul. In a conference which was convened to decide what action to take, three Yugoslavs (Djonović, Tupanjanin and Trbić) and three Britons (Bailey, Bennett and Amery) took part. In that conference, says Trbić, a new participant appeared for the first time "who was simply called Nikolajev [Nikolaev]."[18] Bailey told them that he was instructed to assist Mihailović financially and by sending a mission to him. After a "lengthy discussion" the conference decided to send "two Serbs, one Englishman and one Russian" to Mihailović, and five [Yugoslav] air force officers, led by Radović, to Russia. "A few days later this plan was approved in its entirety by London and Moscow."[19] A few comments must be made. Firstly, Bailey did not come to Istanbul "immediately" after the latest news from Serbia, but sometime between 23 and 31 August, when he sent his review of the situation to London. Secondly, when Bailey was in Istanbul, Amery was in Cairo: on 5 September Amery asked from there for Radović and Trbić. And thirdly, of course, the Russian Project was not finally approved within "a few days" ("*nekoliko dana*"), but took a month, from 4 August to 6 September. These inconsistencies do not imply that Trbić invented the conference, only that his reporting is not reliable. After all, he was a politician, not an administrator. (This brings to mind Djonović's dissatisfaction with Trbić as his agent in Istanbul.)[20]

Fortunately the surviving SOE records contain information which may be used to assess the reliability of Trbić's reporting. On the day after his conference with Djonović and Nikolaev of 6 September, Bailey reported from Istanbul on 7 September that

> Djonović had discussed the plans [agreed to with Nikolaev] with Radović and Trbić who agreed. All stressed the importance of sending a party from Russia 'to secure the adherence of pro-Russian elements, to demonstrate Anglo-Russian co-operation and as a check on Russian intentions.'

Comparison of Trbić's and Bailey's versions confirms that Trbić discussed these matters with Djonović and Radović (in a British context, one would rather say that Trbić was briefed by Djonović). He probably also had a discussion with Bailey; they knew each other. For the rest of Trbić's version all that can be said is that, at best, it sounds like recounting a second-hand story, and at worst, like repeating gossip. But then, we know only the text edited by Marjanović, and not the original reminiscences. Incidentally, the part of Bailey's report about the agreement of 7 September, that the Russian Project would result in "a check on Russian intentions," brings to mind Djonović's claims that right from the start he had so advised his Vice-Prime Minister, Jovanović. It is clear that the *Bullseye* and the *Project* were elements of the same scheme. Throughout the whole event Djonović, the British and the Soviet authorities had in mind a single project—a mission to Mihailović. Yet it was shown that the whole drift of much of the current *Bullseye* historiography is to cast doubt on this basic aim. The *Project* is further evidence that such doubts are misplaced.

Why did the *Project* come to grief? The answer is found with Colonel Radović. He and General Simović, the Yugoslav Prime Minister, were on bad terms. Radović had been Simović's *protégé*,[21] but when Simović was commanding the air force, he had Radović put on the retirement list on 28 March 1938. At the time Radović was commanding the air force brigade at Zagreb, Croatia. As a Colonel (Rtd) he became Director-Manager of the Yugoslav steelworks "Zenica" in Bosnia. Soon after, in the war of April 1941, he put on his uniform and asked for combat posting. On the collapse of Yugoslavia he reached Greece, and on his own initiative assisted a member of the British air attaché's staff in Belgrade, Wing Commander (later Group Captain) Tom Mapplebeck, RAF, in rounding up and evacuating the escaped Yugoslav airmen from Greece to the Middle East.[22] Whatever might have been his disagreements with Simović, Radović was an able and determined man. He entered the First World War as a Cadet in the *k.u.k.* mountain artillery regiment No. 11. In the Austro-Hungarian invasion of Serbia in 1914, as a Serbian nationalist from Bosnia he crossed from the Austro-Hungarian ranks into the Serbian Army. He fought the Central Powers as a Serbian artillery officer until 1917, when he joined the Franco-Serbian air detachment on the Macedonian Front. He came out of the war with the highest Serbian decorations for bravery and gallantry, the Silver and Gold Medals and the White Eagle with Swords.[23] Between the First and Second World Wars he graduated from the *Ecole Supérieure d'Aéronautique et de Construction Mécanique* as an aeronautical engineer in 1921,[24] and in the Yugoslav Army Air Force rose to the rank of (full) Colonel. He and Djonović met for the first time after the Yugoslav *débàcle* when, together with the other Yugoslav airmen, Radović was in the Amman camp, in Transjordan. Djonović found Radović bitter about the lost war, and critical of the Simović government for keeping that pool of trained men in the camp, instead of at war. "He told me," says Djonović, "that, as the Yugoslav government was not using his services as an officer, he offered his services to the English, and asked me to support his application." Djonović discussed this with Bailey on 9 June, but was told that the Yugoslav government would have to allow it first.[25] This agrees with the basis of Bennett's memorandum where it is stated that Bennett introduced Radović to Bailey, who was impressed with him, and the Yugoslav War Minister (General Ilić) was persuaded to agree to Radović's "going to Istanbul to work with Djonović and with the SOE."

Bailey was aware of the animosity between Radović and his Prime Minister, Simović. When Radović refused to leave Istanbul for Cairo after the agreement on the Russian Project, Bailey supported him. He thought the difficulty could be solved by despatching the missions *via* Moscow and Cairo-Malta simultaneously, and posting a British officer to each. In Cairo, on 8 September Amery urged London to persuade Simović to instruct General Ilić, in Cairo, to replace Radović by other officers. Maxwell was anxious to secure "the future collaboration of the Russians and the Yugoslav Communist Party." On 9 September he urged London to ensure that the Russian Project took place, and to obtain Simović's instruction to his people in the Middle East to provide replacement officers. He thought the difficulties could be overcome by seconding the officers to Djonović, instead of attaching them directly "to the British or the Russians." The whole thing grew into a diplomatic issue (that Amery does not mention these interventions in his autobiographical book poses no historical problem: he was a junior officer, and need not have known about it.) London prepared a brief for a meeting with Simović. In an earlier chapter the participation of Yugoslav *émigré* military authorities in despatching Mission *Bullseye* was discussed. On that occasion it was shown that Simović's postwar version of the events was unreliable. This makes it imperative to learn exactly the substance of the British brief which was discussed with Simović, and to get to know his reaction. The summary of the brief reads,

> ...there were two immediate plans for the infiltration of parties into Yugoslavia: (a) via Malta and (b) via Moscow. As regards the Moscow plan the Russians had informed Djonovic that they had a plane 'available in Armenia capable of taking eight persons' and it had been suggested that Radovic together with a British officer and a Yugoslav W/T operator should proceed soon to Moscow for a brief period of instruction before being flown to Suvobor to contact Mihailovic. Radovic should also take with him four couriers in connection with the contacting of 'other bands in Montenegro, Sanjak and Macedonia'; these...should travel to Moscow independently as soon as possible.
>
> ....
>
> It was hoped that Simovic would instruct General Ilic to make (personnel) available as soon as possible.

Simović declined to do it, "saying that Ilic already had the necessary authority." Thus, instead of acting, Simović prevaricated. Furthermore, in the two subsequent meetings with his SOE contacts in London, Simović, still delaying action, started complaining about Radović. He passed on a copy of a telegram sent by Ilić on 11 September, denouncing the British as "planning activity in Yugoslavia without the knowledge of the Yugoslav authorities" and accusing Radović of being the instigator. (Instead of complaining against the British, Ilić should have examined his relationship with his civilian counterpart in the Middle East, Djonović.) In his next meeting with his SOE contacts, Simović used a stratagem which, he thought, would give the *coup de grace* to Radović. London told Cairo that,

> Simovic had gone so far as to suggest that Radovic was 'in the pay of the enemy.'

Meanwhile Radović had chosen four officers in Amman who were to be transported in Soviet aircraft "to different parts of Yugoslavia to get in touch with the local insurgents and establish their liaison with the Allies."[26] This team was to be sent "via Persia [now Iran] to contact the Russians probably at Tabriz." (Tabriz was at the time in the Soviet zone of Iran.)

While the two Generals, Ilić and Simović, were playing personal and diplomatic games instead of getting on with the war effort, the Middle

East SOE was undergoing a crisis of its own. The envoy from London, Frank Nelson, was proceeding to a drastic purge of section leaders there, and installed Terence Maxwell as the new overall head. In this context Simović's antics could not have occurred at a worse time. It was against this background *Bullseye* left Cairo for Malta, and on the same day, Saturday 13 September, Radović departed from Istanbul to Moscow.[50]

How did London react to Yugoslav squabbles? It acted at two levels. The first was a political instruction, *viz.*,

> 'good relations with the Yugoslav Government were more important than the object of (Radovic's) journey.'

The second, the administrative follow-up, was an attempt to stop Radović from reaching Moscow. Simultaneously, Moscow was advised that Radović was "not included" in the team of officers "for infiltration into Yugoslavia."[27] An explanation was needed, and Moscow was advised that Simović had expelled Radović from the Yugoslav Air Force "on suspicion of corruption and of being in the pay of the French." Now came the crux of the matter. Moscow wanted to know if the case against Radović had been proven, and were told that "there was no concrete evidence against" him:

> In the face of this the Russians declined to take any actions vis-a-vis Radovic.

It is not known to what extent Radović was aware of these events—that his own Prime Minister had literally marked his head for the chopping block. In any case, after he returned from Moscow in January 1942, Radović stated that "He was treaty very well (*vrlo dobro*) in Russia."[28] But this is not the end of the story. In chapter 9 of this study it was noted that one of the historical issues regarding the *Bullseye* team is its briefing. *Inter alia*, it was shown that Major Lalatović is reported to have stated in 1942 that, in his briefing, General Ilić, the Yugoslav War Minister, asked the two Majors to locate a Colonel in Yugoslavia and "kill him."[29] Since he wrote this, the original reporter of this detail, Plećaš, specified that General Ilić asked Majors Lalatović and Ostojić to locate and kill *Colonel Dušan Radović: Ilić* thought Radović had already returned to Yugoslavia.[30] Thus we have witnessed here a sequence of events where the British and the Soviets, both waging war, were fair in their dealings, and the two Yugoslav refugee Generals, who played at being soldiers, carried on a private vendetta.

London had a second go at the *Project*. After securing the promise of another team of four officers from Ilić, it approached Moscow again, but was rejected:

> The Russians were angry, considering that they had been made fools of, first in accepting Radovic, then in being told he was a suspected enemy agent and finally in discovering that here had been no evidence against him.

As an historical assessment of the damage caused by the Radović affair, the summary of the SOE man in Moscow cannot be bettered. He closed this file with the masterly understatement that "as a first exercise in co-operation with the Russians this had been a most unfortunate affair."

CHAPTER 11

HUDSON AND MIHAILOVIĆ—
A REVISED HISTORICAL JUDGMENT

Hudson's adventures have an historical interest beyond the British *genre* of boys' own stories. The "case Hudson" is also the case of the British response to the Serbian uprising of 1941. From the moment he met Tito at Užice, and reported to Mihailović at Brajići, the Partisans as well as Četniks entered British political and diplomatic calculations. In the Partisan rout of December 1941 Hudson left Tito, returned to Mihailović, and came off air. This was the turning point. His silence caused concern to the British authorities. Was he dead? Or was he captured? SOE missions were sent to Yugoslavia to find Hudson, but failed before reaching Serbia. A few months later this incident solved itself, and under normal circumstances the episode would have been forgotten. However, in the pro-Tito post-war historiography historians turned it from a small incident into a major affair. Pro-Partisan propositions that Mihailović was an untrustworthy ally dominated accepted interpretations. This, of course, implicates the whole army organization commanded by Mihailović. Mihailović, it is said, when faced with the overwhelming might of the *Wehrmacht's* "punishment expedition," prevented Hudson from communicating with the British authorities, or, more destructively—Mihailović, now a collaborator, stopped Hudson contacting his people. These issues have maintained interest in Serbian events of 1941-42. They form a test case to assess the validity of the existing historiography—a study centered in the relationship of Hudson and Mihailović. A recreation of what really happened in the field will throw a new light on the degree of reliability of the post-war speculations of historians, and enable us to reach a revised historical judgment.

It has been demonstrated that the section of this historiography which deals with the events of 1941 went astray. This waywardness is best seen in Deakin's *Embattled Mountain*. There, in addition to telling his own adventures in war-torn Yugoslavia, he endeavoured to "piece together" the history of earlier British missions. His methodology should be noted. He says,

> ...(I) have sought a collective and provisional reconstruction of the historical record of these events, which...may prove to stand in some measure the test of the release of the remaining evidence.[1]

It is unfortunate for Deakin that his followers have taken his "provisional reconstruction" and his articles for historical gospel, and that the original sources about the events in 1941, now accessible, discredit his account and interpretation of Operation *Bullseye's* record. The simple story of Hudson's mission has become adulterated by attributing sinister political connotations to the "travels" of his radio sets, and to his later radio silence. Even professional historians have become sidetracked. Howard, writing thirty years after the event, stated that

> early in 1942 S.O.E. lost contact with Hudson for the very simple reason that Mihailovic had confiscated his radio set; being unwilling, in his equivocal position, to associate himself closely with the Allies.[2]

By 1977, the popular international understanding of these events, especially of the role of Mihailović, was reflected in *The Historical Encyclopedia of World War II*:

> ...Mihailovich organized a resistance group known as the Chetniks after Germany invaded Yugoslavia in 1941. Almost from the start this group clashed with Tito's partisans, and through an understanding with the Nazi occupation forces, his army drove the partisans out of Serbia....[3]

Of the claims made in these two quotations, the question of Hudson's radio set(s) has been amply discussed. The rout of the Partisans at the hands of the German 342nd Infantry Division and *not* at the hands of the Chetniks has been established. Nevertheless, what was Mihailović doing during the anti-Partisan operation of the 342nd Division, and why did Hudson maintain radio-silence? The answers to these questions will show also if any reference to Mihailović's "equivocal position" is justified or not.

It has been shown that Hudson and Ostojić reached Tito's HQ at Užice on 23 October 1941. Following his instructions, Major Ostojić immediately went on to report to Colonel Mihailović. In contrast, Ostojić's travelling companion, Captain Hudson, stayed behind. Mihailović, a regular officer awaiting the arrival on duty of his allied liaison officer, seems to have taken exception to what in his eyes must have seemed Hudson's unauthorized action. Consequently he instructed Ostojić to return to Užice and bring Hudson to the Yugoslav Army's Guerrilla ("Četnik") Headquarters. Ostojić contacted Hudson; the two men left Užice on 25 October and on the same day arrived at Mihailović's HQ at Brajići. There the Colonel reprimanded his liaison officer for having loitered on the way and for having hobnobbed with the "Communist rabble" as he termed it.[4] Hudson could not have known that this expression was used as an expression of disgust at the illegal Communist Party's constant undermining of the government in pre-war Belgrade society and amongst army officers. He must have felt bewildered at this reception as, in his mind, he was simply adhering to his briefing to explore the situation in occupied Serbia.

In their comments on this misunderstanding some writers tend to ascribe Mihailović's reaction to his being cross with Hudson for having formed a "favourable impression" of Partisans.[5] It is suggested however that, if there is any substance to this speculation, this could not have been Mihailović's primary motivation. One should recall that Mihailović was a regular army officer. Anyone familiar with military procedure would give priority to the assertion that Mihailović,

> considered Hudson to be exclusively a liaison officer between himself and the English, and that his competence was strictly circumscribed by his function.[6]

Had Hudson been more discreet, or a regular officer trained in the ways of the military, he would not have exercised such an initiative which amounted at least to discourtesy. It was his staying behind and not any views he may have entertained about the Partisans that upset Mihailović. However, whichever interpretation one adopts regarding this specific incident, further events show that Mihailović distinguished between a disciplinary matter involving protocol for military attachés and liaison officers, and the business of waging the war. This can be established from Mihailović's attitude toward Hudson's radio set.

Hudson's wireless set was still on the road to Serbia. Contrary to many claims, Mihailović allowed Hudson the use of his own (i.e. Mihailović's) transmitter to establish contact with the British authorities.[7] When it became evident that Hudson's set had been retained at Tito's HQ in Užice, Mihailović allowed Hudson further access to the Četnik transmitter.[8] Nevertheless their relationship did not run smoothly. Mihailović resented Hudson's refusal to reveal his cypher after being requested to do so.[9] The worst incident flowing from the use of independent cyphers, involving Mihailović and Hudson, followed Hudson's wire to Cairo on 13 November 1941. On that occasion he requested the withholding of further supplies to Mihailović, unless "an attempt is made to incorporate all anti-fascist elements under his command."[10] As the open civil war between Mihailović and Tito had just started, commentators usually interpret the request to indicate that Hudson wanted to prevent Mihailović from using this material against Tito. What really happened in the field is indicated from accounts given by an Australian and a British Lieutenant, neither of whom was a regular army officer. The Australian was an escaped prisoner of war (POW) hiding in occupied Serbia, Lieutenant R. H. Jones of the AIF, who probably is the main non-Serb eyewitness of Mihailović's work in 1941. In occupied Serbia Lt. Jones was known as "Radovan Radović" and as "Captain Radovan," and was issued false identity papers by Mihailović's HQ.[11] He described the result of the above request to another escapee, Lieutenant Christie Lawrence of the No. 8 (British) Commando,[12]

> ...(Hudson) had cancelled the convoy, but did not tell Mihailovic what he had done until twenty-four hours later, when Mihailovic and his men had waited the whole of one bitterly cold night, with their [landing site] flares burning, in expectation [of RAF aero-

planes]. On top of Mihailovic's disappointment, (Hudson's) blow was bitter.[13]

When later Lawrence met Mihailović, the latter gave him an account which was "substantially the same"as Jones's version.[14] Lawrence's report is the only published testimony in English of the event and of Mihailović's reaction. Deakin agrees that the British accepted Hudson's recommendation to "withhold further air sorties." Nevertheless, these interpretations are at variance with the currently accepted view that the sorties were stopped due to technical problems. The only account in the Četnik historiography simply says that Mihailović "never forgave" Hudson for his attempt "to interfere in internal Yugoslav politics,"[15] but this is not elaborated, and it does not claim to be based on Mihailović's own words. Despite their differences, Mihailović allowed Hudson to continue using the Četnik transmitter, while his own was retained at Tito's headquarters. Mihailović's transmitter was a field-made contraption, working from "about five hundred pocket batteries."[16] When the *Wehrmacht* on 29 November captured Užice, Mihailović, who knew that Hudson was there, awaited his return for a couple of days and then on 1 December signalled that "Hudson was cut off and had not returned to Ravna Gora."[17] He could not have known that Hudson was accompanying Tito and his Partisans on the "rout" to Sandžak. Deakin says that his message was "the last news" Cairo received about Hudson's "whereabouts."[18] (Unfortunately, Deakin's presentation is again neither chronological, nor analytical nor thematical so that, except for the dates and texts of telegrams, it is hard to follow.) Clissold's claim that Hudson joined "Tito and his bodyguard" when "the Chetniks melted mysteriously away before the German onslaught" is nonsense.[19]

After having over-run Užice and expelled the main body of the Partisans from Serbia, the *Wehrmacht* turned against Mihailović and the Četnik Detachments of the Yugoslav Army. Mihailović, who expected this development, ordered his units to disperse in accordance with guerrilla tactics, and to avoid any frontal engagements with the enemy.[20] Many Army Četniks returned to their villages and pretended to be peaceful peasants. Some units and part-units apparently blended with the "loyal"[21] Četnik bands accompanying German units, and, as "legalised Četniks"[22] took an active part in the subsequent mopping-up of Partisan remnants.[23] Regarding the so-called "legalized Četniks," it is necessary to note an exchange of views in Cairo on 25 September 1941 between the Yugoslav Minister for War, General Ilić, and Colonel Masterson of the SOE:

> (Ilić)... at present in the country [read Serbia] 16 battalions are being formed; we ought to infiltrate our men into those units to endeavour ("*koji će raditi na tome*") to bring them to our side at the right moment. It is [also] necessary to infiltrate men who will gain German confidence and occupy important posts: radio stations, power stations and so on, and who are prepared at the right moment either to seize them or destroy.'
> (Masterson) I agree.... [24]

An historian should keep in mind attitudes peculiar to the combatants in any civil war, and in Serbia a Četnik-Partisan civil war was going on despite the sudden German counter-guerrilla operations. Hence both Četnik soldiers and Partisan fighters were the temporary immediate enemy to one another, and not the Germans. Meanwhile Mihailović remained at the village of Brajići, at the foot of Ravna Gora. When some German troops appeared in that area on 5 December, he moved with his staff and headquarters troops to the village Struganik, at the other end of the Ravna Gora.[25] On the same day Mihailović "radioed" that "he was retreating," could not receive "any [air-] supplies," and was "continuing guerrilla warfare" but "could not maintain radio communication"; that was "his last contact with Malta"[26] in 1941. From the German side, on 3 December 1941 the German Plenipotentiary Commander in Serbia instructed the 342nd Infantry Division "to disarm and take prisoner" the main body of "*Mihajlovic-Cetnikis*" [sic], which had concentrated 20km South-East of Valjevo, and if they resisted, to "destroy them."[27] This order was received by the 342nd Division and entered into its War Diary on the same afternoon.[28] The execution of the operation was ordered for 7 December.[29] Mihailović's HQ at Struganik was over-run on 6-7 December.[30] This explains what Mihailović was doing during the anti-guerrilla drive of the 342nd Division. From the point of view of guerrilla warfare Tito committed the blunder of keeping his people concentrated, lost them, and was expelled from Serbia *by the Germans*. Conversely, Mihailović ordered dispersal of his troops, outwitted the enemy, and remained in Serbia. When he dispersed his troops, Mihailović returned to his usual haunt at Struganik, which was probably the worse thing he could have done. This poses the puzzle why did he allow himself with his staff and the headquarter troops to return there, the obvious place for the Germans to search? (Unless, of course, at the time the Četniks had no agreed subsidiary assembly areas.) Three further points remain of special interest here. They are the manner and saga of Mihailović's escape, the policy and change of tactics (or the vacillations) of the German command, and, the initial and the second German offer of reward for Mihailović's head and the impact of journalism in presenting the case of a guerrilla leader.

When the 342nd Division over-run Struganik, Mihailović jumped into a ditch and covered himself with leaves. The *Wehrmacht* missed him, but captured Major Aleksandar Mišić, a Serb, and General Staff Major Ivan Fregl, a Slovene. The critical few moments Mihailović needed to escape were provided by Mišić telling his captors he was Mihailović.[31] Mišić and Fregl were taken to Valjevo, the main town in that district, and some days later the Germans shot them.[32] The intelligence officer who interrogated Mišić and Fregl at Valjevo, says Živanović, was a "German Captain by the name of Štencl,"[33] who was a regular Lieutenant Colonel in the legal corps of the Yugoslav Army until the German occupation. However, my investigation shows that in identifying this officer a serious mistake occurred, and that the German Captain "Štencl" was confused with the Yugoslav Colonel (not Lt. Colonel) Štencl, who was a prisoner of war in Germany.[34] In the event, Majors Mišić and Fregl were imprisoned together with a number of other Yugoslav army officers. According to surviving witnesses, on returning to their cell after the sentences were passed on them, Mišić and Fregl each in turn simply told their cell-mates: "Gentlemen, I have been sentenced to death."[35] This is the stuff from which national myths are made. Mišić's self-sacrifice shows how circumstances affect national memories. When Mihailović lost the civil war to Tito, Mišić's deed became politically irrelevant. If Mihailović had won, Mišić would have been a national martyr.

Regarding the policy and vacillations of the German Command in Serbia, observers seem to have overlooked the essential difference in the character of military operations of the 1941-45 war in the European East, and the 1939-45 war in the West. In the East, there was a civil war between the Nazis and the Communists ("Bolsheviks"), with no holds barred on either side. After 22 June 1941 this was the case in Serbia in the relationship between the German occupation authorities and Tito. Mihailović and his army officers however, were bound by the western rules of civilized warfare as proclaimed in the Hague Convention (IV) of 1907, *viz.*,

> the inhabitants and *the belligerents remain under* the protection and *the rule of the Law of Nations,* as they result from the usages established among civilized peoples, . . the laws of humanity, and the dictates of the public conscience.[36]

Technically, in the eyes of the *Wehrmacht,* Serbian Partisans were *illegal* irregular belligerents or *franc-tireurs* in the terms of international law.[37] However, the local German Command vacillated in its acceptance of Mihailović's men as *legal* irregular belligerents. In the final stage of the *Wehrmacht* operattion which expelled the Partisans from Serbia, on 30 November the German Plenipotentiary Commander instructed that everybody carrying identity papers authorised by Mihailović (*"Mihajlovic-Ausweisen"*) should be treated as a prisoner of war.[38] On 3 December 1941, a few days before the start of the drive against the Army Četniks, code-named "Operation Mihailović" (*"Unternehmen Mihajlovic"*), it was ordered again that any Mihailović men captured were to be disarmed and treated as prisoners of war.[39] On 5 December, the war diary of the 342nd Division reveals the policy in practice. It reads, "86 Cetniks disarmed, 8 Communists shot."[40] At the start of Operation Mihailović, in the Divisional Diary for 6 December the promise is recorded that any man who captures Mihailović will be given six weeks leave of absence.[41] On 7 December it was discovered that Mihailović had escaped the dragnet. On 8 December the Plenipotentiary Commander in Serbia notified the Division that a reward of *200,000 dinars* had been offered for Mihailović's head.[42] On the same day the capture (*"gefangen zu nehmen"*) of Mihailović's and Mišić's wives was ordered.[43] On 16 December the 1st Battalion of the Infantry Regiment 699 was ordered anew to "tidy up" (*"Saeuberung"*) the Ravna Gora area.[44] On the 17th the Battalion burned down all buildings (*"saemtliche Gebaeude"*) there,[45] including Field Marshal Mišić's villa and museum.[46] Finally on the same day, reversing his original order that captured soldiers of Mihailović should be treated as prisoners of war, the Plenipotentiary Commander in Serbia ordered that thay be treated as rebels.[47] In this manner, he stripped them of the protection of the Hague Convention of 1907 respecting the Laws and

Customs of war on land, and made then *franc-tireurs* like the Partisans, liable to be hanged or shot.[48] The vacillations of the German Command illustrate the perenial conflict between conducting a ruthless anti-guerrilla war by sheer force and terror, and offering enticements of decent treatment when captured ("stick and carrots"). Although the "stick and carrots" approach was not officially applicable to Tito's followers in 1941, its general impact (not to say "appeal") may be seen from the Partisans' own information that some of their men deserted ranks to join the Army Četniks.[49] Obviously, they wanted to profit from leniency if it came to the worst. After all, Tito was at that stage still an inept guerrilla leader, who kept his followers grouped and therefore vulnerable.

Despite claims to the contrary, Mihailović's order to his troops to disperse was the proper one under the circumstances. It enabled his forces to survive the enemy's onslaught and remain in Serbia. Mihailović was now hiding from further pursuit, which, of course, is part of an irregular belligerent's life.

On 8 December when the German Command decided to offer a reward for the capture of Mihailović, leaflets containing the proclamation of this award were to be scattered over Serbia from the air,[50] the Belgrade paper *Novo vreme* of 9 December 1941 published the reward,[51] and posters were put up.[52] This was the first instance of a German price for Mihailović's head. The allied world knew nothing about it then or later. In July 1943 a price for Mihailović's head was offered for the second time. On this occasion, the German Commander in Serbia promised "100,000 *Reichsmark* in gold" each ["100,000 rajhsmaraka u zlatu"] for Tito and Mihailović, "dead or alive." The Allied press disregarded the part of the price concerning Mihailović, and publicized exclusively the reward offered for Tito.[53] The media in that case played a major role in the unmaking of Mihailović and the making of Tito. As a general proposition this is an example of the importance of a good allied press for the success of a national guerrilla leader.

But to revert to hapless Hudson.

Hudson returned from Sandžak on the night of 7-8 December 1941 "during the German encircling assault on Mihailović's headquarters."[54] Although some other writers differ about this date,[55] it is irrelevant. The basic fact is that he returned after the German anti-guerrilla operation had compelled Mihailović to come off air, and when his fortunes in 1941 were at their nadir. To describe this situation, Deakin quotes from a Hudson telegram, sent in early 1943. It reads[56]

> I found no remains of Mihailović's men except himself and a few officers. Everyone else having converted themselves to Nedic men[57] and departed to the complete frustration of the Boche.

Deakin adds that [on this occasion],

> Mihailović refused to see Hudson after the German withdrawal, and denied him the use of radio communications.[58]

As to the radio link with the outside world, the matter was not as simple as that. Despite Deakin's earlier claim that Hudson on this occasion brought with him his own radio set, it has been shown that this claim is at least questionable. Thus, beside being unable to prevent Hudson from using a radio set which he (Hudson) did not posses, Mihailović could not given him the use of the Četnik transmitter when for sound military reasons he was himself off air.[59] However, after Hudson returned to Mihailović from Tito, the Colonel refused to deal further with Hudson and withdrew permission for his presence.

The event cannot be judged in simple black-and-white, neither had it anything to do with "equivocation." This can be demonstrated by summing up Mihailović's disciplining of Hudson. There is Mihailović, a regular soldier who, before banishing Hudson on the third occasion, had had strong disagreements with him twice before. On this occasion, Hudson had actually left the Partisans and voluntarily returned to Ravna Gora, thus finally complying with Mihailović's earlier admonishments. Mihailović was at that moment a harrassed man at the nadir of his guerrilla enterprise in 1941, and must have been labouring under considerable stress. So he seems to have missed the essence of Hudson's action of returning to him, and pinned his attention on Hudson *again* having been with the Partisans. In his eyes that must have been the last straw. Thus Mihailović committed a classic administrative blunder, and disciplined Hudson for the wrong reason. Considering that Hudson apparently lacked diplomacy, it is quite possible that the whole incident can be reduced to a clash of personalities. When later Hudson's own transmitter was found and dug out from where he buried it on parting with Tito, Mihailović relaxed his orders. Captain Perhinek was instructed to return the radio to Hudson. He did so in early May 1942.

Most of Deakin's next claim cannot be sustained either. He says,

> Mihailović vanished with a small band into East Bosnia, leaving Hudson as a lone fugitive in peasant clothes to pursue a bare and hunted existence in the scattered settlements of Ravna Gora for the following months.[60]

From there, says Deakin, Hudson "slowly" moved south-east, and eventually ended up "in the remote township of Ivanjica, in the far south-eastern corner of Sandžak..." where he had "dragged out an appalling existence."[61] Granted that in the first days after the *Wehrmacht* overran Ravna Gora Hudson was a fugitive (but so also was Mihailović with his staff), Deakin's claim is open to challenge on two main grounds. Firstly, Mihailović did not go to East Bosnia. True, such an assumption was first made in the German announcement of 200,000 *Dinars* price on Mihailović's head.[62] But the German intelligence conclusion, made in the heat of the battle, was wrong. It is not clear where Deakin obtained his information. Did he rely on secondary sources which repeated wrongly the original speculation of the German military intelligence? And secondly, Deakin claims that Hudson spent "nearly four months" at Ivanjica, whilst Mihailović was "in a village on Čemerno mountain, near the town of Gacko in Hercegoniva."[63] Deakin's geographical construction is refuted by Karchmar, who draws attention to this—

> Deakin incongruously claims that this was Mt. Cemerno in Herzegovina[64]

whereas it was Mt. Čemerno near Ivanjica,[65] and—ad Deakin says himself—Hudson was at Ivanjica. In other words, in the period when it is claimed that Mihailović was "unwilling, in his equivocal position, to associate himself too closely with the allies,"[66] he was in fact a hunted man. He was wanted by the Germans, who had even put a price on his head. All the while, he and Hudson were living in close proximity to each other.

It must be repeated that the historiography of Hudson's mission to Yugoslavia revolves around a number of incidents. They are the organization and field record of Mission Bullseye, Mihailović's reception of

Hudson on his late arrival on duty, the issue of radio-communications, action and reaction pertaining to the decisive German anti-guerrilla operation, and Hudson's hunted existence. To this should be added the apprehension in Cairo about Mihailović's possible equivocation after the *Wehrmacht* stamped out guerrilla warfare in 1941 Serbia, caused by radio-silence about Hudson's whereabouts. The latter point has been seized upon, adulterated and exploited in the post World War II committed pro-Tito historiography. On this and other concrete examples it has been shown repeatedly that only too often historical reconstructions and assessments of these issues suffer from weak research, and a cavalier treatment of chronology, political geography and even of basic topography. By contrast, here there has been established a thoroughly documented reconstruction of events and a revised historical judgment.

CONCLUSION

It has been shown that the resistance and uprisings were a Serb phenomenon. Let us now make a critical overview of the whole topic. This will provide an additional dimension for a better understanding of the consequences of the events of 1941. The immediate or the "First Wave" British response was to support Mihailović and his troops. When they learned that the communists were also taking part in the uprising in Serbia, Whitehall intervened in Moscow to have the communist leadership accept Mihailović's command. But, says Deakin, because this attempt failed, British support was transferred from Mihailović to Tito in 1943. He says that Britain had no choice as Stalin had turned down British efforts to have Tito reach an accord with Mihailović.[1] Ironically, the decision to support the Partisans, taken in Tehran on 1 December 1943, marks also the twenty fifth anniversary of the establishment of the Kingdom of the Serbs, Croats and Slovenes on 1 December 1918. Two intense thrusts of British propaganda followed immediately. In retrospect, one can say that both propaganda thrusts were based on wrong premises. Nevertheless, in the long run they laid the basis of the myth of Tito.

The first propaganda thrust was ostensibly derived from the politico-military background of the Tehran decision. Mihailović and his troops were concentrated in Serbia and eastern Yugoslavia, that is, in the "Greek hinterland." As there was to be no Allied invasion through Greece, Mihailović's geo-political location lost its strategic importance to the Partisans, who were in western Yugoslavia. Pro-Partisan propaganda and military succour had to reach such a pitch that Berlin would construe them as a harbinger for an Allied landing on the Dalmatian coast. The expected

German response would be that they should control the Dalmatian hinterland before this supposed landing. Thus, these German forces would not be available as a reserve for the Italian or the Eastern Front.

It must be said that this argument flies in the face of logic. Surely, the succour of the Allied campaign in Italy required the provocation of a concentration of German forces away from the borders of Italy (to Mihailović's location), and not at the borders (in Tito's location). Had the concentration of German troops on the Italian border occurred, *the powerful* Red Army's drive via Romania into Serbia and the Balkans would have met no German reserves. By constrast, the *weakened* Italian campaign forces of Generals Sir Harold Alexander and Mark Clark of the 5th US Army would have been potentially in a worse position. But the proverbial "British luck" held despite the wrong policy. The strategic deployment of German divisions was in no way affected by the post-Tehran propaganda. The *Wehrmacht* had been concerned with an "English" landing in the Balkans from late 1940. It was this constant threat that dictated the employment of German forces. Even the numerical increase of German troops in Yugoslavia in the closing stages of the war had nothing to do with the new British pro-Partisan policy or with Tito. It was the result of the belated retreat of the German army Group from Greece and Albania and its consequent transit through Yugoslavia.

The second propaganda thrust was designed to obviate the political embarrassment of having interfered in Yugoslav internal matters without the agreement of the allied and sovereign Yugoslav government. Under wartime circumstances this action was wrong as it signified taking sides in a civil war against the legal government of that country. What would be the reaction of the other lesser allies? The solution which was adopted was to discredit the Royal Yugoslav Government, and thus justify the new political course. As this government had its own guerrilla forces in the country, commanded by General Mihailović, the brunt of the propaganda was to be directed against him. The tone of British anti-Mihailović propaganda was prescribed by the political warfare experts. The prominent British Labourite, R.H.S. Crossman, described it as follows:

> I remember, ...the awkward moment when the Government dropped Mihailovitch and backed Tito. 'In future,' our directive ran, 'Mihailovitch forces will be described not as patriots but as

Conclusion

> terrorist gangs; we shall also drop the phrase 'red bandits,' as applied to partisans, and substitute 'freedom fighters.'
>
> . . . .
>
> I assumed that the men far above me, who made the policy decision, were as cynical about the distinction between patriots and bandits as we were. Only later did the truth dawn on me that British Cabinet Ministers, Archbishops and newspaper editors actually believed our propaganda and took this moral doubletalk seriously.[2]

British propagandists started now calling Mihailović a collaborator, although Churchill in Parliament never questioned Mihailović's personal integrity. Tito meanwhile emerged from the shadows and asserted himself in opposition to Mihailović. The erstwhile "Communists," later known as "Partisans," now became known as "Tito's Partisans." Note the date: Late 1943—early 1944 (not 1941 to late 1943).

Whereas the former or strategic propaganda thrust was based on the current British evaluation of military prospects, the latter propaganda was wrong in that it degenerated from a possible British wartime need into a definite *political* partisanship. Instead of remaining within the bounds of building up an alternative Yugoslav guerrilla or military leader, this aim was lost from sight, and Tito's protagonists started building him up as someone with exceptional endowments. This went in tandem with the unrelenting efforts to destroy Mihailović's reputation. One wonders if the balance was lost because propaganda was handled by young enthusiasts, temporary wartime appointees, who lacked the prerequisite of peacetime experience in holding responsible senior posts. Thus, the first step in creating Tito's myth was taken.

The Tehran decision of 1943 was not only a revolutionary step in the "Grand Strategy" regarding Yugoslavia, it marked also the formal end of the original or the "first wave" British response, and the official advent of the "second wave" British response. The antecedents of this event can be traced from the middle of 1942:[3] Tehran was only the final curtain, although Mihailović was irrevocably abandoned only six months later. The major protagonsts of the Second Wave have since given the tone to British-Yugoslav historiography. This makes it imperative to understand the role of its protagonists in the rise of the Second Wave, and the characteristics of their postwar writing. The starting point is—again—

operation *Bullseye* of "the Hudson case." When the historiography of Hudson's story is viewed in its Serbian setting, a crucial question arises. If this is the best effort of these historians when writing about their man in Serbia, how much credibility should they be accorded when writing of local events in the Serbian uprising? The answer is straightforward: here also, the shortcomings of their research have been repeatedly demonstrated. Furthermore, they also disregarded the influence of their formative background on the chief actors in the Serbian drama. But the events of 1941 were not self-generated. They, Mihailović, and even Tito, were in the first place Yugoslav "products" and must be studied in that context. The present book has tackled this issue. The problem which remains is—what caused the historiographical failings? The first indicator is that wartime creators of the myth of Tito finished by believing their own propaganda. But there are three more interlocked factors.

The first factor which adversely affected the quality of British-Yugoslav historiography arises from pre-World War II British-Yugoslav relations. Viewed from London, in the Europe of Versailles Yugoslavia was too far west of Istanbul and the Suez, and too far east of Paris and the Rhine. Thus, from 1919 to 1939 Yugoslavia was outside the sphere of any direct British interest. British policy was in the hands of Whitehall professionals, and a cautious middle-of-the-road line was observed. Consequently, when Hitler turned his attention to the Balkans, the British political, cultural and newspaper establishments had no worthwhile knowledge of Yugoslav matters. However, except for Churchill's venture into Greece and Yugoslavia in 1941, no lack of Yugoslav expertise caused any untoward problems at that time. When the Serb uprisings flared across occupied Yugoslavia, they were the only known, organized anti-Axis force in those parts. The British official response was to support the man of the legal government, Mihailović, and his Serbs. Concurrently, as the Serb anti-Axis resistance caught the imagination of the allied world, the need arose for instant experts to explain this phenomenon. The need to do so urgently was reinforced by the perception of the Allies that this would also boost the morale of their home front. So it became necessary to obtain and disseminate printed and broadcasted words glorifying the Serb and anti-Axis guerrilla warfare. Mihailović became "hot news." For its own reasons, this was agreeable also to the exiled Yugoslav government. But there was no time for study, neither was much

Conclusion

material readily available for this purpose. Some instant experts rose to the challenge, others failed. Current historiography still suffers from it.

As to methodological shortcomings of this historiography, they can be best illustrated by pointing out two intermittent failings. Firstly, some authors are not too scrupulous in their regard for chronology and/or respect for the impact of political geography upon the understanding of events. This, added to a tendency to be too formal and insufficiently responsive to the fast pace of the events in 1941, affects their ability to reach proper analytical assessments. Secondly, since the abandonment of Mihailović and the elevation of Tito as the "hot news," the protagonists, and later historians of the Second Wave, have become carried past the point of maintaining the myth of Tito, and into waging a private vendetta on Mihailović. It has been pointed out that their wartime age might be responsible. Indeed, as time went by, some of them seem to write of the personal commitments in their youth as if these comprised the wartime history of Yugoslavia. They have turned a past strategic decision into a private crusade, and, in order to hit better, they have also involved Mihailović's brother officers. One gets the impression that, in their eyes, Mihailović and the other Serbs who were Yugoslav officers of the old army were corrupt (whatever that might mean) and simply unable to do an honest thing. Even the fringe-dwellers of this school of history contribute to it. Thus, for instance, Wiskemann, in her "Partitioned Yugoslavia,"[4] offers the following formula: "the Great-Serb chauvinism of the politically aggressive cliques of officers" (which of course, says more of Wiskemann than of the officers). This selfopinionated school of history lacks an understanding of human nature, hence its lack of understanding of officers' motivations and actions.

The second factor deals with the genesis of this event and centres on Deakin's role in the rise of the Second Wave, as well as in the historiography. He says he was the man who influenced Churchill to switch his support from Mihailović to Tito. This claim of Deakin's has never been challenged. "As I talked," said Deakin,

> I knew that I was compiling the elements of a hostile brief which would play a decisive part in any future break between the British government and Mihailović.[5]

The implication is, of course, that despite the Tehran decision of 1 December 1943, Mihailović would not have been fully cast aside but for Deakin's intervention. The above interview occurred in the same month in Cairo. Churchill had stopped there on returning to London from Tehran, and summoned Deakin in order to interrogate him about his mission at Tito's HQ.[6] The following observations have to be made. Firstly, it has been shown that on another occasion Deakin claimed that the change of policy was due to the failure of British efforts in Moscow to have the Yugoslav Communists accept Mihailović's command. But this is a minor point in relation to the other. The second observation is that this was not the first occasion on which Deakin reported adversely on Mihailović to Churchill. Another staunch advocate of the Partisans, Basil Davidson, revealed this in his review of Deakin's *The Embattled Mountain* in the *Times Literary Supplement* in October 1971.[7] There he chided his friend Deakin for having "once more chosen discretion" in that he did not mention that he had aroused Churchill's interest in the Partisans when Churchill was in Cairo *in January* 1943.[8] Deakin has not denied Davidson's revelation. It is clear that he did not intercede with Churchill for the first time only after he had formed his eyewitness opinion of the Partisans, but eleven months earlier.

This points to Deakin's prejudice in the matter. However, even if Deakin was already against Mihailović in January 1943, this does not necessarily make him an early partisan of Tito. At the time of Deakin's first intervention, British authorities dealing with occupied Yugoslavia considered that there was relative calm in occupied Serbia, and that guerrilla warfare was going on in wartime Croatia. But they were perplexed at not being able to discern whether the "Croat Partisans" were led by Communist leadership, or by Maček's Croat Peasant Party (or the HSS).[9] It was hoped that the latter was the case. It turned out however that the "Croat" Partisans were Serbs from Dalmatia, Montenegro, west Bosnia and Croatia who were organized by the Communist Party of Yugoslavia.[10] Further developments led to Tehran. Unfortunately Deakin's personal involvement in these events has prevented him from maintaining a proper detachment in his post-war reconstruction of the road to Tehran. Had he combined his knowledge of British problems with his experiences in the *Embattled Mountain,* he could have produced a balanced historical work. Instead, he adopted the "Partisans'" (that is,

Conclusion

the KPJ's) *political* interpretation of the complex Yugoslav issues, and became the advocate of a committed view.

How is this reflected in his treatment of the events in Serbia of 1941? The style of his book is reminiscent of Dedijer's. Both are disjoined and repetitious in presentation and lacking in chronology. In Dedijer's work this can be explained by his need to suit the Party-line regardless of the evidence. One of his ways of doing so is his methodology of projecting backwards comments based on the later events. He did so in his wartime *Diary* also. Thus, parts of his diary were written after the event, but he has not told his English reader about it. On the contrary: in the Preface to the English edition of his diary,[11] he made the point that he started keeping his notes on the day of the "Axis assault on Yugoslavia" (6 April 1941), and that he always found time to carry on. For him, he says, keeping the diary was "a sacred task." Yet in the Foreward to the first edition of his *Dnevnik*.[12] he wrote that in the [northern] summer of 1941, while in German-occupied Belgrade, "I could not write anything" (*"ništa nisam mogao da pišem"*), and wrote about that period only after he escaped from Belgrade. The Partisan historian, Marjanović, made the following assessment of Dedijer's work:

> (Dedijer wrote his Diary) in different parts of the country [during the Partisans' long march across Yugoslavia]. His writing is often influenced by the opinion the leaders of the uprising held about the events, and this makes his Diary exceptionally valuable. His Diary would have been even more valuable had he noted the events as they occurred, instead of after a delay and from memory. This, for instance, is the case with all events until mid-September 1941.[13]

On the other hand, Deakin also tends to interpret the events in 1941 Serbia by projecting backwards later and irrelevant considerations. The inconsistencies and contradictions of his version of operation *Bullseye* have been pointed out in appropriate chapters. The same goes for his interpretation of the relationship between Mihailović and Hudson, and his resulting negative picture of Mihailović. In contrast to Dedijer's, Deakin's failures, including the deficient chronology, seem to stem from carelessness due to his prejudices. This makes him a hostile witness.

The third factor flows from the "change of guard" at the Yugoslav Desk, consequent upon Churchill's resolute intervention in 1943. The

Whitehall professionals and the SOE's London HQ lost their control of events. Instead, Churchill's "young set" (people like Deakin and Fitzroy Maclean[14]) stepped in and reported directly to the Prime Minister. They represent the Second Wave British response. Besides Maclean, who was not a SOE man, other non-SOE people also became intimately involved with the new policy, although on a lower level (e.g. Phyllis Auty, Elisabeth Barker, and others). They were ideologically divorced from the realities of the response of 1941. In their turn, they had no prewar knowledge of Yugoslavia either. They learned about the country as they went along, from Yugoslav refugee-politicians and from wartime intelligence intercepts. But intercepts are only a field tool, and cannot satisfy an intelligent person's craving for full understanding of the matter in hand. The refugee politicians, waging an armchair guerrilla war against each other, could not help. Eventually the "young set," through admiration for the feats of the Partisans, became responsive to the political arguments of the Partisan leadership in the same way as Deakin. These arguments were used as the basis of a re-oriented, pro-Partisan propaganda, but were put in abeyance during the 1945-48 British-Yugoslav estrangement.

When Stalin expelled Tito from the Cominform in 1948, the main works on partisan Yugoslaia emerged from the ranks of Churchill's young people. It is symptomatic that all these works were published for the first time only after 1948. With the exception of Maclean, who simply describes the job he was doing for the Prime Minister, the other Second Wave writers forced Yugoslav data to fit predetermined historical models. They are busy justifying in absolute terms Churchill's impulsive change of policy. But Tehran was only one of the possible solutions; historians should be responsive to this point. It is known, for instance, that Roosevelt did not share Churchill's view on how to deal with Yugoslavia. In the days when Churchill went out of his way to force the King of Yugoslavia to veer from Mihailović to Tito, Roosevelt wrote to Churchill on 18 May 1944,

> ...do you remember my telling you over a year ago of my talk with Peter [of Yugoslavia] in which I discussed the possibility of three nations in place of the one, he to be the head of a reconstituted Serbia.
>
> . . . .

Conclusion 225

> I think that you and I should bear some such possibility in mind in case the new government does not work out. Personally I would rather have a Yugoslavia, but three separate states with separate governments in a Balkan confederation might solve many problems.[15]

The "new government" alluded to by Roosevelt was Šubašić's, and it did not "work out." It capitulated to Tito, whereas Churchill had in mind saving what could be saved. Despite Roosevelt's conciliatory byline "Personally I would rather have a Yugoslavia" (Yugoslavia was in Churchill's sphere of interest), his conviction about the matter was clear: he advocated independence for Serbs, Croats, and Slovenes. Perhaps, had Roosevelt's approach to this problem prevailed, this issue could have been solved then, instead of still being on the agenda inherited with "Tito's Flawed Legacy." Churchill opted for Tito because he was temperamentally unsuited to Mihailović's cautious regular soldier's strategy. (Wavel and Auchinleck felt Churchill's wrath for the same reason.) Churchill did not study Yugoslav history in order to take his decision. The Second Wave historians do it now for him. This gave rise to a historiography which revolves around three themes. They are the uncritical glorifying of Tito, pillorying of Mihailović as a "traitor," and criticising him as a "pan-Serb" imperialist. Instead of telling us the facts about these men, and allowing us to get to know them, they have turned Tito into an oracle and Mihailović into a scapegoat. This will now be reviewed.

In the matter of Tito's work and person, historical detachment has been sacrificed to hagiographic interpretations. Parts of Auty's biography of Tito show the extent of this adoration. This may be illustrated by a sincere attempt of hers to build further on these shaky foundations. Her uncritical enthusiasm about her subject is seen from her remark in the "Preface" of her biography that,

> Military history [of Tito's achievement] is at present being written by Yugoslav, British and American historians whose books will be available to later biographers of Tito.[16]

In all innocence, Auty wrote this in 1970.[17] This unfulfilled expectation underlines the fact that, except in Yugoslavia, no regular officer of any army, and no military historian, ever penned a work praising Tito or criticising Mihailović. This brings to mind the reaction of Lieutenant General Sir Frederic Morgan; at one stage, in the Second World War he was Chief of Staff to the Supreme Allied Commander Designate (COSSAC). His was not a lonely voice when he pondered about the accusation that Mihailović was a traitor: "Traitor, one asked himself, to whom?"[18]

Another *leitmotiv* in the hagiography of Tito is the claim that, as the leader of the Partisans, he was the one "Yugoslav" in wartime Yugoslavia. This claim, of course, can be refuted in one line: Tito's "National Communism" cannot be dated earlier than his split with Stalin, when from foreign-imposed ruler he became a national leader. It is no use—again—projecting the future backward. As to the history of the Communist Party of Yugoslavia (KPJ), the year 1935 marks the turning point in the Comintern's directives relating to Yugoslavia. Leaving the details aside, until 1935 Yugoslavia was viewed as the southern bastion of the *cordon sanitaire* which the Europe of Versailles had erected against the Soviet Union. Therefore Yugoslavia had to be destroyed. The way to achieve this was to set all the national minorities of the State against Serbia and the Serbs, and co-operate at the same time with any Croat "anti-Belgrade" agitation. With the rise of Fascism, the 7th Congress of the Comintern in 1935 decided to adopt the *Front Populaire* political line. Postwar academic research shows that, concurrently, the KPJ abandoned its "anti-Yugoslav" line and adopted a "pro-Yugoslav" orientation. Not that this was evident in the practice of the day: this has been illustrated by studying their activity at the outbreak of the war in 1939. In any case, Broz's appointment to the General-Secretaryship of the KPJ took place in the *Front Populaire* period when his "Yugoslav" policy was that of an *apparatchik*. The point of this comment is that this development also should have been properly reflected in the historiography, and thus testify to the difference between historical and political writing.

In contrast to claims raised for Tito, Mihailović, it is said, was a "pan-Serb" imperialist. This is not a meaningful historical term; it is borrowed from the political name-calling armoury of Yugoslav in-fighting. It implies that someone is an "anti-Croat." The rejoinder is that the study of Mihailović's background and career revealed no such thing. But the legitimate question may be raised, did he change his views after the big pogroms of the Serbs? There is in existence, and accessible, a document from which this can be studied. It is a "blueprint" for a postwar Yugoslavia, dated

Conclusion

1943, and written under Mihailović's directive; basically it is a military, not a political, document.[19] It outlines the organization and role of the Yugoslav Army in the Fatherland (JVO) under his command, and deals with the transitional issues of a general uprising against the enemy and the liberation of Yugoslavia. It consists of three chapters, clauses and subclauses.

Clauses 1 and 2 of Chapter Three pertain to Mihailović's directives on how to handle the Croat problem. Clause 1 is a general discussion. Clause 2 is technical. The former discusses the different approaches to revenge, and the justified and unjustified applications of "strength" (the unjustified use being termed "bestiality"). The crux of this discussion is the proposition that the Serb people owe it to their selfrespect to revenge themselves on their wartime enemies. But he castigates personal revenge as unlawful and as contrary to a positive impact, and states that the "revenge" must be collective, given a legal form, and executed by obeying the strictest discipline. It is obvious that these arguments are a ready-made gift for whoever would like to cite them out of context. Further reading however shows that this was a *gauche* way of pacifying Serb victims and their families, and arguing for the introduction of judicial processes and outlawing blood feuds. This analysis is confirmed when reading Clause 2.

Clause 2, the technical clause, deals with resolving the issues which the Allies later were to call war crimes and war criminals. The Allies dealt with the Nazis; Mihailović with the Croat Ustašas and sundry other war criminals. This then should be considered to be Mihailović's "policy" on the subject, although not in the literal sense that he actually wrote the document. Keeping this qualification in mind, let us hear Mihailović's policy on the subject. The opening line reads:

> The question of Serbo-Croat relations is one of the most painful ones brought about by the war.

Five pages later, after having discussed the case of Pavelić and his Ustašas, and the harm they have done to both Serbs and Croats, the comment reads

> Our enemy are not the Croat people, but the followers of [the Croat chauvinist ideologue Dr Josip] Frank. . . . The Croat people cannot be held responsible for the crimes committed by the followers of

Frank led by Pavelić, in the same way the Serb people cannot be held responsible for whatever the Ljotićites might do . . . .

And again, on the next page:

The treatment of the Croats must be the same as that of the Serb population.

This is followed by a number of guidelines. A condensed version of the major points is as follows:

- The Croats were to be exhorted to co-operate, 'and from their manpower should be formed purely Croat military units.' [This is a reaffirmation of Mihailović's prewar recommendations.]
- Members of the existing Croat regular army[20] were also to be exhorted to co-operate;
- The Croats were further to be exhorted to surrender the members of the Ustaša 'and all those who had in any way harmed the Serb and Croat peoples.' Such transgressors were to be arrested and brought to a People's Court of Justice with juries consisting of 50-50% Serbs and Croats, and presided over by a regular or reserve Military Judge-Officer from the legal corps of the army;
- Finally, 'Any Ustašas who offered armed resistance' were not to be treated as prisoners of war 'but as traitors.' They were to be dealt with by the Field Court Martials.

At the time, one of the burning questions was how to treat individual Franciscans and other clergy who had participated with arms in hand in the Ustaša genocide. Besides being a delicate question of Yugoslav domestic politics, it also had sensitive diplomatic ramifications. As a matter of fact, later in the war the supposed threat of Mihailović's counter-genocide of the Croats was one of the arguments in the anti-Mihailović propaganda. But what were Mihailović's views insofar as they can be documented? In his guidelines, there is an instruction not to raise religious issues, and a statement that the "transgressors from clerical ranks" should be treated "the same as everybody else." That is, he made it compulsory to extend the protection of trial by jury to the compromised clergy.

Conclusion

Finally it is relevant to review critically the assertion of Mihailović's collaboration with the *Wehrmacht* to quash the uprising and expell the Partisans from Serbia in 1941. It has been shown that, as a matter of fact, this never happened, his meeting with *Oberstleutnant* Kogard at Divci notwithstanding. Still the accusation persists, together with the claim that Mihailović was "equivocating" between the Germans and the British. As this is not so, and his pro-Allied record is unblemished, what is it that triggered this political ploy? The answer, or, at least, the earliest contributory answer to understanding the origin of this happening is to be found in a Foreign Office file.[21] The central item in this file is an English translation of a pamphlet issued by the "partisan Freedom Front" in Slovenia[22] on 1 December 1941. It is a communique of the "G.H.Q. of the partisan Freedom Front in Yugoslavia" [located in Serbia], sent to the executive Committee of the Freedom Front of Slovenes.[23] Its purport was to advise the Slovenes that "fighting broke out between the partisan groups and units of the Četniks of Mihajlović [sic]." Copies of the English translation were sent to at least two senior officials of the Foreign Office by Miha Krek, the Slovene "Vice-Premier Minister" of the Royal Yugoslav government in exile. The Foreign Office advised Lord Glenconner, the new ministerial head of the SOE. (How did it reach Krek in London?)

The contents of the pamphlet, listing names and incidents which were said to have resulted in the civil war in Serbia, were damning for Mihailović. In retrospect, it can be seen that its six clauses became the model for all future assertions that Mihailović was fighting the Partisans and collaborating with the enemy in Serbia. The Foreign Office officials did not know what to make of it. Their reaction can be seen from their annotations in the file. Everybody's consensus was that "we cannot fathom" why Krek distributed this document. On 2 March 1942, C. L. Rose of the Foreign Office's Southern Department wrote that

> The document itself sets out the Communist case against Mihailovic: it looks quite convincing, but without hearing the other side we cannot judge.

One could not be more fair.

The date of the pamphlet is crucial: 1 December 1941. That means that the letter of the Partisan HQ must have left Serbia before that date, but when? The last date mentioned in the text is 2 November. This sets the earliest possible date of the dispatch, and restricts it to between 3 November and at least a few days before 29 November, when the *Wehrmacht* overran Užice and Tito's HQ there, and Tito escaped from Serbia. Yet it is on record that in the same period, following Tito's request to Mihailović of 17 November,[24] there was a meeting of a mixed Partisan—Army Četniks commission in Serbia, charged with investigating their mutual accusations and counter-accusations in the ongoing civil war. Hudson participated in at least some of these investigatory meetings.[25] The last session of the commission was held on 27 November, when it was decided to postpone further meetings till after the German "punishment expedition" (which was underway) was over.[26] But the Partisans escaped from Serbia and this never eventuated. Comparison of Partisan assertions in the mixed commission and those in the pamphlet show them to be similar. Therefore it may be asserted that the letter was a political ploy. They used this to have a "leg" to fight on, if they were to be losers to Mihailović in the field.

This incident adds another additional dimension to conclusions drawn from the field documents of the events and the evidence regarding the British response. Whereas Mihailović and his officers thought that military considerations would decide the outcome, the contrived political missive of 1 December has achieved at least one lasting effect. The final paragraph of Clause 5 of the letter has remained enshrined in much of the current historiography, and certainly in laymen's opinions. The original text in the letter reads:

> Mihajlovic [sic] served two chiefs; he was sending false information to the Government in London and was therefore recognized as the commander of all troops fighting in Serbia for freedom. At the same time he was in communication with Nedic and the Germans . . . .

The other claim of Clause 5 is that Mihailović fought the communists because the enemy paid him moneys to do so. Significantly, even committed historians have exercised discretion on this point, and abstained from disseminating it. By contrast, many of them often enough copied *verbatim* the text of the story about Mihailović "serving two chiefs."

This is not to imply that there was a mole in the Foreign Office who "leaked" this document. Yet it stands to reason that these contrived claims of the Communist Party of Yugoslavia were originally disseminated by

Conclusion

the Stalinist disinformation network of the time. In any case, whereas the British, ever watchful of their own interest, observed the Yugoslav scene with an open mind, the intercession of the Royal Vice-Prime Minister, Krek, is an early documented instance of the political manoeuvring of Yugoslav *émigré* politicians in London and in Cairo. In the final analysis, Mihailović was both exploited and betrayed by his own kind. Both internationally and nationally, politics, not professional military considerations, were the ultimate deciding factor regarding the resistance and the uprising in occupied Yugoslavia.

DIAGRAMS, PHOTOCOPIES, SKETCH-MAPS AND TABLES

LEGEND: D   Diagram   S   Sketch-map
              P   Photocopy   T   Table

YUGOSLAVIA AND SERBIA (S)
    The Territory of Yugoslavia during the Second World War
    Sketch showing relative remoteness of Montenegro
    Territory of the Military Commander in Serbia (Mid June 1941)

YUGOSLAV-GERMAN WAR, April 1941 (T)
    Numbers of Yugoslav POWs in 1941

THE BRITISH SPECIAL AGENCIES (D)
    "Avowable" and "Non-Avowable" Action,
        Agreement Grand–Holland
    Genesis of the British Special or Secret
        Intelligence Service (SIS) including
        setting up of Section 'D'
    SOE establishment and incumbents chart,
        London–Middle East–The Balkans, August 1941

BRITISH-YUGOSLAV COOPERATION (P)
    Memorandum of Ilić–Masterson meeting, Cairo,
        25 September 1941
    Chiefs of Staff to C-in-C Mediterranean,
        Message of 15 October 1941

OPERATION 'BULLSEYE', CAPTAIN HUDSON (D.P.S.T.)
    Hudson's "Bullseye" Instructions
    Bullseye mission in Montenegro
    Perišića Dol. Description of Mission Bullseye's
        landing place (Extract from Commander Woods's Report)

Diagrams, Photocopies

HMS *Triumph:* Special Operation [Operation Bullseye],
(Extract from Commander Woods's report)

Petrovac and Pelješac

Hudson's early movements in Serbia and Sandžak

The two mountains Čemerno:
Where was Mihailović? Where Hudson?

THE SERBIAN UPRISING OF 1941 (D.P.S.)

The German Plenipotentiary Commanding General in Serbia:
Distinguish between the 'loyal Četniks'
and 'enemy Četniks'

Gornji Milanovac: guerrilla attack, 28-29 September 1941

Captain Jovan V. Derok, testimonial of Brigadier
C. D. Armstrong, CBE DSO MC

Order of battle when crushing the Serbian uprising of 1941

The announcement that 2,100 people were shot on 10 October 1941

Meeting Mihailović—The German Command at Divci,
11 November 1941

Calculations as to how many Serbs to shoot (2 sheets)

Zugsfuehrer Josip BROZ (identification by the Austrian
State Archives)

The draft of the first price on Mihailović's head

The announcement of the award of 100,000 RM in gold
for each of Tito and Mihailović

234 BRITISH SPECIAL OPERATIONS

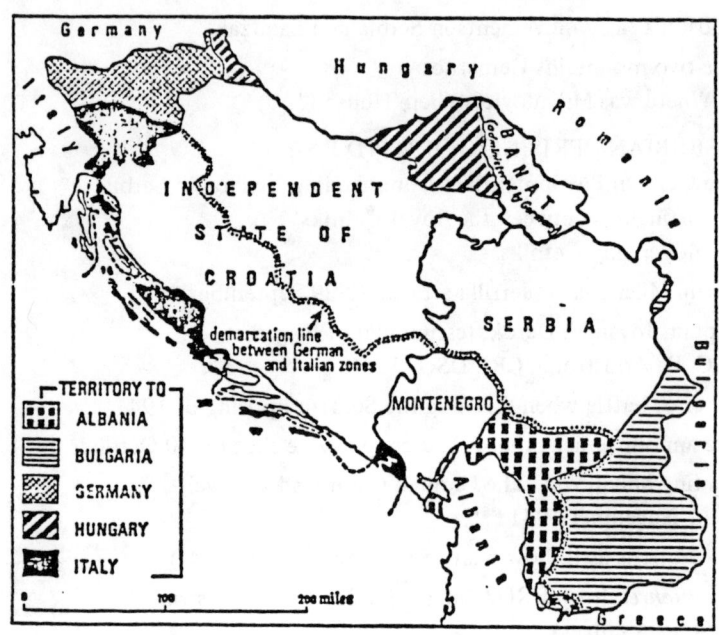

THE TERRITORY OF YUGOSLAVIA DURING THE SECOND WORLD WAR

From Stevan K. Pavlowitch, <u>Yugoslavia</u>,
New York and Washington, Praeger, 1971.

Copied by permission S.K. Pavlowitch.

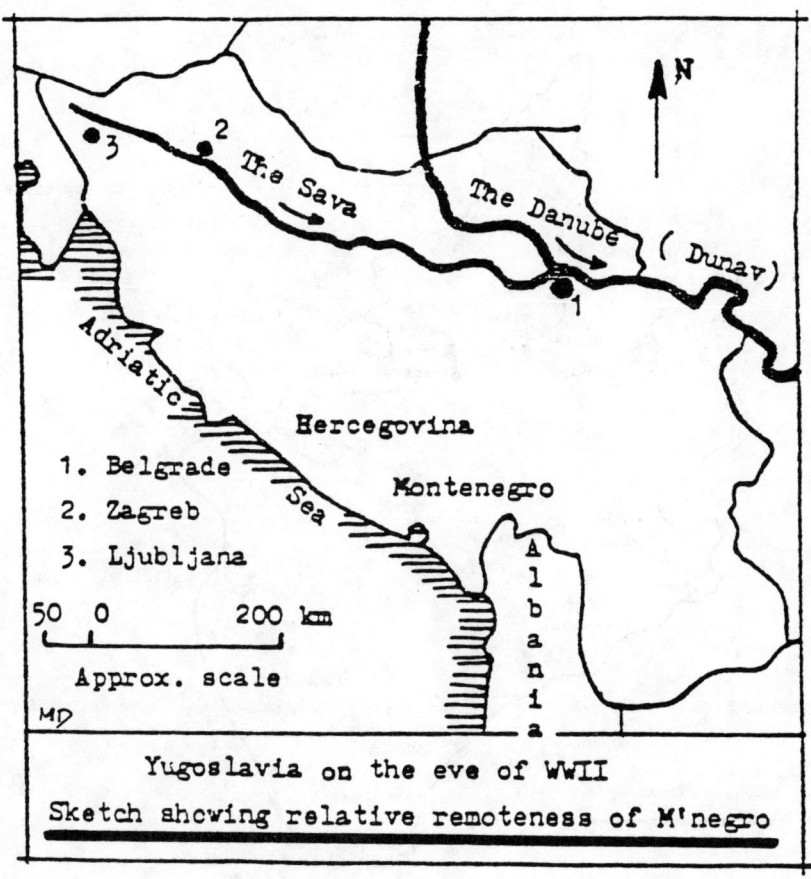

Yugoslavia on the eve of WWII
Sketch showing relative remoteness of M'negro

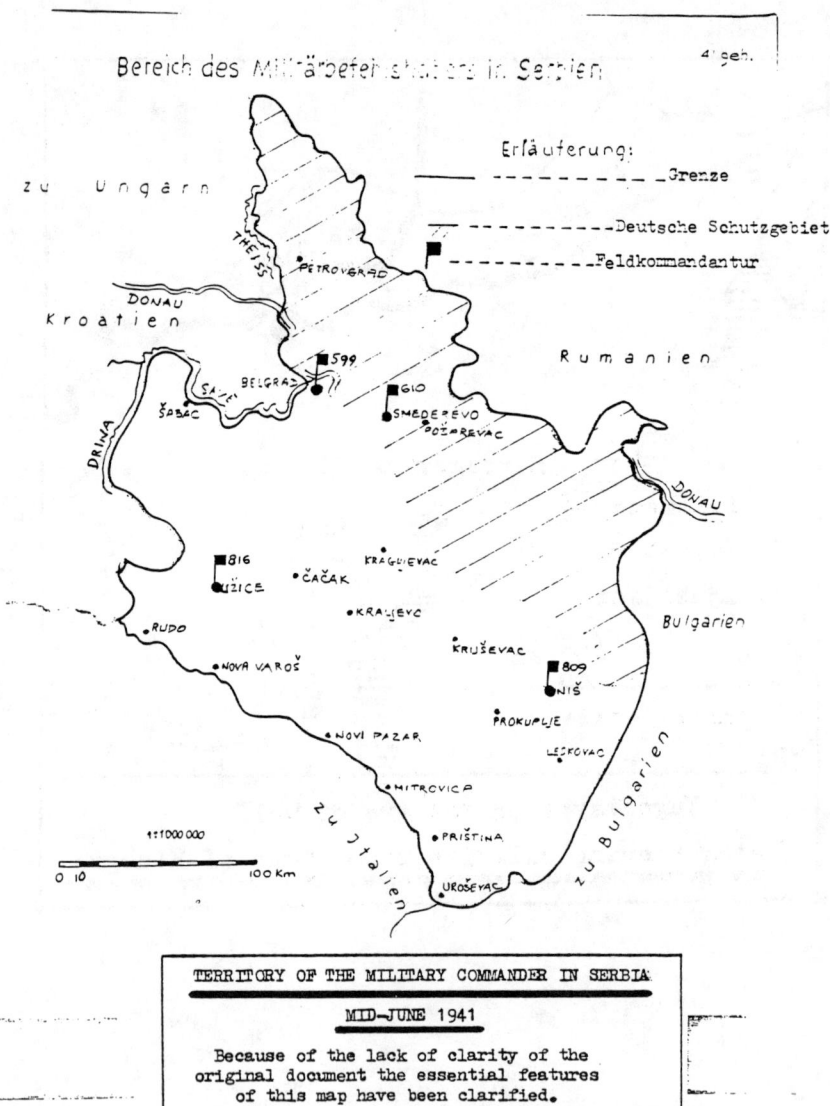

Diagrams, Photocopies

	CAPTURED					
Item (Source)	By the Germans			By the Italians	By the Bulgarians	By the Hungarians
	In Battle	After Capitul.				
a	b	c		d	e	f
1. Tippelskirch, Geschichte p. 150	1,500 officers 224,000 men	334,000 officers and men				
2. Matl in Osteuropa p. 102		344,000 Serbs				
3. Terzić, Jugoslavija p. 575		345,000 eventually retained 200,000 (±)		30,000 10,000 (±)		
4. US Army Pamphlet 20-260 p. 64		254,000 Serbs (±)				
5. See Legend (It.)				Not less than 8,825 of whom "all 2,480 Croats" were released by 12 November (It.)		
REGISTERED WITH THE ICRC						
6. ICRC, letter of 26 May 1981 to MD	As on 1 December 1941 (±) 10,801 officers 155,630 men ――――― 166,431					
7. ICRC, letter of 26 October 1982 to MD				As on 22 Jan 1942 (ß) 6,345	As on 21 Octo 1941 Nil	As on 24 Nov 1941 Nil

Legend:
    ICRC International Committee of the Red Cross.
    (±) [After the Croats et al. were released & the Serbs retained in captivity.]
    (It.) For the release see the Italian Communiqué in The Bulletin of International News, XVIII(24), 29 November 1941, p. 1951, item "12 November". However the Montenegrins were released also, so that the total in Column 5d should be higher.
    (ß) [The Serbians retained only.]

MD

NUMBERS OF YUGOSLAV POWs IN 1941

Chronology and/or event abroad	Foreign Office (FO)	War Office (WO)	Notes
1938 13 March: Germany incorporates Austria September: Munich agreement **1939** 15 March: German army enters Prague Great Britain announces decision to resist further German demands	Late March: Section D set up to study unconventional warfare (sabotage) Due to overlap in activities of their sections, Grand of Section D and Holland of GS(R) agree - "D" to handle actions H.M. Government could not avow (field personnel not in uniform), - GS(R) to handle actions the Government can avow (field personnel in uniform)	In November Major J.C.F. Holland, newly apptd head of the research sectn of the General Staff at WO, GS(R)* steers it to to the research of guerrilla warfare Holland and Grand prepare paper submitted on 20 March to Viscount J.S. Gort, CIGS	*In the spring of 1939 GS(R) is renamed MI R and becomes part of milit. intell. directorate

"Avowable" and "Non-Avowable" Actions
AGREEMENT GRAND - HOLLAND

MD

Diagrams, Photocopies

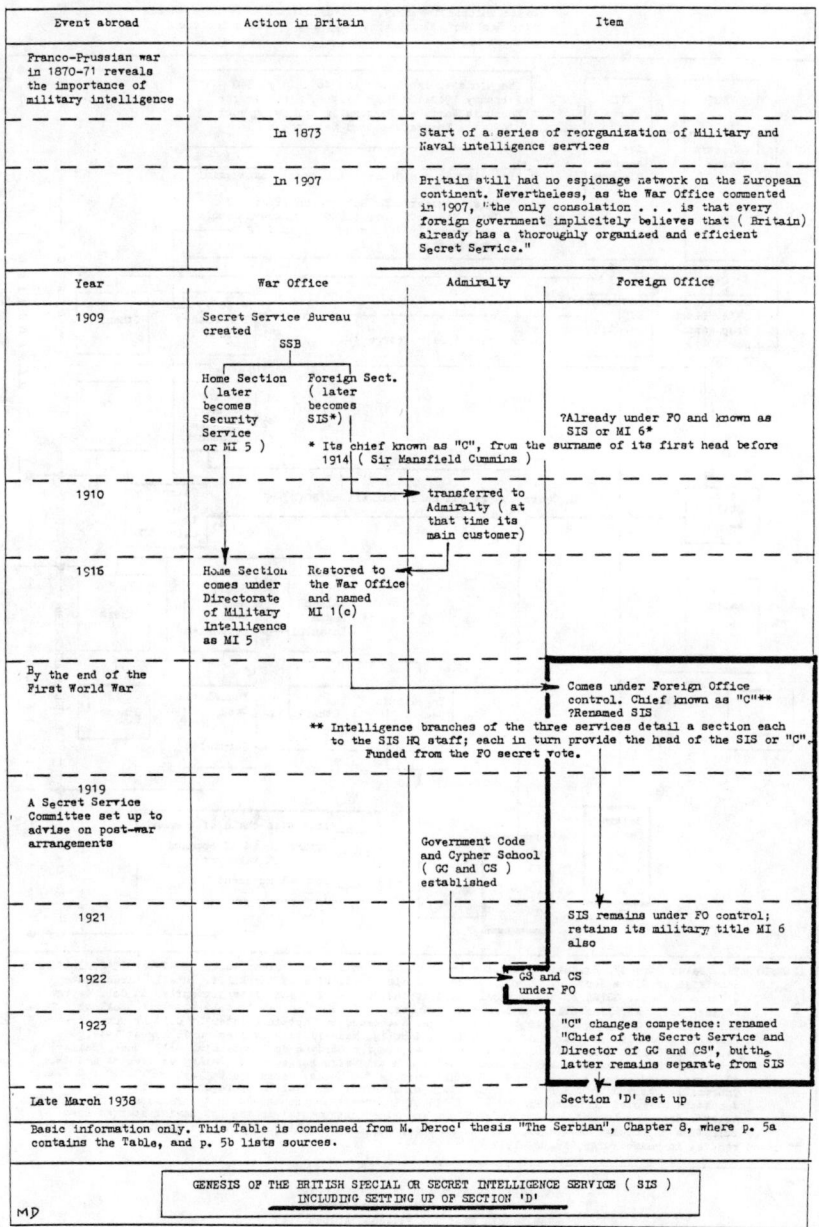

Event abroad	Action in Britain			Item	
Franco-Prussian war in 1870-71 reveals the importance of military intelligence					
	In 1873			Start of a series of reorganization of Military and Naval intelligence services	
	In 1907			Britain still had no espionage network on the European continent. Nevertheless, as the War Office commented in 1907, "the only consolation . . . is that every foreign government implicitly believes that (Britain) already has a thoroughly organized and efficient Secret Service."	
Year	War Office		Admiralty		Foreign Office
1909	Secret Service Bureau created SSB — Home Section (later becomes Security Service or MI 5)	Foreign Sect. (later becomes SIS*) * Its chief known as "C", from the surname of its first head before 1914 (Sir Mansfield Cummins)			?Already under FO and known as SIS or MI 6*
1910			transferred to Admiralty (at that time its main customer)		
1916	Home Section comes under Directorate of Military Intelligence as MI 5	Restored to the War Office and named MI 1(c)			
By the end of the First World War				Comes under Foreign Office control. Chief known as "C"** ?Renamed SIS ** Intelligence branches of the three services detail a section each to the SIS HQ staff; each in turn provide the head of the SIS or "C". Funded from the FO secret vote.	
1919 A Secret Service Committee set up to advise on post-war arrangements			Government Code and Cypher School (GC and CS) established		
1921				SIS remains under FO control; retains its military title MI 6 also	
1922				GC and CS under FO	
1923				"C" changes competence: renamed "Chief of the Secret Service and Director of GC and CS", but the latter remains separate from SIS	
Late March 1938				Section 'D' set up	

Basic information only. This Table is condensed from M. Deroc' thesis "The Serbian", Chapter 8, where p. 5a contains the Table, and p. 5b lists sources.

GENESIS OF THE BRITISH SPECIAL OR SECRET INTELLIGENCE SERVICE (SIS)
INCLUDING SETTING UP OF SECTION 'D'

MD

240 BRITISH SPECIAL OPERATIONS

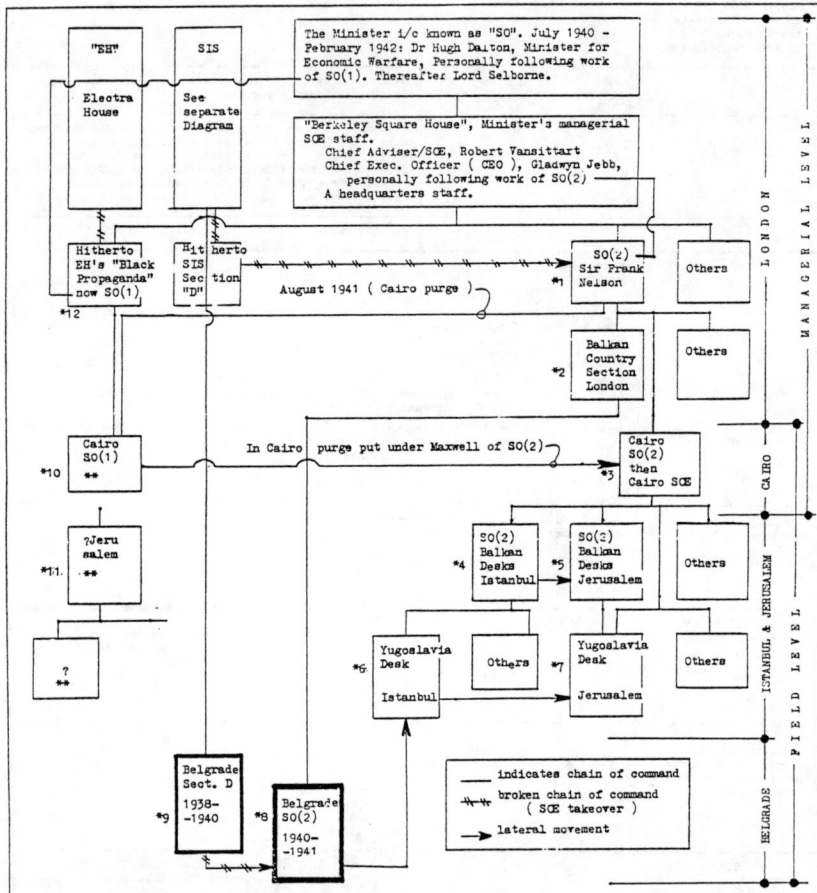

Basic information only, condensed from M. Deroc's thesis "The Serbian", Ch. 8, pp. 6a, b and c, which include sources also.

LEGEND: *1. "Baker Street". Executive Director known as "CD": Sir Frank Nelson August 1940-May 1942. Initially consisted of SIS's Sect. D, later incorporated also Sect. MI R of the Milit. Intell. Directorate (formerly Sect. GS(R) of the General Staff at the WO). - *2. Head, intermittently, Lt. Col. George F. Taylor, and Australian oilman and merchant banker. - *3. SO(2) under Lt Col. George A. Pollock (later Sir George P. QC), August 1940 to Cairo Purge. Succeeded by Captain (later Lt Col) Arthur Terrence Maxwell, a banker, in charge of both SO(2) and SO(1). Maxwell took over as on 15 August 1941. - *4. Heads: Julius Hanau, Stanley William Bailey, George Gardyne de Chastelain. - *5. Under Bailey, who moved there from Istanbul in April 1941 and until Cairo Purge. - *6. Bailey as item *4 and *5. *7. Ibid. - *8. Heads: Bailey and T.S. Masterson. - *9. Heads: Hanau and Bailey. - *10. Col. C.J.M. Thornhill, removed in Cairo Purge. His field of interest was Italian propaganda. - *11. Lt. Col. K. Johnstone, removed in Cairo Purge. His field of interest was propaganda in the Balkans. - *12. "Woburn Alley". Head Rex Leeper, an Australian, who was also instrumental in the BBC having started news bulletins in foreign languages. His Woburn Alley staff were colloquially known as "Leeper's Sleepers".
** means removed in Cairo Purge, August 1941.

SOE ESTABLISHMENT AND INCUMBENTS CHART
London-Middle East-The Balkans, August 1941

MEMORANDUM OF MEETING AT THE YUGOSLAV MINISTRY FOR WAR

25.9.41.

At a meeting held on 25th September, 1941 at the YUGOSLAV Ministry for War between General ILLIC, YUGOSLAV Minister for War, Colonel POPOVIC, YUGOSLAV D.D.K.I., Mr. MASTERSON and Mr. BENNETT, certain decisions were reached regarding future work back into YUGOSLAVIA.

General ILLIC and Mr. MASTERSON will work in complete co-operation on the following questions:-

    A. To establish and ensure lines of communication with YUGOSLAVIA.

    B. To organize restricted sabotage in YUGOSLAVIA. Restricted sabotage meaning sabotage of railway stock - lines - communications and fuel like - which can be carried out without use of explosives and therefore unlikely to bring about reprisals.

    C. Coincident with restricted sabotage, the country to be prepared for a final uprising - food.

MEMORANDUM OF ILIĆ – MASTERSON MEETING
AT THE YUGOSLAV MINISTRY FOR WAR IN CAIRO, 25.9.1941
(Part-photostat, reduced size)

Copied by permission
Colonel Popović

MOST SECRET

MOST SECRET   MESSAGE   OUT

2206/15th October.

TO: Commander-in-Chief,   Date: 15.10.41.
      Mediterranean. 207.

Naval Cypher O.T.T.

FROM: Admiralty.

IMMEDIATE.

Following for Commanders-in-Chief from Chiefs of Staff No.182.

Para.1. King of Yugoslavia has made a personal and urgent appeal to the Prime Minister for assistance to be given to guerilla forces now fighting in his country.

Para.2. From our point of view revolt is premature, but patriots have thrown their caps over the fence and must be supported by all possible means.

Para.3. It is clear that help can only come from the Middle East, and it is important that you should do all that you can as quickly as you can. Please inform us what you are already doing and what further help you can give without prejudice to other operations, also whether we can do anything from this end. Patriots report that aerodromes at Preljina, Chachak and Pozega are in their hands, and their headquarters is at Suvobor.

'B'

2206A/15.

Secretary to V.C.N.S.

1st Lord.
1st S.L.
V.C.N.S.
A.C.N.S.(F)
N.A.1st S.L.
P.A.S.(S)
D.O.D.(F)
D.D.O.D.(F)
D. of P.(2)
Duty Capt.(2)
E.P.S.
Hd. of M.(10)
I.P.(2)
N.I.D.10.Pay.Cdr.Wilson.
W.D.
D.N.I.(4)

PRO DOCUMENT PREMIER 3/510/4
Photocopied by permission, which is gratefully acknowledged. PRO letter 2/CASE 4/1 of 8 February 1985 over the signature of Dr J.B. Post, and PRO letter of 14 July 1986 over the signature of Dr Meryl R. Foster.

CHIEFS OF STAFF TO COMMANDERS-IN-CHIEF

Diagrams, Photocopies

		SOURCE			
Gl. Mihailović (1946)	Jakša V. Djelević (1950)	F.W. Deakin (1971)	Colonel D.T. Hudson (1974)	Colonel S.W. Bailey (1973 - 1975)
(a)	(b)	(c)	(d)	(e)
"I got a message from Hudson. It is the message found in my files. It was a message to the effect that in Yugoslavia a rebellion would not be tolerated, but that the struggle should be waged for Yugoslavia and not become a struggle of the communists for the Soviet Union." . . . . "I got it from Hudson and through the wireless."	"Hudson brought the message that Yugoslavs should fight for own freedom, and not for Soviet or British ends; he demanded intensification of the struggle and a harmonious cooperation with the Partisans."	"(Captain Hudson) received only a very general briefing on what to expect on landing at the point chosen in Montenegro. His directive was in the vaguest terms: to contact, investigate, and report on all groups offering resistance to the enemy, regardless of race, creed or political persuasion." Note: in Proceedings, p.331, Yugoslav section p. "Yug. 5", from "to contact" to "persuasion" Deakin's text is identical with the text above.	"(Hudson) said that when he was sent by S.O.E. in mid-September 1941, as the first British officer into Yugoslavia, he was given a roneod sheet of paper on which the brief for his mission was described as 'to co-ordinate the forces of resistance against the enemy'. He later showed this paper first to Tito, then to Mihailović, . . ." . . . . "Hudson interpreted his brief to mean that he should travel anywhere and meet anyone to further his task of co-ordination."	"(British authorities) did provide a clear and unambiguous British brief. This laid down that in addition to the collection of technical military intelligence about the disposition, strength and armament of Axis forces and related matters, the party's task was to make contact with, investigate and report back on all elements offering resistance to the enemy, regardless of nationality, religion or political belief. No copy of this brief has survived in British hands . . .; but the text may well be in the hands of the present Yugoslav Government . . . ."

NOTES

(a) <u>The Trial of Dragoljub-Draža Mihailović, Stenographic Record</u>, Belgrade, 1946, pp. 123-24. – In a summary of this trial (10 June - 15 July, 1946), <u>Keesing's Contemporary Archives</u> of 17-26 June 1948, p. 9348, it is said that Hudson denied this version, stated that he delivered the message "that the war should be waged for Yugoslavia" and not on behalf of "Russia or Great Britain", and claimed that "the words 'or Great Britain' had been omitted" at the trial. The date of Hudson's statement was probably 12 June 1945 [sic, probably 1946], <u>ibid.</u>, p. 9347.

(b) Jakša V. Djelević, "Iz prvih meseca", ["From the Early Months"], in Knežević, <u>Knjiga 1</u>, p. 185. At the time, the then Lieutenant Djelević was A.D.C. to Colonel Mihailović.

(c) Deakin, <u>Embattled</u>, p. 129. Deakin probably acquired his knowledge while briefed in Cairo to be attached as 2 i/c to Colonel Bailey at General Mihailović headquarters (but was sent, instead, to Tito).

(d) This is Phyllis Auty recounting Colonel Hudson's "own personal account of his mission", which he gave her on 8 July 1974 ("Note on Colonel D.T. Hudson's account of his mission to Yugoslavia 1914 [sic]- 4", in Auty and Clogg, <u>British</u>, p. 91).

(e) S.W. Bailey, "British Policy Towards General Draža Mihailović" in Auty and Clogg, <u>British</u>, pp. 60-61. Colonel Bailey's knowledge is based on his personal involvement in the early stages of Operation Bullseye (prior to Cairo purge in 1941), and on his briefing before being sent to Yugoslavia as the Senior British Liaison Officer to General Mihailović.

MD

HUDSON'S "BULLSEYE" INSTRUCTIONS – COMPARATIVE TABLE OF PRIMARY AND SIMILAR SOURCES

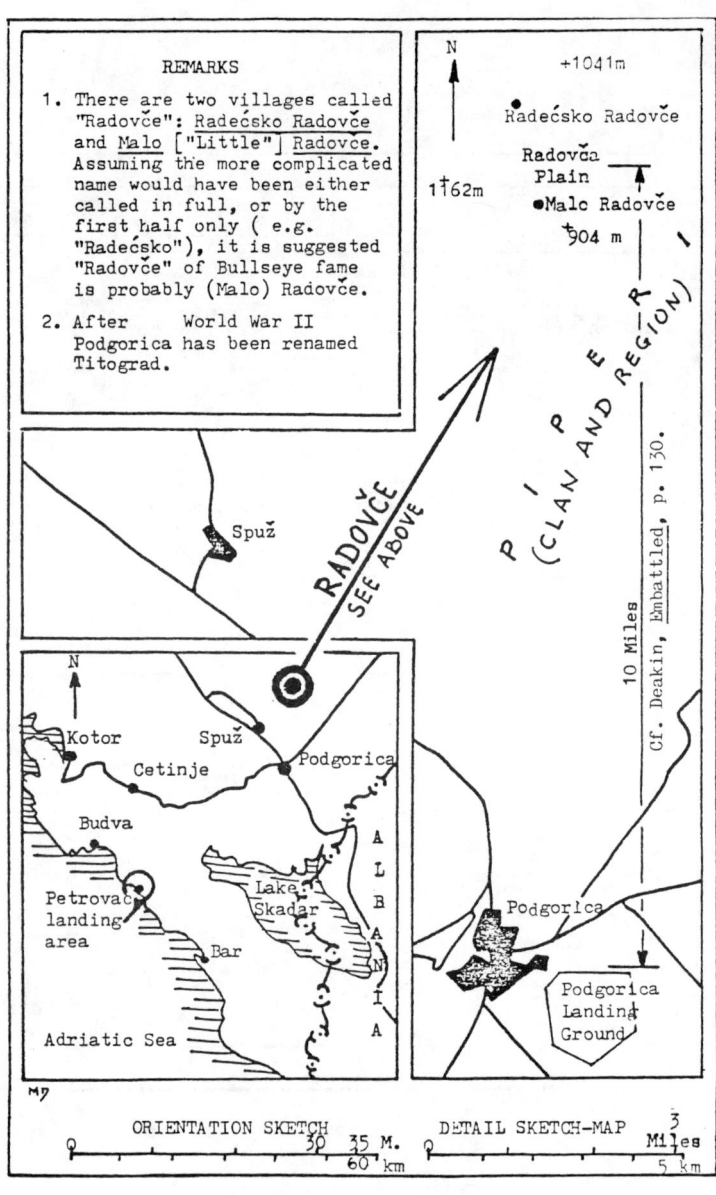

BULLSEYE MISSION IN MONTENEGRO

(1941 TOPOGRAPHY)

DESCRIPTION OF LANDING PLACE

PERISICADOL BAY near PETROVAC

The landing place (PERASICADOL BAY 042.12'9N 018.55'6E) proved ideal. The hills behind it provided adequate leading marks, while a large, light coloured cliff on the southern side made identification easy. The coast is steep to, enabling the submarine to get within 300 yds of the beach if required. The high cliffs round the bay then shield the submarine from view from all points except the actual beach and cliff tops.

The beach, to the left of a large mass of rock in the centre of the bay, is well suited to landing by canoe. Ashore there is good cover close to the beach, a ruined house in which gear can be hidden, and a convenient pathway leading up to the road through good cover.

While the landing was being carried out there was a fresh NE'ly wind with strong gusts, but there was complete shelter from this wind when 500 yds or less from the beach. It is considered that landings by FOLBOT could be carried out on this beach in winds up to force 5 from directions between NW, through N to E.

(Sgd) W.J.W. WOODS
Commander.

PERIŠIĆA DOL
DESCRIPTION OF MISSION BULLSEY'S
LANDING PLACE

Extract from Commander Woods's report

PRO document ADM 236/36
Copied by permission

Special Operation.

Captain HUDSON and his three Serbs set off on what was obviously going to be a very trying few days in great heart, having taken their first experience of submarine travel, which included an attack and subsequent depth charging, completely in their stride.

They had been sent on the expedition at short notice, and their equipment had to be substantially supplemented from Ship's resources. <u>This has been a common feature of all combined operations on which TRIUMPH has been engaged.</u> The actual equipment supplied by TRIUMPH was as follows:-

Webbing Equipment.

- 4 pouches for pistol ammunition.
- 3 pistol carriers.
- 6 rifle equipment braces.
- 2 rifle slings.
- 2 pistol belts.
- 2 sets of pistol braces.

Private property.

- 2 daggers with sheathes.
- 1 pair of binoculars with case.
- 1 pouch for military compass.

Medical.

- 1 tin adhesive tape.
- 20 M & B 693 tablets.
- 24 Halibut liver oil capsules.
- Iodine.

2 pints 6 tots of Rum.

Clothing (supplied by Egyptian Detail, LAZARETTO)

- 3 khaki shirts
- 2 pairs khaki shorts.

HMS <u>TRIUMPH</u>: SPECIAL OPERATION
[OPERATION BULLSEYE]

Extract from Commander Woods's report

PRO document ADM 236/36
Copied by permission

Diagrams, Photocopies 247

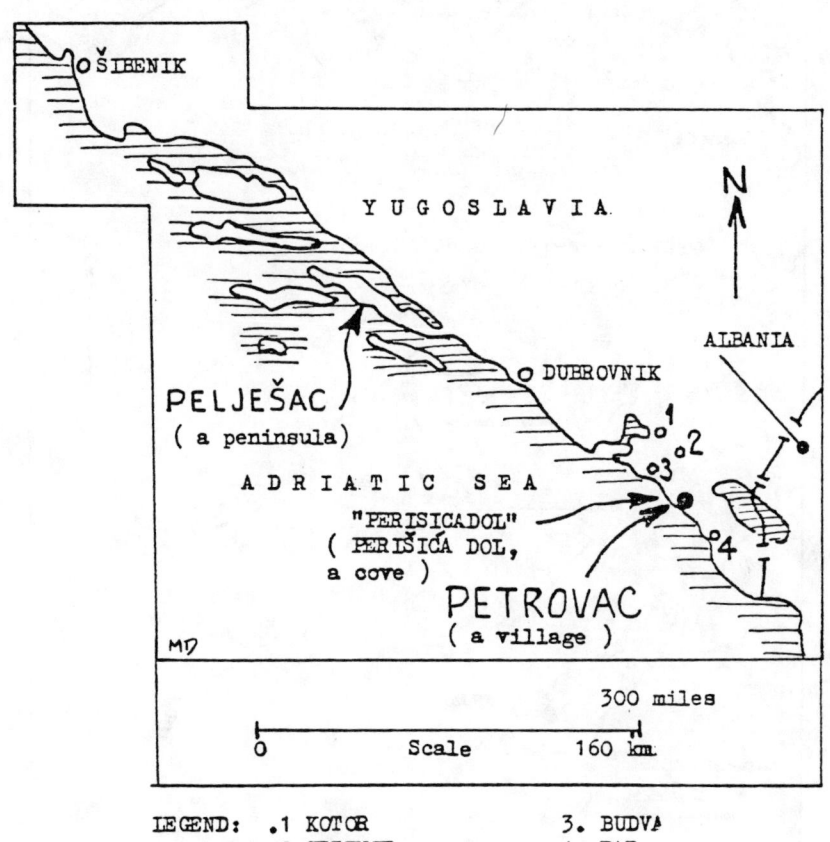

PETROVAC AND PELJEŠAC

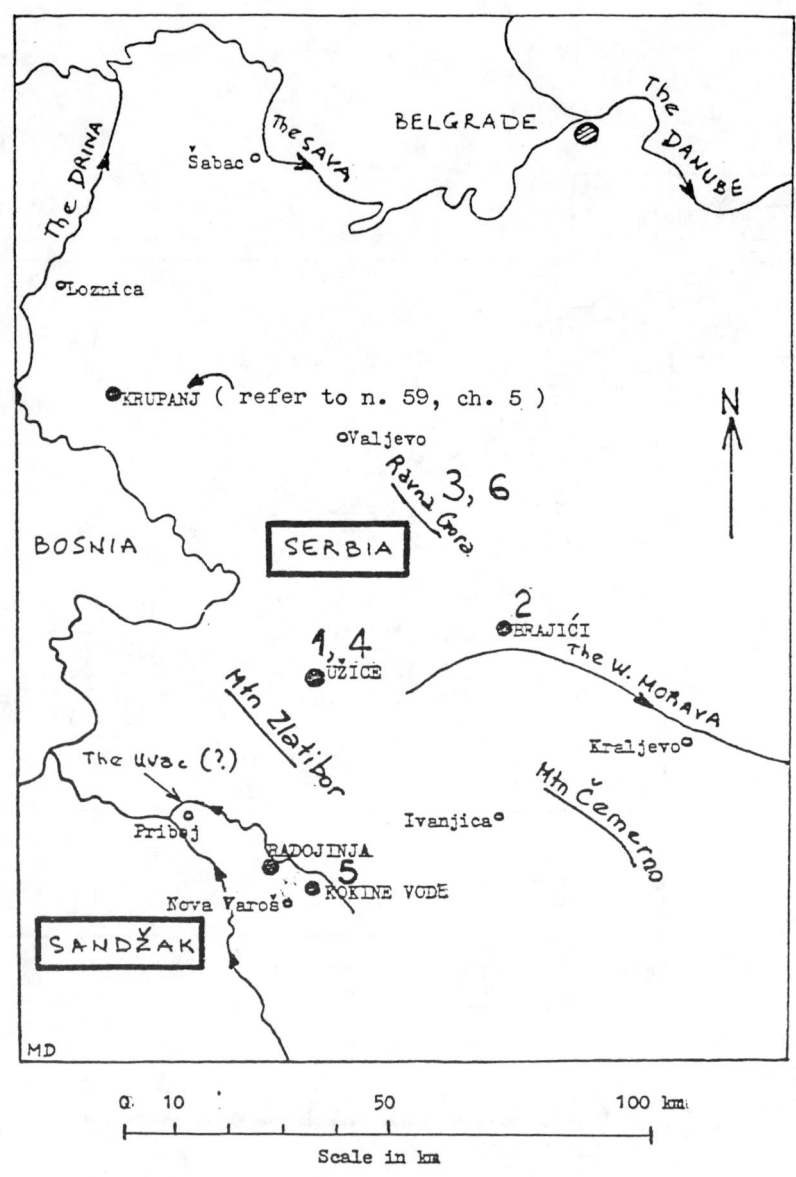

HUDSON'S EARLY MOVEMENTS IN SERBIA AND SANDŽAK
Numerals indicate sequence of movements

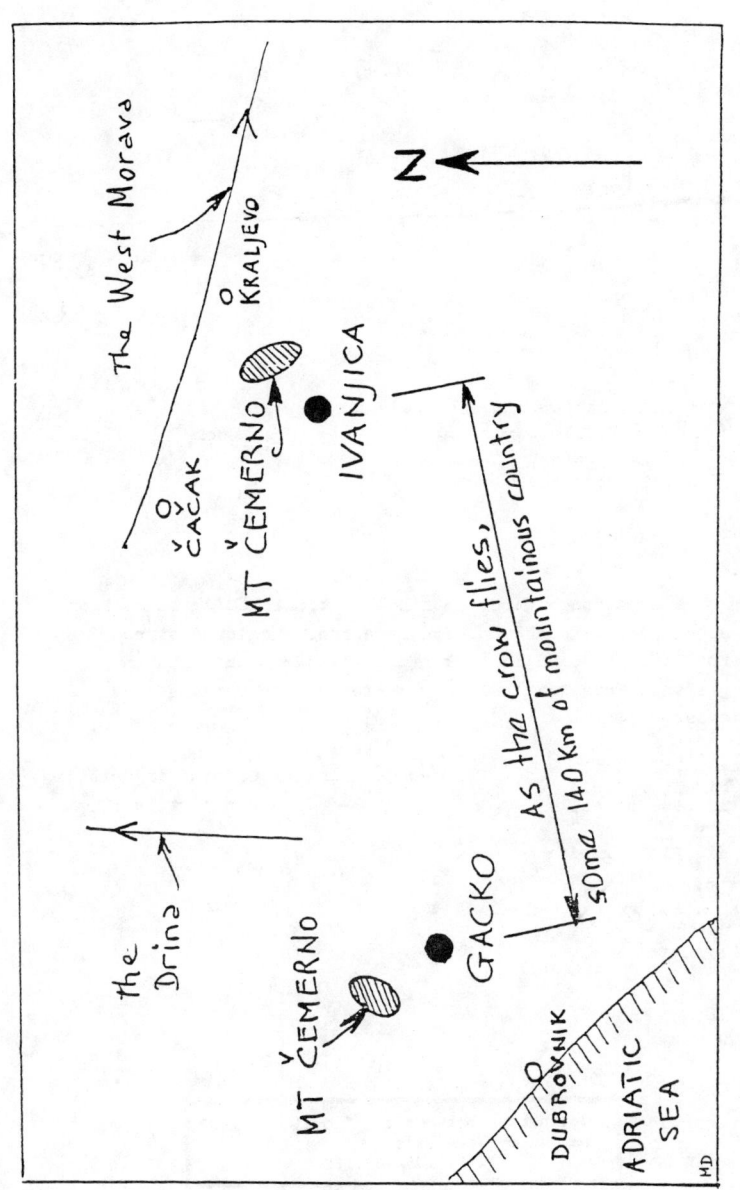

THE TWO MOUNTAINS ČEMERNO
WHERE WAS MIHAILOVIĆ? WHERE HUDSON?

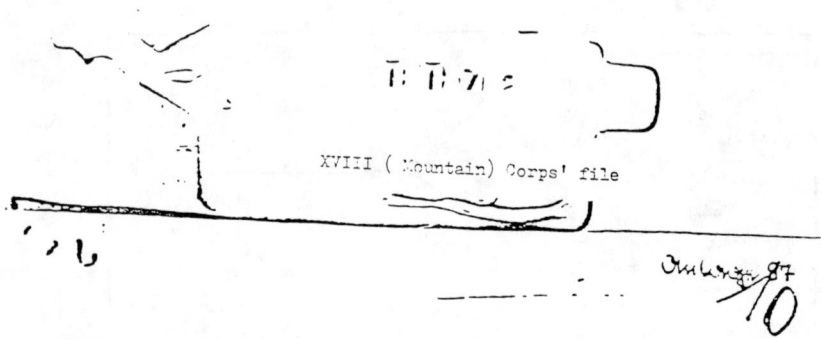

XVIII (Mountain) Corps' file

Der Bevollm.Kommandierende General
in S e r b i e n. Abt. Ic   C...., den 3.11.1941

Betr.: Bezeichnung der
       Cetnik-Verbände.

Da aus Meldungen über Cetnik - Verbände häufig nicht klar
hervorgeht, ob es sich um feindliche oder regierungstreue
Cetniks handelt, sind in Zukunft stets die Bezeichnungen
" regierungstreue Cetniks" bezw. " feindliche Cetniks " zu
verwenden.

Verteiler: Für den Bevollm.Kdr.General in Serbien
B 1 bis Rgt.,Kreis-   Der Chef des Generalstabes:
u.Orts-Kdtren.

Für die Richtigkeit: gez. F e n s e l

Burger
Hauptmann

Distinguish between the "loyal Četniks"
and "enemy Četniks":
T314-1457-001172

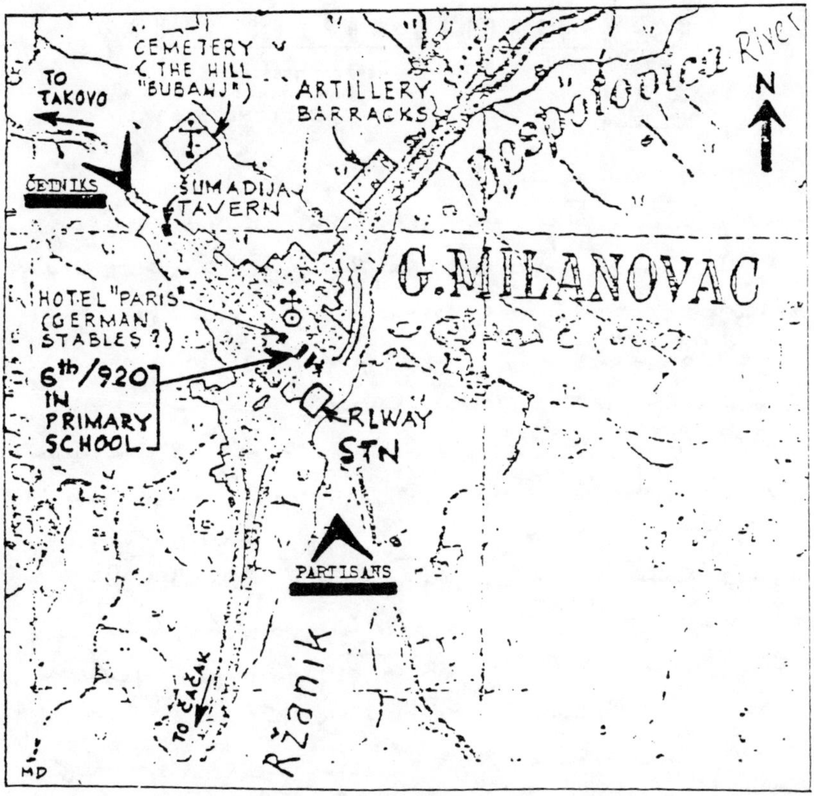

Diagrams, Photocopies

GORNJI MILANOVAC
GUERILLA ATTACK, NIGHT 28-29 SEPTEMBER, 1941

SPECIAL FORCES CLUB

01-589 0490
01-589 4315

8. HERBERT CRESCENT,
KNIGHTSBRIDGE.
LONDON. S.W.1

Captain Jovan Derok was killed in November 1941 after the unprovoked invasion of Jugoslavia by Hitler. At the time of his death he was serving on General Mihailović's staff.

As Head of the British Military Mission to the Royal Jugoslav Army I did not arrive at the General's HQ until some time later: nevertheless I heard of Jovan Derok and of the very high regard the General held for this charming and very brave officer. The other officers at HQ who knew him spoke very highly of his courage, devotion to duty and delightful personality.

May I add my tribute to another very brave Jugoslav who laid down his life for his King and Country.

C.D. Armstrong

CAPTAIN JOVAN V. DEROK

The unsolicited testimonial
of Brigadier C.D. Armstrong, CBE, DSO, MC,
The Head of the last British Military Mission
to the Royal Yugoslav Army (Mihailović)
September 1943 - May 1944

Diagrams, Photocopies 253

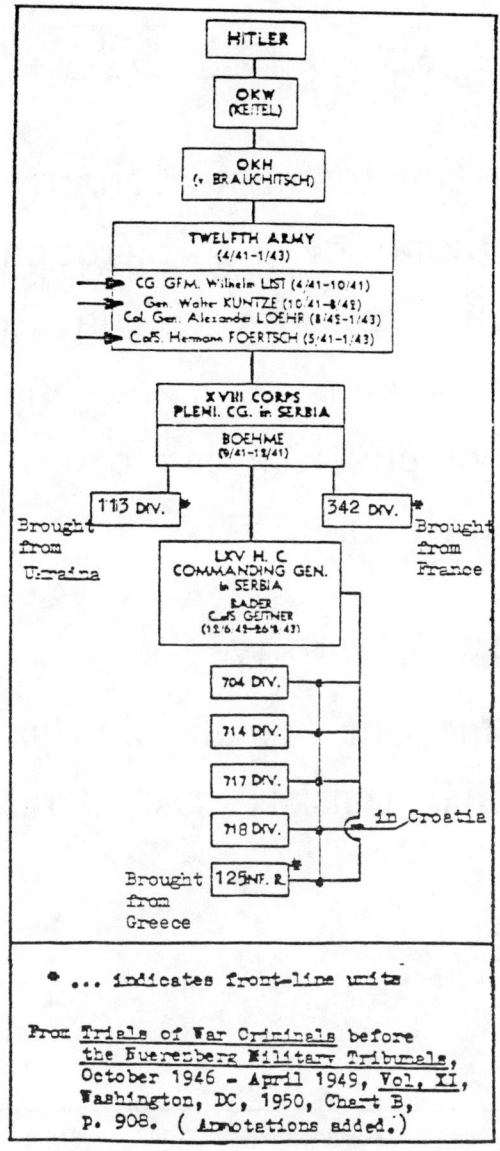

ORDER OF BATTLE

WHEN CRUSHING THE SERBIAN UPRISING OF 1941

ОБЈАВА

Бољшевички бандити убили су 2 октобра ов. год. код Блаца 21 немачког војника на кунавички и животињски начин.

За одмазду

стрељано је 10 октобра 2.100 српских комуниста.

Photocopy of a German announcement in Serbian that
2,100 PEOPLE WERE SHOT ON 10 OCTOBER 1941

Archives of the XVIII (Gebirgs) Armeekorps / Ic
Reports and maps on the resistance, T314-1457-000900

MEETING MIHAILOVIĆ – THE GERMAN COMMAND
11 November 1941 at Divci

Page four of the typewritten transcript in German of the minutes of the meeting. Line nine from top is the beginning of Mihailović's statement.
T314-1457-001317

C.J., den 20. Dezember 1941.

Anlage ..14..

A k t e n n o t i z .

zu den
seit Beginn der Aufstandsbewegung in i.Serbien
bis 5.12.1941 vollzogenen Sühnemaßnahmen.

1.) In Übergab. der Geschäfte des Bevollm.Kdr.Gen.i.Serbien von VVIII. und das XXXXII. .K. sollen mit Wirkung vom 5.12. die bis zu diesem Zeitpunkt vollzogenen Sühnemaßnahmen zusammengefaßt festgestellt werden.

2.) Grundlegende Befehle liegen im Qu.2 Akt (Bevollm.Kdr.Gen.i.C. VIII 7) an.

3.) Auf Grund der Truppenmeldungen ergeben sich folgende Abschlußzahlen:

	J.R.125 + I./A.R.220	342.J.D.	Rfh.Serb. Vers.Btb.	113.J.D.	Höh.Kdo. LXV.	III/697
Eigene a)	11	32	—	—	117	—
b) verwundet	30	130	—	—	218	—
Feindverluste a) im Kampf	369	923	24	—	2246	—
b) Sühnemaßnah.	214	2005	3616	—	4649	—11.1...

Bei dem zugrunde liegenden Schlüssel von 1:100 bzw. 1:50 ergibt sich als zu vollziehende Sühnemaßnahme:

160 x 100 = 16 000
378 x 50 = 18 900
        34 900

CALCULATIONS HOW MANY SERBS TO SHOOT

Balance of the uprising from the beginning to 5 December 1941
34,900 Serbian lives required to atone for 378 wounded and
160 killed German soldiers   T501-251-000843

T 501-251-000844

- 2 -

4.) Durchgeführte Sühnemaßnahme = 11.164
   Abgerechnete tote Feinde = 3.562
   eigene ./. tot Feinde = 36.030
   ———
   31.338

   Damit wären noch zu sühnen: 31.338
                            ./.   11.164
                                   ——————
                                   20.174
                                   ≡≡≡≡≡≡≡≡

5.) Am 16.12. Morgens fehlten zu dieser Meldung noch die Angaben
    der 718.J.D. des III./I.R.697 und 113.J.D.
    Hptm. von Haacke und Hptm. Schuster werden zur
    fernmündlichen Meldung aufgefordert. Für 718.J.D. ist nichts
    veranlaßt.

6.) Es wird einwandfrei festgestellt, daß die Meldungen der unter-
    stellten Einheiten lückenhaft und ungenau sind, da vor allem
    zu Beginn des Aufstandes die Exekutionen ohne schriftliche
    Niederlegung erfolgten und nachträgliche Meldungen ungenau sein
    mußten.
    Die angegebene Zahl von 11.164 durchgeführten Exekutionen ist
    als Mindestzahl zu werten.

7.) Um auf dem Nachgebiet Sühnemaßnahme klare Verhältnisse zu
    schaffen, ist die Ausgabe eines neuen Befehls, der klare Melde-
    verhältnisse schafft, unterwegs. Er ist bereits ausgearbei-
    tet und z.Zt. im Druck.

Österr. Staatsarchiv
  Kriegsarchiv
Wien VII./62, Stiftgasse Nr. 2

Zl. 22.082/1981   Wien, 1981 01 13
Sachbearbeiter Dr.Rutkowski

Herrn
Milan DEROC
~~[address redacted]~~

Australia

In Beantwortung Ihrer Anfrage vom 17.v.Mts wird folgendes
mitgeteilt:
Man nahm und nimmt an, daß der verstorbene Marschall Tito
mit jenem Josip BROZ identisch ist, dem als Zugsführer
(nicht Wachtmeister !) des k.u.Honvéd-Inft.-Rgt.Nr.25 am
.... 1915 für tapferes Verhalten vor dem Feinde die
.... verliehen wurde. Der

Zugsfuehrer Josip BROZ
k.u.Honvéd-Inft.Rgt.Nr.25
(Part-photocopy of the letter
from Austrian State Archives)

SERBEN!

Der Rädelsführer und Aufrührer **Mihajlović**, der das Blut vieler tausender Serben auf dem Gewissen hat, und namenloses Elend über Euer Land gebracht hat, befindet sich nach Zerschlagung seiner Banden auf der

FLUCHT VERMUTLICH NACH BOSNIEN!

Wegen Nichtabgabe der Waffen, Mobilisierung einer illegalen Truppe,

Wegen seines erneuten verbrecherischen Bündnisses mit den Kommunisten und

Wegen der Entfachung des bewaffneten Aufstandes gegen die Deutsche Besatzungstruppe hat er sein Leben verwirkt.

Auf seine Ergreifung wird eine Prämie von

200.000,- Dinar

ausgesetzt.

Das deutsche Oberkommando.

THE DRAFT OF THE FIRST PRICE ON MIHAILOVIĆ'S HEAD
"Because he set ablaze the armed insurrection against the German occupation troops, he has forfeited his life". T501-250-000440

PHOTOCOPY OF THE ANNOUNCEMENT OF THE AWARD

of "100,000 Reichmarks in Gold" for each of Tito and Mihailović, "dead or alive", newspaper Novo vreme, [Belgrade], 21 July 1943.

See Patriot or Traitor: the Case of General Mihailovich, Proceedings and Report of the Commission of Inquiry of the Committee for a Fair Trial for Draja Mihailovich, . . ., Hoover Institution Press, 1978, pp. Photographs.

FOOTNOTES

Notes to Chapter 1

1. *Geographical Handbook, Jugoslavia II,* 190.—The Serbs profess to be plain spoken people (*"Što na umu, to na drumu"*). In this context it is significant that two days before Yugoslavia signed the "Pact" and four days before the *Puč,* General Simović warned Prince Paul on 23 March against joining the Axis powers. The Army was "seething with discontent," said Simović, and "commanding officers were hard put to keep the troops in hand." (Živan L. Knezević, *27. mart.* 103.)

2. Barker, 82-84, 93, 94 and 104-05; Wheeler, 31-33, 37, 50-55; Stafford, "SOE" in *Slavic Review* XXXVI (3), 403 and 407; K. St. Pavlowitch, "Yugoslav-British" in *East European Quarterly,* 332-34 in XII (3) and 431, 433, 434-36, 437, 438-39 in XII (4); St John, 26.—Jukić, 134-36, argues that Maček thougth Yugoslavia should sign the Pact and manage its affairs so as to survive until Hitler gets "swallowed in the vast Russian spaces." (Wisdom of hindsight?)

3. Pomorišac—"Peca," 8-9.

4. People tend to confuse the following terminology: Slovenes or Slovenians (*"Slovenci"*) from Slovenia in Western Yugoslavia, Slavonians (*"Slavonci"*) a mixed Serb and Croatian population in Slavonia in north-central Yugoslavia, and Slovaks (*"Slovaci"*) from Slovakia as in Czechoslovakia.—The Kingdom of the S., C. and S. was renamed "Yugoslavia" by King Alexander I on 3 October 1929.

5. Leffan, in Temperley, *A History IV,* 206.

6. [PRO document] DO (41) 4th, in CAB 69/2—cited by Stafford, "SOE" in *Slavic Review* XXXVI (3), 410 and 410 n. 42.

7. Seton-Watson's letter to Professor R. L. Knežević, published in Živan L. Knežević, *27. mart.* 391.

8. A detailed classification would be as follows: (i) Yugoslavian sources, and (ii) "Exiled" Yugoslav sources of Serbian orientation. (i) Yugoslavian sources from Yugoslavia consist of (a) early works, now discredited, which claimed that the Communist Party of Yugoslavia deserved credit for the *puč,* and (b) later works, which observe a reasonable methodology; (ii) "Emigré" Yugoslav sources are mostly of Serbian orientation and may be mustered into seven groups: (a) writers resolutely supporting the coup: e.g. brothers Radoje and Živan L. Knežević and the monthly periodical *Naša Reč*, Harrow, U.K.: (b) writers who criticise the *"Pučisti"* and the "Government of 27 March" for having deserted the embattled country and escaped abroad, leaving Yugoslavia to the mercy of the Axis (to this group probably belong the majority of the *émigré* officers); (c) writers accusing Great Britain of having provoked the coup without guaranteeing any military aid against Hitler (this group is best represented by the *émigré* press of German collaborators in occupied Serbia); (d) articles by individual authors engaged in research and publishing in American, British, French and other periodicals; (e) reminiscences of participants and exchanges of views in the *Savremenik,* Paris, France; (f) occasional valuable contributions published in *Amerikanski Srbobran—The American Srbobran* and *Glas kanadskih Srba—The Voice of Canadian Serbs* and similar newspapers; and, (g) sundry writings of different quality, including libel and smears, published in all sorts of *émigré* leaflets and mimeographed periodicals, and even books.

9. [PRO document] CAB 69/2, DO (41) 10, citation from Wheeler, 53 and note 156 to p. 53, printed on p. 262. Cf. Stafford in *Slavic Review* XXXVI (3), 417.

10. Wheeler, 16-49 for the diplomatic background, and 49-53 for the coup; it is important to pay attention to Wheeler's footnotes.

11. Stafford, as cited in n. 2.

12. Ibid., 419.

13. For details of the conspiracy see Ž. L. Knežević, cited in n. 7. This book contains also photographs of most of the participating officers.

14. Temperley, *A History IV,* 27 and 28.

15. Wheeler, 57. ["Jankovic" as Lt General Radivoje V. Janković, Yugoslav Director of Operations.]
16. PRO document FO 371/30209, R 3746/73/92, cited in Wheeler, 59 and n. 180 printed on p. 264.
17. St John, 20 and 21.
18. Georgevich, Thesis, "Two Days...," 2.

Notes to Chapter 2

1. Laffan in Temperley, *A History IV*, 195.
2. Churchill, III, 144. *Memoirs of Ernst von Weizsaecker*, 247. (Freiherr von Weizsaecker was the State Secretary in the German Foreign Ministry.)
3. *Diaries of Sir Alexander Cadogan*, 366 (under "Thursday, 27 March") and 365 (for his entry on 21 March).
4. Churchill, III, 149 and 197. Also Woodward, 332 n. 3, 139 n. 2.
5. Terzić, 282.
6. Report of the German Ambassador in Moscow, von der Schulenburg, summarizing his conversation with the Fuehrer on 28 April 1941: *Nazi-Soviet*, 331.
7. *Kriegstagebuch, Wehrmachtfuehrungsstab*, I (1), 368 under "27 Maerz 1941."
8. DGFP, DXII, 372-75 (Document No. 217); detail from p. 373.
9. "Weisung No. 25." In Hitler's system, the *Weisungen* or Directives were his guidelines for subsequent staff elaboration of operational plans. See Percy Ernst Schramm, ed., *Kriegstagebuch des Oberkommandos der Wehrmacht* [OKW], Wehrmachtfuehrungsstab, Vol. IV, Part 1: 1 January 1944–22 March 1945 [and the General Introduction to this Series of Volumes], Frankfurt am Main, 1961.
10. DGFP, DXII, 375 (Minutes, Document No. 217, last paragraph).
11. Operation "Marita" was Hitler's war of April 1941 against Greece and the British and ANZAC troops there. Greece had 26 or 27 divisions (*Australia in the War of 1939-1945*, Series One: Army, Vol. II, *Greece, Crete and Syria* by Gavin Long, Canberra, 1953, pp. 5 and 11). There were some 31,000 British and Anzac troops (ibid., 26 n. 2, for a detailed table see ibid., p. 33 n. 6).
12. DGFP, DXII, 373 (Minutes of Hitler's conference on Yugoslavia).
13. General Glaise-Horstenau's confidence to von Hassell about his talk with Hitler; *Von Hassell Diaries*, 174.

14. DGFP, DXII, document 217 of 27 March 1941, part of the text on p. 374; italics are in the original.

15. Extracts from the proclamation are cited from *Keesing's*, April 5-12, 1941, p. 4549A. In a footnote to the above item, *Keesing's* simply commented "The fighting spirit of the Serbian soldier has always been accounted among the highest in Europe" (ibid., 4550B).

16. DGFP, DXII, document no. 281 on pp. 475-78. Hitler's letter to Mussolini of 5 April 1941, details from p. 476.

17. Terzić, 253, 376 and 378 and 379.

18. Order Dj. No. 2642 of 30 March 1941 (Terzić, 161 and 161 n. 177).

19. St. John, 67-68.—German occupation of Czekia and its "Skoda" armament works, suppliers of Yugoslav motorized equipment, had put a stop to the modernization of Yugoslav forces. Some artillery regiments obtained traction for guns only (15-50 km/hr), so that their ammunition and supply trains remained pulled by oxen and horses (3-5 km/hr). (The case of the No. 115 War Regiment of 105 mm guns: Ž. M. Timotijević to this author, letter of 2 February 1981. ŽMT, now of Sydney, Australia, was Battery Sergeant, 9th Battery, 3rd "Battalion," 115th Artillery). A Yugoslav 4-gun Battery corresponded to a British troop of 4 guns. In Yugoslavia, as in the US, Batteries were grouped by "Battalions": US term, or *"Divizion"*: Serb term, not to be confused with *"Divizija"* or Division.

20. Terzić, 253 and 408.

21. Ibid., 316, 317 and 162.

22. ANZAC for "Australian and New Zealand Army Corps," an abbreviation informally used even when the Australian and New Zealand troops are not formally incorporated in a separate army corps. Common designation for the British and ANZAC troops in Greece was "The Imperial Forces."

23. Long, 192—For the purpose of this argument, wherever the letter "Y" appears in the above quotation, [Y] reads "and Yugoslav."

24. Personal knowledge, MD; Terzić, 505.

25. I am grateful to K. St. Pavlowitch of Cambridge, U.K., for a complete roll-call of the above people; MD.

26. For details Deroc, "When had Simovic" in *The South Slav Journal*, VI, No. 3 (21), 10-12.

27. For the full transcription of the original instruction see Terzić, 553, and Čulinović, 282-83.

28. This act was signed by General von Weichs for the *Wehrmacht*, and Aleksandar Cincar-Marković [not "Marković"] and the Yugoslav Director of Operations, Lieutenant General Radivoje [not "Radivoj"] Janković for the Yugoslav Command. The original document has not been located (Čulinović, 302). For a translation of the German text into Serbo-Croat see ibid., 303-07; Terzić, 568-70. To this document is also appended the signature of the Italian military attaché in Belgrade, Colonel Bonofatti (see Čulinović, 306). In the US Army pamphlet No. 20-260, *German Campaigns*, 64, the Yugoslav military signatory is identified as "General Milojko Jankovic." [It should read Lieutenant General ("Diviziski djeneral") Radivoje Janković; General (*"Armiski djeneral"*) Milojko Janković was commanding the Seacoast Army Area Troops (*"Trupe Primorske armiske oblasti."* I am grateful to Miss Georgianna Watson, Documents Librarian, U.S. Military Academy, for supplying a copy of this pamphlet, MD.—The enclosure to the convention of armistice stipulated that the Yugoslav Armed Forces were "unconditionally capitulating and will be transported into captivity": Čulinović, 303 (document "Supreme Command/Rear Area, O. No. 105 of 19 April 1941"); Terzić, 573 (document "Supreme Command, Operations, O. No. 201, 19 April 1941).

29. Čulinović, 217; emphasis by MD. (Double translation: Čulinović translated the above text from German into Croat, and here it is "re-translated" from Čulinović text into English.)

30. Simović had acted without the knowledge of the government, neither is there any record in the minutes of the government's meeting of 13 April regarding any negotiations and/or armistice with the enemy (Terzić, 553-54). Čulinović, 331-36 (particularly pp. 335-36) allows for the possibility that relevant discussions were not held in the presence of "all ministers."

31. This event gave rise to controversy. Terzić, 562, cites the book by Nikola Milovanović, *Vojni puč i 27. mart*, Belgrade, 1960, pp. 165 and 171-72, whereby the government held a last meeting at Nikšić and approved that the Army capitulate "but not the State." According to this version, Vice-Prime Minister Slobodan Jovanović, a renowned academic lawyer and historian, himself formulated the arguments distinguishing between the "capitulation of the Army" and "capitulation of the State." Yet

Jovanović, *Zapisi,* asserts that at Nikšić there was no meeting of the government. This is corroborated by the statements of Krek and Kosanović, who do not mention any meeting. Jovanović says that Simović maintained the capitulation was a purely military act, not preventing the government from continuing the fight from abroad. Jovanović also says that Simović and the Army Minister (General Ilić) insisted that "capitulation was a final act which cannot be remedied." [Yet all this was happening on the 15th, while the capitulation was signed only on the 17th: Jovanović's testimony, as well as those by King Peter, Krek and Kosanović, raise the question of what instructions exactly were given to Kalafatović?]

32. *Vide* Krizman and Petranović, *Jugoslavenske I,* by Krizman, 98-99, 177 and 118.

33. Terzić, 576.—"Zeta" is, historically, the original name of Montenegro or "Crna Gora" ("Black Mountain").

34. The Supreme Command, O. No. 282 ["O" for "Operations"] — Archives of the Yugoslav Military Historical Institute, Box 3, "registered number" 12/1-1: Terzić, 574.

35. For an account of Simović's government, see K. St. Pavlović, "Jugoslovensko—", in *Glasnik "Njegoš,"* No. 40, June 1978, pp. 34-54; the date of his fall is given on p. 49.

36. Terzić, 504 and 504 n. 113.

37. Čulinović, 282-83, detail (Item 3) on p. 283; Terzić, 553.

38. A photostat of the original document (The Supreme Command, Dj.O. No. 179 of 14 April 1941 at 09.30 hours) is in Čulinović, the set of photostats between pp. 288 and 289; Terzić, 555.

39. Tippelskirch, 150. German losses were 151 killed, 392 wounded and 15 missing. Ibid., 148: "... *aus der Gegend von Skoplje und ostwaerds nach Norden eindrehende Kraefte fanden bei Vranje und am Oberlauf des Ibar starken jugoslawischen Widerstand, den sie bis zur Beendigung des Feldzuges nicht zu brechen vermochten."*

40. Milićević, "Uzroci" in *Glasnik "Njegoš,"* No. 8, December 1961, p. 5.—In the war of April 1941 Milićević was Chief of Staff (CofS) 1st Yugoslav Army.

41. Terzić, 576.

42. In 1946 Lt General Mihailo D. Bodi submitted his report on this abortive mission to the General Staff of the new Yugoslav Army (Čulinović, 289-98; also Terzić, 558-59 and 565-66.) For another account see

[General Staff Lt Colonel] Radmilo [not "Radomir"] S. Trojanović, "Pregovori" in *Glasnik "Njegoš,"* No. 28, June 1972, pp. 9-17.

43. Bodi in Čulinović, detail on p. 291; Terzić, detail on p. 559.

44. See the copy in Vol. 1 of the Enclosure to vol. 1 of the *Kriegstagebuch* of the German Military Commander in [Occupied] Serbia, 20 April–13 November 1941: T501-251-000681 and 000682.

45. "344,000": Matl, "Jugoslawien" in *Jugoslawien, Osteuropa-Handbuch,* 102.–"334,000"; Tippelskirch, 150.

46. Letters of 26 May, 1981 (over the signature of Mrs. C. Rey-Schyrr) and 28 October 1982 (over the signature of Miss Dominique Koull).

47. But not necessarily complete, see International Committee of the Red Cross, *Report* II, 248. Besides the Serbs, these numbers comprise also other individual cases.—It is as well to specify that, in this respect, the International Committee of the Red Cross is only a custodian of statistics. Therefore field—and camp—errors in roll-calls are attributable to the notifying authorities, and not to the ICRC.

48. War diary of the German Commander in Serbia ("Unit 08633"), "Enclosure A2" dated 1 July 1941: T501-245-000542.—Considering that a number of Croat and Slovene loyalists took refuge in Serbia, the above estimate certainly comprises also the latter.

49. Personal knowledge.

50. International Committee of the Red Cross, *Report* I, 527 and 530, and II, 248 and 250. Partisan POWs, arriving from August 1943, had separate camps, mostly in Norway: ibid., I, 530. (I am grateful to Mrs C. Rey-Schyrr of the ICRC for her initiative in forwarding me this documentation, MD.)

Notes to Chapter 3

1. PRO, document FO 371/30215, PWE directive of 19th December 1941. There is apparently no record that Croatia declared war on the USSR, although Croat troops were fighting on the German side.

2. For the regiment at Stalingrad: Djilas, *Conversations,* 39-40.

3. Malaparte, 262. (Unless it is a transcript (as here), elsewhere an "Anglicised" plural form will be used, *viz.* Ustashas instead of *"Ustashis"* or similar.)

4. Maclean, *Disputed*, 162.
5. Marjanović, *Ustanak*, 22 and 22 n. 34.
6. Tomasevich, 106; Jews and Gypsies were outlawed together with the Serbs (Loco cit.). For the persecution of the Serb Orthodox Church, ibid., 177.
7. Wuescht, 52, and, generally, 50-56.
8. Milazzo, 10.
9. Djilas, *Wartime*, 139.
10. Karchmar, *"Draža I"*, 436.
11. Foot, *Resistance*, 188-89.
12. Karchmar, *"Draža I"*, 437; for additional details pp. 436-39.
13. Maclean, *Eastern*, 334-35; Clissold, 98-99.
14. *Report upon the Atrocities*, 179 and 180, and the conclusion on p. 185, that for systematic plunder in Serbian territory "the [Austro-Hungarian] High Command took good care to have the troops accompanied" by armed "fanatical Bosnian Mahommedan peasants. . . ."
15. Tomasevich, 175 and 175 n. 13.
16. Topalović, 52.
17. Broz Tito, *Political Report*, 107.
18. Djilas, *Wartime*, 60.–Note Djilas's elegant turn of phrase: "This disparity *necessitated* the elevation of newcomers. . ." [my italics, MD]. This is a good example of Stalinist "double speak" (*pace*, Orwell), simply meaning "The newcomers took over." Indeed, Djilas himself was sent in to Montenegro by Tito from Belgrade (ibid., 8).
19. Woodward, 332 n. 3.
20. Wuescht, 319-20.
21. Simić, "Jasenovac. . ." in *Nedeljne ilustrovane novine* (NIN), 18 October 1981, pp. 18-19. Ručnov, "Pakao" in *Duga*, No. 313, 22 February to 7 March 1986, pp. 18-19. It appears that, at Jasenovac, most of the victims were either burned in brick-baking furnaces or clubbed to death; those who were slaughtered with a knife or killed by a bullet had a lucky escape (ibid., 19)–Pavelić claimed to act as champion of the Roman Catholic Church. For an appraisal of this point see, for instance, Rhodes, 323-36 (ch. 22).
22. Mihailović to the Yugoslav government in London, telegram No. 377 of 10 August 1942: Živan L. Knežević, *General Mihailović*, 23.

Notes to Chapter 3

23. Broz Tito, "Nacionalno," *Proleter,* XVII (16). December 1942, reprinted in Broz Tito, *Borba,* 129.

24. Rendell, 216.

25. At the same time Nazi persecutions and the *"Eindeutschung"* (germanization) of Slovenes started in Slovenia, which was partitioned between Italy and Germany.

26. *"Abschliessender Bericht der Deutschen Gesandschaft in Zagreb ueber die Umsiedlung der Slowenen vom 20 November 1941,"* published in Wuescht, 315-27, (henceforth cited as *"Bericht"*). *"Bericht,"* the 2nd paragraph (Wuescht, 315).

27. DGFP, DXII, 957-58 (Document No. 589). *"Bericht,"* 3rd and 4th paragraphs (Wuescht, 315-16).

28. DGFP, DXIII, 552-55 (document No. 350 and the Enclosure; my emphasis, MD). *"Bericht"* under 22 September, in Wuescht, 316. Cf. the statistics in DGFP, DXIII, 553, and in the *"Bericht,"* Wuescht, 316.—An additional 6,720 Slovenes were transported to Serbia: DGFP, DXIII, 553 and *"Bericht"* in Wuescht, 316. A question mark remains concerning 60,000 Serbs "resettled" before the date of the first resettlement conference; they are mentioned separately in DGFP, DXIII, 553, but the comments in *"Bericht"* (Wuescht, 315-16) are insufficient to clarify their case.

29. Marjanović, *Ustanak,* 23 n. 35.

30. Slijepčević, 355-57.

31. Ibid., 355-56.

32. Literally: "Meat for the John's Market." "John's Market" was the main market in Belgrade.

33. *Annuaire statistique,* Royaume de Yougoslavie, 1933, Beograd, 1935, p. 39; table quoted in *Geographical Handbook, Jugoslavia II,* 332.

34. Statistics and references are cited in Marjanović, *Ustanak,* 23 and 23 n. 35.

35. "Conversation Between the Fuehrer and Hungarian Minister Sztojay" on March 27, 1941, DGFP, DXII, Document No. 215, p. 370. (Hitler eventually annexed parts of North-West Yugoslavia to Germany, that is, parts of Slovenia only.)

36. Conversation between Hitler and General Edmund Glaise von Horstenau, reported by Ulrich von Hassell, in *Von Hassell Diaries,* 174 (under 5 May 1941).

37. Loc. cit.

38. *Ciano's Diary,* entries on 24 April 1941 (p. 333 and p. 333 n. 235); 28 April (p. 336); 21 and 22 May (pp. 346-47).
39. Extracts from correspondence MD (M. Deroc, this author)– ZJV; later, in his book Vučković, *Sećanja,* 58-60, Vučković had included this information.
40. Bandović, "Ustanak" in Radoje L. Knežević, *Knjiga I,* 74-86, detail on p. 82. Kontić, "Viktor" in *Glasnik "Njegoš,"* No. 4, December 1959, p. 26.–This initial Italian policy is discussed also by Lucien Karchmar, "Draža I," p. 42 and note 8 on p. 64, where beside Kontić, Batrić Jovanović's *Crna Gora u Narodnooslobodilačkom ratu i socijalističkoj revoluciji,* Beograd, 1960, pp. 21-25 and 64-65 is also cited as a source of information.
41. Djilas, *Memoir,* 385.
42. Terzić, 654 and 651.
43. Prince Mihajlo Petrović-Njegoš, "Kako sam" in *Glasnik "Njegoš,"* No. 2, December 1958, pp. 35-37. *Ciano's Diary,* 355 (entry of 7 June 1941).–There are two Frankfurts: Frankfurt am Main (east of Wiesbaden) and Frankfurt an der Oder (east-south-east of Berlin). Serra di Cassano was probably consul at the former.
44. *Ciano's Diary,* 355 (entry of 7 June 1941). The interview took place on the 29th of May (Prince Mihajlo, "Kako sam," op. cit., 35). Mihajlo died in Paris, France, in 1986.
45. *Petrovdan* ("Petersday," actually St. Peter and Paul, 29 June in the Serbian-Orthodox O.S. Calendar).
46. Radoje L. Knežević, comments appended to Bandović's "Ustanak" (op. cit., in n. 40 above), in R. Knežević, *Knjiga I,* 74. Živanović, *Treći srpski I,* 134. Karchmar, "Draža I," 43. Terzić, 652-53, incl. the text of the declaration (*"Deklaracija"*) of 12th July. Djilas, *Wartime,* 18 and 22. Roberts, *Tito, Mihailović,* 24. For an account of the proceedings of the 12th July Assembly, see Zonjić "Petrovdanska" in *Glasnik "Njegoš,"* No. 23, June 1969, pp. 27-32.
47. Laffan, in Temperley, *A History IV,* 202-03.–For an exposition of Montenegrin parties for union with Serbia ("Bjelaši" or the "Whites"), and against ("Zelenaši" or the "Greens"), cf. Laffan, op. cit., 202-04, and Djilas, *Wartime,* 18-19; written at an interval of half a century, the two complement each other.
48. Bandović, "Ustanak" in R. Knežević, *Knjiga I,* 76 and 78. Joksimović, "Ustanak" in *Glasnik "Njegoš,"* No. 1, July 1958, p. 89. (Major

Joksimović was one of the commanders in the uprising.) Živanović, *Treći srpski I*, 134. All these authors ascribe the uprising to the Montenegrin Serb consciousness.—Milazzo in Milazzo, *Chetniks*, 43, ascribes the uprising to the Montenegrin disillusion when they realized the Italians were offering them "personal union" instead of independence; at this stage Milazzo is alone in holding this opinion.

49. Djilas, *Wartime*, 8, 19, 29, 79 and 22.

50. Terzić, 653 (*"narod (je) 13. jula, pod voćstvom Komunističke partije, digao ustanak . . ."*).

51. See, e.g., Bandović as in n. 40, pp. 77-78.—There is a series of articles in the *Glasnik "Njegoš,"* offering different variants on this theme, as well as local details.

52. Karchmar, "Draža I," ch. VI, "The Uprising in Montenegro," 373-74.

53. Ibid., "Draža I," 42.

54. Djilas, *Wartime*, 60-61, where Djilas admits "the disorganization of the party caused by the uprising" and says "a month and a half" was needed to effect reorganization.—As the uprising lasted until the end of August, that means that the Party was being reorganized until—say—mid-October 1941.

55. Broz Tito, *Political Report*, 107.

56. Auty, *Tito*, 173; for details see Dr. Ivan Avakumović, *Mihailović prema*, 27. (Sources differ as to whether this occurred in late 1941 or early 1942.)

57. *The Law for the Protection of the State* of 30 July 1921. For a detailed history see Ivan Avakumović, *History I*, 55-56.

58. General Staff, [British] War Office, Director of Military Intelligence, M.I. 3b, 27 April 1943, Most Secret, "A Short History of the Revolt in Yugoslavia"; PRO archives, document FO 371/33469, pp. 7-8.

59. Biroli's attitude is discussed in ibid., on p. 8. (indirectly) and p. 9 (directly); the use of the VI and XIV Italian Corps by "Djurisic and his friends" [that is, the Mihailović-aligned commanders] is mentioned on p. 9; Mihailović's policy is reviewed on p. 17 and passim.

60. Karchmar, "Draža I," 395-96 and n. 15 types on pp. 427-30.

Notes to Chapter 4

1. For the date of the paper: 25 May in Butler, *Grand II,* 260; 27 May in Cookridge, 5.
2. Butler, *Grand II,* 260; and III (1), p. 42; Cookridge, 5-6; Foot, *SOE,* 6.
3. Butler, *Grand II,* 260; Foot, *SOE,* 6.
4. For Lord Halifax's broadcast of 22 July 1940 in reply to Hitler's speech to the *Reichstag* of 19 July, see *Keesing's,* July 20-27, 1940, p. 4157. Butler, *Grand II,* p. 261; Foot, *SOE,* 9.
5. Butler, *Grand III (1),* p. 42; Foot, *SOE,* 9.
6. Ibid., 8.
7. Sweet-Escott, "S.O.E." Intr. by Major-General Sir Colin Gubbins, in Auty and Clogg, *British,* 3.
8. But cf. Julian Amery's remark that "The local commanders who were in general preoccupied with the Western Desert regarded Yugoslavia very much as a side show" (Amery to this author (MD), letter of 27 November 1981.) Amery was an SOE operative closely linked with Yugoslavia in 1941-42.
9. Dalton, 366.
10. Butler, *Grand II,* 261; Foot, *SOE,* 8-9.
11. Butler, *Grand III (1),* p. 261.
12. Hamilton-Hill, 23 and 39.
13. Sweet-Escott, *Baker,* 53 and 53 n. 1. ("007," was, of course, "James Bond," Ian Flemming's fictitious British Intelligence agent.)
14. Electra House or "EH" was established to study propaganda aimed at Germany (Foot, *SOE,* 1, 2 and 521). "EH" was named after Electra House (on the Thames), where its first head (Sir) Campbell Stuart had his office.
15. Hinsley, *British I,* 278. The "D" was part of SIS is usually only implied. However, that it was a part of the SIS is explicitly stated in Cookridge, 12, and in the obituary of D's first head, L. D. Grand (*The Times,* 28 November 1975, p. 19, col. 8). That Section D was "from the start a part of SIS" is confirmed in the letter of the Foreign and Commonwealth Office (FCO) of 10 March 1982, over the signature of PP—E.G. Boxshall, to this author (MD).
16. Hanau joined Section D in June 1938 and might have been an SIS

before that date (Barker, 37 and Stafford, "SOE" in *Slavic Review,* XXXVI (3), p. 408 n. 38.—(Colonel) S. W. Bailey, a mining engineer who at one stage had considerable influence on D/SOE-Yugoslav relations, was appointed in November 1939 2 i/c Belgrade D Section under Hanau, and then took over and headed the Section from June to August 1940 (Foreign and Commonwealth Office's SOE Adviser, over the signature PP (C. M. Woods), to this author (MD), letter of 7 July 1982, henceforth cited as FCO/SOEA 7 July 1982. Bailey left Belgrade in July 1940.

17. Sweet-Escott, *Baker,* 34; Stafford, "SOE," op. cit., 409.

18. For Masterson's appointment see FCO/SOEA to MD 7 July 1982; also Stafford, "SOE," op. cit., 409. In Tomasevich's *The Chetniks,* his chronology and therefore his interpretation of Belgrade D/SOE postings require revision. Julian Amery was recruited in Belgrade "soon" after his twenty-first birthday (Amery, 158 and 160); he was born on 27 March 1919. His first "D" contact in Belgrade was (Sir) Alexander Glen, who, in his *Footholds,* 44, says that he (Glen) came to Belgrade in January 1940. Consult also Stafford, "SOE" op. cit., in n. 16, 408-09.

19. The SOE were not the only British agency in Belgrade and the Balkans. For instance, "the SIS . . . provided it (SOE) with essential contacts" (Hinsley, *British I,* 369 and 369 n. 120): perhaps under "SIS" is simply meant SOE's predecessor, Section D?

20. Prince Paul was one of the three Royal Regents for King Peter II, a minor. The other two were Dr. Radenko Stanković and Dr. Iv. N. Perović.

21. FCO/SOEA 7 July 1982 as in n. 16.

22. Ibid., and Amery, 185. Bailey's trip occurred in July and early August 1940. General Headquarters, Middle East (GHQ ME), or the British high command in Cairo, was at that time under General Sir Archibald (later Field-Marshal Viscount) Wavel.

23. Amery, 185.

24. In ibid., 233, it is said: ". . . Bailey asked for me to join him in Istanbul." In his letter to this author (MD) of 2 July 1982, Amery explained that he was meant to go to Istanbul but joined Bailey at Cairo, and worked with him "in Cairo and Jerusalem."—According to FCO/SOEA 7 July 1982, as in n. 16, at the end of September 1940 A. G. Gardyne de Chastelain (later Colonel C.) was appointed "number two" to Bailey in Istanbul, and when in April 1941 Bailey moved to Jerusalem, Chastelain remained in charge in Istanbul. (Before his posting to Istanbul, C. was in Romania: Amery, *Approach,* the chapter "The Fall of Rumania.")

25. Starting in July 1940, SZS received £5,000 a month, some other groups in Serbia and Bulgaria were receiving subsidies also (Barker, 45, 45 n. 139, 140, and pp. 85, 85 n. 42). Also E. Barker's paper at the conference on allied governments, London 24-27 October 1977, (see St. K. Pavlović's correspondence in *Naša Reč*, XXXIII (318), October 1980, p. 16).

26. For some instances of smuggling, see Sweet-Escott, *Baker*, 23-24 and 31-32.

27. Mato Rusković to Marjanović, 5 January 1960, in Marjanović, *Ustanak*, 187 n. 304.

28. Deakin, *The Embattled*, 127.

29. Djonović, "Veze" in *Glasnik "Njegoš,"* No. 1, July 1958, p. 41.—Prime Minister Simović notified Foreign Office of Djonović's appointment on 4 June 1941 (K. St. Pavlović, "Srpski" in *Savremenik,* New Series, XXVI (9), August 1980, pp. 59-60, no. 37, citing PRO document [FO (?)] 30291/681/242).

30. Amery, 238.

31. See the chapter 10.

32. Deakin, *The Embattled*, 127.

33. Djonović, "Veze," as in n. 29, pp. 41-42.

34. After the Second World War Rapotec settled in Sydney, Australia, and became a renowned painter.

35. Djonović, "Veze" as in n. 29, 43-44.

36. Glen, 45.

37. It might be that, in the early days of resistance when Mihailović was still an unknown Colonel, the name "Mišić" was the main drawcard in Serbia although Mihailović and not his friend Major Mišić was in charge.

38. Colonel Žarko R. Popović to this author (MD), cassette of 27 October 1981.

39. Djonović, "Veze" as in n. 29, p. 44.

40. Ibid., 44.

41. Amery, 240.

42. Ibid., 240 and 244.

43. Ibid., 244; Glen, 61.—D/SOE officers in Belgrade owed it to "the Director of Military Intelligence, the extrovert and passionately anti-German Jarko [Žarko] Popović" to have "got to know (Colonel Mihailović) quite well" (ibid., 124).

44. Amery, 244.

45. Loc. cit.
46. Sweet-Escott, *Baker*, 70.
47. Ibid., 67-68 and 70.
48. My translation from minutes in Serbian, p. 1, MD. For the Minutes of Meeting Ilić–Masterson see "Colonel Popović's Papers" in the custody of the Hoover Institution on War, Revolution and Peace, Stanford, California 94305.
49. Amery, 244, Sweet-Escott, *Baker*, 70.
50. Ibid., 71-72.
51. Bid., 72.
52. Guedalla, 162.
53. FCO/SOEA, 7 July 1982, as in n. 16.
54. Ibid.: Pollock came to London on 29th December 1940 and "was sent back to Cairo in January [1941]." The above text is published here for the first time.
55. Foreign and Commonwealth Office, letter of 10 March 1982 over the signature pp (E. G. Boxshall) to this author (MD).
56. Sweet-Escott, *Baker*, 74-76.
57. Ibid., 76.
58. Loc. cit.; FCO/SOEA, 7 July 1982, as in n. 16; cf. discussion (Bailey's statement) in Auty and Clogg, 212.
59. Sweet-Escott, *Baker*, 97; Bulter, *Grand III (2)*, p. 517; Cruickshank, 31 and 50; Foreign and Commonwealth Office, letter of 10 March 1982 to this author (MD), as in n. 15; Hinsley, *British II*, PWE note on p. 7.
60. Amery, 245-46.
61. Loc. cit.
62. Ibid., 246.–Julian Amery advised this author on 27 November 1981 that the only reference in his father's diary about a relevant conversation with Churchill is "on 24th August 1941 where he says 'wrote to Julian and Smuts'," but that he could not locate his father's letter; the diary, being a dictated document, would not contain "some things." Churchill's biographer Martin Gilbert has not come across information regarding this intercession of Amery Snr. with Churchill: Gilbert to this author (MD), letter of 22 March 1982.
63. Deakin, *The Embattled*, 126. Deakin does not indicate the source of his information. He had earlier revealed this minute at a Conference on

Britain and European Resistance, organized by St. Antony's College, Oxford, December 10-16, 1962: "Proceedings," general pagination p. 330 (Yugoslav Section, p. "Yug. 4).
    64. Ibid., general pagination p. 330 (Yugoslav Section, p. "Yug. 4").
    65. Deakin, *The Embattled*, 126.
    66. "Proceedings" as in n. 63, general pagination p. 331 (Yugoslav Section, p. "Yug. 5").
    67. Barker, 157.
    68. Ibid., 158.
    69. A superficial reading of Barker's text (Barker, 157) gives the impression that Churchill's minute to Dalton followed upon Simović's intervention of 22 August, *viz.*: "By 22 August Simovic...asked... [etc.]. *But he also asked Churchill to send a submarine....*"; emphasis by this author, MD. This makes the impression that on the 22 August Simović asked "also" that a submarine establish contact with the "working Committee" in Split, but—instead of obliging—Churchill wrote to Dalton in general terms to see what SOE could do for Simović. Yet Barker footnotes the issue of the submarine "45," and this footnote reads "... Simovic letter to Churchill 14.8.41."
    70. Barker, 15.
    71. Amery, 254.
    72. Ibid., 246; Cf. Deakin, *The Embattled*, 131 n. *.
    73. Ibid., 129; Amery, 247; Sweet-Escott, "S.O.E." (in Auty and Clogg, 9).
    74. In Woodward 344, and in Deakin's article "Prva" in *Zbornik radova*, 184, Hudson is introduced as a Major, which he was not at the time; in Maclean's *Disputed* 150 and 475, Hudson is called "William," but his given names are Duane Tyrrell; Auty, in her *Tito*, 186 and 335, gives Hudson the initials "D.H."
    75. Djelević, "Iz prvih" in R. Knežević, *Knjiga I*, 186.
    76. Julian Amery to this author (MD), letter of 2 July 1982.—"Jarko Popovitch" is Colonel Žarko R. Popović. (He might have insisted on inclusion of a British officer in the team in order to start British-Yugoslav cooperation in the field.)
    77. Deakin, "Prva" as in n. 74, p. 184; Auty, *Tito*, 186.
    78. Deakin, *The Embattled*, 130, emphasis by this author (MD).
    79. Bailey, "British" in Auty and Clogg, 60 and 60 n. 3 printed on p. 90. Bailey was given this information when he was briefed in 1942 before

being posted to Mihailović as the Senior British Liaison Officer (loc. cit.).

80. "Popović Papers" at Stanford, as in n. 48. (He still keeps his Diaries and some other papers: Popović to this author (MD), letter of 20 October 1981.)–Bennett brought the above Memorandum to General Ilić on 26 September at noon. (Incidentally, in Bennett's document Ilić's name is spelled "Illic.")

81. Butler, *Grand III (2)*, p. 517; Deakin in "Proceedings"as in n. 63, general pagination p. 328 (Yugoslav Section, p. "Yug. 2").

82. "Proceedings," op. cit., general pagination p. 330 (Yugoslav Section, p. "Yug. 4").

83. Ibid., 331 or "Yug. 5".

84. In none of the "surviving" early messages of Hudson is Tito mentioned either (Deakin, *The Embattled*, 203–Kljaković in his "Velika" in *Vojnoistorijski glasnik*, XXI (2), May-August 1970, pp. 80 and 82, sets Mihailović's signal of 5 November in the context of allied endeavours to have all resistance recognize Mihailović's leadership.

85. Deakin, *The Embattled*, 126. A third version is advanced by Kljaković in 1970. He says that the mission was sent "because it was not known sufficiently about *any of the two* [resistance] organizations"; Kljaković as in n. 84, p. 71, emphasis by this author (MD).

86. Deakin, *The Embattled*, 130 and 136; Sweet-Escott, "S.O.E." as in n. 7, p. 9.

87. Deakin, *The Embattled*, 130, 131, 134, 202; further, Deakin, "Prva," as in n. 74, p. 185. Barker, 158: Hudson "at first had no specific instructions to join Mihailović [and] spent some time. . . ."; Roberts in his *Tito, Mihailović*, 28, interprets the instruction of 9 October to move to Serbia as "the British wanted Hudson to give Mihailović a code."

88. Bailey: in "British" as in n. 79, pp. 59-60, says that in the middle of August 1941 "the Naval monitoring station at Portished" learned about the units of the Royal Yugoslav Army still offering resistance, "under the command of a Colonel Draza Mihailovic, the senior officer present." Similar intelligence reached British ears earlier also. Karchmar in "Draža II," (pp. 758-59 and notes 80-82, typed on pp. 868-69), discusses different dates for the first radio contact.

89. Amery, 245-56. The complete title of his book reads *Approach March, a venture in autobiography*.

90. Deakin, *The Embattled*, 210 n. "+" and p. 214. "Proceedings" as in n. 63, p. 331 or "Yug. 5".

91. Hugh Seton-Watson, *The East*, 158-59.
92. Sweet-Escott, *Baker*, 96.
93. Djilas, *Wartime*, 71; Mitrović, *Zapadna*, 261. Dedijer, in his *Novi Prilozi I*, p. 305, makes an identical statement: when Mission Bullseye met the Partisans, they told the latter "they were going to Draža Mihailović."
94. Julian Amery to this author (MD), letter of 2 July 1982.
95. Petrovac was named after King Peter I of Serbia and of the Serbs, Croats and Slovenes; prior to the First World War Petrovac was known as Castel Lastva. At the time of the arrival of the mission *Bullseye*, Petrovac had about 350 to 400 inhabitants.
96. Deakin, *The Embattled*, 126 n. *; Sweet-Escott, *Baker*, 96. Amery was not supposed to go further than Malta (Amery, 248): it might be that for this reason his name was not entered in *Triumph's* Log.
97. See HMS *Triumph's* Log of 20 September 1941 (PRO document ADM 173/17086). In Amery's *Approach* Woods is mistakenly introduced as Lt Commander. His name was Wilfrid, he was known as Sam (Howarth, 78). Later Admiral Sir W. W.; for his obituary see *The Times*, 3 January 1975, p. 12g.
98. Amery spells has surname DONNE; the spelling used here complies with the Ministry of Defence Naval Historical Branch's letter D/NHB/4/-4/34 of 2 July 1982 over the signature of Michael R. Wilson to this author (MD); Mr Wilson's assistance in this and other matters is gratefully acknowledged.
99. Hudson to Phyllis Auty on 8 July 1974, in Auty and Clogg, 91.
100. Ministry of Defence, Naval Historical Branch, letter D/NHB/4-/4/34 of 30 March 1982 over the signature of M. R. Wilson, to this author (MD); cited by permission.
101. The log of HM Submarine *Triumph* for September 1941 is held in the Public Record Office at Kew, under reference ADM 173/17086: PRO to MD, letter Q 4835 of 20 April 1982 over the signature of Mrs. M. R. Edwards, which is gratefully acknowledged.—This reference is applicable to all extracts from HMS *Triumph's* logs that follow; any emphases in transcribing the original documents are by this author (MD).

Captain's Report, that is, Commander Woods's report for this patrol by HMS *Triumph* is held in the Public Record Office at Kew, under reference ADM 236/36: Naval Historical Branch, letter D/NHB/4/4/34 of 26 April 1982 over the signature of M. R. Wilson, to this author (MD).—This reference is applicable to all extracts of Commander Woods's report that follow;

any emphases in transcribing the original documents are by this author (MD). Lengthy quotations from the document ADM 236/36 are by special permission (PRO letter 2/CASE 4/1 of 8 February 1985, over the signature of Dr. J. B. Post, Copyright Officer) which is gratefully acknowledged.

102. Naval Historical Branch, letter D/NHB/4/4/34 of 30 March 1982 as in n. 100.

Notes to Chapter 5

1. See Bailey's statement, column and footnote (e) in the Table "Hudson's 'Bullseye' Instructions."
2. See Deakin and Bailey's statements, column and foonotes (c) and (e) in the Table "Hudson's 'Bullseye' Instructions."
3. See Mihailović and Djelević's statements, columns and footnotes (a) and (b) in the Table "Hudson's 'Bullseye' Instructions." Further Mihailović reported to his Prime Minister (Slobodan Jovanović in London), on 26 May 1942 that in October 1941 he "received [from Hudson] the British Government's message that the Yugoslavs ought to fight for Yugoslavia, and not change their struggle into a rebellion of Communists for Soviet Union" (Marjanović, *Ustanak,* 307 and 307 n. 379).–However, see Hudson's statement in the Table, footnote (a). Unless Yugoslav archives become freely accessible to western historians, there will always remain the question of "how" Yugoslavs edit the material they publish.
4. Following Bailey, see the Table, column (e); following Deakin, ibid., column (c), the text reads "regardless of race, creed or political persuasion."
5. The legal position and protection of national minorities was a concern of the League of Nations between the first and second world wars. Refer, for instance, to C. A. Macartney's *National States and National Minorities,* Oxford U.P., 1934.–Consult also "The Treaties for the Protection of Minorities" [discussion and details], in Temperley, *A History V.* Any discussion of the post-World War II "solution" of the national problem in Yugoslavia is irrelevant as to the pre-war position.
6. Amery, 158-59, 160, 161 ff.
7. Djilas, *Wartime,* 69. (The third person Hudson enquired about was "the leader of the leftist Agrarians, Dragoljub Jovanović," loc. cit.) –Colonel Radonjić helped Belgrade SOE establish contact with north Albanian tribes (Amery, 30, where his name is spelled Radonitch). For a year

after the collapse of Yugoslavia he was with the Partisans and then joined Mihailović, ibid., 30 n. 1). Radonjić, an M.P., was of the Montenegrin tribe of Kuči on the Albanian border and well known by many Albanian leaders. In Mihailović's GHQ he was i/c liaison with the Albanian resistance, assisted by Captain Savo Vukadinović (Djonović, "Moje veze" in *Glasnik "Njegoš,"* No. 2, December 1958, p. 83).

8. Amery, 250;—FCO/SOEA, letter of 7 July 1982 to this author (MD). For FCO/SOEA letter see ch. 4, n. 16.

9. Amery, passim, and Djonović, "Od zida" in *Glasnik "Njegoš,"* No. 10, December 1962, p. 40 and passim.

10. Amery to this author (MD), letter of 2 July 1982.

11. Perhinek, letter of 14 May 1981 to this author, (MD).

12. Deakin, *The Embattled,* 129. Deakin does not indicate his Serbo-Croat source. However, a part of Simović's statement has been published by Kljaković, "Velika" in *Vojnoistoriski Glasnik,* as in ch. 4, n. 84, p. 72 n. 7, so that one can compare the two quotations.

13. PRO document FO 271/30220.

14. Why stress "dissolved"? Auty writes in the same vein, "two Majors of the Royal Yugoslav forces in exile" (Auty, *Tito,* 186), and "a *former* army officer" (ibid., 185; emphasis by MD). Churchill, Roosevelt, and even Stalin recognized them as an allied belligerent, and had Royal Yugoslav Military Attachés accredited to their governments.

15. Deakin, *The Embattled,* 130.

16. Popović's account of the Bullseye mission is based on Colonel Popović: Cassette of 27 October 1981 to this author (MD).

17. Amery, 246. See also Sweet-Escott, *Baker,* 96.

18. Amery to MD, letter of 2 July 1982.

19. Amery, 247. Djonović's motivation in selecting Trbić may be discerned from his statement that his tour of Yugoslav services in Turkey was due to his dissatisfaction with Trbić's work so that he had to reorganize the whole service; Djonović, "Veze" in *Glasnik "Njegoš," No. 1, July 1958,* p. 42. This should not reflect on Trbić's integrity. There is evidence that he was a very valuable man in the field. Djonović might have been dissatisfied with Trbić's office work? (MD).

20. Amery, 247-48; before the publication of Amery's book, Bennett read the relevant parts (ibid., 15).—Amery assumed that, when they called, Colonel Popović was "not alone" in bed (ibid., 248). Popović says he was

momentarily put out by being awaken and demanded men, and assumes that Amery was writing in this manner "to make the story more interesting" (Popović: Cassette, as in n. 16).

21. "The Minister for Army and Navy." In Yugoslavia, the Military Air Force was an arm of the army, and the Naval Air Force (called "Hydro Air Force") was an arm of the navy, hence the minister's title. Later, in exile, the minister's title was changed to the grandiloquent "Minister for the Army, Air force and Navy."

22. The Minister's appartments were in the GHQ; Brig.-General and Mrs Mirković with their daughter were his house guests (Popović: Cassette, op. cit.).

23. Late in 1942 Stanojlović left the Yugoslav Air Force to join the RAF, where he ended his career as a Wing Commander (Retd.).

24. Roberts erroneously says Djonović selected them for the Operation Bullseye (Roberts, *Tito, Mihailović,* 28). Only later, when the Yugoslav military crisis erupted in Cairo in 1942 and the Yugoslav GHQ became virtually irrelevant, Djonović's stature rose accordingly. He seems to have become the only Yugoslav link cooperating with the British authorities in posting Yugoslav personnel to missions in Yugoslavia.

25. Popović: Cassette, op. cit., The Minister might have seen Bullseye team earlier: General Mihailović testified that Ostojić and Lalatović "made fun of General Ilić himself, who scarcely gave them any message" (*Trial of Dragoljub-Draža,* 123).

26. Amery, 250-51.

27. Plećaš, "S mora" in *Glasnik "Njegoš,"* No. 5, June 1960, p. 37.

28. Auty, *Tito,* 186; emphasis by MD. Deakin, *The Embattled,* 127; emphasis by MD.

29. Howarth, 78. Although Montenegrins are of Serbian Orthodox Faith, the Roman Catholic See of Bar (Antibari, Antivari) in Montenegro dates from the fifth century. Its Archbishops bear also the title *Primas Serbiae* (or *Serviae*); they were often Franciscans.

30. Djilas, *Wartime,* 68. Kljaković, "Velika" in *Vojnoistoriski Glasnik,* XXI (2) p. 72.

31. Djilas, *Wartime,* 7-8, 57-58, 71, 77. Deakin, *The Embattled,* 202.

32. Djilas links the introduction of the term "Partisans" into Montenegro with the return of Captain Arso Jovanović from Serbia, after accompanying mission Bullseye (Djilas, *Wartime,* 77). He returned soon after

the raid on Jelin Dub (ibid., 76-77), which took place on 18 October (ibid., 73).

33. Deakin, *The Embattled*, 131.—Elisabeth Barker is misinformed when saying that, upon landing, the two Yugoslav officers "went straight to Mihailović's headquarters [in Serbia]"; Barker, 158.

34. Deakin, *The Embattled*, 132 n.*

35. Loc. cit. and p. 131. emphasis by MD.

36. Ibid., 131-132; emphasis by MD, except for the word *odreds.*

37. Karchmar, "Draža II," text of no. 88 typed on p. 870; upper case by MD.

As to other authors, Milazzo simply repeats Deakin's version (Milazzo, 33), and Wheeler has an unquestioning but crisp summary of Deakin's version (Wheeler, 85-86). Wheeler ascribes this telegram to Lalatović (ibid., 85), as does Karchmar; this might be due to their telescoping together Deakin mentions Lalatović on p. 131 of *The Embattled* (where the telegram of *13 October* is introduced), and again on p. 133 (where the telegram of *24 October* is—with qualifications—ascribed to him).

38. Kljaković, "Velika" as in n. 30, pp. 72-73; Kljaković's quotation is a Serbo-Croat translation from French.

39. Ibid., 73; emphasis by MD.

40. Ibid., 72; emphasis by MD.

41. Popović Papers as in ch. 4, no. 48, Minutes of the Ilić—Masterson meeting on 25 September 1941, p. 3.

42. Ibid., Memorandum of 25 September 1941 meeting, drafted by John Bennett. Cl. 'B' of this Memorandum embodies agreement on Masterson's proposal.

43. *On 13 October:* Kljaković, "Velika" as in n. 30, p. 73; Hudson signalled his *intention to depart* on 13 October: Wheeler, 71 and 71 n. 22, based on the document "WO 202/128, tel. 1-24, pp. 118-21"; *on or about* 13 October: Deakin, *The Embattled*, 132.

44. Hudson himself, in "Proceedings" as in ch. 4, no. 63, general section p. 339, Yugoslav section p. "Yug. 13"; Djilas, *Wartime*, 72. Djilas remained in Montenegro awaiting news from his [*first*] wife, who was in Serbia (Ibid., 77).

45. Deakin, *The Embattled*, 133.

46. Ibid., 133.—Wheeler reinforces Deakin's version by using forceful expressions but does not add any new information and/or source: Wheeler, 85. Wheeler also confuses Lalatović's signal of 24 October about

preparations for landing at Radovče, and the signal of 13 October pertaining to the "summary of messages" Montenegro-Malta.

47. Deakin, *The Embattled*, 133, emphasis by MD.—Wheeler, apparently referring to the same signla, says that it was received in Malta and London on 22 October (Wheeler, 271 n. 63, based on PRO document "WO 202/128, tel. 31, p. 117").

48. Deakin, *The Embattled*, 133, emphasis by MD.

49. Djilas, *Wartime*, 71.

50. Marjanović, *Ustanak*, 306 n. 376, and 304 n. 369 (in this order). Yugoslav copy of this document is in the Yugoslav archives (ibid., no. 369). According to Marjanović, its British (original) registration is "(Most Secret) M.O. 5/B.M. 1101." The date of the letter is probably 31 October 1941: Auty refers to this document published by Marjanović (Auty, *Tito*, 188 and 188 n. 17, printed on p. 311). Auty says General Dill wrote to Simović "that in a few days *Mihailovic* would be sent. . . [supplies]," yet there is no mention of Mihailović in that letter as published by Marjanović. "General Dill," is General (later Field-Marshal) Sir John Greer Dill (1881-1944, CIGS 27 May 1940–Christmas Day 1941).

51. Deakin in *Proceedings* 332 ("Yug. 6"), emphasis by MD.

52. Auty, *Tito*, 187; emphasis by MD.

53. Roberts, *Tito, Mihailović*, 29 and 29n. 40 printed on p. 328.

54. Karchmar, "Draža II," p. 762 n. 96 (part typed on p. 872) and based on Partisan and pro-Partisan sources.—W/T operator, Sergeant Veljko Dragićević, need not have been a communist. This opinion is fromed from: (i) Colonel Popović in his Cassette to MD; (ii) Djilas, *Wartime*, 71; (iii) Kljaković, "Velika" as in n. 12, p. 77 and p. 77 no. 33.

55. Deakin, *The Embattled*, 136 and 137.—Deakin's assumption that Dragićević fell out with his officers is probably closer to the mark than Karchmar's assumption that Dragićević was a Communist.

56. Hudson in "Proceedings," as in n. 44 above, p. 338, Yugoslav section p. "Yug. 12." Amery says that at Malta "mission's wireless set [-s(?)] proved defective and had to be replaced" (Amery, p. 250).

57. Hudson, in "Proceedings" op. cit., 339, Yugoslav section "Yug. 13."

58. Wheeler, 89 and text of n. 75 printed on p. 274, based on Hudson's signal registered as "WO 202/128, tel. 118, p. 123"; of 27 October.

59. Mitrović, *Zapadna* 261, claims Hudson went to visit Krupanj, a country town where he had worked before the war as a mining consultant,

and witnessed there a Partisan engagement against the Germans. This claim is spurious (Hudson to MD).

60. Wheeler, as per n. 58 above; Kljaković says Mihailović's headquarters signalled on 25 October that Hudson had arrived (Kljaković, "Velika," as in n. 30, p. 77 n. 32).

61. Auty, *Tito*, 186: "Hudson had taken two radio transmitters *and cipher books for himself and Mihailovic*, but was unable to transmit further than Malta" (emphasis by MD). Deakin, *The Embattled*, 138: "It seems that Hudson fulfilled his instructions in *handing over safe codes* for Mihailović's own wireless traffic, which now opened up with Malta in cipher under the code name 'Villa Resta', . . ." (emphasis by MD).

62. Wheeler assumes that Lalatović and Dragicević "left for Serbia at about [22 October]" (that is, when the Radovče telegram had been received at Malta and London): Wheeler, n. 63 printed on p. 271.

63. Hudson in "Proceedings" as in n. 44 above, p. 339, Yugoslav section p. "Yug. 13."

64. Hudson in ibid., p. 339 ("Yug. 13").

65. Wheeler, 89 and n. 75 printed on p. 274.

66. Deakin, *The Embattled*, 137.

67. Ibid., 145 and 146.

68. Ibid., 146, emphasis by MD.—Deakin's reconstruction is based on Hudson's signals transmitted in February 1943 (Ibid., 146n*).

69. Djilas, *Wartime*, 103-05.

70. Ibid., 105 and 108. Did they escape partly on foot, and partly by car? Hudson to MD: on foot all the way.

71. Ibid 112-13, emphasis by MD.

72. Perhinek's letter of 14 May 1981 to this author (MD), emphasis by MD.—"Kokin Brod" ("Kokin's Crossing," "Causeway"?) may be assumed to be at "Kokine Vode" ("Kokin Waters"), which can be located on Ordnance Map Yugoslavia 1:100,000, Sheet 100, *Vardište*, map ref. 78 x 60 (British War Office, Geographical Section, Heliographed from a Yugoslav Map dated 1929).

73. Sheets 1, 2 and 3 of the *Kriegstagebuch:* T315-2123-000765, 000766 and 000767. It is interesting to note that a hand written note has been added to the entry at 1510 hours that the event occurred at 1420 hours. This clashes with the entry at 1500 hours, when the same unit

was ordered to capture Užice with tanks. Had the commander seized the initiative ahead of his orders?

74. Djilas, *Wartime,* 112. The River "Uvca" is *Uvac.* (The ordnance map cited in n. 72. bove, map reference 92 x 41).

75. According to Djilas, it was decided that Serbs from Serbia were to "return immediately," "being homesick" (Djilas, *Wartime,* 112). The "Posavina Regiment," of one hundred men were accompanied on the return trip by Captain Hudson (ibid., 113-114).

76. Deakin, *The Embattled,* 146.

77. Ibid., 146.

78. Perhinek's letter of 14 May 1981 to this author (MD)–This Mountain Čemerno is west of the River Ibar, SW of Kraljevo and East-North-East of Ivanjica, in West Serbia.

79. "Proceedings," as in n. 44 above, p. 338, Yugoslav section p. "Yug. 12."

80. Ibid., p. 337, Yugoslav section p. "Yug. 11."

81. Marjanović in ibid., 350, Yugoslav section p. "Yug. 24."

82. Tito's biographer Dedijer, in ibid., 339-40, Yugoslav section pp. "Yug. 13-14."

Notes to Chapter 6

1. Derok, "Pisma," unpublished material, generally hand-written and mostly addressed to his father, Colonel V.J. Derok (Deroc); formerly in possession of his sister, Madame Yolande Popovitch of Paris. (Mme Popovitch died in Paris in August 1984.)–The extract is from a letter dated 16 August 1929, written in the (Northern) summer training camp at the village Boljare near Vlasotince, Serbia.

2. In the last stages of the Second World War, on 6 September 1944, the birthday of King Peter II, Leskovac was heavily bombed by the allied air force in the so-called *Operation Ratweek;* see Fitzroy Maclean, *Eastern,* 484-87. For a criticism of *Operation Ratweek* see Radoje and Živan L. Knežević, *Sloboda,* 308-09 and 392-93.

3. Derok, *Toplićki.*

4. Lazić, *Titov,* 29.

5. Clarke, "Review" regarding the Yugoslav Army during 1940, dated 30 December 1940, (PRO document FO 371 / 30259), item 16.

6. The summary which follows is from Lieutenant General Živko Pavlović, *Bitka...[The Battle of Jadar in 1914]*, cited by Uglješa Mihailović, "Četnički" in *Kanadski Srbobran–The Canadian Srbobran*, 1 January 1981, p. 8.

7. *Auswertestelle* in Belgrade to the Plenipotentiary Commanding General, 5 November 1941, T314-1457-001203, duplicated in ibid., frame 001213 (the latter is more legible); also *Auswertestelle* in Belgrade to the German High Command (O.K.W.) on 4 September 1941, T314-1457-001218.

8. In Novi Sad (*"Neusatz"* in Ger.), north of Belgrade, were HQ Army Area I (usually termed "The First Army"), and, among other units, also No. 1 Četnik ("Assault") Battalion and the HQ Četnik Command.

9. T 314-1457-001218, item "I." This document is a translation from its Serbian original into German. Therefore it is not certain that the term *"franc-tireurs"* was used in the original. If it was, the writer was not conversant with the terminology of the international law as it stood at the time. (The *franc-tireurs* were illegal, not legal irregular combattants.)

10. Ibid., item "II."

11. Ibid., item "III."

12. The officers were not far off the mark: in the Balkan campaign in 1941, the wear and tear of German motorized vehicles was such that "the panzer and motorized divisions required a rest period of three weeks for technical maintenance." (Seaton, *The German,* 170-171.)

13. For an annotated listing of sources for a biography of Mihailović see M. Deroc, "Sources" in *The South Slav Journal,* Vol. V No. 4(18), Winter 1982-83, pp. 31-34, and M. Deroc, letter to editor, in ibid., Vol. VI No. 1 (19), Spring 1983, pp. 96-97.

14. Mihailović was punished on 1 November 1939 and 3 November 1940 (T314-1457-001206, duplicated in frame 001216).

15. T314-1457-001206, duplicated in frame 001216: this is a German document summarizing Mihailović's personal file in Yugoslav archives.

16. Purković "Dragoljub" in R. Kneževic, *Knjiga I.,* p. 4; Karchmar, "Draža I," pp. 74-75; Stojanović, "Kako je" in *Glasnik "Njegoš",*. No. 9, June 1962, pp. 61-65; Tomasevich, *Chetniks,.* 131; German translation (*"Die Wahrheit"*) of the leaflet "Istina..." [Truth about Draza Mihajlovic (sic)"], p. 5 of the pamphlet (T314-1457-001237).

17. The leaflet as in note 16 above. ("Southern border," as used in the main text above, means primarily the Bulgarian border; MD.)

18. Gavrilović, "Srpski" in *Glasnik "Njegoš,"* No. 17, June 1966, pp. 100-06; Karchmar, "Draža I," p. 74.

19. "[British] Military Attache Belgrade to the War Office," 13 November 1940, item (8); PRO document FO 371/25034. The sentence cited in square brackets, inserted in the text above, is from ibid., (5, b), to which item (8) refers,—*V.q.* Colonel Clarke's "Review," cited in n. 5 above, where on p. 4 item 15, he says, "During the summer of 1940 a start was made with the formation of special fortification detachments for the manning of the frontier defenses.

. . . .

Some of these . . . are in fixed emplacements; others are mobile. The intention is that these fortification detachments should economise troops of the field army, particularly in the area north of the Danube—Sava Line." [The rest of the country is mountainous, the "north of the Danube-Sava line" is flat. [

20. Ibid., cited from item (10).
21. Ibid., item (7, a).
22. PRO document FO 371/25034/181/274, cited in K. St. Pavlowitch, "Yugoslav-British," 2nd instalment, in *East European Quarterly,* XII (4), January 1979, p. 431.
23. Stojanović's article as in n. 16.
24. Purković, "Dragoljub," as in n. 16, detail on p. 4; Marinković, in "Sećanje," (*Glasnik "Njegoš,"* No. 37, December 1976, pp. 26 and 31) claims that Mihailović was his Colonel in the 39th Infantry from the 2nd half of 1937 to the 2nd half of 1938, when he says, Mihailović was posted elsewhere.
25. A five page memorandum based on Mihailović's *"Personalpapiere"* found in the Yugoslav Ministry for Army and Navy: German *Auswertestelle* in occupied Belgrade to the German Cmdg General in Serbia, 5 November 1941 (T314-1457-001203 to 001207, duplicated in T314-1457-001213 to 001217).
26. Ibid., p. 3 of the document (T314-1457-001205, duplicated in 001215).
27. Loc. cit.—Purković, op. cit., in n. 16, says Mihailović was posted from Celje to the High Inspectorate of the Army, but see n. 28 below.
28. In the document *"Die Wahrheit,"* cited in n. 16, leaflet p. 5, it is said Mihailović was punished for the memorandum he submitted when he

was Chief of Staff Fortifications in Slovenia; therefore he was not yet at the High Inspectorate of the Army (cf. Purković in n. 27).

29. Karchmar, "Draža I," pp. 71-72 and 73-75, and notes 4 and 11-14, typed on pp. 96 and 97-99.

30. This is not to deny that he was involved in a brawl with the members of the local German minority [local Nazis?], but the available information is not sufficient to draw any wider conclusions.

31. For the date of punishment see *Auswertestelle* document cited in n. 25, p. 4 (T314-1457-001206, duplicated in 001216).—The German text shows that from 5 March 1940 to 30 October 1940 Mihailović was head of the General Section of the High Inspectorate of the Armed Forces, and from that date Assistant Chief-of-Staff, HQ, Seacoast Army Area [Army Area VI, HQ at Mostar]. As he was punished on 3 November, after an investigation which must have lasted a while, the question is, was his re-posting to the Seacoast Area Command a part of his punishment or not?

32. Stojanović, "Kako je," in *Glasnik "Njegoš,"* June 1962, No. 9, detail on p. 62.

33. The statement of 13 November 1941 by General Nedić to his nephew and future biographer, Stanislav Krakov. (Krakov, *General I,* pp. 272-73.)

34. Loc. cit.

35. A standard Serbian expression meaning to take refuge from the main lines of communications (historically: in the aforested mountains or *"šuma"*), whence to wage guerrilla (or *"četnik"*) warfare. Cf. The French *"le maquis"* and to be a *"maquisard."*

36. Marjanović, Draža I, pp. 47-54.

37. Ibid., 62-63.

38. The assistant Chief of Staff was General Staff Lieutenant Colonel Stefan [S.] Kos, a Slovene (Terzić, 693).

39. Marjanović, Draža I, p. 63; emphasis by MD.

40. Terzić, 327.

41. Vuković, "Sa pukovnikom" in *Glasnik Njegoš,"* No. 34, June 1975, pp. 32-46.

42. Vuković, "Sa pukovnikom," as in n. 41, p. 42.

43. Loc. cit.; Terzić, 693. Osjek, Vrbas and Bosna Divisions were under the 2nd Army (ibid.).

44. Vuković, "Sa pukovnikom" as in n. 41, p. 33.

45. Ibid., 34.
46. Ibid., 34, 35-36 and 38.
47. Ibid., 35, 36 and 38.
48. Ibid., 39.
49. Ibid., 40.
50. Terzić, 396, 397, 430, 465.—Another, earlier, mutiny of Croat reserve troops was that of the No. 106 Infantry Regiment at Karlovac, Croatia, in September 1939: This mutiny was caused "by communist agitators who spread the rumour that the reservists were to be sent to France to the Maginot Line." (See p. 9 of the "Enclosure No. 1" to the report of the British Minister in Belgrade to the Foreign Office of 26 December 1939, PRO document FO 371/23877).
51. Terzić, 480.
52. In possession of his son, Monsieur Zoran Raketitch, of Paris, France, to whom I am obliged for a copy.
53. This was a reasonable question: a field commander's duties, competence and powers depended on it. A precedent in the mind of Yugoslav commanders was the case of Bitolj (now called Bitola). This town, in British sources usually called "Monastir," is north of the Greek border. The Italian air force bombed it on 5 and 6 November 1940 (Hoptner, 186). Yugoslavia did not treat it as a *casus belli*. The British Minister in Belgrade informed the Foreign Office on 9 November that "73 bombs had been dropped, 10 people had been killed and 23 injured, and... material damage was enormous": PRO document FO 371/25034/181/84, cited in K. St. Pavlowitch, "Yugoslav-British" in *East European Quarterly*, XII (3), p. 316 and n. 16 printed on p. 337).
54. S. Rapotec, a Slovene, told this author (MD) in an interview in Sydney in 1982, that he was the commander of the company in which the rebellion started. Rapotec was then a Yugoslav Reserve Lieutenant (later Captain). He says the whole affair started when the mobilized Croats and Slovenes simply left and went home; the small Ustaša gang in the Regiment then took over.
55. T314-1066-000064.
56. T314-1066-000065.
57. T314-1066-000069.
58. T314-1066-000079, cf. T314-1066-000021, 2nd paragraph.
59. Terzić, 502, 503, 506, 518-19, 520 and 531-32.
60. Yugoslav 7th Army in Slovenia disbanded on 11 April (ibid., pp.

518 and 530). At the end of World War II, on 3 May 1945 in Ljubljana a Slovenian State was proclaimed at part of a new Kingdom of Yugoslavia, and the [Prince-] Bishop of Ljubljana, Dr. Gregory Rožman, tried to have General Alexander acquainted with it (Karapandžic, 452-54). Karapandžic is an apologist for the regime in occupied Serbia set up by the Germans. He might have provided the above information to show that his leader, Ljotić, was loyal to Yugoslavia: he ascribes this event to his influence. Be this as it may, the Slovenian act of 3 May should be researched independently.

61. Terzić, 495.
62. Ibid., 517; Stanković, "Sa Dražom" in R. Knežević, *Knjiga I,* pp. 15-27. Čulinović, 219-55, cites many statements about defeatism, treason, desertion and rebellion in the April War.
63. Terzić, 517.
64. Vuković, "Sa pukovnikom,"as in n. 41, p. 41.
65. Ibid., 41-42; Terzić, 529.
66. Vuković, "Sa pukovnikom," op. cit., 41; Stanković, "Sa Dražom," as in n. 62, p. 19.
67. Vuković, "Sa pukovnikom," as in n. 41, p. 41.
68. Ibid., 42. (Vuković spells his name, wrongly, as "Deroko." His war posting was in the 3rd Battalion, Artillery Regiment No. 10, Bosna Division.)
69. Ibid., 42; Stanković, "Sa Dražom,"as in n. 62, pp. 15-18.

I dealt with some of the above events in my article "U ratu" (*Savremenik,* New Series, XXVII (13), October 1981, pp. 108-12.) At the time I did not have all the primary sources I acquired later, so that I had—wrongly—Derok fighting at Doboj-Ševarlija, instead of at Brčko.

70. Vuković, "Sa pukovnikom," as in n. 41, p. 43 (giving a romanticised account); Stanković, "Sa Dražom,"as in n. 62, p. 19.—From Terzić, 540, one gets the impression that the bridge was destroyed on 13 April. However on the sketch-map in the War Diary of the German XLVI Corps, the bridge is shown as already destroyed on the 12th (T314-1066-000030); the corresponding entry is in War Diary of 12 April at 21.30 hours (T314-1066-000094).
71. Vuković, "Sa pukovnikom," op. cit., 43; Milosavljević, "Mihailović" in R. Knežević, *Knjiga I,* detail on pp. 51-52 (Milosavljević was at the time commanding the Vrbas Division of the 2nd Army); Stanković, "Sa Dražom," as in n. 62, p. 18.

72. Vuković, "Sa pukovnikom," op. cit., 43; Stanković, "Sa Dražom," op. cit., 19-20.
73. War Diary of the German XLVI Corps, T314-1066-000094 entry at 21.30 hours, and T314-1066-000023 for losses.
74. Stanković, "Sa Dražom," as in n. 62, p. 19. (Stanković wrongly spells his first name "Feta").
75. Terzić, 515. (Some writers refer to the 46th Corps as an Armoured Corps, but the Motorized 46th was reorganized as a *Panzer* Corps only after the Yugoslav campaign ended.)
76. Terzić, 528-29.
77. Ibid., 540.
78. Vuković, "Sa pukovnikom," as in n. 41, p. 44; Milosavljević, "Mihavilović," as in n. 71, p. 30.—Mihailović reinforced this detachment also by some other units (Stanković, "Sa Dražom," as in n. 62, p. 20.)
79. Vuković, "Sa pukovnikom," op. cit., 40.
80. Milosavljević, "Mihailović," op. cit., 51; Stanković, "Sa Dražom," op. cit., 21-22.
81. Bathe and Glodschey, 169, are wrong in stating that the "Serbs" engaged their own tanks only here in the Yugoslav 1941 campaign. Two other engagements took place on 7 April in Štip-Veles area, south-east of Skoplje, and at Valandovo, north-west of the Lake Dojran on the Greek border (Buchner, 121 and 134). A British patrol "thrust to the north of Monastir [Bitolj]" on 8 April and led back "three Yugoslav tanks and four anti-aircraft guns" (Long, *Greece,* 42); the three tanks might have been the remnants of those engaged in the Štip-Veles area?
82. Terzić, 555.
83. Ibid., pp. 528-29 and 557.
84. Vuković, "Sa pukovnikom," as in n. 41, p. 44. (Milosavljević, as in n. 71, p. 50, says that Miljković discharged all his troops from further service and proceeded to Sarajevo. There is no information available to allow discussion of this point.)—Commander of the II Army Group was General Milutin Dj. Nedić, brother of General Milan Dj. Nedić, who punished Mihailović twice when Minister for the Army and Navy. Milan Dj. Nedić was later "Prime Minister" of German-occupied Serbia.
85. Yugoslav Supreme Command, order No. 0.181: Terzić, 560.
86. Radoje L. Knežević, "Počeci" in R. Kenžević, *Knjiga I,* pp. 7-14, detail on p. 9. (Knežević's article is a critical synopsis of different sources.)

87. Cf. the similarity of outlook between Mihailović and Lt Colonel Clarke, text to notes 19, and 20 and 21.

88. Marjanović, *Draža I,* p. 64 text to n. 19; for n. 19.—Marjanović states this is a verbatim citation from interrogation of Mihailović by [the Partisan] post-war Yugoslav authorities on 6 April 1946 (ibid., pp. 64, n. 96 on p. 343 and n. 19 on p. 344).

89. Knežević, "Počeci," as in n. 86, p. 9.—His reconstruction is based on reminiscences, not on documents, and should not be taken too formally.

90. Marjanović, *Draža I,* pp. 64-65.

91. Gauge and capacity are from Zelenika, *Rat Srbije,* Addendum, Map "Geografski . . ." ["Geographic overview of the Serbian and Montenegrin Battlefield in 1915"].

92. Milazzo, 13 and notes 2-4 on the same page.—In n. 2 Milazzo refers to one of his sources as an article by "Lieutenant Colonel" Mešković, but Mešković was a 2/Lieutenant.

93. Stanković, "Sa Dražom," as in n. 62, p. 25.

94. Loc. cit.—In his n. 5 on the same page, the editor of the *Knjiga,* R. Knežević, draws attention to the fact that Stanković has mistakenly called the nearby village "Žepce," instead of "Žepa." After Mihailović's meeting with the village elders, they were escorted home (Stanković, op. cit., 26). In Stanković's recreation of the address by Mihailović to the two Muslim dignitaries, the following sentence could not have been used at that time by Mihailović: "We are the Yugoslav Army in the Fatherland . . . ." (Ibid., 25.) The "Army in the Fatherland" is an appellation which was given by the *émigré* government to Mihailović's troops only later.

95. Milazzo, 13 n. 2.

96. Loc. cit.

97. Vuković, "Sa pukovnikom," as in n. 41, p. 41; emphasis by this author (MD).

98. Milosavljević, "Mihailović," as in n. 71, p. 50; emphasis by this author (MD).

99. Stanković, "Sa Dražom," as in n. 62, pp. 17-18; emphasis by this author (MD).

100. Mešković, "Od Bosne," in R. Knežević, *Knjiga I,* pp. 28-33.

Notes to Chapter 7

1. "Military Conclusions," Clause 1, Tehran (Teheran) 1 December 1943: FRUS, 652.–Djilas, *Wartime,* 359 (my italics, MD). Significantly, Djilas addes (p. 361): "I applauded zealously and enthusiastically. Only later–but frequently then–would my prolonged applause, like that of many others, be prompted by fears that someone may think I was against the party and Tito." [So much for the democracy Tito introduced when he was in power.] ; Đuretic, Vol. 2, p. 60.

2. This author (MD) to Brezhnev, 30 April 1981, replied to by V. Tushko, Secretary of the USSR-Australia Society in Moscow, 22 June 1981.

3. Auty, *Tito,* "Preface" xii.

4. Dedijer, *Tito Speaks,* London, 1954.

5. Royal Hungarian Honved Regiments, when recruited in Croatia-Slavonia, were known locally as the "Domobran" or Home Guard.

6. Dedijer, *Tito,* 26.

7. Djilas, *Tito,* 16-17.

8. Auty, *Tito,* 31.

9. A *"Zugsfuehrer"* or Section Commander was equivalent to a British Sergeant (Australian Imperial Force, *Notes on the Austro-Hungarian Army,* Government Printer, [1900], "Vocabulary of Military Titles and Terms," p. 57). Some authors claim that Broz was a Sergeant-Major, which is obviously wrong.

10. Oesterreichisches Staatsarchiv-Kriegsarchiv, over the signature of the Director of War Archives (name illegible), prepared by Dr Rutkowski, ZI 22.082/1981 of 13 January 1981 to this author (MD). Dedijer's *Novi Prilozi I,* pp. 59-60, contain Broz's expanded version of his imprisonment. In this version Broz states that shortly after his release his regiment left for the Russian front *in January 1915;* this confirms the later date (My italics, MD.)

11. Djilas, *Wartime,* 103.

12. Maclean, *Disputed,* 20.

13. This doctoring is evident also in Dedijer's *Novi Prilozi I,* where on page 59 is stated "(Broz's) Company should have gone to the Serbian border but was withdrawn."

14. Austrian Archives as in n. 10.

15. Dedijer, *Tito*, 29-30; Auty, *Tito*, 31-32; Maclean, *Disputed*, 23.

16. International Committee of the Red Cross, Central Tracing Agency, letter EOCA/GEN/md of 22 February 1984, over the signature of Mme L. Simonius, Head of the Section, to this author (MD).

17. Austrian Archives as in n. 10, but ref. 2095/0-KA/84 of 28 March 1984 to this author (MD).

18. *Report on the Atrocities*, 173-74.

19. Ibid., 174.

20. Ibid., 181 n. 1: *"Direktionen fuer das Verhalten gegenueber der Bevoelkerung in Serbien"* issued by the *K.u.k. 9. Korpskommando*.

21. Auty, *Tito*, 37.

22. Dedijer, *Novi Prilozi I*, p. 69 n. 1 (text of Tito's letter to Djilas).

23. Auty, *Tito*, 38-39. For details of Broz's service with the Red Guards, see Dedijer, *Novi Prilozi I*, pp. 68-69.

24. Auty is enchanted with Tito as a story-teller. Tito "has an excellent pictorial memory..." she says. He recounted many of the dramatic incidents of his past "in anecdotes that have become fixed...like a collection of old snapshots in a family album." (Auty, *Tito*, "Preface.")— [This shows what flimsy data have some of Tito's biographers taken for historical gospel.]

25. Dedijer, *Tito*, 41.

26. Maček, 90; Stevan K. Pavlowitch, *Yugoslavia*, 62; Slijepčević, 140.

27. Avakumović, *History I*, 49.

28. V. Korać, *Povjest...* [*History of the Workers' Movement in Croatia and Slavonia*], Vol. I, Zagreb, 1929, p. 268, cited in Avakumović, *History I*, 49, n. 82; *v.q.* Minutes of the Constituent Assembly, 17th Session, p. 34, cited in "'Obznana' pred ustavotvornom skupštinom," *Glasnik "Njegoš,"* No. 31, December 1973, pp. 15-16 and p. 16, n. 1.

29. Clause 1 and the last two sentences of the *Obznana* (text in Čulinović, detail on pp. 33 and 34. Emphasis by this author (MD).

30. Dedijer, *Tito*, 41.

31. Avakumović, *History I*, p. 55; S. K. Pavlowitch, *Yugoslavia*, 65.

32. Dedijer, *Tito*, 41.

33. Ibid., 42.

34. Ibid., 43; Auty, *Tito*, 51. Whereas Auty thinks that Šabić was probably a paid agent of the Comintern, according to Dedijer he was a follower of Radić's Croat Republican Peasant Party (HRSS) and Tito made

him join the Communist Party of Yugoslavia (Dedijer, *Novi Prilozi I*, p. 94); nevertheless, Šabić had taken an active part in the Bolshevik Revolution (loc. cit.).

35. Dedijer, *Tito*, 43.
36. Ibid., 44; Auty, *Tito*, 52.
37. Foreign Office/State Department, German War Document Project, Serial 6136H filmed on 9 May 1951; German Foreign Ministry/Zagreb, geheim; *Politische und Kulturelle Geheimakten aus dem Zeitraum 1942-1944*. The folder Pol 4 Nr. 21 contains the information about Tito available to the German Legation December 1942-February 1943, microfilm frames E458403—E458428. Extract from Yugoslav police files (E458406-E458411), detail in E458407. This author (MD) is obliged for copies of this material to the Foreign and Commonwealth Office in London, Reference LRL 425/1, over the signature of K. H. W. Hiscock. (Correspondence of January and February 1981).
38. Avakumović, *History I*, 89; at the time Zagreb had 250 party members (loc. cit., n. 130).
39. Auty, *Tito*, 54.
40. Documentation cited in n. 37, microfilm frame E458407; Avakumović, *History I*, 115 n. 119; Auty, *Tito*, 99 and 101. Cf. Tito's own account in Dedijer, *Tito*, 59-60.
41. Documentation cited in n. 37, microfilm from E458407; Dedijer, *Tito*, 61; Auty, *Tito*, 65-66.
42. Documentation cited in n. 37, microfilm frames E458407, E458410; Dedijer, *Tito*, p. 68; Auty, *Tito*, 68 (the last two authors give 14 November as the date of sentencing).
43. Broz Tito, *Political Report*, 33-34; Dedijer, *Tito*, 75; Auty, *Tito*, 70-73 and the photograph No. 7, opposite p. 62.
44. "Serbs of Mosaic faith" or the Jews of Serbia were of Spanish origin. They were never persecuted in Serbia, assimilated, and became Serbs of Mosaic faith. *V.q.* Djilas, *Wartime*, 356 n. 25: "Pijade had the reputation of being the most zealous Serb among us."
45. Tito's interview in *Politika* of 20 May 1957, cited in Avakumović, *History I*, p. 100 and p. 100 n. 43.
46. Dedijer, *Tito*, 79-81; Auty, *Tito*, 83; Documentation cited in n. 37, microfilm frames E458407, E458408.
47. Dedijer, *Tito*, 88; Auty, *Tito*, 88 and n. 18 printed on p. 302;

Maclean, *Disputed,* 71. Also Dedijer, *Novi Prilozi I,* pp. 212 and 213.
  48. "Invitation" of 24 January 1919, text in Degras, *The Communist I,* p. 3 (Clause I-5).
  49. The "Platform" of 4 March 1919, text in Degras, *The Communist I,* pp. 17-24, detail on p. 19 (Section "1").
  50. Degras, *The Communist II,* pp. 449-50; Avakumović, *History I,* p. 113.
  51. Avakumović, loc. cit.
  52. Avakumović, *History I,* pp. 11-12.
  53. Ibid., 112 n. 100, citing *Istorijski Arhiv Komunističke Partije Jugoslavije,* vol. ii, p. 35.
  54. Belgrade newspaper *Politika* was reporting the court-martial and appeal proceedings; *v.q. The Times* of 4, 17, 21 and 22 June 1932, pp. 9a, 13g, 13g and 11f respectively, and Avakumović, *History I,* p. 112.
  55. Avakumović, *History I,* documentation listed on p. 112 n. 101.
  56. Ibid., 94-98.
  57. Auty, *Tito,* 66.
  58. Broz Tito, *Political Report,* p. 30.
  59. Dedijer, *Tito,* 90, 96-97; Auty, *Tito,* 95 and 99.–Broz had at least 17 aliases and/or *noms de plume:* S. Babić, J. A. Carlson, Dragomir, Jiriček, Klanjčanin, I. Kostanjšek, S. Mekas, Novak, Oto, Petar, Rudi, Timo, Tito, Tomanek, Valter, Fridrih Valter, Viktorov.
  60. Dedijer, *Tito,* 103; Auty, *Tito,* 109.
  61. The Central Committee itself moved to Paris from Vienna "during the last months of 1936" (Auty, *Tito,* 110).
  62. Dedijer, *Tito,* 104, 106, 107; Auty, *Tito,* 109, 111; Kopinič (*alias* "Vokšin" in Moscow and "Valdes" in Spain), when interviewed by Vjenceslav Cenčić in "Enigma Kopinič: Pariski susret s Titom," NIN (*Nedeljne Ilustrovane novine*), 1 May 1983, p. 56.
  63. While in Paris, as Joseph Broz he enrolled as a student in the *Ecole Libre des Sciences Politiques,* later the *Institut d'Etudes Politiques* (personal knowledge by this author, MD). This might have been a stratagem to conceal the reason for his presence there from the *Préfecture de Police.*
  64. Dedijer, *Tito,* 110; Broz Tito, *Political Report,* 36.
  65. Dedijer, *Tito,* 110; Auty, *Tito,* 129.
  66. Ibid., 128.
  67. Dedijer, *Tito,* 98. *V.q.* Maclean, *Disputed,* 82; Auty, *Tito,* 102.

68. Djilas, *Tito*, 11.
69. Loc. cit.
70. Dedijer, *Tito*, Auty, *Tito*, 146-47.
71. Ibid., pp. 115-16. Of the seven names on Auty's list of people who ran the party, the names of Kardelj, Ranković and Djilas are familiar.
72. Dedijer, *Tito*, 115.
73. Ibid., 124-25.
74. Some of the relevant contemporary Comintern directives are printed in Degras, *The Communist III*, passim.
75. Auty, *Tito*, 146 and (for her source), n. 7 printed on p. 307.
76. Avakumović, *History I*, p. 175.
77. A party leaflet of December 1939, cited in Avakumović, ibid., 176-77, where he indicates his source also.
78. H.M Minister in Belgrade to the Foreign Office, No. 292, 33/-109/39 of 26 December 1939: its enclosure entitled "Memorandum on Communism in Yugoslavia," p. 9 (PRO document FO 371/23877, sheet marked 477): *v.q.* this book, ch. 6 n. 50. Cf. Avakumović, *History I*, pp. 180-81.
79. *The Communist*, Belgrade, p. 70, cited in Avakumović, *History I*, p. 180 n. 37.
80. Avakumović, *History I*, pp. 177 and n. 20.
81. Broz Tito, *Political Report*, p. 44.
82. Dedijer, *Tito*, 127-28. Also Dedijer, *Novi Prilozi I*, pp. 262-63.
83. Dedijer, *Tito*, 122. The members of the commission were Tito, Bakić and Vladimir Popović (Djilas, *Memoir*, 361).
84. Broz Tito, *Political Report*, 50. Also Dedijer, *Novi Prilozi I*, p. 250.
85. Auty, *Tito*, 150-51.
86. Ibid., 151-53.
87. Avakumović, *History I*, p. 189 n. 2.
88. Djilas, *Memoir*, 388.
89. Dedijer, *Tito*, 140-41; Djilas, *Memoir*, 388; Broz Tito, *Political Report*, 50.
90. Ibid., 50. (A "war committee," instead of existing "peace time" military committee?)
91. Djilas, *Memoir*, 388; emphasis by this author (MD). In his *Novi Prilozi I*, pp. 270-71, Dedijer gives a similar summary and calls attention to

Djilas's having singled out the central point in Tito's address: that the Communist take-over in Yugoslavia should be effected by passing the intermediary revolutionary stages taught by the Comintern.

92. See the text to footnote 50.
93. Djilas, *Memoir*, 388-89.
94. Ibid., 389.
95. Dedijer, *Tito*, 141-42; emphasis by this author (MD).
96. Auty, *Tito*, 171. [Moscow was concerned about its relations with Great Britain and played down the "Socialist" part of its platform; nevertheless Tito disregarded the admonishments to temper his "socialist" zeal for the time being.]
97. Ibid., 170-71.
98. Ibid., 171.
99. Drachkovitch, "The Comintern" in Drachkovitch and Lazitch, *The Comintern*, 184-213, detail on p. 192; emphasis by this author, MD. In the official English translation of Tito's speech on the same subject at the 5th Congress of the KPJ in 1948, the word *"Prepare"* is rendered as *"Get ready"* (Broz Tito, *Political Report*, p. 52). For the full text of the proclamation in Serbo-Croat, see *Zbornik dokumenata i podataka*, Tom I Part I, Belgrade, 1949, pp. 11-17; the part in question is on p. 12: *"Spremajte se . . . ."*
100. Auty, *Tito*, 172; emphasis by this author, MD.
101. Loc. cit.
102. Auty, *Tito*, ch. 10, passim.
103. In this context both resistance movements, Mihailović's and KPJ's initially occupied themselves with gaining the allegiance of the "First Rifles." The army men and other local "First Rifles" gravitated to Mihailović; the KPJ relied on sending out party activists to the countryside to recruit them.
104. See Auty's text cited to note 98 above.
105. Cited from Drachkovitch, "The Comintern" in Drachkovitch and Lazitch, *The Comintern*, 193.
106. Koštunica (Vojislav) and Kosta Čavoški, *Party Pluralism or Monism, Social Movements and the Political System in Yugoslavia 1944-1949*, East European Monographs, Boulder, 1985. (This monograph is part of a wider project financed by the Republican Science Community of Serbia, Yugoslavia.)

107. Ibid., p. 226 (part of note 1 to Chapter II).
108. *Zbornik dokumenata*, as in n. 99, p. 17; the reprint in the *Zbornik* is in Latin letters of the original typewritten text in the Cyrillic alphabet (for the photostat of the latter see ibid., p. 13).

Notes to Chapter 8

1. A.F.H.Q., G-2 (PB), [Bari?], September 1944: *The Cetniks: A Survey*, 6 (PRO document WO 204/8109). Different authors give different dates. (See, e.g., Marjanović, "Prilozi istoriji" in *Istorija XX veka– Zbornik radova I*, p. 164 n. 39, and Karchmar, "Draža I," part of the text of no. 12 typed on p. 103. A day or two either way has no bearing on discussions here.) Ravna Gora is a "saddle" between mountains Maljen (1,103m) and Povlen (1,346m) on the road from Valjevo to Užice.

2. For a text in English see OKW/L, (IV/QU), number 4434/41 of 3 April 1941: "Provisional Directives for the Partition of Yugoslavia," in International Military Tribunal, Nurenberg, *Trial of the Major War Criminals*, Vol. VII, Nurenberg, Germany, 1947, pp. 238-40 (Document No. 1195-PS). For the text in German see the above document, No. 1195-PS, "Vorlaeufige Richtlinien fuer die Aufteilung Jugoslawiens" in ibid., Vol. XXVII, Nurenberg, Germany, 1948, pp. 60-62 (British exhibit GB-144; this text contains some printing errors, e.g., in C1.7, "Desnien" instead of "Bosnien"). Cf. document No. 291, "General Plans for the later Organization of the Administration in the Yugoslavia [sic] Area" of 6 April 1941, in DGFP, DXII, p. 487.

3. But at one stage only an "*autonomous*" Croatia, "probably under Hungarian influence" was considered (C1.2 of the document No. 291 in DGFP, DXII, p. 487).

4. C1.5 of "Provisional Directives," as in n. 2 above (emphasis by this author, MD).

5. Clause 1 of the document "Oberbefehlshaber des Heeres [OKH], Gen St d H/Befehlsstab Gen Qu, Nr. B/249/41 geh." of 20 April 1941, over the signature of Field Marshal Wilhelm von Brauchitsch: two typewritten pages headed "*Befehl fuer die Einrichtung einer Militaerverwaltung in Serbien.*" A copy is located in the war diary of the "Unit 08633" for April-December 1941 (T501-245-000247 and 000248).

6. DGFP, DXII, March and April 1941, passim.

7. *Generaloberst Halder,* Vol. II, p. 391.
8. Erpenbeck, 265.
9. See n. 5 above (*"Befehl fuer die Einrichtung"*).
10. OKH, *Anordnung* Nr. II 0294/41 g. Kdos. Chefs. (Operation 'Twenty five'" of 31 March 1941, T501-245-000239 to 000246). Note that some clauses of the *"Anordnung"* were virtually replaced by Hitler's directives for the partition of Yugoslavia of 3 April 1941.
11. AOK, 2, O.QU., 19 April 1941: two typewritten pages headed *"Militaerverwaltung im altserbischen Raum and im Raum des deutschen Schutzgebietes."* A copy is located in the war diary of MBS/Ia, 21 April-10 October 1941 (T501-249-001081 and 001082); *Generaloberst Halder,* 363, entry of 13 April 1941 under "Wagner (e)."
12. War diary of "Unit 08633," entry under 22 April 1941 (T501-245-000113). Foerster took over from Schmidt-Logan on 22 April. (T501-245-000235 to 000237).
13. OKH, Gen St d H/Gen Qu, Nr. B/249/41 g., 17 April 1941: *"Dienstanweisung fuer den Militaerbefehlshaber in Serbien"* (T501-245-000249 to 000251).
14. As n. 13; p. 2 of the document (T501-245-000250).
15. War diary of Unit 08633, entries on 9, 17, 20 and 23 April 1941 (T501-245-000112 to 000114).—When "Unit 08633" became the HQ of the MBS, its diary continued as the diary of the latter. Later somebody added to the title page the annotation "Kommandierender General und Befehlshaber in Serbien/Ia."
16. Service instructions as in n. 13 above, p. 1, Item A (T501-245-000249).
17. MBS, *"Kommandobefehl Nr. 1"* of 28 April 1941 (T501-245-000279 and 000280).
18. See MBS circular of 2 May (T501-245-000302). For his request to the higher authorities to do so see his *"Kommandobefehl Nr. 1"* as in n. 17. For the approval of the OKH to introduce this change see T501-245-000289.
19. DGFP, DXII, p. 574, footnotes to the document No. 365.
20. "Befehl" of 20 April as in n. 5 above.—When Field Marshal List was appointed commander in the southeast in June 1941, the MBS came under him, but the direct communication between the OKH and MBS continued. On 24 July List abolished this practice: T501-245-000605.

Notes to Chapter 8

21. See the text to footnote 2 above.
22. Erpenbeck, 9.
23. Some writers call him "Thurner." This spelling might have crept in because Halder used it in his diary.
24. Hitler's War Directive No. 27 of 13 April 1941. For an English translation see Trevor-Roper, 65-68, detail on p. 69. For the original German text see Hubatsch, 112-117. (Trevor-Roper dates the directive "4 April," which is not borne out by the text that follows; Hubatsch dates it "13 April," which is followed here.)
25. Hehn, 18 (with the listing of units). Marjanović, *Ustanak,* 27 (with the listing of units).
26. AOK 2, 825 geh., 26 April 1941, *"Weisungen fuer den Militaerbefehlshaber in Serbien."* Incomplete copy (p. 1 only) in the war diary "Ia" of the MBS for 21 April-10 October 1941 (T501-249-001077). This directive was issued in fulfillment of clause 3 in the *Befehl* of the OKH of 20 April, as in n. 5 above, which stipulated that "a special instruction" was to be issued "regarding the employment of [field] troops" in Serbia.
27. The *Ls-Btl.* soldiers were in the age group 35-45: Erpenbeck, n. 34 typewritten on p. 138.
28. *Generaloberst Halder,* 408-409.
29. Erpenbeck, 15; Marjanović, *Ustanak,* 35-36. Emphasis is by this author (MD).
30. Živanović, Treći I, p. 147. How much did the clash of their per-
31. Erpenbeck, 15 and n. 60 types on p. 139.
32. They were in the age group 29 to 35; Hehn, 18 and 20. For the first mention of these replacement divisions to the "15th wave," see war diary of Unit 08633 on 2 May 1941 (T501-245-000288 and 000289).
33. War diary of Unit 08633 on 17 June 1941 (T501-245-000423). Bader took command of the HK LXV on 13 June at Vrnjačka Banja, a spa in the rich valley of the West Morava in Serbia, and moved his HQ to Belgrade on the day of the takeover from the AOK 2 (War diary of the 717th Infantry Division for 15 May-31 December 1941, entries on 13 and 17 June 1941: T315-2262-000087 to 000093; also War diary of Unit 08633 on 10 June 1941: T-501-245-000421).
34. *Befehl* of 20 April, as in n. 5, Clause 2.
35. War diary of Unit 08633, entries on 19 and 29 July 1941 (T501-245-000530 and 000533).

36. For an English text of Hitler's directive No. 31 of 9 June 1941: Trevor-Roper, 74-77. For a more extensive text, in German: Hubatsch, 122-25 and 127.

37. See the marching survey in the diary of the Unit 08633; T501-245-000289 to 000301.

38. *Generaloberst Halder*, 402.

39. Diary of the 08633, entry of 19 May 1941 (T501-245-000297).

40. Diary of the 08633 under 6 May 1941 (T501-245-000290).

41. Hehn, 20, and n. I(2) printed on p. 148, citing from Bader's own report.

42. War diary of the 08633, "Enclosure A2" (a document dated 1 July 1941; T501-245-000542). The total of 325,000 comprised 316,200 civilians who had been mobilized under Yugoslav laws, 2,000 professional army officers and 6,800 "regular soldiers and unreliable elements."

43. *"Verordnung betreffend die Erfassung von Kriegsgefangenen"*: see the Folder of Enclosures, Vol. I, to the War Diary of the MBS/Abt. Qu., 20 April-13 November 1941 (T501-251-000675); encl. 2 to this document contains the sample of the identity card (ID) to be issued (T501-251-000677). This proclamation was published on 22 May: Marjanović, *Ustanak*, 37.

44. Ibid., p. 37.

45. Loc. cit.

46. Loc. cit.

47. Page 1 of the confidential instruction of how to proceed, Militaer-befehlshaber in Serbien, Kommandostab, Abtlg. Qu. Nr. 38/41 geh., Anlage 3 z. Kriegstagebuch Abt. Qu., 14.4.1941, *"Erfassung, Beurlaubung und Ueberwachung entwichener Kriegsgefangener"* (T501-251-000671).

48. T501-245-000422.

49. *The Trial of Dragoljub-Draža Mihailović*, 113.

50. This text was published in *Hrvatski narod* of 10 April 1941 (Čulinović, 233 and 233 n. 267).

51. For negotiations which led to the passing-over of the Yugoslavia's legitimate power to the Ustasha-Croatia in April 1941, see DGFP, DXII, pp. 513-14 (document No. 311, Kvaternik to Hitler, from Zagreb, 11 April 1941) and pp. 516-17 (Veesenmayer to the Foreign Ministry from Zagreb, 11 April 1941); for a denial of this version by Maček see Maček, 229.

52. The former Kingdom of Serbia incorporated Serbian Macedonia

Notes to Chapter 8   303

or "South Serbia" (now Yugoslav Republic of Macedonia), in 1912-13, and Montenegro and Vojvodina in 1918. In the pre-war Yugoslavia this territory was partitioned into banovinas of the Danube, Drina, Morava, Zeta and Vardar. Hitler left in *"Serbien"* parts of the first three mentioned banovinas.

53. Ironically, the only people with a regulated status and protection were the Serb POWs registered in Axis camps with the International Committee of the Red Cross.

54. MBS, *"Kommandobefehl Nr. 1"* of 28 April, p. 2 (T501-245-000280).

55. "A chronological review of events": War Diary of Unit 08633, item 22 (T501-245-000124 and 000125).

56. By contrast, the appearance of Mihailović signified hope in national rebirth.

57. As in n. 10.

58. Ibid., p. 2 of the document (T501-245-000240).

59. In Woodward, 332-33, Nedić is referred to as "not a 'quisling' in the worst sense of the term; he had submitted to the occupying Powers only because he thought that further resistance would mean useless loss of life."

60. War diary of the 08633, "Tageb. Nr. 23/41" of 22 April 1941 (T501-245-000271).–Benzler advised the External Affairs Department on 27 April that the MBS was setting up a Serbian administration (DGFP, DXII, pp. 654f., document No. 414).

61. Harald Turner, under Schmidt-Logan, was handling Serbian affairs: Erpenbeck, 10.

62. Ibid., text to n. 52 on p. 14; Živanović, *Treći*, p. 146.

63. Kostić, 17.

64. Sugar, "The Role" in *Revue roumaine d'histoire,* XVI (3), 1977, pp. 487-505, detail on p. 504. (The U.S. government contributed $50,000 to this food relief, and Lane added $20,000 out of his own pocket.)

65. Marjanović, *Ustanak,* 32.

66. Kostić, 18; Karapandžić, 22; Parežanin, *Drugi,* 313-14; Živanović, *Treći I,* p. 145.–The first three authors are apologists for Ljotić; Živanović is a Četnik author, and therefore anti-Ljotić.

67. Parežanin, 313-14.

68. Ljotić's private army was called *"Srpski dobrovoljci"* (Serb Volunteers"). They proved themselves a very efficient anti-guerrilla formation.

So it happened that in the Second World War, as well as the two anti-German guerrilla movements (Tito and Mihailović), in Serbia there was also this anti-guerrilla force.

69. Cf. the testimony of a Lieutenant Christie Lawrence, a British escaped POW, who fought with the insurgents in Serbia in 1941: "It will be noticed that [in my book] there is no mention... of Marshal Tito. This is because during the year 1941-2 I never heard his name" (Lawrence, 268).

70. Kostić, 18-19; Marjanović, *Ustanak,* n. 73, printed on pp. 32-33 (citing Kostić); Živanović, *Treći I,* pp. 145-146.

71. The commissioner for the treasury, Dušan Letica, resigned in mid-August on the grounds that he could not provide the 6.5 million *Reichsmark:* Erpenbeck, 73; Benzler's telegram to Berlin of 27 August 1941 (DGFP, DXIII, p. 400, document No. 250).

72. Kostić, 23; Karapandžic, 26.

73. "W. B. Suedost (AOK 12) Ic/AO, Nr. 5876/41 geh." of 29 July 1941 to the MBS (T501-245-000636) transmitting higher orders; emphasis by this author (MD).—From the style of the above order it seems that shooting cum hanging remained applicable for all "non-sabotage" cases (such as rebellion etc.)?

74. Entries and enclosures to the war diary of the 08633: T501-245-000204, 205, 207, 213, 534, 570, 628, 629, 654, 656, 665, 666 and 667. The above reconstruction is based on the report of the A/Cder of the German 64th Police Reserve Battalion of 1 August 1941 (T501-245-000666, 667).

75. *Wachtmeister* Paul Moebes, driving the motorcycle, was killed, and *Rottwachtmeister* Wilhelm Schmidt, his passenger in the side car, disappeared (presumed abducted).—Marjanović, *Ustanak,* 453, fourth entry under 27 July, claims the ambush for the Partisans. However, when interrogated by the German police, local peasants reported having seen a group of 8 to 10 men, some in civilian clothes, others in uniform. Witnesses made no mention either of the Partisan Red Star, nor of any Četnik insignia. Significantly, German police recorded that the corpse had no boots and socks, but *the rifle* of the missing Sergeant was left on the scene of the ambush (T501-245-000666). Still, the fact remains that Marjanović claims it as Partisans' work.

76. T501-245-000667.

Notes to Chapter 8

77. Živanović, *Treći I,* 147-48.
78. T501-245-000667.
79. Benzler's telegram 446 of 1 August 1941 to Berlin: *Auswaertiges Amt,* 2 typewritten pages in "Politisches Archiv des Auswaertigen Amts, Buero Staatssekretaer, Jugoslawien, Band 3" (I am grateful to the AA and Dr Maria Keipert, letter to me over her signature, AA No. 117-251.09/83 of 5 December 1983; MD).
80. Cited in Marjanović, *Ustanak,* 170, indicating his source in Yugoslav archives. Colonel Trišić was an undercover man of Mihailović's. After World War II, Trišić settled in the United States,a nd became an ordained Serb-Orthodox priest *("Pop");* he died in California in the 1970s.
81. As n. 79.
82. On 12 July 1941 the 64th Battalion was ordered to post one company to the "FK Uzice" (that is, to Stockhausen); enclosure A17 to the war diary of the 08633 (T501-245-000570).
83. T501-245-000665.
84. Benzler's telegram as in n. 79.
85. DGFP, DXIII, pp. 400-01, document No. 250.
86. DGFP, DXIII, pp. 411-13, document No. 257 (detail on p. 412).
87. But then, in 1915 the Serbian Army did not capitulate. Outmanoeuvring the encirclement by the Austro-Hungarian, German and Bulgarian armies, it withdrew with the King (Peter I) and the government across the Albanian mountains to the sea, whence it was evacuated by the fleet of the Entente. When reorganized and re-equipped, the Serbian Army was then deployed on the Macedonian or "Salonika" front.

Notes to Chapter 9

1. See ch. 8 n. 68.
2. Cf. the report of the Plenipotentiary Commanding General in Serbia [Boehme] to the Commander South-East, Abt. Ia Nr. 985/41 g. Kdos of 15 November 1941, under "2" (4 typewritten pages, T501-251-000364 to 000367, detail on p. 3 or 000366).
3. *Der Schriftwechsel des Militaerbefehlshabers Serbien* (MBS) *mit der Regierung Nedic:* Mil. Bfh. Suedost, Box 142/170, Nr. 61071, Anlageband zum KTB von 30.XIII.1941–6.X.1944, *Anglage 2* (stamped 283), Bundesarchiv-Militaerarchiv, document RW40/93 (2 pages of

typescript).—There is also an *Anlage 44* which in its own *Beilage 3* contains a transcript of the above document, but wrongly dated "27. August 1942" instead of 1941.

4. The case of the Generals in south-east Europe (*viz.*, The Balkans) was judged by the Tribunal V of the Nurenberg Military Tribunals: *Trials of War Criminals, Vol. XI, passim.*

5. Karapandžić, 86, citing Kostić, 46-47.

6. Marjanović, *Ustanak*, 183.

7. Abwehrstelle Belgrad to the Plenipotentiary Commanding General in Serbia, Tgb. Nr. 7716/10.41 IIIC 2g, 24 October 1941 (6 typewritten pages, T314-1457-0001088 to 0001093, detail on p. 6 or 0001093), and, for Boehme's report, as n. 2, part of Clause "I" typed on p. 3 (T501-251-000366).

8. DGFP, DXIII, pp. 434-35, document No. 267, item 3 (printed on p. 435).—Similar reservations were entertained also in the HQ LXV Higher Command in Serbia (Hehn, 39-40).

9. Extract from Hitler's directive No. 44 1538/41 of 16 September 1941 printed in *Trials of War Criminals, Vol. XI*, pp. 969-71, detail on p. 969 (document NOKW 1492, prosecution exhibit 49).

10. Keitel's order N. 002060/41 of 16 September 1941, printed in *Trials* as in n. 9, pp. 971-72, detail on p. 972 (document NOKW-258, prosecution exhibit 53).

11. Boehme based this order on his own interpretation of the "Balkan mentality" of the Serbs: Boehme's order No. 2848/41, supplement 48 (Qu Section, No. 470/41 of 10 October 1941), partial translation, printed in *Trials* as in n. 9, pp. 977-78 (document NOKW-557, prosecution exhibit 88).

12. *Trials* as in n. 9, pp. 799-801 (documents NOKW 1198 and 1151, prosecution exhibits 5 and 7).

13. "One of the first acts of Boehme in his new post" (NOKW-1048, prosecution exhibit 63) in *Trials* as in n. 9, p. 803.

14. Hehn, 29.

15. *Trials* as in n. 9, pp. 1318-19, further p. 763 n. 1 and p. 782.

16. Glaise von Horstenau to the German Minister in Zagreb, 9 December 1941 (2 typewritten pages; T501-267-000636 and 000637).

17. Glaise von Horstenau's message 431/41 [telephoned or telegraphed?] of 30 December 1941 (3 typewritten pages: T501-267-000593 to 000595, detail on 000593).

18. As n. 3, but *Anlage 44:* Nedić to Bader, 16 September 1942 (eight typewritten pages in German, plus eight pages of enclosures in support of his submission). The same as with the *Anlage 2* in n. 3 above, Nedić's handwritten signature is not appended; therefore they are either a German translation or a copy of the original.

19. Auty, *Tito,* 168 and p. 168 n. 6 printed on p. 309, citing K. Zilliacus, *Tito,* London, p. 122.

20. Folder of the MBS/ Ia, 21 April–10 October 1941, document of 22 June 1941: Turner (for the MBS) to Aćimović, T501-249-000751.

21. Auty, *Tito,* 172; Djilas, *Wartime,* 22.

22. Some examples: The field telephone line was cut at "Nis-Kabanje" [sic; Niška Banja(?)] on 26 May (T501-245-000127); the entry of 8 June reads "Attacks by smaller and larger bands, sabotage of telephone lines increasing" (T501-245-000421).

23. T501-245-000129 and 000130; Avakumović, *Mihailović,* 17.

24. T501-245-000129.

25. MBS/Ia, 283/41 geh., to the Commander South-East/Ic [Enemy Intelligence], 2 August 1941. (T501-249-000755 to 000757).

26. Marjanović, *Ustanak,* 447-507, particularly detail on p. 449. That General Lontscha or Lontschar was involved is corroborated in the German war diary, e.g., entry No. 97 of 18 July 1941 at 16 hours (T501-245-000177).

27. Marjanović, "Prilozi istoriji," in *Istorija XX veka I,* pp. 153-230, p. 182 n. 79.

28. For records of shootings consult the war diary MBS/Ia (microcopy T501-245).

29. Karchmar, "Draža I," pp. 184-85.–Avakumović, *Mihailović* and his articles in *Naša Reč.*

30. This text is cited in Drachkovitch, "The Comintern" in Drachkovitch and Lazic, *The Comintern,* 192. In Auty's quotation of the same instruction this particular paragraph is omitted (Auty, *Tito,* 171).

31. Auty, *Tito,* 173.

32. Enclosure "A 59" to the war diary, T501-245-000662 and 000663.

33. Commander in Serbia to the Commander South-East, 23 July 1941, over the signature of a Dr Kissel (enclosure A35 to the war diary), T501-245-000597 to 000600.

34. Information from émigré Serbs; MD.

35. T501-245-000597 and 000598.
36. *Zbornik dokumenata,* Tom I, Part 1, p. 63 (cited in Živanović, *Treći III,* pp. 11-12). My italics, MD.
37. T314-1457-001172.
38. Maclean, *Eastern,* 313.
39. Djilas, *Wartime,* 96.
40. Chief of Operations (Ia), 1 October 1941: Dr. 804/41/Geheim, p. 1 (Budesarchiv-Militaerarchiv, the file *Hoeh. Kdo* LXV/40111/2).
41. T501-250-000983, 000994 and T501-250-000978, 001041.
42. T501-250-000983, 000994 and 001042.
43. T501-250-001041, 001042 and 001040.
44. T501-250-001039.
45. For the original text in German see T501-250-001039.
46. T501-250-0001033. Further, MBS/Ia, No. 609/41/Geheim, of 27 September 1941 to the 6th/920: T501-250-001028. For the "Flugzeugabwurf" (air-drop of orders) see MBS/Ia of 27 September 1941 to the 6th/920: T-501-250-001026; also the Ia, No. 625/41/Geheim to the Infantry Battalion I/749 at Čačak: T501-250-001021.
47. T501-250-001028 to 001031 incl.; Gravenhorst used to sign simply "Grav," which, in the original, looks rather like "Gia."
48. Vučković's version has been established from his papers and the correspondence with this author (MD) in 1969 and 1970.
49. Djelević, "Iz prvih" in R. Knežević, *Knjiga II,* 184; Živanović, *Treći II,* p. 74. Avakumović, *Mihailović,* 22.
50. Captain Maurice Vitou, "The Truth about Mihailovich? (IV)" in *World Review,* August 1945, pp. 31-37, detail on p. 32.–The German Intelligence HO in Belgrade learned that "two Englishmen" were at Mihailovic's HQ. Document Abwehrstelle Belgrad, No. 6462/10.41-g. I H (Geheim) of 30 October 1941, p. 2 reads "About one hundred German *Landesschuetzen* from Donji [sic] Milanovac seem to be in the school at Planinica (11 km SE from Mionica). Allegedly, they are guarded by two English escapees from Crete" (T501-250-000977).
51. MBS/Ia, "Angelegenheiten Ls. Btl. 920": page 3 of Holstein's report (T501-250-000982), p. 2 for Egger's interrogation of 22 October 1941 (T501-250-000984), and T501-250-000988 and 000995 for Dirnberger's.
52. Egger interrogation, as in no. 50.

53. Nedeljković, "Sećanja" in *Četrdeset godina I*, 298.
54. Page 1 of Hostein's report (T501-250-000980).
55. As n. 48 above; Živanović, *Treći II* p. 96; Miodrag Vasić, in the days of the uprising Mayor of Čačak, to this author (MD), letter of 17 March 1970.
56. T501-251-000843, 844.
57. 113 Inf. Div./Ia, Enclosures to the war diary, Part 2, 30 September 1941–3 January 1942, The Commanding Officer, No. 1637/41 of 26 October 1941 (T315-1290-000267).
58. British CofS to Commander-in-Chief, Mediterranean, 15 October 1941; PRO document Premier 3/510/4.–"Suvobor," mentioned in the last line of the message of 15 October 1941, was Mihailović's HQ.
59. *The Trail of Dragoljub-Draža*, 113.
60. For the Circular: T314-1457-000709 and 710; Major Dangić (referred to as *"Generalmajor"*) identified as the author in T314-1457-000702 to 705).
61. For instance, this author (MD) is obliged to the administration of the *Times* for twice (in 1963 and 1980) assisting his endeavours to get in touch with the "Special Correspondent."
62. Živanović, *Treći III*, citing chronological instances and locations.
63. Ljubičić, 122. (Ljubičić, now a General in the new army, commanded this Detachment in 1941.) In Čačak, partisans hoisted a red flag with a five-pointed star (Vitou, as in n. 50).
64. Marjanović, *Ustanak*, 292; Djilas, *Wartime*, 99.
65. Lazović, "Hiljadu . . . ," ["One Thousand Tine Hundfred Forty One"], 2 instalments, in *Sloboda*, 10 December 1958 (pp. 3 and 5) and 20 December (p. 3).
66. Erpenbeck, 90 and text of n. 25 typed on p. 152; Živanović, *Treći II*,. p. 137; Marjanović, *Ustanak*, 249-50–The early arrests netted 4410 males (see Bundesarchiv/Militaerarchiv, *GenKdo* XVIII A.K./Ic, Anlage zum Kriegstagebuch for September 1941, entry under 27 September: *"Die Aktion gegen Sabac beginnt"*).
67. Karchmar, "Draža I," p. 181.
68. His gallantry had been noticed already on the Macedonian Front (WWI) already. On 23 September 1918 "Infantry 2nd Lieutenant Dragoliub M Michailovitch, Machine Gun Section of 23rd [Serbian] Infantry Regiment" was awarded the British Military Cross (Ministry of Defence,

D/DMS (B) /58/11W/MS/Pt3 of 18 July 1983, over the signature of the Military Secretary, to this author, MD.)—It seems that in the Serbian Army the soldiers voted for recipients of decorations for valour, and so his regiment chose Lt Mihailović for this Allied recognition; MD.

69. "Proceedings of a Conference on Britain and European Resistance 1939-45, organized by St. Antony's College, Oxford, 10-16 December 1962," typed and mimeographed, p. 337.

70. T315-1290-000145.

71. T314-1457-000900.

72. DGFP, DXIII, pp. 708-09 (document No. 432, Benzler to Foreign Office Berlin, telegram No. 841 of 29 October 1941).

73. Derok, *Toplički*, 115.

74. Marjanović, "Prilozi," 210, indicating also his source.

75. Ibid., 178, and p. 178 no. 71 for his source. Živanović, *Treći III*, p. 12 and p. 12 n. 9 for source.

76. *The Trial of Dragoljub-Draža*, 127.

77. Karapandžic, 129-52. Marjanović, "Četničko- nemački," in *Zbornik filosofskog fakulteta*, X (1), Belgrade, 1968, pp. 497-517.

78. In Karapandžic, 132.

79. T314-1457-001314 to 001322. Some pages reproduced from this microfilm are not legible. The Budesarchiv-Militaerarchiv kindly supplied legible Xerox copies of the archival copy of the *Niederschrift ueber das Treffen* (XVIIIAK, 17729/14). Kogard was at the time head of the enemy intelligence (Ic) in Boehme's HQ (T314-1457-001249).

80. The German minutes are a translation of what Mihailović said in Serbian, so the translation given here is made from German.

81. T314-1457-001320.

82. *The Trial of Dragoljub-Draža*, 110.

83. Consult, for instance, the British *Manual of Military Law*, 1929 (valid in the early days of World War II), Chapter XIV, p. 275 (Clause 20 (ii)), and interpretation on pp. 276-77 (Clauses 22 to 28).

84. Roberts, *Tito, Mihailović*, 102 and 106-12, particularly p. 108; Duretic, *Saveznici I*, pp. 248-49, particularly detail on p. 249.

85. Beloff, 81-82.

86. Milica Josimović-Knežević, "Martovski," five instalments, NIN of 10, 17, 24 November and 1, 8 December 1985, detail in the instalment of 17 November (p. 56).

87. T314-1457-000469, T314-1457-001311, and also the cut-out from the *Donauzeitung* of 13 November 1941 in T314-1457-001380. *"Montag"* (Monday) mentioned by the *Donauzeitung* was 10 November 1941 (T314-1457-001310).
88. T314-1457-001239, 001240 and 001311. Matl's letter in Karapandžić, pp. 152-54, detail on p. 153.
89. Ibid., 152. In 1941 a Colonel, Max J. Pemsel reached the rank of a Lieutenant General in the West German Army and is now Rtd.
90. Plenipotentiary Commanding General in Serbia/Ic, No. 3712/41 geh. of 13 November 1941 (T314-1457-001309 to 001313, detail in 001309), and T314-1457-001311.
91. T314-1457-001332 to 001345, detail in 001333.
92. Lee's article in the *Sunday Express* is cited in *General Mihailovich: The World Verdict, A Selection of Articles...*, With an Introduction by the General's Friends and a Foreward by F.A. Voigt, Gloucester, 1947, pp. 63d66; details from pp. 63 and 64. (The Editor of this collection was K. St. Pavlowitch, who wrote also the Introduction "by the General's Friends." This procedure was adopted to prevent Pavlowitch's persecution by the Yugoslav Communist Government of the day. K.St.P. to this author (MD), letter of 4 September 1983).

Notes to Chapter 10

1. FCO/SOEA, letter of 12 October 1982 to this author (MD), C.M. Woods; *V.q.* note 11.
2. Amery, 244 and 259.
3. See ch. 4.
4. Amery, 259.
5. Ibid., 259.
6. Loc. cit.
7. Djonović, "Veze" in *Glasnik "Njegoš,"* No. 1, July 1958.
8. By his letters of 3 August 1983 and 4 June 1984 to Academician A.L. Narochnitsky, director of the Institute of History of USSR, this author (MD) requested assistance and/or advice to identify Colonel Nikolaev. No reply was received.
9. Djonović, as in n. 7, p. 45.
10. G.H.N. Seton-Watson's statement in Auty and Clogg, 290; Sweet-Escott's statement in ibid., 210; Sweet-Escott, *Baker,* 73.

11. Permission to publish the information contained in this chapter has been obtained from the Foreign and Commonwealth Office (FCO), in a letter of 10 March 1982 to this author, over the signature of D. Salter, pp. (E.G. Boxshall); and from FCO, SOE Adviser (FCO/SOEA), in a letter of 7 July 1982 to this author, over the signature of C.M. Woods. For permission to publish the information contained in PRO documents refer to PRO letter Q 12625 of 1 December 1981 to this author, over the signature of Nicholas Cox, Head of Search Department. All of it is gratefully acknowledged.

This author (MD) bears full responsibility for use he made of this material, and it should be clearly understood that all opinions expressed are the author's own and nothing should be construed to imply any responsibility of H. M. Government.

12. Sweet-Escott, *Baker,* 117.
13. Cf. the earlier chapters on the *Bullseye.* The issue of radio communications bedevilled not only relations between Hudson and Mihailović, but it was also a running sore in British-Yugoslav governmental relations.
14. Amery was not aware of it. In his letter of 2 July 1982 to this author (MD) Amery stated that Hudson "was only called upon to go [with the *Bullseye*] because Jarko [sic] Popovitch insisted that there must be a British officer."
15. See ch. 5.
16. Marjanović, *Draža I,* pp. 79-90 and 97-99. These memoirs are deposited with the National Library of Serbia in Belgrade, and registered under R 571, Vols I, II and III (Marjanović, ibid., n. 63 printed on p. 345).—This author (MD) could not obtain from Belgrade a Xerox of another copy of Trbić's memoirs, as this work was "at present [21 November 1983] receiving conservation treatment."
17. Marjanović as in n. 16, pp. 80, 82 and 83.—I was not able to identify Thompson, MD.
18. Ibid., pp. 83-84.
19. Loc. cit.
20. Cf. chapter 5 n. 19.
21. Colonel Žarko R. Popović to this author, (MD), letter of 14 January 1983.
22. Plećaš, *Ratne,* 29-30. [Mapplebeck seems to have been given this rank and appointment as a cover for his other work; MD.]

23. Radović's obituary notice by [Colonel] Petar Vukčević of the former Yugoslav Air Force, *Vazduhoplovni Glasnik,* London, February 1972, pp. 2-4; Radović's US immigration and naturalization file: US Department of Justice, Immigration and Naturalization Service, San Francisco, Cal., letter 76-39-c NBA of 21 October 1983 to this author (MD); Oesterreichisches Staatsarchiv—Kriegsarchiv, letter Z129.808/1983 of 15 December 1983 to this author (MD).

24. Association des Anciens Elèves de l'Ecole Nationale Supérieure de l'Aéronautique et de l'Espace, letter of 19 September 1983 to this author (MD).

25. Djonović, "Od zida" in *Glasnik "Njegoš,"* 31-32.

26. Plećaš, as in n. 22, p. 59.—Lieutenant (later Captain) Plećaš was one of the officers who were to follow Radović' to the Soviet Union. (Plećaš died in the US in 1984.) Whereas his chronology is not always reliable, his information about the choice of four officers is correct.

27. Masterson (who came to Cairo on 15 September 1941) and the SOE man in Moscow were charged with executing the administrative steps.

28. Plećaš as in n. 22, p. 60.—Colonel R. died in the US in 1970.

29. See the text to n. 27 in ch. 5.

30. Plećaš, as in n. 22, p. 123.

Notes to Chapter 11

1. Deakin, *The Embattled,* xii.
2. Butler, *Grand IV,* p. 386 and 386 n. 44 printed on p. 393.
3. *The Historical Encyclopedia of World War II,* French edn (Casterman), English edn (Macmillan), American edn (Facts on File, 1980).
4. Deakin, *The Embattled,* 136; repeated, inter alia, in Wheeler, 86 and p. 87 n. 66 printed on p. 271, and in Milazzo, 33 and p. 33 n. 87.
5. E.g., Deakin, *The Embattled,* 136—Incidentally, Deakin, Elisabeth Barker et al. are wont to be critical of British authorities for not having heeded Hudson's intelligence favourable to the Partisans. But, at that time, it was official British policy *not* to deal with the malcontents, be they Yugoslavs, or exiled Czechs, Poles or Greeks (Colonel Bailey to J. Djonović, see Djonović, "Od zida" in *Glasnik "Njegoš"* No. 10, December 1962, pp. 31-32).

6. Djelević, "Iz prvih" in R. Knežević, *Knjiga I,* p. 185. (At that time, Lieutenant Djelević was Mihailović's ADC.)

7. PRO document WO 202/128, tel. 118, p. 123, cited in Wheeler, 89 and p. 89 n. 75, printed on p. 274. This telegram shows that Hudson arrived at Užice on 23 October, and moved on the "Ravna Gora" [actually to Brajići at the foot of Ravna Gora] on 25 October.

8. From an "Extract of a letter dated 11 December from the Minister for Economic Warfare to the Prime Minister," it is seen that, "the British officer whom we sent to Yugoslavia in a submarine" has been in touch by wireless ever since. (PRO document PREM 3/510/1, headed *"Most secret,* D.O. (41) 36, 14 December 1941, War Cabinet, Defence Committee (Operations), Yugoslav Revolt.")

9. Lawrence, 227, citing an eyewitness: "Mihailovic wanted X [that is, Hudson] to part with the British code, but he, of course, refused."– In London and in the Middle East the Yugoslavs were asking to use their own cypher, and the British denied it (Barker, *British,* 158). However, the Secret Intelligence Service (SIS) was opposing not only an independent Yugoslav cypher, but also opposed SOE's demand "to be allowed its own codes and signal network" (Hinsley, *British I,* p. 178).

10. Date and text are from Deakin, *Embattled,* p. 139.

11. I am obliged to the Director of the Australian War Museum at Canberra, and to the Australian Minister for Veteran Affairs, who forwarded my letters to Mr. Jones when I wanted to interview him. It is unfortunate that such an interview never took place. (MD)

12. As an escaped POW, Lt. Lawrence spent part of 1941 in occupied Serbia, where he introduced himself as a Captain (Lawrence, 46).

13. Ibid., 228.

14. Ibid., 231.

15. Živanocić, *Treći III,* p. 52. Deakin, *Embattled,* 140. Karchmar says that in retaliation for his action Mihailović denied Hudson "further use of the radio channel" (Karchmar, "Draža II," p. 762), which seems to be a free interpretation of a statement in Lawrence, 227.

16. Loc. cit.

17. Deakin, *Embattled,* 146.

18. Ibid., 147.

19. Clissold, 74.

20. Živanović, *Treći III,* pp. 157-58.

21. Official German terminology in occupied Serbia. A circular issued on 3 November 1941 over the signature of [Colonel Max J.] Pemsel, CofS of the German Plenipotentiary Commanding General in Serbia reads, "As it is often not clear from the reports regarding Četnik Detachments whether it is a question of enemy (*"feindliche"*) četniks or of those loyal (*"regierungstreue"*) to the Government [of occupied Serbia], in future the designations *"regierungstreue Cetniks"* and *"feindliche Cetniks"* should be used."–Cf. the commentary on "legal" and "illegal" Cetniks in A.F.H.Q., G-2 (PB), *The Cetniks*, 6-7 n. 10 and p. 7 n. 11.

22. The term used to describe Mihailović's soldiers who pretended to be "loyal Četniks."

23. Marjanović. *Ustanak*, 388-89.

24. Popović Papers, Minutes of the Meeting, p. 3 (deposited with the Hoover Institution). It is symptomatic that in Serbia this was done. E.g., a German-appointed Commander of the Gendarmerie, Colonel Trišić, was eventually arrested by the Germans when it was discovered that he was an officer of Mihailović supplying Army Četniks with materiel, and Lieutenant Zoran Vasiljević was planted in the Belgrade telephone exchange, where he was discovered and shot by the Germans (Živanović, *Treći I*, pp. 98-103).

25. Živanović, *Treći III*, p. 161-64.

26. Deakin, *The Embattled*, 146.

27. T501-250-000442.

28. T315-2123-000743.

29. T501-250-000442, item 2, and T315-2123-000743, entry at 18.00 hours.

30. The 342nd Infantry Division, War Diary, Operations, 6 December 1941, entry at 17.00 hours: *"Major Misic mit Stab gefangen genommen"* (T315-2123-000729), and the Diary for 7 December, p. 2, entry at 13.30 hours: *"Unternehmen durchgefuehrt. Mihajlovic* [sic] *entflohen"* (T315-2123-000726).–By coincidence, Colonel Mihailović's promotion to General Staff Brigadier General is also dated 7 December 1941 (Decree of the King of Yugoslavia, Dj. No. 83, [Yugoslav] Official Gazette, (*"Službeni list"*), No. 3, London; see R. Kneževic, *Knjiga I*, p. 218.

31. Mešković, "Mišićeva žrtva" in R. Knežević, *Knjiga I*, p. 197; Živanović, *Treći III*, p. 165, and Avakumović, *Mihailović*, text to n. 39 printed on p. 33.

32. Živanović, *Treći III*, pp. 171 and 172.

33. Ibid., p. 169. Živanović wrote in Serbian Cyrillic alphabet, which is phonetic; spelling "Štencl" could be in German spelling either "Stenzel" or "Stentzel."

34. I reached this conclusion on the following basis: (i) A *Hauptmann Dr Stenzel* was in the HQ German 342nd Division in Valjevo at that time (T314-1457-001343 and 001349), (ii) the *Deustche Dienststelle* confirmed that a *Hauptmann Dr Erich Stentzel* or Stenzel was at one stage serving on staff of the 342nd Division: their letter to this author (MD), "VI/A-677" of 9 February 1984) over the signature Swatzina, but, (iii) in Dimitrijević, *Djeneralštabni*, is listed a *Colonel Dragutin Z. Štencl, a Serb who was a POW in Germany, and after WWII settled in South America.* My endeavours to contact Colonel Štencl remained fruitless.

35. As n. 32.

36. Preamble to "Hague Convention of 1907 respecting the Laws and Customs of War on Land"; see Carnegie Endowment for International Peace, Division of International Law, *The Hague Conventions and Declarations of 1899 and 1907,* New York, 1915, the above citation in the main text is from ibid., 101-02 (emphasis by MD).

37. *Franc-tireurs* (an expression from the 1870-71 Franco-Prussian War) were not legally recognized belligerents. For "legal" and "illegal" irregular belligerents in World Wars I and II consult Article I of the Annex to the Convention IV of 1907. *V.q.* Heilbrunn, *Partisan,* passim.

38. T315-2123-000760.

39. T315-2123-000743.

40. T315-2123-000735.

41. This was probably a Divisional initiative (not the Commander's in Serbia), T315-2123-000731.

42. T315-2123-000722, T315-2123-000715.—The draft of the reward is in the Plenipotentiary Commanding General's War Diary, Operations (T501-250-000440).

43. T315-2123-00721.

44. T315-2123-000691.

45. T315-2123-000687.

46. In Živanović, *Treći III,* p. 165, the date is mistakenly given as 11 December.

47. T315-2123-000721.

Notes to Chapter 11

48. The German High Command issued its liberal *Manual* in 1944, which extended the protection of being treated "as prisoners of war" to "all bandits in enemy uniform or in civilian clothes" (Heilbrunn, 147-48). Since World War II British anti-guerrilla operations in Malaya and Africa have proven a liberal procedure to work satisfactorily. Its success depends on credibility of the anti-guerrilla Power in the eyes of the insurgents: the British earned it, the Germans never did (ibid., passim).

49. Lola Ribar to Tito, 7 January 1942, cited in Živanović, *Treći III*, p. 176, item "g."

50. T315-2123-000722 (mentioning also the announcement made over the Belgrade radio); T315-2123-000718.

51. S.K. Pavlowitch, *Yugoslavia*, 121 and p. 121 n. 16.

52. Avakumović, *Mihailović*, 31.

53. Ibid., 128; *The Times*, 24 July 1943, 4th edn. p. 3e; Martin, *Ally Betrayed*, 78 and 218-19; Roberts *Tito, Mihailović*, 122; S.K. Pavlowitch, *Yugoslavia*, 156 n. 57.—This is an extremely sensitive issue with the Serbs. I am obliged to Nora Beloff for the information in her letter of 28 October 1985, that the full reprint of the German announcement was published in No. 69 of *The Second Great War, A Standard History*. [This was a monthly published in London by The Amalgamated Press Ltd., 1939—.] As Miss Beloff points out, "at that time the switch [from Mihailovic to Tito] was not yet complete!"

54. Deakin, *The Embattled*, 146.

55. In his *Treći III*, Živanović says Hudson rejoined Mihailović on 14 December (p. 171).

56. Deakin, *The Embattled*, 146 and 195. There is a similar quotation in A.F.H.Q., *The Cetniks* (as in n. 21) p. 17.

57. "Nedić men" is yet another expression used for the "loyal" or "*regierungstreue*" Četniks.

58. Deakin, *The Embattled*, 146.

59. Mihailović's next radio-message was "picked up" by the British on 7 January 1942. (Ibid., 149).

60. Ibid., 146.

61. Ibid., 147 n.

62. See text to n. 53 above.

63. Deakin, *The Embattled*, 147-48.

64. Karchmar, "Draža II," n. 10 typed on p. 366.

65. Ibid., 283.
66. As n. 2 above.

Notes to Conclusion

1. *The Observer*, 3 February 1980, p. 35: Deakin, "Tito—Why Churchill backed the Partisans."—Some commentators argue that it was his sop to Stalin, while he waited for a proper Second Front. This school of thought is best represented in Radoje and Živan L. Knežević, *Sloboda*, 210. For a review of this book see M. Deroc's review "Iz slobode" in *Savremenik*, New Series XXVIII (16), Autumn 1982, p. 104.
2. Crossman, "The Ethics" in *The New Statesman and Nation*, LII (1344), 15 December 1956, p. 794.
3. See various papers and discussion in Auty and Clogg.
4. Wiskemann, "Partitioned" in A. and V. Toynbee, *Hitler's*, 656.
5. Deakin, *The Embattled*, 262-63. (He was able to influence Churchill because of their special relationship: before the war he was Churchill's "literary assistant"; ibid., 80.)
6. Ibid., 261.
7. *TLS*, Friday 22 October 1971, pp. 1301-03: "Partisans of Tito." The original article does not carry the name of the author; only later was it learned that it was Davidson.
8. The first to comment on the import of Davidson's revelation was a former Major in the Political Warfare executive (PWE), Vane Ivanović, in his book *LX—Memoirs*, 257).
9. Deakin, *The Embattled*, 207-09 and 211; Seton-Watson's "Afterword" in Auty and Clogg; Wiskeman, as n. 4, pp. 665 and 665 n. 3.
10. In addition to Tito's own statement in the text to ch. 3 n 23 of this book, see Seton-Watson, *The East*, 123 and 130 n. 3.
11. Dedijer, *With Tito*. (For the original work see n. 12 below.)
12. Dedijer, *Dnevnik I*.
13. Marjanovic, *Ustanak*, 7.
14. Fitzroy Maclean MP, for the occasion given the rank of Brigadier (later Major-General, Sir F.). Churchill's personal ambassador to the Yugoslav Partisans and the man who—on Churchill's orders—provided Tito with the decisive support.
15. Elliot Roosevelt, *The Roosevelt Papers III*, p. 500. That Peter did not like Roosevelt's proposed solution is beside the point. He did

not like Churchill's solution either, but gave in.—It is interesting to note that in the presence of General Mihailović, A Yugoslav national congress at Ba, Serbia, in January 1944 resolved that future Yugoslavia should be a federation of three units: Serbia, Croatia and Slovenia.

16. Auty, *Tito,* xii.

17. Auty is an historian of Yugoslavia, and one is entitled to expect that her statements in *Tito* should have been better researched. For instance, she persistently refers to the *International* Macedonian Revolutionary Organization (IMRO) instead of to the *Internal* (etc.)—in the Bulgarian abbreviation VMRO, not IMRO; Pašić, PM of Serbia and the SHS, she titles "Regent"; Barthou, the unfortunate French Foreign Minister who bled to death on the occasion of the assassination of King Alexander I of Yugoslavia in 1934, she called "French premier," etc.

18. Morgan, *Peace and War,* 232.

19. A German translation of this material is filed in Bundesarchiv-Militaerarchiv under No. RH19XI/17 (formerly German Army Group "F" registration 66135/5). Bundesarchiv-Militaerarchiv kindly supplied copies of this material.—The annotation of the SS Police and Security Chief in Serbia of 15 July 1943 reveals that the original was clandestinely obtained from a D[raža] M[ihailović] HQ, copied, and returned. The English translation, made by this author (MD), is from the German translation of the material in Serbian.
traitor who collaborated with the SS was probably in the Vojvodina HQ.] The English translation, made by this author (MD), is from the German translation of the material in Serbian.

20. In Pavelić's Croatia there existed Ustaša formations, "regular army" or the *Domobran,* and Croat divisions under direct German command. The officer corps of the *Domobran* was composed of Croat Yugoslav officers and former Croat Austro-Hungarian officers who had not volunteered for the SHS army in 1918-20. This mixed *Domobran* officer corps of Croats proved to be much less viable than the former SHS/Yugoslav mixture of Serbs, Croats and Slovenes.

The fact that the Yugoslav government in London dishonourably discharged from Yugoslav Forces those Croat Yugoslav officers who had joined the *Domobran* went against Mihailović's efforts to solve their problem. Therefore, those Croat officers who intended to rejoin the Allied camp after the collapse of Italy, had no choice but to join Tito.

21. Miha Krek to Bruce Lockhart and George Rendell, 24 February 1942, and the accompanying British memoranda: FO Registry No. R 1375/. . . , PRO document FO 371/33465.

22. The Slovenian "Freedom Front" was—under the occupation—the *front populaire* type of organization of the KPJ in Slovenia.

23. The original was published in *The Slovene Reporter* II (29) of 1 December 1941.—Krek had the Slovene text translated into English.

24. Karchmar, "Draža I," p. 262 and discussion in n. 79 typed on pp. 356-57. His listing of sources is exhaustive.

25. Deakin, *The Embattled*, 141-42; A.F.H.Q., *The Cetniks*, items 21 and 22 (with the footnotes) on p. 10. (In item 21 it is said that Tito's request to Mihailović for a "parley" occurred on 14 November; the date goven in the main text above—17 November—is from Karchmar, see n. 24 above.)

26. Živanović, *Treći III*, p. 124.

SOURCES

Articles, Letters to Editor, Monographs and Reviews

Bailey, S. W. "British Policy Towards General Draza Mihailovic" in Phyllis Auty and Richard Clogg, eds., *British Policy Towards Wartime Resistance in Yugoslavia and Greece*, London, Macmillan, 1975, pp. 59-90.

Bandović, Milan. "Ustanak u Crnoj Gori" ["The Uprising in Montenegro"] in Radoje L. Knežević, ed., *Knjiga o Draži [The Book on Draža]*, Volume 1, Windsor, Canada, Srpska Narodna Odbrana, 1956, pp. 75-86.

Bosnitch, Sava. Review of *Le Operazioni delle unita italiane in Jugoslavia (1941-1943)* [by Salvadore Loi], Roma, Ufficio storico, Stato Maggiore dell'Esercito, 1978, in *The South Slav Journal*, VI No. 1 (19), Spring 1983, pp. 112-20.

Broz-Tito, Josip. "Nacionalno pitanje u Jugoslaviji u svjetlosti narodno-oslobodilačke borbe" ["National Question in Yugoslavia Interpreted through the Struggle for National Liberation"], *Proleter*, XVII (16), December 1942, as reprinted in Josip Broz-Tito, *Borba za oslobodjenje Jugoslavije, članci i govori 1941-1944 [The Struggle for Liberation of Yugoslavia, articles and speeches, 1941-1944]*, Beograd, Državni izdavački zavod, 1945, pp. 121-130.

———. *Political Report of the Central Committee of the Communist Party of Yugoslavia*, Report delivered at the Vth Congress of the CPY, [English edn.], Beograd, [no publisher shown], 1948; [A monograph].

Cenčić, Vjenceslav. "'Enigma Kopinič': Pariski susret s Titom" ["'Enigma Kopinič': His Paris Encounter with Tito"] an interview with Josip

Kopinič, *NIN (Nedeljne Ilustrovane novine)*, five instalments: 1 May 1983 (pp. 55-56), 8 May 1983 (pp. 50-52), 15 May 1983 (pp. 50-52), 22 May 1983 (pp. 50-52) and 29 May 1983 (pp. 50-52).

Crossman, R. H. S. "The Ethics of Terrorism," *The New Statesman and Nation*, LII (1344), 15 December 1956, p. 794.

Cvetković, Dragiša J. "Kako se imao dalje razvijati srpsko-hrvatski sporazum" ["How the Serbo-Croat Agreement (of 1939) was Meant to Develop Further"], in *Dokumenti o Jugoslaviji*, No. 5, Paris, 1954, pp. 9-10.

Deakin, F. W. "Prva britanska vojna misija kod Tita (maj-septembar 1943)" ["The First British Military Mission to Tito (May-September 1943)"] in *Zbornik Radova "Neretva-Sutjeska" 1943*, Beograd, 1969, pp. 184-195.

Deroc, Milan. "Demise of the Yugoslav Army," *East European Quarterly*, accepted for publication.

———. "The Former Yugoslav Army," *East European Quarterly*, XIX (3), September 1985, pp. 363-374.

———. "Iz slobode u smrt" ["From Freedom into Death"], A review of *Sloboda ili smrt [Freedom or Death]* by Radoje and Živan L. Knežević, in *Savremenik*, New Series, XXVIII (16), Autumn 1982, pp. 103-06.

———. "Letter to Editor" [Additional information to article "U ratu treba ratovati"] *Savremenik*, New Series, XXVIII (16), Autumn 1982, pp. 123-24.

———. "Sources for Draža Mihailović's Biography: Basic Data and Peacetime Events Only," *The South Slav Journal*, V No. 4 (18), Winter 1982-83, pp. 31-34.

———. "U ratu treba ratovati" ["When at War make War"], *Savremenik*, New Series, XXVII (13), October 1981, pp. 108-12.

———. "When had Simović fled the country?", *The South Slav Journal*, VI (3), Autumn 1983, pp. 10-12.

Djelević, Jakša, V. "Iz prvih meseca" ["From the Early Months"], in Radoje L. Knežević, ed., *Knjiga o Draži [The Book on Draža]*, Volume 1, Windsor, Canada, Srpska Narodna Odbrana, 1956, pp. 177-89.

Djonović, Jovan. "Moje veze sa Dražom Mihailovićem sa Srednjeg istoka" ["My Liaison from the Middle East with Draža Mihailović"], *Glasnik Srpskog istorisko-kulturnog društva "Njegoš,"* No. 2, December 1958, pp. 82-98.

———. "Od zida plača do postojbine faraona" ["From the Wailing Wall to the Country of the Pharaoh"], *Glasnik Srpskog istorisko-kulturnog društva "Njegoš,"* No. 10, December 1962, pp. 28-42.

———. "Veze s Dražom Mihailovićem sa Srednjeg i bliskog istoka i severne Afrike" ["Liaison with Draža Mihailović from the Middle and Near East and North Africa"] *Glasnik Srpskog istorisko kulturnog društva "Njegoš,"* No. 1, July 1958, pp. 41-65.

Drachkovitch, Milorad M. "The Comintern and the Insurrectional Activity of the Communist Party of Yugoslavia in 1941-1942" in Milorad M. Drachkovitch and Branko Lazitch, eds., *The Comintern,* Historical Highlights..., Stanford, Cal., Hoover Institution, 1966, pp. 184-213.

Gavrilović, Dr. Milan. "Srbi i Jugoslavija" ["The Serbs and Yugoslavia"], *Glasnik Srpskog istorisko-kulturnog društva "Njegoš,"* No. 46, June 1981, pp. 37-70.

———. "Srpski duh od Kosova do Ravne Gore" ["Serbian Idea from Kosovo to Ravna Gora"], *Glasnik Srpskog istorisko-kulturnog društva "Njegoš,"* No. 17, June 1966, pp. 100-06.

Ivanović, Vane. "Basil Davidson, *Special Operations Europe,* London, 1980," a review by Vane Ivanović in *The South Slav Journal,* III (3), September 1980, pp. 46-50.

———. "Britanske veze sa našom gerilom" ["British Relationship with Our Guerrilla Movement"], *Naša Reč,* XXXVI (341), January 1983, pp. 6-8.

Joksimović, Milorad. "Ustanak u Vasojevićima i prva veza Crne Gore sa Dražom Mihailovićem" ["The Uprising in Vasojevići and the First Contact with Draža Mihailović"] in *Glasnik Srpskog istorisko-kulturnog društva "Njegoš,"* No. 1, July 1958, pp. 88-105.

Josimović-Knežević, Milica. "Martovski pregovori 1943." ["The Negotiations of March 1943"], *NIN,* five instalments: 10, 17, 24 November and 1, 8 December 1985.

Kljaković, Vojmir. "Velika Britanija, Sovjetski Savez i ustanak u Jugoslaviji 1941. godine" ["Great Britain, USSR, and the Uprising in Yugoslavia in 1941"], *Vojnoistoriski Glasnik,* XXI (2), May-August 1970, pp. 69-103.

Knežević, Radoje L. "Počeci pokreta otpora" ["Beginnings of the Resistance Movement"], in Radoje L. Knežević, ed., *Knjiga o Draži [The Book on Draža],* Volume 1, Windsor, Canada, 1956, pp. 7-14.

Konjhodžić, Alija S. "Muslimani i Treći srpski ustanak" ["The Moslems and the Third Serbian Uprising"], *Glasnik Srpskog istorisko-kulturnog drustva "Njegoš,"* No. 16, December 1965, pp. 47-61.

Kontić, Jovan M. "Jovan Djonović" [an Obituary], *Glasnik Srpskog istorisko-kulturnog drustva "Njegoš,"* No. 11, June 1963, pp. 1-11.

―――――. "Viktor Emanuilo na Cetinju" ["Victor Emmanuel at Cetinje"], *Glasnik Srpskog istorisko- kulturnog društva "Njegoš,"* No. 4, December 1959, pp. 26-41.

Laffan, R.G.D., "The Liberation of New Nationalities, Part I, The Yugo-Slavs" in H.W.V. Temperley, ed., *A History of the Peace Conference of Paris,* Vol. IV, London, Henry Frowde and Hodder &Stoughton, 1921, Ch. IV, pp. 171-212.

Lazović, Drag, D., "Hiljadu Devet Stotina Četrdeset Prva" ["One Thousand Nine Hundred Forty One"], 2 instalments, *Sloboda,* 10 December 1958 (pp. 3 and 5) and 20 December (p. 3).

Marinković, Živorad Ž. "Sećanje na komandanta puka, pukovnika Dragoljuba Mihailovića" ["Remembering my Regimental Commander, Colonel Dragoljub Mihailović"], *Glasnik srpskog istorisko- kulturnog društva "Njegoš,"* No. 37, December 1976, pp. 26-31.

Marjanović, Jovan, "Četničko-nemački pregovori u selu Divci 1941. godine" ["Četnik-German Negotiations in the Village of Divci in 1941"], *Zbornik filosofskog fakulteta,* X (1), Beograd, 1968, pp. 497-517.

―――――. "Prilozi istoriji sukoba Narodnooslobodilačkog pokreta i četnika Draže Mihailovića u Srbiji 1941 godine" [Further Documentation Regarding the Conflict in Serbia between the People's Liberation Movement and the Četniks of Draža Mihailović in 1941"], in *Istorija XX veka–Zbornik radova I,* Beograd, "Kultura," 1959, pp. 153-233.

Matl, Dr Josef "Jugoslawien im zweitem Weltkrieg" in Werner Markert, ed., *Osteuropa-Handbuch, Jugoslawien,* Koeln-Graz, Boehlau Verlag, 1954, pp. 99-121.

Meneghello-Dincic, Kruno . . . "L'état 'Oustacha' de Croatie, 1941-1945," *Revue d' histoire de la deuxième guerre mondiale,* XIX (74), April 1969, pp. 43-65.

Meškovic, Pavle "Mišićeva žrtva" ["Mišić's Self-Sacrifice"] in Radoje L. Knežević, ed., *Knjiga o Draži* [*The Book on Draža*], Volume 1, Windsor, Canada, Srpska narodna odbrana, 1956, pp. 196-98.

―――――. "Od Bosne do Ravne Gore" ["From Bosnia to Ravna Gora"], in Radoje L. Knežević, ed., *Knjiga o Draži* [*The Book on Draža*], Volume 1, Windsor, Canada, Srpska narodna odbrana, 1956, pp. 28-33.

Mihailović, Uglješa "Četnicki odredi 1914. godine" ["The Četnik Detachments in 1914"]. *Kanadski Srbobran,* 1 January 1981, p. 8.

Milićević, General Staff Brigadier General T.K. "Uzroci nase vojničke propasti 1941" ["The Causes of our Military Debacle in 1941"], *Glasnik Srpskog istorisko- kulturnog društva "Njegoš,"* No. 8, December 1961, pp. 5-49.

Milosavljević, Dragoslav V. "Mihailović do Ravne Gore" ["Mihailović prior to Ravna Gora"] in Radoje L. Knežević, ed., *Knjiga o Draži* [*The Book on Draža*], Volume 1, Windsor, Canada, Srpska narodna odbrana, 1956, pp. 44-52.

Nedeljković, Radisav "Sećanja iz narodnooslobodilačke borbe u čačanskom okrugu" ["Reminiscences from the People's Liberation War in Čačak District"], in *Četrdeset godina,* Volume 5, Beograd, 1961, pp. 295-314.

Nikitović, Časlav "'Obznana' pred Ustavotvornom skupštinom" ["Constituent Assembly's Debate on 'Obznana'"], *Glasnik Srpskog istorisko-kulturnog društva "Njegoš,"* No. 31, December 1973, pp. 15-28.

Nurik (Lester) and Robert M. Barrett "Legality of Guerrilla Forces under the Laws of War," *American Journal of International Law,* XL (3), July 1946, pp. 563-83.

Pavlowitch, Kosta St. "Srpski političari prema britanskim dokumentima" ["Serb Politicians in the light of British Documents"], *Savremenik,* New Series, XXVI (9), August 1980, pp. 45-66.

―――――. "Jugoslovensko-britanski odnosi 1939-1945: Simovićev pad prema britanskim izvorima" ["Yugoslav-British Relations 1939-1945: the Fall of Simović as seen from British Sources"], *Glasnik Srpskog istorisko-kulturnog društva "Njegoš,"* No. 40, June 1978, pp. 34-55.

―――――. "Yugoslav-British Relations 1939-1945 as seen from British Sources," *East European Quarterly,* XII (3), pp. 309-339 and XII (4), pp. 425-41.

Pavlowitch, Stevan K. "How many Non-Serbian Generals in 1941?", *East European Quarterly,* XVI (4), January 1983, pp. 447-52.

―――――. "Još se plaća 27 mart" ["It is still claimed the Coup d'Etat of 27 March 1941 was Paid For"], *Naša Reč,* XXXIII (318), October 1980, p. 16.

Petrović-Njegoš, Prince Mihajlo "Kako sam odbio da primim presto" ["How I refused the offer of the Throne"], *Glasnik Srpskog istorisko-kulturnog društva "Njegoš,"* No. 2, December 1958, pp. 33-37.

Plećaš, Nedjeljko B. "S mora i iz vazduha u porobljenu Otadžbinu" ["From the Sea and the Air into the enslaved Fatherland"], *Glasnik srpskog istorisko-kulturnog društva "Njegoš,"* No. 5 June 1960, pp. 36-48.

Pomorišac, Nikola "26-27 mart u dvorskom vozu" ["The 26-27 March [1941] in the Royal Train"], typewritten monograph, mimeographed in a restricted number of copies, Sydney, Australia, 1981.

Purković, Dr. Miodrag Al. "Dragoljub Mihailović, kratka biografija" ["A Short Biography of Dragoljub Mihailović"], in Radoje L. Knežević, ed., *Knjiga o Draži* [*The Book on Draža*], Volume 1, Windsor, Canada, 1956, pp. 1-5.

Ručnov, Marko, "Pakao desetog kruga" ["The Hell of the Tenth Circle"], *Duga*, 22 February–10 March 1986, pp. 18-19.

Simić, Zvonko "Jasenovac juče i danas: dodji, vidi i ne zaboravi" ["Jasenovac yesterday and today: come, inspect it, and do not forget"], *NIN* (*Nedeljne ilustrovane novine*), 18 October 1981, pp. 18-19.

Stafford, A.T. "SOE and British Involvement in the Belgrade Coup d'Etat of March 1941," *Slavic Review*, XXXVI (3), 1977, pp. 399-419.

Stanković, Mirko "Sa Dražom od Brčkog do Ravne Gore" ["With Draža from Brčko to Ravna Gora"] in Radoje L. Knežević, ed., *Knjiga o Draži* [*The Book on Draža*], Volume 1, Windsor, Canada, 1956, pp. 15-27.

Stojanović, Milan K. "Kako je kažnjavan Draža Mihailović" ["Draža Mihailović's Punishments"], *Glasnik srpskog istorisko-kulturnog društva "Njegoš,"* No. 9, June 1962, pp. 61-65.

Strugar, Colonel Vlado "Die jugoslawische Armee 1918-1964," *Oesterreichische militaerische Zeitschrift*, Vols 5 / 1964 (pp. 305-08), 6 / 1964 (pp. 403-09), 2 / 1965 (pp. 104-10) and 3 / 1965 (pp. 197-200).

Sugar, Peter F. "The Role of U.S. Minister Plenipotentiary, Arthur B. Lane, in Belgrade (June 1940–April 1941)," *Revue romaine d'histoire*, XVI (3), 1977, pp. 487-505.

Sweet-Escott, Bickham "S.O.E. in the Balkans," intr. by Major-General Sir Colin Gubbins, in Phyllis Auty and Richard Clogg, eds. *British Policy towards Wartime Resistance in Yugoslavia and Greece*, London, Macmillan, 1975.

Trojanović, Radmilo S. "Pregovori za primirje sa Nemačkom 16. i 17. aprila 1941" ["Armistice Negotiations with Germany on 16 and 17 April 1941"], *Glasnik srpskog istorisko-kulturnog društva "Njegoš,"* No. 28, June 1972, pp. 9-17.

Vitou, Captain Maurice "The Truth about Mihailovich? (IV)" in *World Review,* August, pp. 31-37.

Voinović, Stevo [His autobiographical letter] in *Zbornik* [Paris, Momčilo, M. Matić, ed.], No. 48, 1983, pp. iv to v.

Vuković, Miodrag M. "Sa pukovnikom Dražom Mihailovićem od 6. do. 14. aprila 1941. godine" ["With Colonel Draža Mihailović from 6 to 14 April 1941"], *Glasnik srpskog istorisko-kulturnog društva "Njegoš,"* No. 34, June 1975, pp. 32-46.

———. "Sa pukovnikom Dražom Mihailovićem od 6. do 14. aprila 1941." ["With Colonel Draža Mihailović from 6 to 14 April 1941"], *Savremenik,* New Series, XXVII (12), July 1981, pp. 103-15.

Wiskemann, Elizabeth, "Partitioned Yugoslavia" in Arnold and Veronica Toynbee, eds., *Hitler's Europe,* O.U.P., 1954, pp. 648-74.

Zonjić, Miličko "Petrovdanska tragedija na Cetinju 1941. godine" ["St Peter's Day Tragedy at Cetinje in 1941"], *Glasnik srpskog istorisko-kulturnog društva "Njegoš,"* No. 23, June 1969, pp. 27-32.

Books

Amery, Julian *Approach March,* A Venture in Autobiography, London, Hutchinson, 1973.

Auty, Phyllis, *Tito,* A Biography, London, Longman, 1970.

———. Yugoslavia, New York, Walker, 1965.

Auty (Phyllis) and Richard Clogg, eds., *British Policy towards Wartime Resistance in Yugoslavia and Greece,* London, Macmillan, 1975.

Avakumovic, Ivan *History of the Communist Party of Yugoslavia,* Volume 1, The Aberdeen U.P., 1964.

Avakumović, Dr. Ivan *Mihailović prema nemačkim dokumentima* [*Mihailović as seen from the German documents*], London, Savez "Oslobodjenje," 1969.

Barker, Elisabeth *British Policy in South-East Europe in the Second World War,* London, Macmillan, 1976.

Bathe (Dr. Rolf) and Erich Glodschey *Der Kampf um den Balkan,* Chronik des jugoslawischen und griechischen Feldzugs, Oldenburg/Berlin, Gerhard Stalling, 1942.

Beloff, Nora *Tito's Flawed Legacy, Yugoslavia and the West: 1939-84,* London, Victor Gollancz, 1985.

Boehme, K.W. *Die deutschen Kriegsgefangenen in Jugoslawien 1941-1949,* Volume I/1, Muenchen, Ernst & Werner Gieseking, 1962.

Broz-Tito, Josip *Borba za oslobodjenje Jugoslavije,* Članci i govori iz narodno-oslobodilačke borbe 1941-1944. [*The Struggle for Liberation of Yugoslavia, Articles and Speeches 1941-1944*], 2nd edn, Beograd, Državni izdavački zavod, 1945.

Buchner, Alex *Der deutsche Griechenland-Feldzug,* Operationen der 12. Armee 1941, Heidelberg, Scharnhorst Buchkameradschaft, 1957.

Burgess, Alan *The Lovely Sergeant,* London (etc.), Heinemann, 1963.

Butler, J.R.M., ed., *History of the Second World War,* United Kingdom Military Series, *Grand Strategy,* 6 volumes, London, HMSO, 1956-1976: *Volume II, September 1939—June 1941,* by J.R.M. Butler, London, HMSO, 1957; *Volume III (1),* June 1941—August 1942, by J.M.A. Gwyer, London, HMSO, 1964; *Volume III (2),* June 1941—August 1942, by J.R.M. Butler, London, HMSO, 1964; *Volume IV,* August 1942—September 1943, by Michael Howard, London, HMSO, 1972. *Volume V,* August 1943—September 1944, by John Ehrman, London, HMSO, 1956.

Četrdeset godina, Zbornik sećanja aktivista jugoslovenskog revolucionarnog radničkog pokreta [*Forty Years, . . .*], Volume 5: 1941-1945, Beograd, Kultura, 1961.

Churchill, Winston S. *The Second World War,* 6 volumes, Vols 1-5, First Australian Edn, London (etc.) 1948-1952, Vol. 6, London (etc.). 1954: *Volume III,* The Grand Alliance, London (etc), Cassell Co., 1950; *Volume VI,* Triumph and Tragedy, London (etc.), Cassel & Co., 1954.

Clissold, Stephen, *Whirlwind,* An Account of Marshal Tito's Rise to Power, London, The Cresset Press, 1949.

Cookridge, E.H. *Inside SOE,* The Story of Special Operations in Western Europe 1940-1945, London, Arthur Baker, 1966.

Cruickshank, C[harles] G[reig] *The Fourth Arm, Psychological Warfare 1939-1945,* London, Davis-Poynter, 1977.

Čulinović, Dr Ferdo *Slom Stare Jugoslavije* [*The Downfall of Old Yugoslavia*], Zagreb, Školska knjiga, 1958.

Dalton, Hugh *The Faithful Years, Memoirs 1931-1945*, 2nd impression, London, Frederick Muller, 1957.
Deakin, F.W. *The Embattled Mountain*, Oxford U.P., 1971.
Dedijer, Vladimir *Dnevnik I, 1941-1942* [*Diary I, 1941-42*], Beograd & Sarajevo, Prosveta & Svijetlost, 1945.
———. *Novi prilozi za biografiju Josipa Broza Tita* [*Further Contributions to a Biography of Josip Broz Tito*], 1953–; Vol. I, 1980 Reprint of the 1953 edn, "Mladost"Zagreb (et al.), 1980.
———. *Tito Speaks, His Selfportrait and Struggle with Stalin*, London, Weidenfeld and Nicolson, 1954.
———. *With Tito Through The War, Partisan Diary 1941-1944*, [tr. Alex Brown], London, 1951.
Derok, Captain Jovan V. *Toplički ustanak i oružani otpor u okupiranoj Otadžbini 1916-1918 godine* [*The Uprising in Toplica and the Armed Resistance in the Occupied Fatherland 1916-1918*], Beograd, Biblioteka Ratnika, 1940.
Djilas, Milovan *Conversations with Stalin*, tr. M.B. Petrovich, London, Rupert Hart-Davis, 1962.
———. *Memoir of a Revolutionary*, tr. Zdenka Willen, New York, Harcourt Brace Jovanovich, 1973.
———. *Tito, The Story from Inside*, tr. Vasilije Kojic and Richard Hayes, London, Weidenfeld and Nicolson, 1981.
———. *Wartime*, tr. M.B. Petrovich, New York and London, Harcourt Brace Jovanovich, 1977.
Dokumenti o Jugoslaviji [a collection of articles in defence of the Cvetković Government, edited by Dragiša J. Cvetković, former PM of Yugoslavia], Paris, France, 1951-58.
Drachkovitch (Milorad M.) and Branko Lazitch *The Comintern: Historical Highlights, Essays, Recollections, Documents*, Stanford, Cal., Hoover Institution, 1966.
Duretic, Veselin *Saveznici i jugoslovenska ratna drama* [*The Allies and the Yugoslav War Drama*], 2 vols, 2nd edn. Belgrade, Balkanological Institute of the Serbian Academy of Sciences and Arts, 1985.
Foot, M.R.D. *Resistance, An Analysis of European Resistance to Nazism 1940-1945*, London, Methuen, 1977 reprint with corrections.
———. *SOE in France, An Account of the Work of the British Special Operations Executive in France 1940-1944*, London, HMSO, 1966.

General Mihailovitch: The World's Verdict, A Selection of Articles..., With an Introduction by the General's Friends [actually K. St. Pawlovitch] and a fwd by F.A. Voigt, Gloucester, UK, John Bellows Ltd., 1947.

Glen, Alexander *Footholds against a Whirlwind,* London, Hutchinson, 1975.

Guedalla, Phillip *Middle East 1940-1942,* A Study in Air Power, London, Hodder and Stoughton, 1944.

Guikovaty, Emile *Tito,* Paris, Hachette, 1979.

Hamilton-Hill, Donald *SOE Assignment,* New English Library, May 1975 Reprint.

Heilbrunn, Oto *Partisan Warfare,* fwd by Colonel C.M. Woodhouse, London, Allen &Unwin, 1962.

Hoptner, J.B. *Yugoslavia in Crisis 1934-1941,* Columbia, U.P., 1963.

Howarth, Patrick *Undercover,* The Men and Women of the Special Operations Executive, London, Routledge &Kegan Paul, 1980.

Istorija XX veka—Zbornik radova I, Beograd, "Kultura," 1959.

Ivanović, Vane *LX—Memoirs of a Yugoslav,* New York and London, Harcourt Brace Jovanovich, 1977.

Jaszi, Oscar *The Dissolution of the Habsburg Monarchy,* The University of Chicago Press, 1961.

Jovanović, Slobodan *Zapisi o problemima i ljudima, 1941-1944* [*Notes about Problems and People 1941-1944*], fwd by Radoje L. Knežević, London, Society of Serbian Writers and Artists Abroad, 1976.

Jukić, Ilija *Pogledi na prošlost, sadašnjost i budućnost hrvatskog naroda* [*Observations regarding the Past, Present and Future of the Croat People*], London, Hrvatska politička knjižnica, 1965.

Karapandžic, Bor. M. *Gradjanski rat u Srbiji 1941-1945* [*The Civil War in Serbia, 1941-1945*], Cleveland, Ohio, Pte Edn, 1958.

Kemp, Peter *No Colours or Crest,* A Panther Book (Cassell), 1958.

Knežević, Radoje L. (ed.) *Knniga o Draži* [*The Book on Draža*], 2 Volumes, Windsor, Canada, Srpska narodna odbrana, 1956.

Knežević (Radoje) and Živan L. *Sloboda ili smrt* [*Freedom or Death*], Seattle, USA, Pte Edn, 1981.

Knežević, Živan L. *27. mart 1941* [*The 27th of March, 1941*], fwd by Radoje L. Knežević, New York, Pte Edn, 1979.

Kostić, Boško N. *Za istoriju naših dana* [*A Contribution to the History of Our Times*], Lille, France, Pte Edn, 1949.

Koštunica (Vojislav) and Kosta Čavoski. *Party Pluralism or Monism.* East European Monographs, Boulder, 1985.

Krakov, Stanislav. *General Milan Nedić,* 2 volumes. Muenchen, "Iskra": Volume I—*Na oštrici noža.* "Iskra": 1963.

Lawrence, Christie. *Irregular Adventure,* intr. by Evelyn Waugh. London, Faber and Faber, 1947.

Lazić, Branko, *Titov pokret i režim u Jugoslaviji 1941-1946 [Tito's Movement and Regime in Yugoslavia, 1941-1946],* N.P., Pte Edn. 1946.

Lockhart, Bruce. *Comes the Reckonning.* London, Putnam, October 1947.

Ljubičić, Nikola. *Uzički Narodnooslobodilački partizanski odred "Dimitrije Tucović,"* Beograd, IRO "Narodna Knjiga," 2nd edn., 1981.

Long, Gavin. *Greece, Crete and Syria;* Australian War Memorial: *Australia in the War of 1939-1945,* Series one—Army, Volume II, Canberra, 1953.

Maček, Vladko. *In the Struggle for Freedom,* tr. Elizabeth and Stjepan Gazi, New York, Speller and Sons, 1957.

Maclean, Fitzroy. *Disputed Barricade,* The Life and Times of Josip Broz-Tito, 2nd impression, London, Jonathan Cape, August 1957.

———. *Eastern Approaches,* 2nd impression, London, Jonathan Cape, 1949.

Malaparte, Curzio. *Kaputt,* tr. Cesare Foligno, London, Alvin Redman, 1948.

Marjanović, Jovan. *Draža Mihailović izmedju Britanaca i Nemaca [Draža Mihailović between the British and the Germans],* Volume I: *Britanski štićenik [The British Protégé],* Zagreb and Beograd, Globus (etc.), 1979.

———. *Ustanak i narodno-oslobodilački pokret u Srbiji 1941 (The Rising and the National Liberation Movement in Serbia in 1941),* Beograd, Institut društvenih nauka, I (3), 1963.

Martin, David. *Ally Betrayed,* The Uncensored Story of Tito and Mihailovich, fwd by Rebecca West, New York, Prentice-Hall, 1946.

Milazzo, Matteo J. *The Chetnik Movement and the Yugoslav Resistance,* Baltimore and London, John Hopkins U.P., 1975.

Mitrović, Dojčilo. *Zapadna Srbija 1941 [West Serbia in 1941],* Beograd, Nolit, 1975.

Morgan, Lieut. General Sir Frederick. *Peace and War,* A Soldier's Life, London, Hodder & Stoughton, 1961.

Parežanin, Ratko. *Drugi svetski rat i Dimitrije V. Ljotić [The Second World War and Dimitrije V. Ljotić],* N.P., Pte Edn., 1971.

Pavlowitch, Stevan K. *Yugoslavia,* New York and Washington, Praeger, 1971.
Peter II of Yugoslavia. *A King's Heritage,* the Memoirs of..., London, Cassell, 1955.
Plećaš, Nedjeljko B. *Ratne godine 1941-1945 [The War Years 1941-1945],* Columbus, Ohio, Kosovo Publishing Co., 1983.
Rendell, Sir George. *The Sword and the Olive,* Recollections of Diplomacy and Foreign Service, 1913-1954, London, John Murray, 1957.
Rhodes, Anthony. *The Vatican in the Age of the Dictators, 1922-1945,* London (etc.), Hodder and Stoughton, 1973.
Roberts, Walter R. *Tito, Mihailović, and the Allies, 1941-1945,* 2nd printing, Rutgers U.P., 1973.
Roosevelt, Elliot, Ed. *The Roosevelt Letters, Being the Personal Correspondence of Franklin Delano Roosevelt,* 3 vols (1887-1945), London (etc.), George G. Harrap, Vol. 1 (1949), Vol. 2 (1950), Vol. 3 (1952).
Rootham, Jasper. *Miss Fire,* The Chronicle of a British Mission to Mihailovic, 1943-1944, London, Chatto and Windus, 1946.
Seton, Albert. *Germany Army 1933-45,* London, Wakefield and Nicolson, 1982.
Seton-Watson, Hugh. *The East European Revolution,* London, Methuen, 1950.
Slijepčević, Dr. Djoko. *Jugoslavija uoči i za vreme drugog svetskog rata [Yugoslavia at the Eve and During the Second World War],* Muenchen, "Iskra," 1978.
St. John, Robert. *From the Land of Silent People,* London (etc.), George G. Harrap, 1942.
Sweet-Escott, Bickham. *Baker Street Irregular,* London, Methuen, 1965.
Temperley, H. W. V., ed. *A History of the Peace Conference of Paris,* 6 *volumes,* London, Henry Frowde and Hodder & Stoughton: Volume IV, 1921; Volume V, 1924.
Terzić, Velimir. *Jugoslavija u aprilskom ratu 1941 [Yugoslavia in the War of April 1941],* Titograd, Grafički zavod, 1963.
Tippelskirch, Kurt von. *Geschichte des zweiten Weltkrieges,* 3rd edn., Bonn, Athenaeum, 1959.
Tomasevich, Jozo. *The Chetniks,* Stanford U.P., 1975.
Topalović, Dr. Živko. *Pokreti narodnog otpora u Jugoslaviji 1941-1945 [National Resistance Movements in Yugoslavia, 1941-1945],* Paris, Pte Edn., 1958.

Toynbee, Arnold and Veronica (eds.). *Hitler's Europe*, O.U.P., 1954.
Vučković, Zvonimir. *Sećanja iz rata [War Reminiscences]*, London, Naše delo, 1980.
Wheeler, Mark C. *Britain and the War for Yugoslavia, 1940-1943*, East European Monographs, Boulder, 1980.
Wuescht, Johann. *Jugoslawien und das Dritte Reich.* Stuttgart, Seewald Verlag, 1969.
Zelenika, Lt Colonel-General M[ilan]. *Rat Srbije i Crne Gore 1915 [The War of Serbia and Montenegro 1915]*, Beograd, "Vojno delo," 1954.
Živanović, Lt Colonel Sergije M. *Treći srpski ustanak 1941 [The Third Serbian Uprising in 1941]*, 3 volumes, Chicago, Ill., Pte edn–Vol. I: 1962, Vol. II: 1962, Vol. III: 1966. (Note: on the outer cover page the title reads *Djeneral Mihailović i njegovo delo*.)

Correspondence with the Wartime Participants

(i) Showing their wartime rank:
Captain Julian Amery
Lieutenant Colonel Ž. L. Knežević
Mr K. St. Pavlowitch, *Chef de Cabinet* to The Yugoslav PMs in London
Major R. K. Perhinek
Major N. D. Pomorišac–"Peca"
Colonel Ž. R. Popović
Captain A. A. Povhè
Captain S. Rapotec
Captain Z. (James) Vučković
Major R. P. Wade;

(ii) Messrs Amery and Lieutenant Colonel Hudson read the original draft of the "Bullseye" chapters;

(iii) The other correspondence is mentioned in footnotes only.

Diaries (Published), and Diaries-MS (Unpublished)

(i) Published:
Ciano's Diary 1939-1943, Malcolm Mugeridge ed. and intr., London and Toronto, Heinemann, 1947.

Diaries of Sir Alexander Cadogan, 1938-1945, David Dilks, ed., First American Edn, New York, 1972.

Generaloberst Halder: Kriegstagebuch, Hans-Adolf Jacobsen ed., Volume II, Stuttgart, 1963.
Kriegstagebuch des Oberkommandos der Wehrmacht, Wehrmachtfuehrungsstab, 7 Volumes, Frankfurt a/M. Bernard & Graefe Verlag, 1961-1965:
    Vol. I Part 1, August 1940-31 December 1941, H. A. Jacobsen, ed., 1965;
    Vol. 4 Part 1, January 1944-22 March 1945 [incl. the general introduction to this series]. Ernst Schramm, ed., 1961.
Memoirs of Ernst von Wiezsaeker, tr. John Andrews, London, Gollancz, 1951.
Von Hassell Diaries 1938-1944, London, Hamish Hamilton, 1948.

(ii)   Unpublished MS:
Lieutenant General Ratko Raketić, Commanding Slavonia Division, typewritten "Diary, April 1941," in the custody of his son, Monsieur Zoran Raketitch of Paris, France.

Dissertations (Theses), MS, Unpublished

Deroc, Milan. "The Serbian Uprising of 1941 and the British Response," unpublished PhD thesis, The University of New England, N.S.W., Australia, 1985. (Used an original copy.)

Erpenbeck, Dirk-Gerd. "Serbien 1941: deutsche Militaerverwaltung und serbischer Widerstand," [an administrative state thesis]. The University of Muenster/Westf., unpublished typewritten MS, Muenster/Westf., 1968. (A xerox copy.)

Ford, Thomas Kirkwood, Jr. "Pawns and Powerbrokers: OSS and the Yugoslav Resistance during the Second World War," unpublished PhD thesis, University of Southern Mississippi, 1980. (Used a University Microfilm International Copy.)

Georgevich, Dragoslav. "Two Days in Yugoslav History, March 25 and 27, 1941," typewritten, unpublished MA Thesis, San Jose State College, California, 1967. (Used a xerox copy.)

Karchmar, Lucien. "Draža Mihailović and the Rise of the Četnik Movement, 1941-1942," 2 volumes, typewritten, unpublished PhD thesis, Stanford University, 1973. (A University Mircofilm International copy.)

Sources

Documents:

(i) Published—
  (ia) Published collections of documents,
  (ib) Published individual documents;
(ii) Unpublished—
  (iia) Microfilms of unpublished collections,
  (iib) Unpublished individual documents.

(1a) *Published collections of documents*

Biber, Dr Dušan, ed., *Tito-Churchill,* Strogo tajno; Beograd-Zagreb, Arhiv Jugoslavije & Globus (1981).

Degras, Jane, ed. *The Communist International 1919-1943, Documents,* 3 Volumes: *Volume I,* 1919-1923, Oxford U.P., 1956; *Volume II,* 1923-1928, Oxford U.P., 1960; *Volume III,* 1928-1943, Oxford U.P., 1965.

Documents on German Foreign Policy 1918-1945 (DGFP), *Series "D":* Volume XII (1 February to 22 June 1941), London, HMSO, 1962; *Volume XIII* (23 June to 11 December 1941), London, HMSO, 1964.

Foreign Relations of the United States (FRUS), *Diplomatic Papers,* The Conferences at Cairo and Tehran [in] 1943, Washington, D.C., US Printing Office, 1961.

Hague Conventions and Declarations of 1899 and 1907 (The), New York, Carnegie Endowment for International Peace, Division of International Law, 1915.

Hubatsch, Walther, ed. *Hitlers Weisungen fuer de Kriegsfuehrung 1939-1945,* Dokumente der Oberkommando der Wehrmacht, Frankfurt a/M. Berbard und Graefe, 1962.

Knežević, Lieutenant Colonel Živan L. *General Mihailović and U.S.S.R.,* with Official Memoranda and Documents, Pte edn in the USA, deposited with the Foreign Agents Registration Section of the Department of Justice, 1945.

Krizman (Bogdan) and Branko Petranović. *Jugoslavenske vlade u izbjeglištvu,* Dokumenti, 2 Volumes, Zagreb, Globus, 1981: *Volume I,* 1941-1943, by Bogdan Krizman.

Lemkin, Raphael. *Axis Rule in Occupied Europe.* Washington, Carnegie Endowment for International Peace, 1944.

Nazi-Soviet Relations 1939-1941. Documents from the Archives of the German Foreign Office, ed. by Raymond James Sontag and James Stuart Beddie, US Department of State, 1948.

Šišić, Dr Ferdo, ed. *Dokumenti o postanku Kraljevine Srba, Hrvata i Slovenaca 1914-1919. [Documents regarding the Creation of the Kingdom of the Serbs, Croats and Slovenes, 1914-1919]*, Zagreb, Matica hrvatska, 1920.

Trevor-Roper, H. R., [tr. and ed.]. *Hitler's War Directives 1939-1945*, Texts from Walter Hubatsch, *Hitlers Weisungen fuer die Kriegsfuehrung 1939-1945*, London, Sidgwick and Jackson, 1964.

Zbornik dokumenata i podataka o narodnooslobodilačkom ratu jugoslovenskih naroda [Collection of Documents and Data about the War of National Liberation by the Yugoslav Peoples], Beograd, 1949-1968, Volume I Part 1, 1949.

(1b) *Individual documents published by private authors,* all as cited in the text and footnotes.

(iia) *Microfilms of unpublished collections of German wartime military documents,* as catalogued by the US National Archives:

Microcopy T314 Roll 1066—
Records of German Field Commands: Corps.
XLVI Panzerkorps in the Yugoslav Campaign of April 1941.

Microcopy T314 Roll 1457—
Records of German Field Commands: Corps
XVIII (Gebirgs) Armeekorps.
Various war diaries and reports about the guerrilla warfare in Serbia in 1941.

Microcopy T315 Roll 2262—
Records of German Field Commands: Divisions.
717. Infanterie Division.
Documentation regarding the occupation and guerrilla warfare in Serbia in 1941.

Microcopy T501 Roll 245—
Records of German Field Commands: Rear Areas, Occupied Territories, and others.
Various war diaries of the Commander South-East and of the Command in Serbia in 1941.

Microcopy T501 Roll 249–
Records of German Field Commands: Rear Areas, Occupied Territories, and others.
Various war diaries and other folders of the Command in Serbia, including political matters, 1941-1943.

Microcopy T501 Roll 250–
Records of German Field Commands: Rear Areas, Occupied Territories, and others.
Folders of the Command in Serbia pertaining to various anti-guerrilla field operations, 1941-1942.

Microcopy T501 Roll 251–
Records of German Field Commands: Rear Areas, Occupied Territories, and others.
Various war diaries of the Commander in Serbia, 1941-1942.

The advice received in the search for appropriate records from Mr George Wagner of the US National Archives, Military Archives Division, is gratefully acknowledged (MD).

(iib)   *Unpublished individual documents* are from the archives of
Auswaertiges Amt (AA), Staatssekretaer, Bonn, West Germany
Bundesarchiv-Militaerarchiv, Freiburg i/B, West Germany
Department of Defence, Naval Historical Branch, London, U.K.
Deutsche Dienststelle, Berlin, West Germany
Foreign and Commonwealth Office, Political Archives, London, U.K.
Foreign and Commonwealth Office, SOE Adviser, London, U.K.
Public Record Office (PRO), Kew, London, U.K.
Staatsarchiv-Kriegsarchiv, Vienna, Austria
U.S. Department of Justice, Immigration Branch, San Francisco, Calif.

Reference to and/or citing of documents, in part or wholly, has been done following permission of the respective managements, which is gratefully acknowledged. All use commentaries and conclusions remain the responsibility of this author (MD), and no managements, archives or governments are responsible for any of it.

Crown Copyright documents from the Public Record Office appear by permission of the Controller of Her Majesty's Stationery Office.

Encyclopaediae, Handbooks and Reference Works

Australian Imperial Force, *The Notes on the Austro-Hungarian Army*, Melbourne, Government Printer, [1900 (?)].

Cetniks (The). A Survey of Cetnik Activity in Yugoslavia, April 1941-July 1944, A.F.H.Q., G-2 (PB), [Bari (?)], September 1944.

Darby, H. C. et al., *A Short History of Yugoslavia*, Cambridge U.P., 1966.

Dimitrijević, Djordje J., *Djeneralštabni oficiri Kraljevine Jugoslavije [General Staff Officers of the Kingdom of Yugoslavia]*, London, Pte Edn., 1974.

Geographical Handbook Series, Jugoslavia, 3 Volumes, [British] Naval Intelligence Division, 1944-45, *Volumes I & II:* October 1944.

German Campaigns in the Balkans (The). Spring 1941 [US] Department of the Army, Pamphlet No. 20-260, Washington, November 1953.

Hehn, Paul N., *The German Struggle against Yugoslav Guerrillas in World War II*, German Counter-Insurgency in Yugoslavia 1941-1943, Columbia U.P., 1979. Hehn's work is an edited and expanded translation of a German internal report. Hehn refers to its author as "General Wisshaupt." According to the Bundesarchiv-Militaerarchiv, Ernst Wisshaupt was an *Oberheeresarchivrat* who wrote this report for the Commander South-East. The title of the original report is "Die Bekaempfung der Aufstandsbewegung im Suedostraum"; its present archival registration is RH XI/81.

Hinsley, F. H. et al., *British Intelligence in the Second World War*, Its Influence on Strategy and Operations, 3 Volumes: Volume I, London, HMSO, 1979; Volume II, London, HMSO, 1981; Volume III (Part 1), New York, Cambridge U.P. for HMSO, 1984.

Historical Encyclopedia of World War II (The), French, English and American Edns; American Edition, Facts on File, 1980.

International Committee of the Red Cross, *Report of the ICRC on its Activities during the Second World War* (September 1, 1939–June 30, 1947), 2 Volumes, Geneva, May 1949: Volume I: General Activities, Volume II: The Central Agency for Prisoners of War.

Jugoslawien, Werner Markert ed.: *Osteuropa-Handbuch*, Koeln-Graz, Boehlau Verlag, 1954.

Macartney, C. A., *National States and National Minorities*, Oxford U.P., 1934.

Sources

New Catholic Encyclopedia

Podhorsky, René, Commander (Retd), *Ranglista osoblja Kraljevske mornarice na dan 6. aprila 1941 godine* [*Seniority List of the Commissioned Personnel of the Royal* [Yugoslav] *Navy on Active Service on 6 April 1941*]. Zuerich, Pte edn. 1970.

Podhorsky, René, Commander (Retd), *Ukazno osoblje Kraljevske mornarice koje na dan 6. aprila 1941 nije više bilo u aktivnoj službi* [*Commissioned Personnel of the Royal* [Yugoslav] *Navy, who were not on the Active List on 6 April 1941*], Zuerich, Pte edn, 1972.

Report upon the Atrocities committed by the Austro-Hungarian Army during the First Invasion of Serbia [in 1914], submitted to the Serbian Government by R. A. Reiss, tr. F. S. Copeland, London, Simpkin Marshall Hamilton and Kent & Co., 1916.

Vojna enciklopedija, 2nd edn, Beograd, Redakcija Vojne enciklopedije, 1970-1976, *Volume IV.*

Woodward, Sir Llewellyn, *British Foreign Policy in the Second World War,* London, HMSO, 1962.

Journals and Periodicals

American Journal of International Law
Amerikanski Srbobran, Pittsburgh, Pa, USA
Bulletin of International News (BIN), The.
Duga, Beograd, Yugoslavia.
East European Quarterly.
Glas kanadskih Srba, Windsor, Ont., Canada.
Glasnik Srpskog istorisko-kulturnog društva "Njegoš," Chicago, Ill., USA.
Kanadski Srbobran, Hamilton, Ont., Canada.
Keesing's Contemporary Archives (Keesing's).
Naša reč, Harrow, U.K.
New Statesman and Nation (The).
NIN (Nedeljne ilustrovane novine), Beograd, Yugoslavia.
The Observer.
Oesterreichische militaerische Zeitschrift.
Politika, Beograd, Yugoslavia.
Revue d'histoire de la deuxième guerre mondiale.
Revue romaine d'histoire.

Savremenik, Paris, France.
Slavic Review.
Sloboda, Chicago, Ill.
Službeni Vojni list [*The Official Military Gazette*], Beograd, Kingdom of the Serbs, Croats and Slovenes.
South Slav Journal (The), London, U.K.
The Times.
Times Literary Supplement.
Vazduhoplovni glasnik, London, U.K.
Vojnoistorijski glasnik, Beograd, Yugoslavia.
World Review.
Zbornik (Paris, M. M. Matić, ed.).
Zbornik filosofskog fakulteta, Beograd, Yugoslavia.

Private Papers, Unpublished MS and Cassettes

Derok, Captain Jovan V., "Pisma, dnevnici i pribeleške 1928-1940" [Letters, Diaries and Other Papers, 1928-1940"], unpublished material in the custody of his sister, Madame Yolande Popovitch of Paris, France. Generally hand-written. (Mme Popovitch died in August 1984.)

Popović, Colonel Žarko R., "Notes and Papers": (1) Deposited with the Hoover Institution, Stanford University, California, USA, (ii) Remainder still in his possession in London, U.K. (iii) Dictated Cassette about the events in Cairo in 1941 to this author.

Rapotec, Stanislaus (Stanislav), "Papers and Documents pertaining to his Intelligence Missions in 1941," a mixed set of copies and originals given by Mr Rapotec to this author (MD).

The access to this material is gratefully acknowledged.

Proceedings of Conferences and Similar

"Proceedings"...
Conference on Britain and European Resistance, organized by St Antony's College, Oxford [U.K.], December 10-16, 1962. "Proceedings," typewritten, mimeographed.

Martin, David, ed., *Patriot or Traitor: the Case of General Mihailovich,* Proceedings and Report of the Commission of Inquiry of the Committee for a Fair Trial for Draja Mihailovich, Introductory Essay by David Martin, fwd by Frank J. Lausche, Stanford, California., Hoover Institution Press, 1978.

Trials (Stenographic Records)

Trial of Dragoljub-Draža Mihailović, [Edited] Stenographic record, Beograd, The Union of the Journalists Associations, 1946.

Trials of the Major War Criminals..., International Military Tribunal, Nurenberg, Germany, *Vols VII, 1947, and XXVII, 1948.*

Trials of War Criminals before the Nuernberg Military Tribunals under Control Council Law No. 10, Nuernberg, October 1946–April 1949, *Volume XI* ("The High Command Case" and "The Hostage Case"), Washington, Gvt Printing Office, 1950.

INDEX

of persons mentioned in the main text and in footnotes

Aćimović, Milan, pp. 10, 16, 18, 22, 167; notes Ch. 9: 20

Alexander I, pp. 3, 4, 7, 8, 9, 36, 56, 93, 119-121; notes Ch. 1:4, Conclusion: 17

Alexander Karadjordjevic, Crown Prince (later King A. I), p. 7

Alexander, Sir Harold, p. 218; notes Ch. 6: 60

Amery Jnr, see Amery, Julian

Amery, Julian, pp. 56, 60, 61, 63, 65, 68-71, 74, 76, 79, 91, 195-199, 201; notes Ch. 4: 8, 18, 24, 62, 76, 94, Ch. 5: 10, 18, Ch. 10: 14 and p. 333.

Amery, Leopold, p. 65.

Amery Snr, (see also Amery, Leopold), pp. 64, 65

Arasaratnam, Professor Sinnapah, p. xi

Auchinleck, Sir Claude ("Auk"), pp. 61, 62, 225

Auty, Phyllis, pp. 49, 66, 70, 81, 86, 87, 114-118, 121, 123, 125, 128, 131-134, 167, 168, 171, 191, 224, 225; notes Ch. 4: 99, Ch. 7: 24, 34, 71, Ch. 9: 30; Conclusion 17

Avakumović, Dr. Ivan A., pp. 126, 128, 170, 176

Bader, Paul, pp. 142, 143, 145, 165, 166, 175; notes Ch. 8: 33, Ch. 9: 18

Bailey, Stanley William ("Bill"), pp. xv, 56-59, 61, 62, 65, 66, 77, 195-201; notes Ch. 4: 16, 22, 24, 79, Ch. 11: 5

Bakić, Mitar, pp. 84, 87, 88, 127; notes Ch. 7: 83.

Bandović, Milan, p. 46

Barker, Elisabeth, pp. 64, 224; notes Ch. 5: 33, Ch. 11: 5

Barthou, Louis, notes Conclusion 17

"Beli", Serbian spelling and pronounciation: see Bailey

Beloff, Nora, p. 191; notes Ch. 11: 53

Beloussova, Pelagia (Polka), p. 118

Bennett, John, pp. 60, 66, 67, 74, 79, 194-199, 201; notes Ch. 4: 80, Ch. 5: 20, 42

Benzler, Felix, pp. 138, 153, 161, 164; notes Ch. 8: 59

Biroli, Pirzio, p. 51; notes Ch. 3: 59

Bodi, Mihailo D., p. 31

Boehme, Franz, pp. 140, 142, 160, 162-166, 172, 183, 192; notes Ch. 9: 2, 11, 13, 79

Bonofatti, Luigi, notes Ch. 2: 28

Boxhall (spelling error), see Boxshall

Boxshall, E. G. notes Ch. 4: 15, 55, Ch. 10: 11

Braushitsch, Wilhelm von, p. 137; notes Ch. 8:5

Index

Brezhnev, Leonid I., p. 114; notes Ch. 7: 2
Brož, Josip or Josef, p. 117, see also Broz-Tito, Josip
Broz-Tito, Josip (see also "Valter") pp. vii, viii, xii, 3, 6, 12, 20, 28, 39, 41, 49, 51, 67, 78, 81, 86-88, 90, 92, 113-135, 151, 157, 167, 170-174, 178, 182-184, 186, 191, 205-222, 224-226, 230; notes Ch. 4: 84, Ch. 7: 1, 9, 10, 13, 22-24, 34, 37, 59, 63, 83, 91, 96, 99, Ch. 8: 67, 68, Ch. 11: 49, 53, Conclusion 10, 14, 20, 25
Butler, J. R. M., p. 54

Cadogan, Sir Alexander, pp. 2, 19
Campbell, Ronald Ian, p. 98
"Captain Radovan", see Jones, R. H.
Casertano, Raffaele, p. 36
Cassano, Sera di, p. 47
Čavoški, Dr. Kosta, p. 134
Chamberlain, Neville, p. 54
Chambermaid from Herceg Novi, Anonymous, p. 46
Chandos, Lord (see also Lyttelton), p. 62
Churchill, Winston S., pp. vii, viii, 13, 18, 19, 21, 22, 26, 54, 63-65, 67, 78, 113, 114, 130, 193, 219-225; notes Ch. 4: 62, 69, Ch. 5: 14, Conclusion, 5, 14, 15
Ciano, Count Galeazzo, p. 47
Čižinski, Josip, p. 124
Clark, Mark, p. 218
Clarke, C. S., pp. xv, 97-100, 112; notes Ch. 6: 19, 87
Clausewitz, Karl von, pp. 124, 125
Clissold, Stephen, p. 209
Collishaw, R. ("Collie"), p. 61
Coningham, Sir Arthur, p. 61
Cox, Nicholas, notes Ch. 10:11
Crew, Mrs. Jennifer, p. xi

Crossman, R. H. S., p. 3; notes Conclusion 2
Čulinović, Dr. Ferdo, p. 27
Cvetković, Dragiša, pp. 4, 9, 12; notes p. 329

Dalton, Dr. Hugh, pp. 13, 14, 54, 55, 61-65, 67, 68; notes Ch. 69
Danckelmann, Heinrich, pp. 140, 142, 157, 158, 162, 164, 166
Dangić, Jezdimir S., pp. 180, 181; notes Ch. 9: 60
Davidson, Basil, p. 222; notes Conclusion 7, 8
Davies, a Corporal (British No. 2 Commando), p. 73
Deakin, F. W. D. (later Sir-), pp. 57, 64-71, 74, 77, 78, 81-90, 206, 209, 214, 215, 217, 221-224; notes Ch. 11: 5, Conclusion, 5
Dedijer, Vladimir, pp. 114-116, 119, 121, 122, 124, 125, 127-130, 133, 233; notes Ch. 7: 34, 91
Denić, Branko, p. 58
Derok, Jovan V., pp. 94, 95, 105, 107, 178 (v.q. 45), 184; notes Ch. 6: 68, 69
Derok (Deroc), V. J. notes Ch. 6: 1
Deroko (wrong spelling), see Derok
Dill, Sir John Greer, pp. 17, 85; notes Ch. 5: 50
Dimitrov, Georgi *alias* Deda p. 131
Dirnberger, an *Unteroffizier*, p. 177
Djelević, Jakša V., Ch. 11: 6
Djilas, Milovan, pp. 12, 37, 39, 46, 47, 51, 69, 76, 82, 85, 88-90, 113, 116, 124, 125, 128-130, 168, 173, 174; notes Ch. 5: 44, Ch. 7: 71, 91
Djonović, Jovan Dj., pp. 56, 58-60, 65, 79, 195-202; notes Ch. 4: 29, Ch. 5: 24, Ch. 11: 5

Djuretić, Dr. Veselin ("Dj" is used here due to the lack of a special type Đ with diacritic marking), pp. 113, 114
Djurić, Radoslav Dj., p. 184
Djurišić, Pavel I., pp. 49, 51; notes Ch. 3: 59
Djuro, a Montenegrin, Military Academy Cadet, p. 94
Don, Douglas, pp. 70, 73
Donne, see Don
Dragićević, Veljko, pp. 66, 84-86, 88; notes Ch. 5: 54, 55, 62
Draža, See Mihailović, Dragoljub-Draža M.
Duretić, Dr. Veselin, see Djuretić

Eden, Anthony, pp. 20, 78
Edwards, Mrs. M. R., notes Ch. 4: 101
Egger, an *Unteroffizier*, p. 177
Elena of Italy (born Petrović-Njegoš), pp. 45, 47

Fischer-Galati, Professor Stephen, p. xii
Flemming, Ian, notes Ch. 4:13
Foerster, Helmut, pp. 137, 142, 143, 148; notes Ch. 8: 12, 30
Foertner, Johann, p. 165
Foertsch, Hermann, p. 164
Foot, M. R. D., pp. 38, 54
Frank, Dr. Josip, p. 227
Francis-Joseph I, p. 117
Fregl, Ivan E., p. 211
Frunze, Mikhail Vassilievich, p. 124

Gani-Beg Kryeziu, pp. 76-77
Gardyne de Chastelain, A. G., notes Ch. 4: 24
Gavrilović, Dr. Milan, p. 57
Gilbert, Martin, Ch. 4: 62

Glen, Alexander (later Sir-), notes Ch. 4:18
Glenconner, Lord, p. 229
Goebbels, Dr. Paul Joseph, pp. 23, 34
Goering, Hermann, p. 138
Golubović, Mihailo St., p. 29
Gorkić, Milan—see Čižinski, Josip
Gradišnik, Ferdo, F., p. 29
Grand, L. D., pp. 55, 95; notes Ch. 4:15
Gravenhorst, an *Oberstleutnant*, p. 175; notes Ch. 9:47
Grdanički, Jovan, p. 198
Gubbins, Sir Colin, p. 54
Guinness, Bobby, p. 197

Hadžidamjanović, see Hadži-Damjanović
Hadži-Damjanović, Jovan S., p. 101
Hadži-Djordjević, Ljubomir, p. 58
Halder, Ritter Franz von, pp. 137, 141, 143; notes Ch. 8:23, 30
Halifax, Lord, p. 54; notes Ch. 4:4
Hamilton-Hill, Donald, p. 55
Hanau, Julius ("Ceasar"), pp. 55, 56; notes Ch. 4:16
Hart, Liddell, p. 59
Heeren, Viktor von, p. 100
Heydrich, Reinhard, p. 55
Hill, George, p. 197
Hindenburg, Paul von, p. 16
Hiscock, K. H. W., notes Ch. 7:37
Hitler, Adolf, pp. viii, 1, 2, 8, 10-12, 15, 16, 18-24, 28, 32, 33, 35, 37, 42, 44, 54, 56, 57, 93, 95, 100, 126, 131, 136, 137, 139, 140, 142, 143, 146-149, 154, 160-162, 176, 190, 195, 220; notes Ch. 1: 2, Ch. 2:9, 11, Ch. 3: 36, Ch. 4: 4, Ch. 8, 10, 50

Index

Holland, J. C. F., pp. 55, 95
Holstein, Prinz von, pp. 177, 178
Horstenau, Edmund Glaise von, pp. 165, 166; notes Ch. 3: 36
Howard, Michael, p. 206
Howarth, Patrick, p. 82
Hubbatsch, Walther, notes Ch. 8:24
Hudson, Duane Tyrel (Bill), pp. viii, xii, 52, 53, 65, 67-71, 73-77, 79, 82-92, 173, 180, 184, 196, 198, 205-209, 213-216, 220, 223, 230; notes Ch. 4: 74, 84, 87, 99, Ch. 5:3, 43, 44, 59-61, 68, 75, Ch. 10:13, 14, Ch. 11: 5, 7, 9, 15, 55, and p. 333
Hyson, Miss Madeleine, p. xii

Ilić, a Lieutenant from the 1st Assault Btn., p. 168
Ilić, Bogoljub S., pp. 27, 66, 67, 70, 74, 77, 79, 80, 84, 198, 201-203, 210; notes Ch. 2: 31, Ch. 4:48, 80, Ch. 5:25, 41
Illic, Bogoljub, see Ilić, Bogoljub
Ivanović, Vane, notes Conclusion 8

Janković, Milojko B., notes Ch. 2:28
Janković, Radivoje V., p. 17; notes Ch. 1:15, 28
Jerković, Nebojša, p. 183
Johnstone, Kenneth, p. 63
Jones, R. H., p. 208; notes Ch. 11: 11
Jovanović, Arso R., pp. 84, 87, 88, 134, 173; notes Ch. 5: 32
Jovanović, Dragoljub, notes Ch. 5:7
Jovanović, Dragoslav-Dragi, p. 148
Jovanović, Slobodan, pp. 195, 200; notes Ch. 2: 31, Ch. 5:3
Jovović, Jakov N., p. 14

Kachel, Mrs. Noelene, p. xii
Kalafatović, Danilo S., pp. 26, 27, 29, 31, 107; notes Ch. 2:31

Kalaitović, Vuk K., p. 90
Karapandžić, Bor. M., p. 187; notes Ch. 6:60
Karchmar, Lucien, pp. 37, 38, 48, 51, 83, 84, 86, 99, 109, 170, 183, 215; notes Ch. 11: 15, Conclusion 25
Karadelj, Edvard, p. 113; notes Ch. 7:71
Keipert, Dr. Maria, notes Ch. 8:78
Keitel, Wilhelm, pp. 136, 162, 163
Kent, David, p. xi
Kewisch, an *Oberst*, p. 164
Kiessel (or Kissel?), Dr. Georg, p. 188; notes Ch. 9:33
Kissel, see Kiessel
Kljajić, Krsta, p. 178
Kljaković, Vojmir, p. 83
Knežević, Radoje L., pp. 27, 109, 110; notes Conclusion 1
Knežević, Živan L., p. 3; notes Conclusion 1 and p. 333
Kogard, an *Oberstleutnant*, pp. 175, 188-190, 192, 229; notes Ch. 9:79
Kogart, see Kogard
Koghart, see Kogard
Kolchak, Aleksandr Vasilieyevich, pp. 117, 118
Kontić, Jovan, p. 46
Konvalinka, Sava, p. 10
Kopinič, Josip, notes Ch. 7:62
Kos, Štefan Š., notes Ch. 6:38
Kosanović, Sava N., pp. 27; notes Ch.2:31
Koštunica, Dr. Vojislav, p. 134
Koull, Miss Dominique, notes Ch. 2:46
Kragujević, Milan P., p. 103
Krakov, Stanislav, notes Ch. 6:33
Krek, Dr. Miha, pp. 27, 229, 231; notes Ch. 2:31, Conclusion 21, 23
Kren, Vladimir, p. 10

Kvaternik, Slavko, p. 146; notes Ch. 8:50

Lalatović, Mirko I., pp. 66, 77, 78, 80, 81, 83-88, 92, 198, 203; notes Ch. 5:25, 46, 62
Lane, Arthur Bliss, p. 149
Lawrence, Christie, pp. 208, 209; notes Ch. 8:68, Ch. 11:9, 12, 15
Lazović, Drag. D., p. 182
Lecco, see Leko
Lees, Michael, p. 193; notes Ch. 9:92
Leko, Jovan M., p. 4-5
Leković, Mišo, p. 191
Letica, Dušan, notes Ch. 8:70
Letica, Stanoje, p. 176
List, Sigmund Wilhelm, pp. 143, 161, 164; notes Ch. 8:20
Ljotić, Dimitrije V., pp. 150, 158, 185; notes Ch. 6:60, Ch. 8:65, 67
Lockhart, R. H. Bruce, notes Conclusion 21
Loehr, Alexander, p. 40
Lontscha or Lontschar, a *Wehrmacht* General, pp. 169, 170; notes Ch. 9:26
Ludendorff, Erich Friedrich Wilhelm, p. 16
Luxardo, von (a *Generalmajor*), p. 116
Lyttelton, Oliver (see also Chandos, Lord), p. 62

Macdonald, A. H. H., p. 17
Maček, Dr. Vladko, pp. 4, 19, 21, 103, 146, 222; notes Ch. 1:2, Ch. 8:50
Mackensen, August von, p. 164
Maclean, Fitzroy (later Sir-), pp. xv, 36, 116, 173, 224; notes Conclusion 14

Maglić, Bogdan, D., pp. 101, 102, 105
Maisky, Ivan M., p. 78
Malaparte, Curzio, p. 36
Mapplebeck, Tom G., p. 220; notes Ch. 10:22
Marjanović, Dr. Jovan, pp. 43, 57, 85, 101, 109, 143, 144, 150, 154, 169, 187, 200, 223; notes Ch. 8:74
Marko (*nom de guerre*), see Hudson, D. T. ("Bill")
Martinović, Ratko, p. 168
Masterson, Thomas S., pp. 55, 60, 63, 66-68, 70, 74, 84, 210; notes Ch. 4:18, 48, Ch. 5:41, 42, Ch. 10:27
"Matel," see Matl
Matern, a *Sonderfuehrer*, p. 188
Matić, Momčilo M., notes p. 327
Matl, Dr. Josef, pp. 32, 33, 187, 188, 192; notes Ch. 9:88
Matsuoka, Yosuke, pp. 2, 20
"Mattel," see Matl
Maxwell, Arthur Terence, pp. 61-65, 69, 79, 194, 198, 201, 203
Menzies, Stewart (later Sir-), p. 55
Mešković, Pavle, p. 111; notes Ch. 6:92
Michailovitch MC, Dragoliub, notes Ch. 9:68—see also Mihailović, Dragoljub-Draža M.
Mihailović, Dragoljub-Draža M., pp. vii, viii, xii, xiv, xv, 18-20, 27, 33, 40, 45, 51, 52, 58-60, 63-69, 75, 77-79, 81-84, 86-93, 97-103, 105-113, 130, 133, 134, 136, 141, 144, 145, 150, 152, 156, 158, 160, 168-70, 172, 173, 176, 178-193, 195, 196, 198-200, 202, 205-231; notes Ch. 3:22, 59, Ch. 4: 37, 43, 84, 87, 93, Ch. 5:3, 25, 50, 60, 61, Ch. 6: 13, 14, 15, 24, 25, 26, 27, 28,

Index

31, 78, 84, 87, 88, 94, Ch. 7: 103, Ch. 8: 55, 67, 79, Ch. 9: 68, 80, Ch. 10:13, Ch. 11: 9, 15, 22, 24, 30, 53, 59, Conclusion 15, 19, 20, 25
Mihailović, Jelica (Mrs. Dragoljub M.), p. 212
Mihailović, Mihailo, p. 97
Mihajlo Petrović-Njegoš, Prince, p. 47
Milazzo, Matteo J., pp. 37, 109, 110
Milenković, Ljubiša, p. 176
Milićević, Todor K., p. 29
Miljković, Dragoslav S., pp. 101, 102, 108; notes Ch. 6:84
Milosavljević, Dragoslav V., p. 111; notes Ch. 6:71, 84
Mirković, Borivoja-Bora, pp. 3, 17, 26, 80; notes Ch. 5:22
"Mišić", notes Ch. 4:37
Mišić, Aleksandar Z., pp. xv, 59, 168, 187-189, 211; notes Ch. 11:30
Mišić, Milena (Mrs. Aleksandar M.), p. 212
Mišić, Živojin, pp. 16, 58-59, 168, 212
Misita, Veselin V., p. 107
Mitrović, Nenad, p. 188
Mitrović, Ratko, p. 184
Moebes, Paul, notes Ch.8:74
Morgan, Sir Frederic, p. 226
Mussolini, Benito, pp. 1, 8, 23, 35, 46

Narochnitsky, A.L., notes Ch. 10:8
NCO (non-commissioned officer), a Croat, anonymous, pp. 168, 169
Nedić, Milan Dj., pp. 99, 100, 148, 150, 154, 156-161, 214, 230; notes Ch. 6:33, 84, Ch. 8: 58, Ch. 9:18, Ch. 11:57

Nedić, Milutin DJ., p. 99; notes Ch. 6:84
Nedić, Neško, p. 184
Nelson, Sir Frank, pp. 61, 62, 203
Neuhausen, Franz, p. 138
Nicolas I, p. 45
Nikolaev, a Soviet Colonel, pp. 195, 197-199; notes Ch. 10:8
Nikolajev, see Nikolaev
Novaković, Ljubomir-Ljubo, p. 101

Oklobdžija, Bogdan, p. 175
Orwell, George, notes Ch. 3:18
Ostojić, Zaharije I., pp. 66, 77, 80, 84-88, 198, 203, 207; notes Ch. 5:25

Palošević, Miodrag P. ("Paloš"), pp. 97, 107, 168
Pantić, Branislav J., pp. 187-189
Pašić, Nikola, notes, conclusion 17
Paul Karadjordjević, Prince, pp. viii, 4, 5, 8-11, 21, 56, 98, 99, 127; notes Ch. 1:1, Ch. 4:20
Pavelić, Dr. Ante, pp. 36, 40, 58, 157, 180, 228; notes Ch. 3:21, Conclusion 20
Pavlović MP, Pavle, p. 120
Pavlović, Živko, notes Ch. 6:6
Pawlovitch, Kosta St., notes Ch. 2: 25, Ch. 9:92, and pp. 330, 333
Pećanac, Kosta, p. 172
Pemsel, Max J., pp. 172, 192; notes Ch. 9:89, Ch. 11:21
Perhinek, Rudolf-Rudi, pp. 51, 77, 89-91, 215; notes Ch. 5:11, 72, 78 and p. 333
Perović, Boža (Božidar?), p. 105
Perović, Dr. Ivo N., notes Ch. 4:20
Pešić, Petar, p. 100
Petain, Philippe, pp. 157, 158
Peter I, p. 7; notes Ch. 4:95, Ch. 8: 86

Peter II, pp. 2, 4, 26, 27, 30, 47, 151, 159, 172, 224; notes Ch. 2: 31, Ch. 4:20, Conclusion 15
Petrović, Momčilo, p. 58
Picht, a *Rittmeister*, p. 171
Pijade, Moša, p. 121; notes Ch. 7: 44
Plećaš, Nedjeljko B., pp. 81, 203; notes Ch. 10:26
Polish officers (two, anonymous), pp. 59, 80, 81
Pollock, George A., pp. 61-63; notes Ch. 4:54
Pomorišac, Nikola D. ("Peca"), p. 5; notes p. 333
Popović, Vladimir, notes Ch. 7:83
Popović, Žarko R., pp. 58, 59, 66, 79-81, 84; notes Ch. 4:38, 43, 76, 80, Ch. 5:16, 54, Ch. 10:14, 21, Ch. 11:24, and p. 333
Popovitch, Jarko-see Popović, Žarko R.
Popovitch, Mme Yolande, notes Ch. 6:1, and p. 340
Post, Dr. J. B., notes Ch. 4:101
Povhe, Alojz, A., notes p. 333
Protogueroff, p. 33
Publican from Gornji Milanovac, a woman (anonymous), p. 176

Quaiffe, Geoff, p. xi

Račić, Dragoslav S., p. 183
Radić, Stjepan, p. 119; notes Ch. 7: 34
"Radonić"–see Radonjić
Radonjić, Miljan, p. 76; notes Ch. 5:7
Radosavljević, Mole ("Abas"), p. 184
"Radovan Radović"–see Jones, R. H.

Radović, Dušan M., pp. 196-204; notes Ch. 10:23, 26, 28
Radunović, Milo, p. 29
Raketić, Ratko R., pp. 103, 104
Raketitch, Zoran R., notes Ch. 6: 52 and 334
Rakić, Branko, p. 175
Rakić, Dragomir, pp. 58-60
Ranković, Aleksandr, p. 133; notes Ch. 7:71
Rapotec, Stanislav-Stanislaus, p. 58; notes Ch. 4:34, Ch. 6:54, and 333
Rashid-Ali, p. 60
"Rasovic, Milan" in Z. Vučković's *Sećanja iz rata* is identified as Rašović, Miloš (whom see)
Rašović, Miloš, p. 45
Reljić, Milenko, p. 168
Rendell, Sir George, p. 41; notes Conclusion 21
Rey-Schyrr, Mrs. C., notes Ch. 2: 46, 50
Ribar, Ivo-Lola, notes Ch. 11:49
Ribbentrop, Joachim von, p. 161
Ribnikar (family), pp. 131, 133
Rice, Brian, p. xi
Roberts, Walter R., p. 86
Rolf, a Corporal (British No. 2 Commando), p. 73
Rommel, Erwin, pp. 142, 196
Roosevelt, Franklin D., pp. 113, 224, 225; notes Ch. 5:14; Conclusion 15
Rose, C. L., p. 229
Rožman, Dr. Greogory, notes Ch. 6:60
Rusković, Mato (Mate?), notes Ch. 4:27
Rutkowski, Dr., notes Ch. 7:10

Šabić, Stevo, p. 120; notes Ch. 7: 34

Index

Salter, D., notes Ch. 10:11
Sandes, Flora, p. 6
Savić, Milunka, p. 7
Schmidt, Wilhelm, notes Ch. 8:74
Schmidt-Logan, a *Wehrmacht* General, p. 137, 148; notes Ch. 8:60
Seton-Watson, G. Hugh N., p. 68; notes Ch. 10:10, Conclusion 9, 10
Seton-Watson, R. W., pp. 3, 13
Simonius, Mme L., notes Ch. 7:16
Simović, Dušan T., pp. viii, 3, 4, 11, 12, 17, 23, 25-30, 58, 60, 64, 65, 77, 78, 85, 107, 186, 198, 200-203; notes Ch. 1:1, Ch. 2:30, 31, Ch. 4:29, 69, Ch. 5:12, 50
Slijepčević, Dr. Djoko, p. 10
Smiljanić, Momcilo, p. 10
Smuts, Jan Christian, notes Ch. 4: 62
Spajić, Eta J., p. 106
Spajić, "Feta"—see Spajić, Eta J.
Stafford, A. T., p. 14
Stalin, Iosif ("Joseph")—born Dzugashvili, Iosif Vissarionovich pp. 56, 100, 113, 114, 124, 130, 131, 135, 151, 167, 172, 182, 217, 224, 226, 231; notes Ch. 5: 14, Conclusion 1
Stanković, Mirko, pp. 106, 110, 111; notes Ch. 6:62, 94
Stanković, Dr. Radenko, notes Ch. 4:20
Stanojlović, Boško R., p. 80; notes Ch. 5:23
"Štencl", notes Ch. 11:23
Štencl, Dragutin Z. (a Yugoslav Colonel), p. 211; notes Ch. 11: 34
"Štencl," a *Hauptman*—see Stentzel
"Štencl", wrong identification, p. 211
Stentzel or Stenzel, Dr. Erich, notes Ch. 11:34

St. John, Robert, pp. 17, 23
Stockhausen, von, pp. 152, 153; Ch. 8:81
Stojadinović, Dr. Milan, pp. 8, 148
Stojadinović, Dr. Miloslav, p. 148
Stojanović, Milan K., p. 99
Stuart, Sir Campbell, notes Ch. 4: 14
Šubašić, Dr. Ivan, pp. 26, 225
Svetlana, Stalin's daughter, p. 172
Swatzina, an official, notes Ch. 11: 34
Sweet-Escott-Bickham, pp. 56, 61, 62, 69; notes Ch. 10:10

Tarović, an engineer-officer, p. 105
Tenant, Sir C. G.—see Glencorner, Lord
Terzić, Ljubiša T., p. 107
Terzić, Velimir I., pp. 20, 27, 30, 31, 47, 134, 173
Thompson, an official, p. 199; notes Ch. 10:17
Thornhill, C. J. M., p. 62
"Thurner," notes Ch. 8:23. See also Turner
Timotijević, Žika M., notes Ch. 2: 19
Tippelskirch, Kurt von, pp. 29, 32, 33
Tito—see Broz-Tito, Josip
Todorović, Boško P., p. 180
Tolstoy, Lev (Leo), p. 125
Tomasevich, Jozo, pp. 37-39
Topalovic, Dr. Živko, pp. 38, 39
Tribić, Vasilije, pp. 79, 196-200; notes Ch. 5:19, Ch. 10:16
Trevor-Roper, H. R., notes Ch. 8: 24
Trišić, Jovan, p. 152; notes Ch. 8: 79, Ch. 11:24
Trojanović, Radmilo S., p. 31
Tsolakoglou, George, p. 25
Tupanjanin, Miloš, pp. 56, 199